The Mind and Art of Abraham Lincoln, Philosopher Statesman

The earliest known photograph of Lincoln, dated 1846. From the Library of Congress.

The Mind and Art of Abraham Lincoln, Philosopher Statesman

Texts and Interpretations of Twenty Great Speeches

David Lowenthal

LEXINGTON BOOKS
Lanham • Boulder • New York • Toronto • Plymouth, UK

Published by Lexington Books
A wholly owned subsidiary of The Rowman & Littlefield Publishing Group, Inc.
4501 Forbes Boulevard, Suite 200, Lanham, Maryland 20706
http://www.lexingtonbooks.com

Estover Road, Plymouth PL6 7PY, United Kingdom

British Library Cataloguing in Publication Information Available

Library of Congress Cataloging-in-Publication Data
Lincoln, Abraham, 1809-1865.
  [Speeches. Selections]
  The mind and art of Abraham Lincoln, philosopher statesman : texts and interpretations
of twenty great speeches / David Lowenthal.
      pages cm
  Includes index.
  ISBN 978-0-7391-7125-7 (cloth : alk. paper) -- ISBN 978-0-7391-7126-4 (pbk. : alk.
paper) -- ISBN 978-0-7391-7127-1 (electronic)
  1. United States--Politics and government--1815-1861. 2. United States--Politics and
government--1861-1865. 3. Lincoln, Abraham, 1809-1865--Political and social views. 4.
Lincoln, Abraham, 1809-1865--Oratory. 5. Speeches, addresses, etc., American. I.
Lowenthal, David, 1923- II. Title.
  E457.92 2012a
  973.7092--dc23
                                                                    2011049225

Abraham Lincoln

Best for a land, you clearly saw,
Is freedom strictly bound by law,
Yet no one barred—you knew this too—
From doing what his mind can do,
Free to fly high as he can
And bridled to no other man.
But you're unique in that your thought
Your country's form has newly wrought
With reason, vividly expressed,
And baleful passions all suppressed,
A better whole in every part
And you eternal in its heart.

Contents

Preface

How moving and inspiring, how filled with ironies, contraries, tragedies and triumphs is the epic of Lincoln's life. The barely educated country boy—"the aggregate of all his schooling did not amount to one year," he later said—studies books of literature and law and becomes a master of the English language. Still while a young man, and within his own mind and bosom, the rustic genius turns to reflecting relentlessly on the nature of things. The self-made lawyer, in prior office mounting no higher than one-term congressman and four-term Illinois legislator, stubbornly struggles to keep the territories free of slavery and at last ascends to the presidency. The gangling youth, who can lick almost anyone and wants to fight no one, finds himself directing the Union in a great civil war. The weaver of tales and jokes, who keeps his listeners convulsed in laughter for hours on end, bears a four-year burden of fretful sorrow as North and South clasp each other in deadly embrace. We see the loving husband tend unremittingly a loving but difficult wife, and the loving father looking on helplessly as two of his children fall early victim to death's stern decree. We see, with rising hopes, the Great Emancipator, adored for so long by those he liberated, and, with victory finally achieved, the savior of his country—of a Union freed from the scourge of slavery in keeping at last with the Declaration of Independence. But then, suddenly: the lover of Shakespeare martyred by a single shot from the gun of a fanatical Shakespearean actor. As his body failed, "It is all over," they said, in the dimly lit room across the street from the theater. "The President is no more." Such was his rise, and such his fall, but in the hearts of his countrymen no fall at all but a rise to everlasting glory.

This is Lincoln's most obvious legacy: his own life, his extraordinary deeds and accomplishments, and, as their source, an extraordinary nature and character that combined all the virtues, intellectual and moral. Like the fictitious nanny of the children's movie, *Mary Poppins*, he was "practically perfect in every way." And it is a tribute to our democracy that it could recognize, encourage and exalt such a man. I know there are those who do not share my high estimate of Lincoln and might feel my encomium wholly unwarranted. Some descendants of those he emancipated now think of him as nothing more than a hypocritical racist, others criticize as despotic his suspension of the writ of *habeas corpus* during the Civil War, and there are even some still attached to the Confederacy who

regard him as having unnecessarily caused that war. All three charges are utterly
false and will be shown to be so in one speech after another, if we read on ahead
with a modicum of patience and understanding. Instead, we find in Lincoln a
man struggling with the racial prejudice around him who himself did not have a
racist bone in his body, and whose premature loss was a terrible blow to the
cause of growing equality in this country. We find that no one was more careful
than Lincoln to act in accordance with the Constitution, and that suspending the
writ of *habeas corpus* had the most complete justification it could possibly receive. And we see that by preventing secession Lincoln freed the South of the
burden of black slavery in a way that would have been unlikely, for decades if
not centuries to come, had secession succeeded and the South been left to deal
with slavery on its own, only those anxious to preserve slavery would prefer
such an outcome. What is more, the Lincoln who saw the Civil War to its end
opposed all efforts at punishment and retribution and sought only the South's
swift return to an equal status within the Union. That's the meaning of "With
malice toward none, with charity for all," and little else than these final lines
from his Second Inaugural are needed to give us the true measure of this extraordinary man.

This is the Lincoln all Americans should study again and again, along with
our other great men. He has been celebrated in memoirs, biographies and histories, in books and articles almost without count. But another vital part of the
legacy Lincoln left, in his own hand and voice, so to speak, are his writings, of
which his speeches form the best-known but not the only part. The speeches are
great accomplishments in themselves and remind us of the struggles and challenges of which they were a part, especially once the slavery issue came to the
fore. We forget how much argument, originality of research, ingenuity, resi-
lience, unflagging persistence in the face of powerful and popular opposition—
how much sheer intellectual, emotional and physical exertion was needed to
make Lincoln's cause victorious. We take that victory for granted and treat it as
if it were easy to attain and well nigh inevitable—since we enjoy its fruits without having to engage in the struggle ourselves. Lincoln's speeches will set us
right. Without his extraordinary capacity to teach and persuade, usually face to
face with his audiences, there is a good chance his cause would not have succeeded, and the country would have moved toward a more ominous destiny.

Roy Basler's nine-volume edition of *The Collected Works of Abraham Lincoln* contains his letters, memoranda, reports, proclamations, newspaper material, even poetry, along with his speeches. But it is the speeches we continue to
celebrate—not many, since not many are known to the public; in fact, very few,
our acquaintance rarely extending beyond the *Gettysburg Address* and the final
paragraphs of the *Second Inaugural*. (It is remarkable how little Americans learn
about Lincoln in college as well as in school.) There are many more we would
celebrate if we knew them, and this volume is intended to convey texts and interpretations for the twenty I have found most important. Included are those of
obvious historical importance, such as the *House Divided* speech, the *Gettysburg*

Address, and the two *Inaugurals*, along with many that are much less known, such as the *Perpetuation* and *Temperance* speeches, and a small number, such as the *Handbill on Infidelity*, the *Emancipation Proclamation* and a few letters, that, strictly speaking, aren't speeches at all but vital for understanding Lincoln. Most of these would appear on anyone's list of his greatest speeches; the rest I hope will prove their importance in the reading and incline the reader to reach out on his own to others he may find even better. For convenience I have separated my selections into three categories: the early speeches, those just before the Civil War, and the wartime speeches. In each case the text of the speech is followed by its interpretation.

The reader may wonder why interpretations are at all necessary in reading Lincoln. We all know that this poor undereducated descendant of simple farm folk developed powers of thought and expression so extraordinary that to this day he has not only had few if any American equals but has also, with his *Gettysburg Address,* won a place among the foremost rhetoricians of the world. Even so, in describing Lincoln we must go beyond rare rhetorical ability. There have been many tributes to his mental capacity generally, but his writings reveal a power of thought even his closest friends did not suspect. I do not hesitate to say that, just as Plato's *Republic* had its philosopher kings, so our republic had in Lincoln a philosopher president, and before that a philosopher statesman. To show as much, nothing more will be needed than two of his earliest writings— the speeches on *Perpetuation* and *Temperance*. These turn out to be miniature masterpieces of political philosophy, and his so-called *Handbill on Infidelity*, a few years later, serves as their capstone.

Some philosophizings are couched in recondite or technical language, but not Lincoln's. On the contrary, his speeches are addressed to matters of common concern, expressed in the clearest possible language and organized for direct practical effect. So how can it be difficult to penetrate their depths? Very early in life (we have his own testimony for this in the *Handbill on Infidelity*), Lincoln learned to distinguish between developing his thoughts privately and telling them to the world. To think is to question, and to think deeply is to question dearly held beliefs most people assume to be true. But what if some of these beliefs are salutary or necessary or simply too powerful to confront directly? What if they would be fruitlessly damaged by critical thought openly expressed? And wouldn't an open attack on them also arouse serious hostility not only to the offending thought but to the thinker himself? What then can a man like Lincoln do, assuming he was such a man? With respect to tender or sensitive subjects of this kind, he has only two options: either to be silent or to express himself in such a way as to preserve a conventional surface while indicating a deeper unconventional meaning. This latter mode of writing, this combination of revealing and concealing, requires the most careful use of words, and the concealing must be done in such a way as also to reveal, otherwise we could not know a deeper message was there at all. From an early point onward, even before he was thirty years old, this is the mode of writing and speaking Lincoln adopted. Great minds before him, living in times much less free and much more dangerous, had adopted the same approach. Lincoln, living under the protection of the First Amendment, discovered by his own thought and experience that—particularly for one entering public life—the free air of American democracy did not obviate the necessity for politic self-restraint.

So it's often not easy to ascertain Lincoln's deeper meaning, but this raises another question: is it right or wise for the interpreter to reveal what Lincoln saw fit to conceal? If our object is to understand Lincoln, to get at the deepest wellsprings of his thought and action, there's no alternative: the interpreter must be willing to say what he sees. We all start by admiring the man, his almost unique combination of virtues and capacities, his wisdom, his magnanimity, and we wonder what makes for such qualities. We want to know the full unvarnished truth about him, come what may, and however unconventional. Especially in connection with religion, Lincoln's mode of expression makes for great difficulties. As he well knew, there is no more delicate subject, and even during his lifetime his beliefs became a matter of controversy. At one point he even had to defend himself, with his *Handbill*, against the charge of infidelity—i.e., complete disbelief.

What was Lincoln in matters of religion? Answers have ranged from extreme skeptic to devout believer. Was he a church-goer? He himself admits he was not. Was he a Christian? Many think he had to be, but some who knew him well said no. Did he believe in divine providence? Most are sure he did. One hesitates to leap into this thicket, where pleasing one group is bound to disappoint and even anger others, despite (or because of) the bond all share as admirers of this great man. But he must be permitted to be himself, despite our fondest desires. Keenly aware, then, of the complexity of the task, doing my best not to err but gladly open to correction if I have, I will follow the truth angel wherever she leads. At times I will find myself drawing from Lincoln's texts views some will deny he could possibly hold, or subtleties and complications we might all be tempted to think were surely beyond him. That Lincoln had an intimate and exhaustive knowledge of the Bible is beyond dispute, and his references to, and evocations of, the deity are as moving as they are plentiful. But I see no advantage in suppressing the radical views undergirding some speeches in order to accommodate or strengthen the religious expressions abounding in others, especially the later ones. Differences of this magnitude cannot be resolved here, but at least the outlines of their extent will become somewhat clearer.

Religion is not the only subject on which Lincoln exercised this kind of caution. Over the years he had to confront many others—the temperance movement, slavery, race relations, the rebellion, even the nature and political principles of the country itself—where frank speech was not prudently possible and where much greater harm than good would have come from it. This is why Lincoln's writings need interpretation. Wherever I thought them straightforward and in little need of interpretation, I provided little, although I have often had recourse to simple summaries for the sake of clarification or to set the stage for points of particular interest. In a few cases I had to confess I was unable to provide an adequate interpretation at all.

The earliest accounts of Lincoln's life, as well as the latest, refer to his unremitting dedication to reading and studying, the unusual love of solitude that was the counterpart of his delight in discussion and story-telling, his thinking things through and working them out on his own. This most people could easily see in his actions, his conversation and the products of his thought, such as legal briefs and speeches. But they could not see all that was going on in his mind. We must realize that, for men like Lincoln, even their closest friends in the practical world may not be confidants in the philosophical one, the world of ideas. This is why trying to find corroborations or clarifications of his deeper thoughts in the writings of friends like William Herndon or Joshua Speed—or even in Lincoln's own letters—is of little avail. So the interpreter of Lincoln is on his own. He must do his best with the facts of the speeches as they lie before him. Nor must he place undue reliance on his own conjectures about the contemporary influences or events he thinks Lincoln must have had in mind when he wrote. Follow the words of the speeches, their implications and internal logic, above all else! Skip over nothing, question everything! That's what we'll do as we try to become philosophical friends of Lincoln.

The addressees of this book are all those, young and old, amateur and professional, who, loving Lincoln, want to understand him better, and, loving their country, want to understand it better. I hope my analyses contribute to both ends. I have avoided the full panoply of scholarly citations, references, agreements and disagreements in order to complicate my interpretations as little as possible. That way they will be more easily grasped, if sound and convincing, and more easily doubted and subject to refutation, if not. My thinking about Lincoln was originally inspired by Harry Jaffa's *Crisis of the House Divided*—the book that more than any other I know brought into salience Lincoln's early speeches and revolutionized the appreciation of his intellectual and rhetorical ability. Since then I've taught many courses and seminars for undergraduate and graduate students, using Richard Current's *The Political Thought of Abraham Lincoln* and Roy Basler's large one-volume edition of Lincoln's *Speeches and Writings*, my copy of both having by now been leafed through so often that only a strong rubber band can hold their pages together. As to those who have written on Lincoln and his speeches, my impression is that they constitute a distinguished group, serious and thoughtful in their analyses. (Standing alone in scope is John Channing Briggs' *Lincoln's Speeches Reconsidered*.) Yet my interpretations remain sufficiently different as to make me think them worth submitting to the public.

In doing my work, I have especially valued the intellectual freedom and devotion to serious scholarship prevailing at Boston College and the other Catholic colleges at which I have taught. A good friend, Charles Fish, deploying his skeptical turn of mind, ardent hostility to defect and gift for aptness of expression, helped substantially strengthen the argument and writing throughout. I have debated many an interpretation with another good friend, Edward Lev, and of course over the years enjoyed discussions with students at Boston College, and, more briefly, Assumption College, who were always surprised and impressed by the Lincoln they found in these speeches. I'm grateful to Hilail Gildin, old friend and editor of *Interpretation*, for permission to reprint my article, "How Lincoln Defended Himself against the Charge of Religious Infidelity" (Winter 2009) in chapter 3 of this book. Many thanks also to the ever-buoyant Carmella Murphy, compositor supreme, and to Erin Walpole of Rowman & Littlefield for helpful editorial advice. Finally, I must express my appreciation for the financial support provided by the Earhart Foundation to help me begin this project. It took longer to finish than anticipated, but I hope my ability to read and write suffered no decline with age.

A word about Lincoln's texts. In the main their source is Roy P. Basler's edition of *The Collected Works of Abraham Lincoln* (Rutgers University Press, 1953), with an occasional detail of spelling or punctuation from the same editor's one-volume, *Abraham Lincoln, His Speeches and Writings* (Da Capo Press). The difficulties of editing Lincoln are summarized in the latter's introduction.

I. Early Speeches

Chapter 1

The Perpetuation Address, January 27, 1838

Lincoln was in his third term as a member of the Illinois House of Representatives when he delivered this address to the Young Men's Lyceum of Springfield—a society his friend Herndon said "contained and commanded all the culture and talent of the place."

Text

As a subject for the remarks of the evening, *the perpetuation of our political institutions* is selected.

In the great journal of things happening under the sun, we, the American People, find our account running, under date of the nineteenth century of the Christian era.—We find ourselves in the peaceful possession, of the fairest portion of the earth, as regards extent of territory, fertility of soil, and salubrity of climate. We find ourselves under the government of a system of political institutions, conducing more essentially to the ends of civil and religious liberty, than any of which the history of former times tells us. We, when mounting the stage of existence, found ourselves the legal inheritors of these fundamental blessings. We toiled not in the acquirement or establishment of them—they are a legacy bequeathed us, by a *once* hardy, brave, and patriotic, but *now* lamented and departed race of ancestors. Their's was the task (and nobly they performed it) to possess themselves, and through themselves, us, of this goodly land; and to uprear upon its hills and its valleys, a political edifice of liberty and equal rights; 'tis ours only, to transmit these, the former, unprofaned by the foot of an invader; the latter, undecayed by the lapse of time and untorn by usurpation, to the latest generation that fate shall permit the world to know. This task gratitude to our fathers, justice to ourselves, duty to posterity, and love for our species in general, all imperatively require us faithfully to perform.

How then shall we perform it?—At what point shall we expect the approach of danger? By what means shall we fortify against it?—Shall we expect some transatlantic military giant, to step the Ocean, and crush us at a blow? Never!—

All the armies of Europe, Asia and Africa combined, with all the treasure of the earth (our own excepted) in their military chest; with a Buonaparte for a commander, could not by force, take a drink from the Ohio, or make a track on the Blue Ridge, in a trial of a thousand years.

At what point then is the approach of danger to be expected? I answer, if it ever reach us, it must spring up amongst us. It cannot come from abroad. If destruction be our lot, we must ourselves be its author and finisher. As a nation of freemen, we must live through all time, or die by suicide.

I hope I am over wary; but if I am not, there is, even now, something of ill-omen, amongst us. I mean the increasing disregard for law which pervades the country; the growing disposition to substitute the wild and furious passions, in lieu of the sober judgment of Courts; and the worse than savage mobs, for the executive ministers of justice. This disposition is awfully fearful in any community; and that it now exists in ours, though grating to our feelings to admit, it would be a violation of truth, and an insult to our intelligence, to deny. Accounts of outrages committed by mobs, form the every-day news of the times. They have pervaded the country, from New England to Louisiana;—they are neither peculiar to the eternal snows of the former, nor the burning suns of the latter;—they are not the creature of climate—neither are they confined to the slave-holding, or the non-slave-holding States. Alike, they spring up among the pleasure hunting masters of Southern slaves, and the order loving citizens of the land of steady habits.—Whatever, then, their cause may be, it is common to the whole country.

It would be tedious, as well as useless, to recount the horrors of all of them. Those happening in the State of Mississippi, and at St. Louis, are, perhaps, the most dangerous in example and revolting to humanity. In the Mississippi case, they first commenced by hanging the regular gamblers; a set of men, certainly not following for a livelihood, a very useful, or very honest occupation; but one which, so far from being forbidden by the laws, was actually licensed by an act of the Legislature, passed but a single year before. Next, negroes, suspected of conspiring to raise an insurrection, were caught up and hanged in all parts of the State: then, white men, supposed to be leagued with the negroes; and finally, strangers, from neighboring States, going thither on business, were, in many instances subjected to the same fate. Thus went on this process of hanging, from gamblers to negroes, from negroes to white citizens, and from these to strangers; till, dead men were seen literally dangling from the boughs of trees upon every road side; and in numbers almost sufficient, to rival the native Spanish moss of the country, as a drapery of the forest.

Turn, then, to that horror-striking scene at St. Louis. A single victim was only sacrificed there. His story is very short; and is, perhaps, the most highly tragic, of anything of its length, that has ever been witnessed in real life. A mulatto man, by the name of McIntosh, was seized in the street, dragged to the suburbs of the city, chained to a tree, and actually burned to death; and all within a single hour from the time he had been a freeman, attending to his own business, and at peace with the world.

Such are the effects of mob law; and such are the scenes, becoming more and more frequent in this land so lately famed for love of law and order; and the stories of which, have even now grown too familiar, to attract any thing more, than an idle remark.

But you are, perhaps, ready to ask, "What has this to do with the perpetuation of our political institutions?" I answer, it has much to do with it. Its direct consequences are, comparatively speaking, but a small evil; and much of its danger consists, in the proneness of our minds, to regard its direct, as its only consequences. Abstractly considered, the hanging of the gamblers at Vicksburg, was of but little consequence. They constitute a portion of population, that is worse than useless in any community; and their death, if no pernicious example be set by it, is never matter of reasonable regret with any one. If they were annually swept, from the stage of existence, by the plague or small pox, honest men would, perhaps, be much profited, by the operation.—Similar too, is the correct reasoning, in regard to the burning of the negro at St. Louis. He had forfeited his life, by the perpetration of an outrageous murder, upon one of the most worthy and respectable citizens of the city; and had not he died as he did, he must have died by the sentence of the law, in a very short time afterwards. As to him alone, it was as well the way it was, as it could otherwise have been.—But the example in either case, was fearful.—When men take it in their heads to day, to hang gamblers, or burn murderers, they should recollect, that, in the confusion usually attending such transactions, they will be as likely to hang or burn some one who is neither a gambler nor a murderer as one who is; and that, acting upon the example they set, the mob of to-morrow, may, and probably will, hang or burn some of them by the very same mistake. And not only so; the innocent, those who have ever set their faces against violations of law in every shape, alike with the guilty, fall victims to the ravages of mob law; and thus it goes on, step by step, till all the walls erected for the defense of the persons and property of individuals, are trodden down, and disregarded. But all this even, is not the full extent of the evil.—By such examples, by instances of the perpetrators of such acts going unpunished, the lawless in spirit, are encouraged to become lawless in practice; and having been used to no restraint, but dread of punishment, they thus become, absolutely unrestrained.—Having ever regarded Government as their deadliest bane, they make a jubilee of the suspension of its operations; and pray for nothing so much, as its total annihilation. While, on the other hand, good men, men who love tranquility, who desire to abide by the laws, and enjoy their benefits, who would gladly spill their blood in the defense of their country; seeing their property destroyed; their families insulted, and their lives endangered; their persons injured; and seeing nothing in prospect that forebodes a change for the better; become tired of, and disgusted with, a Government that offers them no protection; and are not much averse to a change in which they imagine they have nothing to lose. Thus, then, by the operation of this mobocractic spirit, which all must admit, is now abroad in the land, the strongest bulwark of any Government, and particularly of those constituted like ours, may effectually be broken down and destroyed—I mean the *attachment* of the People. Whenever this effect shall be produced among us; whenever the vicious portion of population shall be permitted to gather in bands of hundreds and thousands, and burn churches, ravage and rob provision-stores, throw printing presses into rivers, shoot editors, and hang and burn obnoxious persons at pleasure, and with impunity; depend on it, this Government cannot last. By such things, the feelings of the best citizens will become more or less alienated from it; and thus it will be left without friends, or with too few, and those few too weak, to make their friendship effectual. At such a time and under such circumstances, men of sufficient talent and ambition will not be wanting to seize the opportunity, strike the blow, and overturn that fair fabric, which for the last half century, has been the fondest hope, of the lovers of freedom, throughout the world.

I know the American People are *much* attached to their Government;—I know they would suffer *much* for its sake;—I know they would endure evils long and patiently, before they would ever think of exchanging it for another. Yet, notwithstanding all this, if the laws be continually despised and disregarded, if their rights to be secure in their persons and property, are held by no better tenure than the caprice of a mob, the alienation of their affections from the Government is the natural consequence; and to that, sooner or later, it must come.

Here then, is one point at which danger may be expected.

The question recurs, "how shall we fortify against it?" The answer is simple. Let every American, every lover of liberty, every well wisher to his posterity, swear by the blood of the Revolution, never to violate in the least particular, the laws of the country; and never to tolerate their violation by others. As the patriots of seventy-six did to the support of the Declaration of Independence, so to the support of the Constitution and Laws, let every American pledge his life, his property, and his sacred honor;—let every man remember that to violate the law, is to trample on the blood of his father, and to tear the character of his own, and his children's liberty. Let reverence for the laws, be breathed by every American mother, to the lisping babe, that prattles on her lap—let it be taught in schools, in seminaries, and in colleges; let it be written in Primers, spelling books, and in Almanacs;—let it be preached from the pulpit, proclaimed in legislative halls, and enforced in courts of justice. And, in short, let it become the *political religion* of the nation; and let the old and the young, the rich and the poor, the grave and the gay, of all sexes and tongues, and colors and conditions, sacrifice unceasingly upon its altars.

While ever a state of feeling, such as this, shall universally, or even, very generally prevail throughout the nation, vain will be every effort, and fruitless every attempt, to subvert our national freedom.

When I so pressingly urge a strict observance of all the laws, let me not be understood as saying there are no bad laws, nor that grievances may not arise, for the redress of which, no legal provisions have been made.—I mean to say no such thing. But I do mean to say, that, although bad laws, if they exist, should be repealed as soon as possible, still while they continue in force, for the sake of example, they should be religiously observed. So also in unprovided cases. If such arise, let proper legal provisions be made for them with the least possible delay; but, till then, let them, if not too intolerable, be borne with.

There is no grievance that is a fit object of redress by mob law. In any case that arises, as for instance, the promulgation of abolitionism, one of two positions is necessarily true; that is, the thing is right within itself, and therefore deserves the protection of all law and all good citizens; or, it is wrong, and therefore proper to be prohibited by legal enactments; and in neither case, is the interposition of mob law, either necessary, justifiable, or excusable.

But, it may be asked, why suppose danger to our political institutions? Have we not preserved them for more than fifty years? And why may we not for fifty times as long?

We hope there is *no sufficient* reason. We hope all dangers may be overcome; but to conclude that no danger may ever arise, would itself be extremely dangerous. There are now, and will hereafter be, many causes, dangerous in their tendency, which have not existed heretofore; and which are not too insignificant to merit attention. That our government should have been maintained in its original form from its establishment until now, is not much to be wondered at. It had many props to support it through that period, which now are decayed, and crumbled away. Through that period, it was felt by all, to be an undecided experiment; now, it is understood to be a successful one.—Then, all that sought celebrity and fame, and distinction, expected to find them in the success of that experiment. Their *all* was staked upon it:—their destiny was *inseparably* linked with it. Their ambition aspired to display before an admiring world, a practical demonstration of the truth of a proposition, which had hitherto been considered, at best no better, than problematical; namely, *the capability of a people to govern themselves.* If they succeeded, they were to be immortalized; their names were to be transferred to counties and cities, and rivers and mountains; and to be revered and sung, and toasted through all time. If they failed, they were to be called knaves and fools, and fanatics for a fleeting hour; then to sink and be forgotten. They succeeded. The experiment is successful; and thousands have won their deathless names in making it so. But the game is caught; and I believe it is true, that with the catching, end the pleasures of the chase. This field of glory is harvested, and the crop is already appropriated. But new reapers will arise, and *they*, too, will seek a field. It is to deny, what the history of the world tells us is true, to suppose that men of ambition and talents will not continue to spring up amongst us. And, when they do, they will as naturally seek the gratification of their ruling passion, as others have so done before them. The question then, is, can that gratification be found in supporting and maintaining an edifice that has been erected by others? Most certainly it cannot. Many great and good men sufficiently qualified for any task they should undertake, may ever be found, whose ambition would aspire to nothing beyond a seat in Congress, a gubernatorial or a presidential chair; *but such belong not to the family of the lion, or the tribe of the eagle.* What! think you these places would satisfy an Alexander, a Caesar, or a Napoleon?—Never! Towering genius distains a beaten path. It seeks regions hitherto unexplored.—It sees *no distinction* in adding story to story, upon the monuments of fame, erected to the memory of others. It *denies* that it is glory enough to serve under any chief. It *scorns* to tread in the footsteps of *any* predecessor, however illustrious. It thirsts and burns for distinction; and, if possible, it will have it, whether at the expense of emancipating slaves, or enslaving freemen. Is it unreasonable then to expect, that some man possessed of the loftiest genius, coupled with ambition sufficient to push it to its utmost stretch, will at some time, spring up among us? And when such a one does, it will require the people to be united with each other, attached to the government and laws, and generally intelligent, to successfully frustrate his designs.

Distinction will be his paramount object, and although he would as willingly, perhaps more so, acquire it by doing good as harm; yet, that opportunity being past, and nothing left to be done in the way of building up, he would set boldly to the task of pulling down.

Here then, is a probable case, highly dangerous, and such a one as could not have well existed heretofore.

Another reason which *once was*; but which, to the same extent, is *now no more*, has done much in maintaining our institutions thus far. I mean the powerful influence which the interesting scenes of the revolution had upon the *passions* of the people as distinguished from their judgment. By this influence, the jealousy, envy, and avarice, incident to our nature, and so common to a state of peace, prosperity, and conscious strength, were, for the time, in a great measure smothered and rendered inactive; while the deep-rooted principles of *hate*, and the powerful motive of *revenge*, instead of being turned against each other, were directed exclusively against the British nation. And thus, from the force of circumstances, the basest principles of our nature, were either made to lie dormant, or to become the active agents in the advancement of the noblest of cause—that of establishing and maintaining civil and religious liberty.

But this state of feeling *must fade, is fading, has faded*, with the circumstances that produced it.

I do not mean to say, that the scenes of the revolution *are now* or *ever will* be entirely forgotten; but that like every thing else, they must fade upon the memory of the world, and grow more and more dim by the lapse of time. In history, we hope, they will be read of, and recounted, so long as the bible shall be read;—but even granting that they will, their influence *cannot be* what it heretofore has been. Even then, they *cannot be* so universally known, nor so vividly felt, as they were by the generation just gone to rest. At the close of that struggle, nearly every adult male had been a participator in some of its scenes. The consequence was, that of those scenes, in the form of a husband, a father, a son or a brother, a *living history* was to be found in every family—a history bearing the indubitable testimonies of its own authenticity, in the limbs mangled, in the scars of wounds received, in the midst of the very scenes related—a history, too, that could be read and understood alike by all, the wise and the ignorant, the learned and the unlearned.—But *those* histories are gone. They *can* be read no more forever. They *were* a fortress of strength; but, what invading foeman could *never do*, the silent artillery of time *has done*; the leveling of its walls. They are gone.—They *were* a forest of giant oaks; but the all-resistless hurricane has swept over them, and left only, here and there, a lonely trunk, despoiled of its verdure, shorn of its foliage; unshading and unshaded, to murmur in a few more gentle breezes, and to combat with its mutilated limbs, a few more ruder storms, then to sink, and be no more.

They *were* the pillars of the temple of liberty; and now, that they have crumbled away, that temple must fall, unless we, their descendants, supply their places with other pillars, hewn from the solid quarry of sober reason. Passion has helped us; but can do so no more. It will in future be our enemy. Reason, cold, calculating, unimpassioned reason, must furnish all the materials for our future support and defence.—Let those materials be moulded into *general intelligence, sound morality*, and in particular, *a reverence for the constitution and laws*: and, that we improved to the last; that we remained free to the last; that we revered his name to the last; that, during his long sleep, we permitted no hostile foot to pass over or desecrate his resting place; shall be that which to learn the last trump shall awaken our WASHINGTON.

Upon these let the proud fabric of freedom rest, as the rock of its basis; and as truly as has been said of the only greater institution, *"the gates of hell shall not prevail against it."*

Interpretation

In some ways the two little-known speeches Lincoln made in Springfield, Illinois—the first to the Lyceum, early in 1838 (when he was twenty-nine), the other to the Washingtonian temperance society four years later—are the most important he ever made. The former has as its subject mob lawlessness and its consequences, the latter the temperance movement itself. Not only his comparative youth but his very limited education and wholehearted devotion to the law and politics might tempt us to think him incapable of, as well as little inclined to, serious theoretical reflection. But genius does not require years, nor great learning, nor the outward appearance of thinking profoundly. These two speeches prove as much. They deserve to be ranked with the best political reflection produced by any American and no less with the minor political masterpieces of world literature. But the care with which we read them must match the politic care with which they were composed. Never again, as his prominence grew, would Lincoln attempt to compose such discourses.

The earlier speech begins with these words: "As a subject for the remarks of the evening, *the perpetuation of our political institutions* is selected." Selected by whom? The peculiar phrasing of this sentence leaves us unsure as to whether it was the Lyceum or Lincoln himself who chose the subject. It seems likely that it was Lincoln, for if it had been chosen by the Lyceum, he could have said that he had been asked to speak on that subject, or, using his own locution, that the subject *has been* selected—suggesting previous selection by the Lyceum. Moreover, the very boldness involved in undertaking so lofty, deep and unusual a subject suggests its origin with him rather than the Lyceum. Nevertheless, by not speaking in the first person, Lincoln seems somewhat unwilling to admit as much. He may have considered that a statesman ought not to speculate about the mortality of his own society, or even admit to this possibility. Perhaps the topic also bespoke a degree of difficulty, requiring weighty and extensive experience, that so young a man could hardly lay claim to.

The framework for understanding the speech as a whole is given in the next sentence: "In the great journal of things happening under the sun, we, the American people, find our account running, under date of the nineteenth century of the Christian era." The sun is the outer boundary that, by its revolutions around the earth, establishes the great "journal" (a daily record) of things in which we Americans have a running account. The order is a natural order, with the sun almost looking down on it, and "the Christian era" has a place within that order as part of its running account. This way of referring to the period of Christian dominance has a peculiarly historical ring to it. It might suggest that, just as there was a pre-Christian era, there will also be a post-Christian era, and this would certainly be true if the outer limit of things is natural—i.e., if the whole order of things is set by nature rather than by a supernatural God. This in turn suggests the possibility, given an order set by nature alone—indeed the likelihood or even necessity, that all human things are perishable, that they have not been here for all time past and cannot remain for all time future, that our political institutions are also perishable and perhaps even the presiding entity—the sun itself.

This supposition seems utterly outrageous: how could Lincoln have even considered such a thing? How could he hint at a thought that, right at the outset, would nullify the project of perpetuation on which he has just embarked? And why only hint? Did he think people incapable of tolerating so lamentable and even tragic a prospect as our ultimate perishing? That we could not bear the thought that no matter how hard we strive, our political institutions cannot keep enduring? Not too likely, but not impossible either. Let's call it a mere possibility, to be verified or proven false by what lies ahead in the speech. But if the possibility thus opened up—by inference, of course—is verified, if Lincoln is shown to have really meant so grim and paradoxical a conclusion, then we have here the first case where prudence must have led him to conceal the mordant truth deep beneath the very optimistic position taken in his title.

II

Just as we must beware of reading into Lincoln thoughts that aren't there, so must we be wary of clamping limits on his intellect that aren't there. The vice of under-interpreting is as bad as the vice of over-interpreting. The slight hints of Lincoln's independence of mind that we have seen will soon be strengthened and corroborated. Let us assume, tentatively, that the beginning of the first paragraph shows at least that Lincoln's orientation will be natural, in keeping with the reference to sun and earth, rather than supernatural, as the reference to Christian era might open as a possibility. The political counterpart to this critical beginning occurs at the end of the same first paragraph, where Lincoln again shows his independence by distancing himself from the very basis of our institutions, the Declaration of Independence, and thereby from modern liberal philosophy generally. He gives four reasons for transmitting "our political edifice of liberty and equal rights" to the latest generation that fate shall permit the world to know." They are: "gratitude to our fathers, justice to ourselves, duty to posterity and love for our species in general," all of which "imperatively require us faithfully to perform" the task of transmittal.

In contrast to the Declaration, these reasons emphasize not the inalienable rights of the individual but the ties that bind us to others, past, present and future. We have ties of gratitude to our forefathers, from whom we have inherited our political institutions, of justice to ourselves, who now enjoy them, of duty to our children and their children and theirs, to whom we must transmit them, and even to the whole human "species" (a word with a scientific ring) for reasons as yet undetermined. Even what we owe to ourselves is described in terms of justice rather than the protection of our rights as individuals, and one source of obligation—love for mankind—entirely transcends the bounds of political life as such. But clearly, although only one duty (to posterity) is called that, it is what we owe, not what we are owed, that will be the basis of our political perpetuation. And is it not strange that the terminus of our endeavors will be determined by "fate," and stranger still—though perfectly consistent for an order symbolized by the sun—that among our obligations no duty to God is mentioned?

Somewhat reluctantly, I conclude from this sentence that Lincoln found deficiencies in the philosophy of the Declaration, deficiencies that he was never to make explicit here or at any other point in his career, that he would never openly refer to, and that even now had to be implied rather than stated. The Declaration bases society on the God-given and inalienable rights of the individual—the individual concerned primarily about himself—but such an individual will be preoccupied with the present. He will have difficulty looking backward gratefully to past generations, even to the great founders, as well as far, far into the future for the needs of future generations. He will therefore have difficulty assuming the perspective of Lincoln's own speech, which is that of the enlightened statesman concerned more with the distant future of the society than self-interested individuals are likely to be, and concerned about the rest of mankind as well. The motives of such a statesman will themselves be hard to understand on the basis of the psychology inherent in the primacy the Declaration gives individual rights.

Nevertheless, throughout his political career Lincoln insisted that his fundamental political feelings all came from the Declaration of Independence. Whatever its defects, the Declaration is the statement of our philosophy and the intellectual foundation for Americans of their belief in liberty and equality—ends Lincoln considered good and noble in themselves—i.e., independently of the Declaration. Later in the speech he will even use the superlative, referring to "the noblest of causes—that of establishing and maintaining civil and religious liberty." Lincoln might well have concluded that for a cause so noble he must cherish and publicly espouse the Declaration's great principles while at the same time understanding, and finding ways of ameliorating, its inherent defects—without openly pointing an accusing finger at them. This approach will prove to be the key to his greatest political accomplishments later in life.

The sub-solar setting with which Lincoln began suggested that the proper framework for understanding human affairs—and among them the problem of perpetuating our political institutions—is natural rather than religious or supernatural. In accord with this premise, the speech makes a completely natural—i.e., a scientific or philosophical—analysis of the causes of possible breakdown in American society and adds a religious thought only in its very last words. It even goes so far as to omit from the analysis the fact that Americans are Christians and influenced in their behavior by Christian beliefs—a point preoccupying Lincoln in his later speech on temperance.

After this beginning, deeper and more far-reaching than it seems on the surface, the overall logic of the perpetuation speech is not difficult to follow. Our institutions are those of "civil and religious liberty," but if civil liberty is stretched so far as to encourage and allow the kind of mob violence then spreading in the country, its ultimate consequence will be the overthrow of democracy by despotism. This dismal prospect can only be avoided by instituting, in support of our political edifice, what Lincoln is bold enough to call a "political religion," at the same time adding a new pillar for the edifice derived from "reason, cold, calculating, unimpassioned reason." With their help we can successfully endure as a free society until "the last trump" sounds—hence his ringing conclusion: "Upon these let the proud fabric of freedom rest, as the rock of its basis; and as truly as has been said of the only greater institution, *the gates of hell shall not prevail against it.*"

III

Just before the end of the first paragraph, Lincoln specifies three possible ways for a breakdown of our institutions to occur: conquest by an invader, decay and usurpation. The possibility of invasion is immediately dismissed: "As a nation of freemen we must live through all time or die by suicide." But does suicide include both decay and usurpation, apparently so different from each other? It turns out that both, working in tandem, have an important role in Lincoln's analysis.

The story begins with a vivid description of the mob outrages that were spreading through the country. He gives an account—two different accounts, in fact—of two such outrages, one in Mississippi, the other in St. Louis. In Mississippi the mob began by hanging "regular gamblers," then negroes suspected of raising an insurrection, then white men supposed to be assisting the negroes, and finally strangers entering the state. The corpses dangling from trees were seen "in numbers almost sufficient, to rival the native Spanish moss of the country, as a drapery of the forest"—a grotesque but unforgettable simile. Lincoln calls the gamblers "a set of men certainly not following for a livelihood a very useful or very honest occupation," but one licensed by the legislature the year before.

The "horror-striking scene" at St. Louis involved a mulatto man named McIntosh who was a freeman minding his own business one minute and burned to death by a mob the next. Now, with the strange assertion that "Abstractly considered, the hanging of the gamblers at Vicksburg, was of but little consequence," Lincoln begins a quite different account of both outrages. This time Lincoln calls the gamblers "a portion of the population that is worse than useless" (rather than not very useful) and their death (by hanging) no matter of "reasonable regret" for anyone. "Honest men would be much profited if they could be annually swept away by a plague." So, too, in St. Louis. This time we are told that the negro (not "mulatto" now, and no longer named) had forfeited his life by an outrageous murder: "As to him alone, it was as well the way it was as it could otherwise have been."

What? As well that the man was dragged through the streets, chained to a tree and burned to death? How could Lincoln possibly say something like this?

Why is the second account of these two events so much harsher on the victims than the first? In trying to answer this question, let us assume that the first account is from the point of view of the law, and to some extent that of the overly optimistic supporter of the law, who tends to view all citizens as law-abiding: a man is innocent until proven guilty. The second account looks at the actual crimes or evils involved and calls for immediate and severe punitive justice: let us call it the attitude of the just mob, the mob that would constitute the best case for mob action because it acts swiftly, accurately and justly. By the evident sympathy Lincoln shows for the latter—to the point of agreeing with the harsh treatment of McIntosh—Lincoln makes the best case possible for it. The mob and not the Mississippi legislature was right in its judgment of the gamblers, and the mob that lynched McIntosh was right in its judgment—and punishment—of his guilt as a murderer. Having evinced his sympathy for these mobs and their on-the-spot justice, Lincoln is now in the best position to demonstrate his point: that, however right in the circumstances, mob action is wrong because it makes way for mobs that are not so punctilious in their harm-doing, that wreak havoc on the innocent and their possessions and thereby create the conditions for the overthrow of democracy itself.

And now Lincoln becomes realistic in characterizing the far-from-just mobs—consisting of "the vicious part" of the population—that were burning churches, robbing provision stores, throwing printing presses into rivers, shooting editors and thereby starting the country on the road to despotism. Succeeding in their lawlessness by their very numbers, the outbreak of mob action encourages those Lincoln calls the "lawless in spirit," who are always awaiting the breakdown of law, to become lawless in practice. This in turn causes those he calls "lovers of tranquility"—whose primary concern is for their own property, family and persons, and who comprise most of the nation—to start losing their attachment to the government. At some point, the true friends of the government, by whom Lincoln must mean those who love it—with its liberty and equality—for itself rather than for its effects in terms of personal security, will find themselves too few and too weak to protect it. Although he does not say so, Lincoln gives the impression of numbering himself in this group—as his later reference to the cause of liberty as the noblest suggests. When lawlessness increases, and the lovers of tranquility become increasingly alienated from a government that cannot protect them, men of "talent and ambition" will come forth to rend and replace this "fair fabric" of liberty, which for the last half century—i.e., since 1789—has been "the fondest hope of the lovers of freedom throughout the world." The combination of widespread disorder among the people and the ambition of a few will bring our government to an end and prove to the world that the people are incapable of governing themselves.

IV

Lincoln had included the love of our species among the duties to perpetuate our form of government, and here we see it at work in his conviction that the fate of mankind as a whole depends on the fate of freedom in this country. As for the men of talent and ambition who threaten to bring the fabric down, Lincoln will postpone for a while his closer examination of them in order to present his prescription for countering mob action. This prescription takes the form of an innovation he calls a "political religion," which requires swearing by the "blood of the Revolution" never to violate the laws nor tolerate their violation by others. "As the patriots of seventy-six did to the support of the Declaration of Independence, so to the support of the Constitution and laws let every American pledge his life, his property and his sacred honor."

After stipulating this pledge, borrowed in its language from the conclusion of the Declaration of Independence, Lincoln offers one of the most remarkable passages in our political literature, beginning with the words "Let reverence for the laws" and completing the paragraph. It calls for this political religion to be taught in the home by mothers, in all educational institutions, in primers, but also "preached from the pulpit, proclaimed in legislative halls, and enforced in courts of justice." And all of us (including all "colors and conditions") must "sacrifice unceasingly upon its altars." From this novel urging on Lincoln's part we would conclude that the founders of the country made a serious error in not providing such reverential support for the institutions they devised. But the difficulties involved in this political religion are almost transparent. For one thing, Lincoln's mentioning the Declaration and the Constitution side by side is bound to bring to mind the subject of slavery. To obey the Constitution and laws on the subject of slavery is not to obey the Declaration, but the Declaration is generally regarded by Americans as the more basic document—the statement of the truths underlying all just government. For the Declaration clearly considers slavery unjust, while the Constitution recognizes its legal existence. Which is to be obeyed? Further, how can Lincoln ask those of "all colors and conditions"—a category that must surely include black slaves—to obey the Constitution but not the Declaration?

That Lincoln understands the slavery issue to be at the bottom of most if not all of the mobs at that time is clear from his general description of their actions. These mobs are mainly anti-abolitionist or pro-slavery mobs, not anti-slavery mobs. Having called for strict obedience to the law as a necessity, Lincoln explains just how far he means this to go. Allowing for a limited set of exceptions, in which obedience to bad laws becomes unnecessary, he takes up the issue of what to do about the "promulgation of abolitionism" that has precipitated much of the mob violence. Either, he tells us, such promulgation is right in itself and deserves the protection of the law, or it is wrong and should be prohibited by law. In neither case is mob action called for. But the expression "right in itself" already illustrates the problem. Judged by the Declaration, such promulgation is

right, since all men are endowed with the right to liberty. Judged by the Constitution, it is wrong, since slavery is protected by it in several places (without the
word "slavery" ever being used). Now if abolitionism is taken to mean acting
contrary to or beyond the Constitution's protection of slavery to put an end to it,
how can abolitionists be blamed for taking up the standard of the Declaration
against the Constitution? Strictly speaking, a political religion defined in terms
of obeying the Constitution and laws would support outlawing the promulgation
of abolitionism. Who can blame the patriotic and knowledgeable American for
being torn on this issue?

Another great difficulty with the idea of a political religion comes from its
comprehensive nature. When Lincoln says, "Let every man. . . ," is he simply
expressing a wish that there be such a religion, or is he calling for its actual im-
plementation through laws? Is it an exhortation or a command? To enforce such
requirements—to stand guard over mothers, schools, primers, ministers—
nothing less than an all-embracing despotism will do. It would imitate the old
religions in all-pervasive controls that included political and legal enforcement.
If the "Let every man. . ." is just an exhortation—and that alone would be consistent with our liberal democracy—we would be settling for a very imperfect
instilling of reverence for the Constitution and laws and therefore allowing a
serious and possibly fatal flaw to remain in the system. This by itself is enough
to nullify the prospect of perpetuation. We should note, incidentally, that Lincoln never proposed a system of regulation in the form of actual laws, nor ever
again even in the form of exhortation. His aim (in this speech, but perhaps not in
some later ones) seems to have been more theoretical than practical—to indicate
a weakness in our system that it can never fully eliminate, necessitating, in the
long run, our inability to perpetuate it.

The most obvious feature of this political religion, and the reason for its
name, is Lincoln's conscious use of the beliefs, feelings and practices of religion
(and especially Christianity) itself. This political religion, consisting of reverence for the Constitution and the laws, is to be taught in seminaries and
preached from the pulpit, requires an oath swearing by the blood of the Revolution, and demands that everyone "sacrifice unceasingly upon its altars." This
comes as close to idolatry as Lincoln possibly could without using the term, and
would certainly conflict with the worship of a God transcendent to the laws.
Perhaps this is one reason why Lincoln suppresses the identification of the
American people as Christian, and fails to introduce their religion until the very
end of the speech.

Compared to Biblical religion, the obvious central weakness of Lincoln's
political religion is its lacking a real God to support and enforce it. If its requirements are to be understood as exhortations, those who fail to abide by them
can only be punished by social pressures of various kinds, and those who abide
by them superbly can be praised and honored. If, on the other hand, political
religion is required by law (and then "enforced by courts of justice"), legal punishments will be available and honors as well. In neither case are its punish-

ments and rewards comparable in power to those associated with the Biblical God, which with all of God's might are still imperfectly heeded. So, to expect perpetuity from the human enforcement mechanisms available to political religion is hardly realistic. Like all other things in nature, extending indefinitely the life of our society by natural means is not possible. We can only conclude that Lincoln's daring invention of political religion is both inconsistent with free society and incapable of doing the job. This radical theoretical solution to the problem of lawlessness turns out to be no solution at all.

V

After this, Lincoln recurs to the political problem from which he began, asking why there should be any greater danger to our political institutions now than in the first fifty years of our national existence. Something has changed. Those of the founding generation who sought "celebrity and fame and distinction" could find them in setting up the new political experiment testing the capability of a people to govern themselves. It was their "ambition" (not their justice or dedication to the common good or to liberty itself) that moved them to find satisfaction in this endeavor: "If they succeeded they were to be immortalized. . . ." But this "field of glory" has already been harvested, and similar men now arising will seek to gratify the same "ruling passion," but this time not by adding to the political edifice built by others but by tearing it down. In particular, those belonging to "the family of the lion or the tribe of the eagle" will not be satisfied by even the highest positions within a system established by others. "What! Think you these places would satisfy an Alexander, a Caesar or a Napoleon? Never! Towering genius disdains a beaten path." It "thirsts and burns for distinction." With these words Lincoln seems to enter the very souls of these paragons of ambition, just as earlier he had displayed a good sense of what animated raging mobs. The whole range of humanity seems available to him.

Here we have a kind of "lawlessness of spirit" different from that of the low criminals who are just waiting for law and order to break down. We may call these much greater figures men of lawless ambition. That such men exist, however rarely, may be taken for granted, but we are startled to find Lincoln attributing to our own founding fathers the very same kind of motive, nothing higher. Why does he imply (though without directly stating it) that they too were only men of ambition? Were none of them to be numbered among those true lovers of freedom whose existence Lincoln has already acknowledged and among whom he no doubt numbered himself? Did none love the noblest of causes for its own sake? Were all seeking "celebrity, and fame, and distinction?" Is there no essential difference between a Washington and a Caesar? And how can Washington deserve the position Lincoln accords him at the end if he is not the very embodiment of republican dedication and justice? Why does Lincoln wax Machiavellian or hard-boiled in his general ascription of motives to political men?

Lincoln's analysis suggests a hierarchy of ambition among men. Those of greatest ambition aim at glory born of distinction—of going far beyond what other men can do. The lion is the king of the jungle, the eagle king of the air— both beasts of prey, and the mightiest of beasts. The height of ambition, in such as Alexander, Caesar and Napoleon is empire—ruling over their own and other peoples as well. It is essentially a form of war or domination. The founders were men of lesser ambition and talents, and under them are those "whose ambition would aspire to nothing beyond a seat in Congress, a gubernatorial or a presidential chair. . . ." Finally, at the bottom of the hierarchy are those of little or no ambition, who aspire to only minor positions or who look to others to produce the security they want for themselves and their families.

Let us venture a suggestion as to why Lincoln treats ambition as if it is never subservient to aims like justice, the common good or liberty itself. Ambition has a power of its own, and in the circumstances of lawlessness is bound to surge forth acting against the republic. Like the founders themselves, Lincoln seems to have little confidence in the power of reason or virtue to control the passion of ambition—except in the few who remain true to their love of liberty. But he does not single out the founders as themselves such friends: rather he attributes sheer ambition even to them. If this has the effect of lowering the popular respect that can be paid them, it may also enlarge the sense of present danger from ambition amid mob lawlessness most needed now.

Lincoln may also have had in mind another consideration. When the country was to be founded, the love of fame in the leaders would have the same constructive effect as the love of the common good, or the love of liberty itself: in both cases it would lead them to create and strengthen the new society. Nor would it have been easy to discover whether it was ambition or dedication that moved them. At present, however, ambition—at least in its strongest form—will seek to tear down the government. Two of the great men Lincoln names— Caesar and Napoleon—overthrew republics. But now ambition will have to mask itself more than before, posing as savior of the people when it intends their suppression. So to be wary of ambitious men—to suspect ambition everywhere—would be wise counsel.

If great fame is to be found in tearing down the republic, would not even greater fame be found in saving it from such men? Just as Lincoln seems to rule out the possibility of disinterested devotion to liberty among the founders, so he seems to rule it out for himself—a man, possibly of an ambition matching Caesar's, who nevertheless remains steadfast in his devotion to liberty and saves the Union from the usurpations and depredations of the Caesars and Napoleons. A little less than two years later, on December 26, 1839, Lincoln gave a speech (on the topic of the Sub-Treasury) that had a spectacular ending. Here is what he said:

> *Many free countries have lost their liberty, and ours may lose hers; but if she shall, be it my proudest plume, not that I was the last to desert, but that I never*

deserted her. . . . The probability that we may fall in the struggle ought not to deter us from the support of a cause we believe to be just; it shall not deter me. If ever I feel the soul within me elevate and expand to those dimensions not wholly unworthy of its Almighty Architect, it is when I contemplate the cause of my country, deserted by all the world beside, and I standing up boldly alone, and hurling defiance at her victorious oppressors. Here, without contemplating consequences, before High Heaven, and in the face of the world, I swear eternal fidelity to the just cause, as I deem it, of the land of my life, my liberty and my love. . . .

After this remarkable statement, no one can doubt Lincoln's wholehearted devotion to liberty. We cannot rule out the possibility that he sought great distinction for himself, right to the end, but in him that aim was subservient to the noblest of causes, that of obtaining and maintaining civil and religious liberty. For him the highest human end is not distinction but nobility, as determined by judgment or reason. Achieving liberty for others is a higher end than the distinction gained from dominating them.

Lincoln's Machiavellian and less than flattering portrayal of the founders' motives may have yet another basis. It concentrates on the real but often hidden power of ambition in human affairs, treating it not as deriving from sinfulness but as a powerful force of our nature. He does not rely on prayer or God to help against would-be despots: to the extent that religion is to be used it will be not Biblical religion but a religion of his own invention—a political religion that inculcates reverence for the laws.

VI

Lincoln finds an additional source of danger in the passing of the Revolutionary era. Its wholesome effect on the nation has faded with time. The passions of "jealousy, envy and avarice incident to our nature" were temporarily rendered inactive, and the "deep-rooted" passions of hatred and revenge were turned against the British rather than against ourselves. Thus, the "basest principles of our nature" were either "made to lie dormant, or to become the active agents in the advancement of the noblest of cause—that of establishing and maintaining civil and religious liberty."

The base passions of our nature have great political importance, since they affect the possibility of national cohesion and stability. Whether their baseness comes wholly from their ill effects Lincoln does not say, but clearly a moral judgment is being invoked on the passions. Lincoln had also distinguished the judgment from the passions of the people, and by his reference to the "basest principles of our nature" implies that some natural passions are not base, just as judgment (or reason) is not base. So the problem of human governance will come down to strengthening reason and the good passions relative to the base ones, and finding ways to quell or re-channel the base passions. In this respect the disappearance of the British enemy engenders a serious threat to our national well-being. It is also notable in this analysis that Lincoln fails to call upon virtue or moral education to restrain the passions but instead assumes their constant independent strength, alterable only by other forces, such as political religion. The "realism" shown in his analysis of the passions resembles the way he treated the motivation of the founders, allowing little independent strength to the desire for justice or love of freedom as compared to ambition and the passion for distinction.

However great the strength of the passions, and the difficulty of controlling them, they do not exhaust the human picture for Lincoln. The noble and the base, the just and the unjust are equally real. Murdering the innocent is wrong. We really do owe gratitude to the founding fathers. We have a real duty to posterity. To be carried away by the base passions is base. We should love the human species as a whole. These are connected with our judgment, our rational mind. Without these objective sources of guidance, human life would be tossed to and fro by the passions, abetted by reason only in the calculating of means to their ends.

The fading of the Revolutionary scene and experience from the minds of Americans is the central theme of the third from last paragraph in the speech, with its beautiful and moving descriptions of the death and disappearance, one by one, of all who participated in the Revolution. The sense of relentless physical change and decline is strong in these lines. Those who fought for freedom can no longer testify to the struggle in which they played a part. Lincoln hopes that these Revolutionary scenes "will be read of, and recounted, so long as the bible shall be read," but their influence must nevertheless weaken. Is it possible that the Bible itself will not always be read, that it itself is subject to change? Nevertheless, by bringing to our attention this comparison with the Bible, and stressing the fact that these living histories of the Revolution are gone and "can be read no more forever," Lincoln encourages us to ponder the difference between political and religious histories. Why is it that the Bible can celebrate events and keep their memory alive long after their participants have died? As the divine record—God's own book—the Bible can prolong the existence of everything in its pages. Compared to this, the events of the Revolution, preserved at best in human narratives, can never evoke the same interest. The memory and meaning of the Revolution must fade; one of the strongest props of the new society must weaken. This is why the first fifty years of the republic are not an adequate basis for judging its present and future susceptibility to collapse.

VII

We come now to the conclusion. The survivors of Revolutionary battles were "pillars of the temple of liberty," and now that they are gone, other pillars must be put in their place. "Passion has helped us, but can do so no more. Reason—cold, calculating, unimpassioned reason—must furnish all the materials for our future support and defence." At this point Lincoln had offered himself ample opportunity to call upon religion and religious faith to assist the vulnerable republic: he does not. It is reason, described in the coldest terms, that must furnish all the materials needed for our support and defence. "Let those materials be moulded into general intelligence, sound morality, and, in particular, a reverence for the Constitution and the laws. . . ." It is not that these three supports of the republic consist of reason. Like reverence for the laws, which is a kind of passion, they are devised by reason, just as Lincoln is doing in this speech. In a similar way, we may expect morality and "general intelligence" to be devised by reason (without deriving from faith). Again, all must share in political religion, morality and "general intelligence": these are democratic in their character. But the reason from which they are derived cannot be a capacity of the whole people. It must therefore come from democratic leaders like Lincoln himself who serve the people but are superior to it in capacity. But how will they reach the people, teach them? Will the people accept them? Is even our highest political office capable of allowing such guiding wisdom? Democracy seems to be in need of something it itself cannot provide.

It is this stress on reason as the source of our political salvation that gives a special character to the short remainder of the speech. Suddenly, Washington— "our Washington"—is introduced to indicate that with the help of reason's products only at Judgment Day will he be roused from his long sleep without a "hostile foot" (foreign or domestic) ever desecrating his resting place. And it is immediately after this that the juxtaposition of our destiny and that of Christ's church ends the speech. Lincoln's grand final sentence explicitly likens the temple of liberty (giving a religious character to our political institutions by the word "temple") to what he calls "the only greater institution"—he does not identify it as the church of Christ: "the gates of hell shall not prevail against it." Nor does he identify these words as those of Christ himself, in the Gospel according to St. Matthew (16:18-19). He probably expected his audience to do this for themselves. In some translations the phrase "powers of death" is used instead of "gates of hell," but Lincoln meant us to connect this ending (using the King James or a similar version) with the "last trump" finally awakening "our WASHINGTON" that he had spoken of just before. He maintains that, if we are wise enough to adopt the measures he recommends, hell and death can be staved off for our political institutions so that they last until that "last trump" sounds.

It is somewhat anomalous to speak of the gates of hell not prevailing against the temple of liberty. First, strictly speaking it is not a temple, and the only religion called for to support it is not Christianity but what Lincoln calls a "political religion." Secondly, how can merely human institutions be made perpetual without the kind of miraculous powers Christ provides for his church in Matthew to stave off the "gates of hell?" Are civil and religious liberty almost as dear to Christ as his church? If hell cannot prevail against this liberty, can this liberty also, like the church, keep its believers out of hell and put them on the pathway to heaven? Or does Lincoln's reference to "the proud fabric of freedom" suggest freedom's rivalry to, and even defiance of, Christ and his church?

Does the reference to "our WASHINGTON" work to the same effect by treating him as something like a savior? In short, is there a harmony between Washington and Christ, or is there a fundamental opposition between the "temple of liberty," founded on reason, and the church, founded on faith? Finally, when Lincoln uses the phrase "as truly as has been said of the only greater institution," to affirm our perpetuation as a society, does he not make it contingent on the truth of Christ's statement, which within the natural framework he adopts for the speech as a whole must be subject to doubt? Is that why he refrains from identifying the speaker as Christ?

Many questions have come thronging in. Certainly what is demanded of Christ's church—of His followers—and what is demanded of the citizens of a liberal democracy are different and in some ways diametrically opposed. God demands loving and humble obedience, whereas "civil and religious liberty" makes everyone independent, self-determining—to the point of choosing his own religion rather than following the one true religion—and even proud. The church rests squarely on duties, liberty on rights. Perhaps this is why, for the sake of this discourse, Lincoln omitted a duty to God as one of the reasons for perpetuating our political institutions. While Christ can be relied upon to preserve his church till Judgment Day, we may not be able to say that he is concerned about preserving civil and religious liberty in the same way. Is there anything in the gospel Lincoln quotes, or in any part of the New Testament, to show such a concern? After all, Christ did say that his kingdom is not of this world.

This is a most peculiar ending to the speech. Outwardly, Lincoln claims in it that we can perpetuate our political institutions, that to do so we need political religion and reason (along with reason's products), and that we can thereby last as a free society until Judgment Day. Until the last two sentences, orthodox religion had played no role in the effort to perpetuate. Even then, in fact, it is not made part of that effort but used only for a rather incongruous and incredible comparison between the prospects for perpetuation of the "only greater institution" and the "temple" of liberty.

On reading this ending, which, with its deep religious significance, has burst so suddenly upon us, we cannot help but return to the comparison between natural and supernatural things that we glimpsed at the beginning. There Lincoln refers to the nineteenth century of the Christian era, but now we can ask whether the Christian era is friendly or hostile to the cause of civil and religious liberty? Clearly liberty of this sort was not sought by Christ, who went so far as to require his followers to obey Caesar in everything that did not clash with God's word. This implies that all regimes, including the most despotic, are to be obeyed unless they compel a Christian to violate God's commandments. By calling Christ's church the "only greater institution," Lincoln forces us to compare the two and realize that our political cause must depend completely on our own efforts: unlike the church, it will not be helped to persevere by Christ. And by elevating civil and religious liberty to a place just beneath that of Christ's church, Lincoln in effect denies the political elements of Christ's teaching calling for obedience to Caesar. A quiet but challenging defiance underlies his outward submissiveness to that teaching.

Conclusion

Had Lincoln wanted to confront the growing mob violence in a practical way, he could simply have confined himself to showing its harms and dangers and making practical recommendations to cope with it. Instead, he uses the occasion to delve into the problem more deeply and ends up making recommendations, however helpful, that must fall short of achieving perpetuation in the strict sense. At the very outset he lets us know that his guiding star—his sun—will be reason and philosophy rather than the Bible and religion. He will attempt to understand the nature of things, using cause and effect naturally arrived at, and this remains his approach to the very end.

Lincoln's lesson for American democracy (and all other modern democracies) is simple. When mobs take the law into their own hands, sensing their collective power as an active part of the people and abusing their liberty in the name of justice, the violence to individuals and property that they do can ultimately spell the doom of democracy. To restrain the base passions involved, Lincoln prescribes a political religion—a reverence for the constitution and laws—that in its fullness is obviously inconsistent with democracy and beyond its reach, just as he knows that the reason he also calls for as a second and necessary support is all too rare and unavailable. If this is so, his final optimism about our prospects for enduring until judgment day cannot be meant seriously. The full truth about American institutions is not sanguine, but, by implication, other forms of government fare no better. All are subject to growth and decay. All are perishable.

This morbid prospect does not keep Lincoln from regarding the cause of "civil and religious liberty" as the noblest of all causes, nor lull him into political quietism. The good statesman will never flag in his devotion, but he must understand the real situation in which he finds himself. He must know the elements of human nature, distinguishing noble from base passions and noble from base ends. He must appreciate the range of human ambition and the changes wrought to the country by its increasing distance in time from the great revolution of 1776. He must understand the ills to which democratic liberty and equality are prone in order to find ways of extending their existence. At this stage Lincoln may not have foreseen the complete splitting of the country with which he was faced in 1861, but no one saw more clearly, even as far back as 1838, the divisive power of the slavery issue, nor the need for heroic action to keep men of supreme ambition from putting an end to democracy.

Chapter 2

The Temperance Address, February 22, 1842

In his last year as an Illinois legislator, and having just turned thirty-three, Lincoln was invited to speak to the Springfield branch of the Washington Temperance Society on Washington's birthday. The nature, aims and methods of the organization are conveyed in the speech.

Text

Although the Temperance cause has been in progress for near twenty years, it is apparent to all, that it is, *just now,* being crowned with a degree of success, hitherto unparalleled.

The list of its friends is daily swelled by the additions of fifties, of hundreds, and of thousands. The cause itself seems suddenly transformed from a cold abstract theory, to a living, breathing, active, and powerful chieftain, going forth "conquering and to conquer." The citadels of his great adversary are daily being stormed and dismantled; his temple and his altars, where the rites of his idolatrous worship have long been performed, and where human sacrifices have long been wont to be made, are daily desecrated and deserted. The trump of the conqueror's fame is sounding from hill to hill, from sea to sea, and from land to land, and calling millions to his standard at a blast.

For this new and splendid success, we heartily rejoice. That that success is so much greater *now* than *heretofore,* is doubtless owing to rational causes; and if we would have it to continue, we shall do well to inquire what those causes are. The warfare heretofore waged against the demon of Intemperance, has, some how or other, been erroneous. Either the champions engaged, or the tactics they adopted, have not been the most proper. These champions for the most part have been Preachers, Lawyers, and hired agents.—Between these and the mass of mankind, there is a want of *approachability,* if the term be admissible, partially, at least, fatal to their success. They are supposed to have no sympathy of feeling or interest, with those very persons whom it is their object to convince and persuade.

And again, it is so easy and so common to ascribe motives to men of these classes, other than those they profess to act upon. The *preacher,* it is said, advocates temperance because he is a fanatic, and desires a union of the Church and State; the *lawyer,* from his pride and vanity of hearing himself speak; and the *hired agent,* for his salary. But when one, who has long been known as a victim of intemperance, bursts the fetters that have bound him, and appears before his neighbors "clothed, and in his right mind," a redeemed specimen of long lost humanity, and stands up with tears of joy trembling in eyes, to tell of the miseries *once* endured, *now* to be endured no more forever; of his once naked and starving children, now clad and fed comfortably; of a wife, long weighed down with woe, weeping, and a broken heart, now restored to health, happiness, and renewed affection; and how easily it is all done, once it is resolved to be done; however simple his language, there is logic, and an eloquence in it, that few, with human feelings, can resist. They cannot say that *he* desires a union of church and state, for he is not a church member; they cannot say *he* is vain of hearing himself speak, for his whole demeanor shows, he would gladly avoid speaking at all; they cannot say *he* speaks for pay for he receives none, and asks for none. Nor can his sincerity in any way be doubted; or his sympathy for those he would persuade to imitate his example, be denied.

In my judgment, it is to the battles of this new class of champions that our late success is greatly, perhaps chiefly, owing.—But, had the old school champions themselves, been of the most wise selecting, was their *system* of tactics, the most judicious? It seems to me, it was not. Too much denunciation against dram sellers and dram drinkers was indulged in. This, I think, was both impolitic and unjust. It was *impolitic,* because, it is not much in the nature of man to be driven to anything; still less to be driven about that which is exclusively his own business; and least of all, where such driving is to be submitted to, at the expense of pecuniary interest, or burning appetite. When the dram-seller and drinker, were incessantly told, not in the accents of entreaty and persuasion, diffidently addressed by erring man to an erring brother; but in the thundering tones of anathema and denunciation, with which the lordly Judge often groups together all the crimes of the felon's life, and thrusts them in his face just ere he passes sentence of death upon him, that *they* were the authors of all the vice and misery and crime in the land; that *they* were the manufacturers and material of all the thieves and robbers and murderers that infested the earth; that *their* houses were the workshops of the devil; and that *their persons* should be shunned by all the good and virtuous, as moral pestilences—I say, when they were told all this, and in this way, it is not wonderful that they were slow, *very slow,* to acknowledge the truth of such denunciations, and to join the ranks of their denouncers in a hue and cry against themselves.

To have expected them to do otherwise than as they did—to have expected them not to meet denunciation with denunciation, crimination with crimination, and anathema with anathema, was to expect a reversal of human nature, which is God's decree, and never can be reversed. When the conduct of men is designed to be influenced, *persuasion,* kind, unassuming persuasion, should ever be adopted. It is an old and a true maxim, that a "drop of honey catches more flies than a gallon of gall."—So with men. If you would win a man to your cause, *first* convince him that you are his sincere friend. Therein is a drop of honey that catches his heart, which, say what he will, is the great highroad to his reason, and which, when once gained, you will find but little trouble in convincing his judgment of the justice of your cause, if indeed that cause really be a just one. On the contrary, assume to dictate to his judgment, or to command his action, or to mark him as one to be shunned and despised, and he will retreat within himself, close all the avenues to his head and his heart; and though your cause be naked truth itself, transformed to the heaviest lance, harder than steel, and sharper than steel can be made, and tho' you throw it with more than Herculean force and precision, you shall be no more able to pierce him, than to penetrate the hard shell of a tortoise with a rye straw.

Such is man, and so *must* he be understood by those who would lead him, even to his own best interest.

On this point, the Washingtonians greatly excel the temperance advocates of former times. Those whom *they* desire to convince and persuade, are their old friends and companions. They know they are not demons, nor even the worst of men. *They* know that generally, they are kind, generous, and charitable, even beyond the example of their more staid and sober neighbors. *They* are practical philanthropists; and *they* glow with a generous and brotherly zeal, that mere theorizers are incapable of feeling.—Benevolence and charity possess *their* hearts entirely; and out of the abundance of their hearts, their tongues give utterance. "Love through all their actions runs, and all their words are mild." In this spirit they speak and act, and in the same, they are heard and regarded. And when such is the temper of the advocate, and such of the audience, no good cause can be unsuccessful.

But I have said that denunciations against dram-sellers and dram-drinkers are *unjust* as well as impolitic. Let us see.

I have not enquired at what period of time the use of intoxicating drinks commenced; nor is it important to know. It is sufficient that to all of us who now inhabit the world, the practice of drinking them, is just as old as the world itself,—that is, we have seen the one, just as long as we have seen the other. When all such of us, as have now reached the years of maturity, first opened our eyes upon the stage of existence, we found intoxicating liquor, recognized by everybody, used by everybody, and repudiated by nobody. It commonly entered into the first draught of the infant, and the last draught of the dying man. From the sideboard of the parson, down to the ragged pocket of the houseless loafer, it was constantly found. Physicians prescribed it in this, that, and the other disease. Government provided it for its soldiers and sailors; And to have a rolling or raising, a husking or hoe-down, any where about without it, was *positively insuffer-able.*

So too, it was everywhere a respectable article of manufacture and of merchandise. The making of it was regarded as an honorable livelihood; and he who could make most, was the most enterprising and respectable. Large and small manufactories of it were every where erected, in which all the earthly goods of their owners were invested. Wagons drew it from town to town—boats bore it from clime to clime, and the winds wafted it from nation to nation; and merchants bought and sold it, by wholesale and by retail, with precisely the same feelings, on the part of the seller, buyer, and bystander, as are felt at the selling and buying of flour, beef, bacon, or any other of the real necessaries of life. Universal public opinion not only tolerated, but recognized and adopted its use.

It is true, that even *then,* it was known and acknowledged, that many were greatly injured by it; but none seemed to think the injury arose from the *use* of a *bad thing,* but from the *abuse* of a *very good thing.*—The victims to it were pitied, and compassionated, just as now are the heirs of consumptions, and other hereditary diseases. Their failing was treated as a *misfortune,* and not as a *crime,* or even as a *disgrace.*

If, then, what I have been saying be true, is it wonderful, that *some* should think and act *now,* as *all* thought and acted *twenty years ago*? And is it *just* to assail, contemn, or despise them, for doing so? The universal *sense* of mankind, on any subject, is an argument, or at least an *influence,* not easily overcome. The success of the argument in favor of the existence of an over-ruling Providence, mainly depends upon that sense; and men ought not, in justice, to be denounced for yielding to it in any case, for giving it up slowly, *especially,* where they are backed by interest, fixed habits, or burning appetites.

Another error, as it seems to me, into which the old reformers fell, was, the position that all habitual drunkards were utterly incorrigible, and therefore, must be turned adrift, and damned without remedy, in order that the grace of temperance might abound to the temperate *then,* and to all mankind some hundred years *thereafter.*—There is in this something so repugnant to humanity, so uncharitable, so cold-blooded and feelingless, that it never did, nor ever can enlist the enthusiasm of a popular cause. We could not love the man who taught it—we could not hear him with patience. The heart could not throw open its portals to it. The generous man could not adopt it. It could not mix with his blood. It looked so fiendishly selfish, so like throwing fathers and brothers overboard, to lighten the boat for our security—that the noble minded shrank from the manifest meanness of the thing.

And besides this, the benefits of a reformation to be effected by such a system, were too remote in point of time, to warmly engage many in its behalf. Few can be induced to labor exclusively for posterity; and none will do it enthusiastically. Posterity has done nothing for us; and theorise on it as we may, practically we shall do very little for it, unless we are made to think, we are, at the same time, doing something for ourselves. What an ignorance of human nature does it exhibit, to ask or expect a whole community to rise up and labor for the *temporal* happiness of *others,* after *themselves* shall be consigned to the dust, a majority of which community take no pains whatever to secure their own eternal welfare, at a no greater distant day? Great distance, in either time or space, has wonderful power to lull and render quiescent the human mind. Pleasures to be enjoyed, or pains to be endured, *after* we shall be dead and gone, are but little regarded, even in our *own* cases, and much less in the cases of others.

Still, in addition to this, there is something so ludicrous in *promises* of good, or *threats* of evil, a great way off, as to render the whole subject with which they are connected, easily turned into ridicule. "Better lay down that spade you are stealing, Paddy;—if you don't you'll pay for it at the day of judgment." "By the powers, if ye'll credit me so long, I'll take another, jist."

By the Washingtonians, this system of consigning the habitual drunkard to hopeless ruin, is repudiated. *They* adopt a more enlarged philanthropy. *They* go for present as well as future good. *They* labor for all *now* living, as well as all *hereafter* to live.—*They* teach *hope* to all—*despair* to none. As applying to *their* cause, *they* deny the doctrine of unpardonable sin. As in Christianity it is taught, so in this *they* teach, that

> While the lamp holds out to burn,
> The vilest sinner may return.

And, what is a matter of most profound gratulation, they, by experiment upon experiment, and example upon example, prove the maxim to be no less true in the one case than in the other. On every hand we behold those, who but yesterday, were the chief of sinners, now the chief apostles of the cause. Drunken devils are cast out by ones, by sevens, and by legions; and their unfortunate victims, like the poor possessed, who was redeemed from his long and lonely wanderings in the tombs, are publishing to the ends of the earth how great things have been done for them.

To these *new champions*, and this *new* system of tactics, our late success is mainly owing; and to *them* we must chiefly look for the final consummation. The ball is now rolling gloriously on, and none are so able as *they* to increase its speed, and its bulk—to add to its momentum, and its magnitude.—Even though unlearned in letters, for this task, none others are so well educated. To fit them for this work, they have been taught in the true school. *They* have been in *that* gulf, from which they would teach others the means of escape. *They* have passed that prison wall, which others have long declared impassable; and who that has not, shall dare to weigh opinions with *them,* as to the mode of passing.

But if it be true, as I have insisted, that those who have suffered by intemperance *personally,* and have reformed, are the most powerful and efficient instruments to push the reformation to ultimate success, it does not follow, that those who have not suffered, have no part left them to perform. Whether or not the world would be vastly benefitted by a total and final banishment from it of all intoxicating drinks, seems to me not *now* to be an open question. Three-fourths of mankind confess the affirmative with their *tongues,* and, I believe, all the rest acknowledge it in their *hearts.*

Ought *any,* then, to refuse their aid in doing what the good of the *whole* demands?—Shall he, who cannot do *much,* be, for that reason, excused if he do *nothing*? "But," says one, "what good can I do by signing the pledge? I never drink even without signing." This question has already been asked and answered more than millions of times. Let it be answered once more. For the man to suddenly, or in any other way, to break off from the use of drams, who has indulged in them for a long course of years, and until his appetite for them has become ten or a hundred fold stronger, and more craving, than any natural appetite can be, requires a most powerful moral effort. In such an undertaking, he needs every moral support and influence, that can possibly be brought to his aid, and thrown around him. And not only so; but every moral prop, should be taken *from* whatever argument might rise in his mind to lure him to his backsliding. When he casts his eyes around him, he should be able to see, all that he respects, all that he admires, and all that [he?] loves, kindly and anxiously pointing him onward; and none beckoning him back, to his former miserable "wallowing in the mire."

But it is said by some, that men will *think* and *act* for themselves; that none will disuse spirits or anything else, merely because his neighbors do; and that *moral influence* is not that powerful engine contended for. Let us examine this. Let me ask the man who would maintain this position most stiffly, what compensation he will accept to go to church some Sunday and sit during the sermon with his wife's bonnet upon his head? Not a trifle, I'll venture. And why not? There would be nothing irreligious in it: nothing immoral, nothing uncomfortable.—Then why not? Is it not because there would be something egregiously unfashionable in it? Then it is the influence of *fashion;* and what is the influence of fashion, but the influence that *other* people's actions have on our actions, the strong inclination each of us feels to do as we see all our neighbors do? Nor is the influence of fashion confined to any particular thing or class of things. It is just as strong on one subject as another. Let us make it as unfashionable to withhold our names from the temperance pledge as for husbands to wear their wives' bonnets to church, and instances will be just as rare in the one case as the other.

"But," say some, "we are no drunkards; and we shall not acknowledge ourselves such by joining a reformed drunkards' society, whatever our influence might be." Surely no Christian will adhere to this objection.—If they believe, as they profess, that Omnipotence condescended to take on himself the form of sinful man, and, as such, to die an ignominious death for their sakes, surely they will not refuse submission to the infinitely lesser condescension, for the temporal, and perhaps eternal salvation, of a large, erring, and unfortunate class of their own fellow creatures. Nor is the condescension very great.

In my judgment, such of us as have never fallen victims, have been spared more from the absence of appetite, than from any mental or moral superiority over those who have. Indeed, I believe, if we take habitual drunkards as a class, their heads and their hearts will bear an advantageous comparison with those of any other class. There seems ever to have been a proneness in the brilliant, and warm-blooded, to fall into this vice—the demon of intemperance ever seems to have delighted in sucking the blood of genius and of generosity. What one of us but can call to mind some dear relative, more promising in youth than all his fellows, who has fallen a sacrifice to his rapacity? He ever seems to have gone forth, like the Egyptian angel of death, commissioned to slay if not the first, the fairest born of every family. Shall he now be arrested in his desolating career? In that arrest, all can give aid that will; and who shall be excused that *can*, and will not? Far around as human breath has ever blown, he keeps our fathers, our brothers, our sons, and our friends prostrate in the chains of moral death. To all the living every where we cry, "come sound the moral resurrection trump, that these may rise and stand up, an exceeding great army"—"Come from the four winds, O breath! and breathe upon these slain, that they may live."

If the relative grandeur of revolutions shall be estimated by the great amount of human misery they alleviate, and the small amount they inflict, then indeed, will this be the grandest the world shall ever have seen.—Of our political revolution of '76, we all are justly proud. It has given us a degree of political freedom, far exceeding that of any other of the nations of the earth. In it the world has found a solution of the long mooted problem, as to the capability of man to govern himself. In it was the germ which has vegetated, and still is to grow and expand into the universal liberty of mankind.

But with all these glorious results, past, present, and to come, it had its evils too.—It breathed forth famine, swam in blood and rode on fire; and long, long after, the orphan's cry, and the widow's wail, continued to break the sad silence that ensued. These were the price, the inevitable price, paid for the blessings it bought.

Turn now, to the temperance revolution. In *it,* we shall find a stronger bondage broken; a viler slavery manumitted; a greater tyrant deposed. In *it,* more of want supplied, more disease healed, more sorrow assuaged. By *it* no orphans starving, no widows weeping. By *it,* none wounded in feeling, none injured in interest. Even the dram maker, and dram seller, will have glided into other occupations *so* gradually, as never to have felt shock of the change; and will stand ready to join all others in the universal song of gladness.

And what a noble ally this, to the cause of political freedom. With such an aid, its march cannot fail to be on and on, till every son of earth shall drink in rich fruition, the sorrow quenching draughts of perfect liberty. Happy day, when, all appetites controlled, all passions subdued, all matters subjected, *mind,* all conquering *mind,* shall live and move the monarch of the world. Glorious consummation! Hail, fall of Fury! Reign of Reason, all hail!

And when the victory shall be complete—when there shall be neither a slave nor a drunkard on the earth—how proud the title of that *Land,* which may truly claim to be the birth-place and the cradle of both those revolutions, that

shall have ended in that victory. How nobly distinguished that People, who shall
have planted, and nurtured to maturity, both the political and moral freedom of
their species.

This is the one hundred and tenth anniversary of the birthday of Washington.—We are met to celebrate this day. Washington is the mightiest name of
earth—*long since* mightiest in the cause of civil liberty; *still* mightiest in moral
reformation. On that name, an eulogy is expected. It cannot be. To add brightness to the sun, or glory to the name of Washington, is alike impossible. Let
none attempt it. In solemn awe pronounce the name, and in its naked deathless
splendor, leave it shining on.

Interpretation

The artistry of this speech is on a par with that of its counterpart, the perpetuation speech, and while its subject seems more limited, it makes up in depth for any lack it may have in scope. Together they deal with the most important features of American society—the one with its constitutional nature as a country based on "civil and religious liberty," the other with its extra-constitutional nature as predominantly Christian. Lincoln wrote no additional speeches of the same character: he may have thought these two were enough to reveal the fundamentals (and problems) of American society.

In this fascinating and rather peculiar work, Lincoln cannot be said to discuss Christianity directly by name, but he makes it plain, from beginning to end, that the spirit of the temperance movement in both its older and newer phases derived from Christianity. Why else would he say that the movement called for fighting the "demon," drink, by completely abstaining from the use of alcohol? The group he was addressing was the Springfield Washingtonians—a branch of the national temperance movement that had adopted Washington's name. The speech is peculiar because of its powerful support for that movement—a support we would not have expected from Lincoln, who otherwise seems to have had no trouble accepting the drinking habits of others, however little inclined to drink he was himself. Just as in the perpetuation speech, Washington himself plays an important role at the end of this one, with Lincoln again heaping praise on him despite the fact that Washington was never known for supporting the temperance cause during his lifetime. This use of Washington in both speeches is almost an open invitation to examine the relation between the "civil liberty" Washington was instrumental in bringing about in one speech and this new "moral reformation" in his name in the other. That relation is really vital to the speech.

Even more peculiar than Lincoln's espousing the temperance cause are the reasoning and rhetoric he uses. He begins by telling us that the temperance movement was a failure for its first twenty years and only now, due to great changes in the movement, has it turned into a resounding and growing success—a success so great that Lincoln refers to it as " the temperance revolution." This new success Lincoln describes as a great conquest aimed not only at the "citadels" of its great adversary but at "his temples and his altars," his "idolatrous worship" and "human sacrifices." The mode of description is clearly drawn from the Bible, where the conqueror—the Hebrew nation, or Jehovah—overcomes the idol-worshippers. The tone of the description is epic, even to the point of gross exaggeration, as in this sentence: "The trump of the conqueror's fame is sounding from hill to hill, from sea to sea, and from land to land, and calling millions to his standard at a blast." Notice also that what calls millions to his standard is the conqueror's *fame* rather than the intrinsic qualities of the standard itself. And we must remember that this warlike language of conquest is being

applied not to the older and more objectionable phase of the temperance movement that failed but to its new and more successful phase.

The next short paragraph indicates that the kind of analysis of this revolution Lincoln will provide is wholly philosophical or scientific: "doubtless," he
says, the movement's change from failure to success is due to "rational causes,"
by which he must mean causes intelligible to human reason. But could they not
have been due to a miracle, like the Biblical events from which he draws his
initial comparison? Could not the entire temperance movement be divinely inspired and produced? By quietly stipulating "rational causes," even while supposing them the only possible kind of causes (by the word "doubtless"), Lincoln
shows his independence of the Biblical tradition against the background of
which he sets his analysis.

What follows is a plainly outlined and carefully executed argument, filled
with surprises. Heretofore, the warfare against the demon intemperance has
failed, and this must be due either to its champions or their tactics. Its champions
were mostly "preachers, lawyers and hired agents." By depending on the tactic
of denunciation, these champions were both impolitic and unjust. They were
impolitic because denouncing the sellers and imbibers of drink was not likely to
get them to quit. They were unjust because up till then (meaning until the very
point that the temperance advocates appeared on the scene) society as a whole
treated drink not as an evil to be avoided but as a good thing capable of abuse,
and it is unjust to denounce people for doing what was so long and so universally accepted. A further error made by the old reformers was to consider all habitual drunkards incorrigible, and, for the long-range good of all the others, need-
ing to be cast adrift as damned. Proceeding systematically from one point to the
next, Lincoln shows the superiority of the new champions and new tactics to the
old, comparing the thought behind them both.

The second and shorter part of the speech discusses what others can do to
help drunkards reform, which is simply to pledge to abstain from the use of alcohol themselves. To get them to do this, Lincoln asks them to keep in mind the
infinitely greater condescension shown when Omnipotence took on the form of
sinful man and suffered an ignominious death for him. Then, after unexpectedly
praising the kind of people habitual drunkards are, Lincoln turns to his conclusion. He compares "our political revolution of '76" with the "temperance revolution," which has the superior merit of doing no harm as it proceeds toward good
ends. In the name of the entire species, Lincoln congratulates the new movement
for adding moral freedom to our political freedom. He even makes use of some
expressions from Shakespeare's *Macbeth,* and ends by remembering, in the most
glorious terms, Washington, whose birthday they were gathered to celebrate.
Through the Washingtonians, Washington's name has now been made "mightiest in moral reformation", just as it had already been "mightiest in the cause of
civil liberty."

That's the overall picture. Returning now to the beginning, it is apparent
that the preacher (and not the lawyer or hired agent) was the heart of the original

movement. That is why not only dram-drinkers but dram-sellers were the object, and used against them the "thundering tones of anathema and denunciation, with which the lordly judge often groups together all the crimes of the felon's life, and thrusts them in his face just ere he passes sentence of death upon him." With all the vice and crimes of the world blamed on them, they were to be cut adrift as incorrigible and damned. So when it was commonly said that this preacher is a "fanatic" who "desires a union of the Church and state," it may not have been far from the truth. Given these suspicions and charges, what more natural than for the preacher to rid the devout of these sinners? He would be sorely tempted to use the arm of the state to purify the body politic, which to him is essentially a holy congregation meant to follow God's will.

Just as the harsher side of Biblical morality is reenacted with these words, so the softer side of Christianity appears with the new phase of the movement—with the Washingtonians, who make the reformed drunkard himself their champion. How this man is persuaded to stand up before those who are still drunkards is left unclear, for we are told he would "gladly avoid speaking at all"—perhaps out of shame at having been a sot, or because much that he says would necessarily involve condemning himself, or possibly because he prefers not to lord it over his erstwhile brethren. Lincoln does not give the reason. He does say it is by an act of resolution that such men save themselves: "how easily it is all done, once it is resolved to be done." But this implies that it is really not by divine intervention or grace that the change to sobriety takes place. Nevertheless, the Washingtonians teach "*hope* to all—*despair* to none." They deny the doctrine of "unpardonable sin," insisting that "while the lamp holds out to burn, The vilest sinner may return." And Lincoln describes the movement in terms of the Gospels casting out of demons (Matthew 12:27-28; Mark 5:15). "On every hand," he says, "we behold those, who but yesterday, were the chief of sinners, now the chief apostles of the cause." And "Drunken devils are cast out by ones, by sevens, and by legions," and those thus saved "are publishing to the ends of the earth how great things have been done for them."

With these rather hyperbolic descriptions, Lincoln shows that in his mind the temperance movement has lost none of its Christian inspiration, although in some ways this feature has become more muted than before. And while we are explicitly told that the reformed drunk is not a church member—perhaps out of antipathy to those earlier temperance preachers, or because sobriety requires it—he seems nevertheless to be moved by the gospel spirit of charity. Perhaps it is by an appeal to this spirit that he is made to overcome his reluctance to speak and come to the aid of his still-bemired brethren. And if the greatest sinners have become the greatest apostles (the word "apostles" implies some special zeal in spreading the word), it may be that they are thereby helped to remove the guilt and opprobrium of their earlier life.

But I have yet to mention the greatest surprises in this speech. In explaining why the denunciatory approach of the preachers had to fail, Lincoln says that the natural tendency of the people denounced was to resist, to fight back, rather than to "join the ranks of their denouncers, in a hue and cry against themselves." To expect otherwise was to expect "a reversal of human nature, which is God's decree, and never can be reversed." "Such is man," Lincoln continues, and "so *must* he be understood by those who would lead him, even to his own best interest." Now it becomes clear why Lincoln was convinced that the failure and success of the temperance movement had to be explained by "rational causes." There is a human nature, decreed by God, and it can never be reversed. It is fixed—forever. It is even fixed for God himself, and hence (by implication) never to be reversed or interfered with by miracles. This principle is the foundation of rational scientific analysis, and at the same time of rational statesmanship. We are able to understand man through reason because he (and perhaps all other things as well) has a fixed and intelligible nature.

But we have already passed the place in the text—so easily overlooked—that in the context of this speech supporting the temperance cause should have given us an even greater jolt. In explaining why the old system of denunciation was impolitic, Lincoln had said that "it is not much in the nature of man to be driven to anything; still less to be driven about that which is exclusively his own business; and least of all, where such driving is to be submitted to, at the expense of pecuniary interest, or burning appetite." In this sentence it is the middle assertion that should intrigue us most. What? To be driven about that which is exclusively his own business? Why the whole temperance movement presumes that one's drinking or not drinking (and with it the manufacturing and selling of alcoholic beverages) is a matter of interest to God and everyone else, that drink is one of the main causes of sin and crime, and that these are hardly private affairs. But drinking is a private affair if it is exclusively your own business.

We must remember that in making this easily neglected statement, Lincoln speaks in his own name, and that, if this is his view, he cannot possibly be in agreement with the temperance movement. Now the mock epic description—the second such description—given later to prove the injustice of the old system takes on new importance. It begins at the place where Lincoln reminds his listeners (or readers) that he has not inquired when the use of intoxicating beverages began. He then launches into a description much more natural in its detail and gentle in its appeal than the "conquering" one with which the speech began. Lincoln paints a picture of what life was like when such beverages were universally regarded as good and valuable. In those days the injury coming from the use of alcohol was thought to arise not from a bad thing, "but from the *abuse* of a *very good thing*."—a misfortune, not a crime, and given special emphasis by the addition of the word "very" to what had been said before.

The injustice of the older reformers—the preachers—derived from the fact that twenty years ago everyone shared this opinion about alcohol (it was the "universal *sense* of mankind") and therefore could not justly be denounced for it. This allows Lincoln to interject an even more momentous comparison, for he adds—apparently to strengthen his case—that "The universal *sense* of mankind on any subject is an argument, or at least an *influence*, not easily overcome. The success of the argument in favor of the existence of an overruling Providence, mainly depends upon that sense. . . ." By saying that the argument for a providential God "mainly" depends for its success on its being the universal sense of mankind, Lincoln weakens rather than strengthens that argument. For the sense that such a God exists may derive from a hope and need for divine protection, universally felt, and in this case would hardly constitutes proof for the existence of such a being. What all men believe is not really an argument, though it may well be what Lincoln calls an "influence," for it leaves unanswered the question as to what grounds there are for thinking the belief true. "All men believe so and so" falls short of proving that what they believe is true. And an "influence" is a social power or pressure, not a matter of proof at all.

Yet this universal sense is said to be the main argument for divine providence—which means that all other arguments for it are weaker still. Even so, taking note of this universal sense is most important as an "influence," for it reveals the source, strength and necessity of religion in human life. The religion of Americans is Christianity, with its roots in the Bible, and this Christianity—whatever its good points and however great its necessity—contains elements capable of leading to the extremes of the temperance movement and threatening liberty.

But Lincoln does not rest satisfied with having jarred the complacency of his readers this much. His final criticism of the older phase of the temperance movement is that it damned and cut adrift "all drunkards in order that the grace of temperance might abound, to the temperate *then*, and to all mankind some hundred years *thereafter*." He has two objections to this. First, the idea of cutting the drunkards off and damning them is inhuman, uncharitable, and selfish: "the noble minded shrank from the manifest meanness of the thing." The second objection is to the impracticality of getting many people to act for the sake of benefits far off in time: "What an ignorance of human nature does it exhibit, to ask or to expect a whole community to rise up and labor for the *temporal* happiness of *others*, after *themselves* shall be consigned to the dust, a majority of which community take no pains whatever to secure their own eternal welfare, at no more distant day?"

Lincoln says that the "grace of temperance might abound to the temperate then" as well as "to all mankind some hundred years thereafter." I assume the first refers to the favor of God won by abstention, and that the hundred years thereafter" refers to judgment day. Men will not act for the distant good of others, he says; they will not even act for their own distant good. By way of illustration, Lincoln tells the only joke in the speech, the nub of which is that Paddy will steal a second spade after stealing the first if he learns that all he is threatened with is paying for it (punishment) on judgment day. For Lincoln had led into the joke by making the extreme claim, a claim in itself farfetched, that "there is something ludicrous in *promises* of good, or *threats* of evil, a great way off, as to render the whole subject with which they are connected, easily turned into ridicule." He says that such promises *are* ludicrous, not that they may be *considered* ludicrous by some. In other words, he takes the side of the short-sighted, of those who a moment before had seemed defective in not considering their own eternal welfare, let alone that of others. So, it seems, it is not Paddy who is ludicrous but the promises of eternal reward and punishment made to him. In short, Paddy—the butt of the joke—knows what he is doing.

The effect of this passage is to accommodate and support the short-range selfishness of men—the opposite of Lincoln's previous appeal to the generosity and highmindedness of others, and against selfishness, in his earlier objection to the harsh treatment of the sinning drunkard. Why did Lincoln find it necessary to ridicule as nugatory the very idea of eternal salvation and damnation that he knew was in fact so powerful in motivating Christian believers? It may have been for this very reason. If the preachers, rather than representing an aberration, in fact derived their denunciatory spirit from some deep element in Christianity itself, they can only be countered at the same depth. The point is made by the way Lincoln describes the preachers as having used "the thundering tones of anathema and denunciation, with which the lordly judge often groups together all the crimes of the felon's life" before sentencing him to death. The connection with Judgment Day is made all too apparent here. Broadly speaking, the intolerance of evil or sin Lincoln attributes to Christianity receives its most powerful sanction from the idea of eternal rewards and punishments. So in this speech Lincoln does the opposite of what he did in the *Perpetuation* speech. There he tried to get near-sighted men to be far-sighted, considering the distant time horizon needed for perpetuating the republic. Here he gets far-sighted Christians to be near-sighted, so that they will look to immediate rather than future goods and evils.

In the second half of the speech, Lincoln aims at showing what those who are not drunkards can do for the movement. He begins by summing up the situation: the new champions and new tactics have caused "our" late success, and "to *them* we must look for the final consummation." But the metaphor he adopts at this point is the momentum of a moving ball, described in terms drawn from modern physics. There is something mechanical about it, compared to the description of the same movement, at its onset, with which the speech began, where it is likened to a conquering chieftain. But this descent to a calmer perspective soon meets with another bombshell. "Whether or not the world would be vastly benefitted by a total and final banishment from it of all intoxicating drinks seems to me not *now* to be an open question. Three-fourths of mankind confess the affirmative with their *tongues*, and, I believe, all the rest acknowledge it in their *hearts*."

Since the very soul of the temperance movement is for the abolition of such beverages, how can Lincoln say this is not now an open question? Does he mean not open here and now in the presence of the abolitionists? Is it a closed question, well and properly closed? Or should it be an open question if it is to receive a well-grounded answer? Why raise the point at all? In fact, Lincoln has already given us good reason to believe that the abolitionists are wrong, but it cannot be said to *them*. This is a lesson in prudence: one cannot always pronounce the truth publicly. But it then becomes a mystery why Lincoln—in reality a staunch opponent of abolitionism—accepted the invitation to speak to the abolitionists at all, and why he gives the appearance of being so solidly behind them. Was it not irresponsible to add fuel to a misguided and even dangerous crusade? And why not come right out in opposition to the movement if he thought it wrong and dangerous?

Before attempting to answer these questions, let us follow the text to the end. When Lincoln says that three-quarters of mankind confess the affirmative (to the desirability of totally banishing intoxicating drinks), we might ask how he knows. Surely he exaggerates in speaking of all mankind. And if so large a fraction expresses as much with their tongues and the rest with their hearts (but not their tongues), is it not possible that the vast majority who favor it verbally do not favor it in their hearts? And may not confessing it with their tongues have another meaning, for if we look at those who actually drink (with their tongues) we will find a vast majority—even all, if we add the three quarters and one quarter together—of the world favoring the retention of alcoholic beverages, not their abolition. Given the growing pressures in America to conform in the new direction, Lincoln wants us to realize that in this super-charged atmosphere what counts is not what people say but what they really believe and what their actions reveal about their real preferences.

Next Lincoln tries to show why the non-drunkards—the vast majority of the population—should join the temperance movement, and he takes up the case of those who never drink: why should they sign the pledge? To break the hold of alcohol on him, the drunkard must make "a most powerful moral effort," which requires that the rest of the community assist by their example. To the charge that men will not give up the use of spirits because of their neighbors, he answers with another bit of humor, asking the man making this charge "what compensation he will accept to go to church some Sunday and sit during the sermon with his wife's bonnet upon his head?" Such is the power of fashion. Lincoln draws the conclusion that it can be made unfashionable for people not to take the pledge, but he seems to have been heading toward a much more relevant and radical application of the point. For to what extent is our becoming moral itself a matter of fashion—of following the example of others or of the community generally? If social fashion is what makes us moral, it would seem that all moral beliefs and virtues are only matters of convention, without a natural basis of their own. Does Lincoln really want to go this far? The picture he had drawn of the earlier attitude toward drink (a good thing, a very good thing) had suggested that this was the more natural practice, that it had a sounder basis in nature, so he could not have believed that social pressures as such were sufficient to determine what was really good or right. As for making it unfashionable to withhold names and not take the pledge, Lincoln's stress on supplying pledges for the cause distracts from the main point—that the person taking the pledge agrees to banish liquor from his life completely.

Lincoln moves on to the case of the non-drunkards (a category that includes moderate drinkers) who refuse to join a society of reformed drunkards, regardless of whether their influence is needed for freeing drunkards from their habit. These men, we may assume, are animated by a certain pride. To persuade them to take the pledge, Lincoln goes to the heights of moral appeal for Christians, using the example of Omnipotence itself. Without mentioning Christ by name, or even the son of God, he reminds them of the condescension shown by Omnipotence in taking on the "form of sinful man" and dying "an ignominious death for their sakes." Is not the condescension required of the non-drunkard in taking the pledge for the drunkards' sake infinitely less than that? Lincoln comes just short of calling pledge-taking an obligation of every Christian.

It is hard to know how to assess this appeal by Lincoln to the greatest event in Christian belief. The example seems much too powerful for its application here, or the cause much too slight. Getting non-drunkards to give up their use of alcohol does not seem to demand a very great sacrifice from them, certainly nothing heroic. Hadn't Lincoln already told us "how easily it is done, once it is resolved to be done?" Nevertheless, it could be a sacrifice on two counts—either because the giving up of a great appetite, however evil, at least seems a sacrifice to the one whose appetite it is, or because alcohol is not only a good but a very good thing, as Lincoln said is still the universal belief, and then a real sacrifice is involved in giving it up. In addition, there is a question as to what the example of Omnipotence signifies as a general guide for human action. By God's condescension Lincoln probably means his lowering himself and suffering for the sake of an inferior being. Does this signify that men are obliged to give up everything for others? Are they obliged to give up large benefits they possess for small gains to others? Is Christ's suffering itself a model for men to follow—in this case by giving up the natural pleasure of drink? Is there no case to be made for selfishness and self-interest—a case that might extend to the taking care of one's own problems as well as interests? Remember, Lincoln had said that drinking is a man's own business! Assuming what cannot be assumed, that taking the pledge by non-drunkards is an important factor in saving alcoholics, is this a sufficient reason for those who enjoy drinking moderately to give it up? We can conclude that, under it all, Lincoln did not mean seriously this appeal to the non-drunkard to stop drinking.

The discussion takes an unexpected twist when Lincoln proceeds to raise the status of drunkards in our eyes, just as earlier he had praised those who had already reformed. Drunkards are not sinners: "their heads and their hearts will bear an advantageous comparison with those of any other class." "Brilliant genius and warm-blooded generosity," he tells us, have always been susceptible to this vice. He does not say why. It is possible that the world, with its follies and cruelties, disappoints and depresses them deeply and drives them to drink. Lincoln does speak of the "demon of intemperance" delighting in sucking their blood, but the demon is not *in* them. Now, instead of looking down on drunkards, as we are prone to do, and condescending to help them, as Lincoln himself had requested a moment before, we are inspired to look up to and admire them! Almost imperceptibly, Lincoln departs from this interesting sally. Again in epic Biblical tones he calls for saving the drunkards—our close relatives and friends—from moral death. The specific issue of the pledge has been dropped, and we end with a praise of this revolution as the "grandest the world shall ever have seen"—if the "relative grandeur of revolutions" is estimated by the large amount of misery they eliminate and the small amount they cause.

This allows Lincoln to turn, for comparison and linkage, to our political revolution of '76, i.e., from general considerations to the character of our own country. This revolution has given us a greater freedom than exists anywhere else, and by proving man's ability to govern himself has furnished the germ for the "universal liberty of ranking." But it also took its toll in bloodshed, whereas the temperance revolution, he tells us, has broken a stronger bondage, freed men from a viler slavery, and deposed a greater tyrant. No one has been hurt by it, either in his feelings or interest. Even dram-makers and dram-sellers "will have glided into other occupations so gradually as never to have felt the change. . . ." And what an ally to the cause of political freedom, which with its help shall be expanded to every human being: "Happy day, when, all appetites controlled, all passions subdued, all matters subjected, *mind*, all-conquering *mind*, shall live and move, the monarch of the world. Glorious consummation! Hail, fall of fury! Reign of Reason, all hail."

This is probably the climactic passage of the whole speech. To celebrate the temperance revolution is to celebrate the victory of mind over all appetites, all passions, all matters (I take "matters" to mean all material things): "Mind, all-conquering mind shall live and move, the monarch of the world." But, if nothing else, the final line of the passage—"Hail, fall of Fury! Reign of Reason, all hail!"—should put us on our guard, for it paraphrases the witches' prophetic and ominous greetings in *Macbeth* (I, 3:48-50), the Shakespearean play Lincoln liked best. This suggests that the whole idea of a complete conquest by mind is a witches' brew, and Lincoln's seeming praise wholly ironical. How can this be? If we rephrase the point so that its reference to Christianity becomes more recognizable, the basic difficulty consists in the effort to make mind, reason, spirit or soul the complete ruler over everything material or connected with bodies, without allowing sufficiently for the needs of those material things themselves. Here is the idea underlying the complete abstention from alcohol that the temperance movement, in both its earlier and later phases, seeks to bring about. Compared to this, the moderate and more natural situation preceding the temperance movement, in which alcohol was considered a good rather than an evil thing, although capable of abuse, represents a better understanding of the general relation between mind and matter.

Lincoln's next paragraph is ironical as well, and for the same reason. When the victory of mind is complete, with not a single slave or drunkard left on earth, our land can be proud of having brought both political and moral freedom to the whole species. But the absence of drunkards would be insufficient as a way of describing this ultimate and extreme condition, for even moderate drinking would be gone. Not only that, the freedom to choose moderate drinking would be gone too, even though, to that point, the movement had used only social pressure to achieve abstention and not yet resorted to legal prohibition. So the "moral freedom" thus celebrated is not quite compatible with political freedom. They do not go hand in hand.

And now the conclusion, taking us back to the birthday of Washington being celebrated by the occasion: "Washington is the mightiest name of earth—long since mightiest in the cause of civil liberty, still mightiest in moral reformation." Lincoln is not so gauche as to suggest that Washington himself was not a Washingtonian—that he did not espouse the abolition of drink sought by the Washingtonians. He compares Washington to the sun, his glory to the brightness of the sun. He speaks of the solemn awe with which the name should be pronounced, and of its deathless splendor. This final paean to Washington has a distinctly religious aura. In it Lincoln remains within the horizon of nature—of the sun and the earth, and the example of a man who comes closest to being divine while remaining a man. Washington has the same status at the end of both the *Perpetuation* and *Temperance* Addresses.

Let's summarize our findings. Lincoln writes this speech in such a way as apparently to praise the temperance revolution while, deeper down, criticizing it, and what he feared most was its subjecting man's physical needs to a kind of asceticism. Then why make the speech at all? Why engage in such rank (though well-concealed) hypocrisy? He probably could not refuse to speak without becoming an object of suspicion and disfavor, if not opprobrium, to this growing movement. For the few readers who would study his words carefully, he revealed a deeper analysis of the movement, laying bare its Christian foundations, stressing dangers more than advantages, and giving many lessons in philosophy along the way. For others, he at least kept alive the picture of the earlier, and sounder, use of alcoholic beverages, broadening sympathies and trying to make sure that the older more persecutory form of the movement, with its greater threat to liberty, would never regain control of it. After this speech, the temperance movement would be more likely to run its course in the least dangerous way.

Chapter 3

The Handbill on Infidelity, August 11, 1846

This is Lincoln's response to the charge of infidelity circulated against him by his opponent, the Reverend Peter Cartright, in the 1846 election for a seat in the United States House of Representatives. Despite winning, Lincoln was concerned that the rumors had "succeeded in deceiving some honest men" and asked the Illinois Gazette to publish this handbill and give it a much broader distribution than it had received before the election.

Text

TO THE VOTERS OF THE SEVENTH CONGRESSIONAL DISTRICT.

Fellow Citizens:

A charge having got into circulation in some of the neighborhoods of this District, in substance that I am an open scoffer at *Christianity*, I have by the advice of some friends concluded to notice the subject in this form. That I am not a member of any Christian Church, is true; but I have never denied the truth of the Scriptures; and I have never spoken with intentional disrespect of religion in general, or any denomination of Christians in particular. It is true that in early life I was inclined to believe in what I understand is called the "Doctrine of Necessity"—that is, that the human mind is impelled to action, or held in rest by some power, over which the mind itself has no control; and I have sometimes (with one, two or three, but never publicly) tried to maintain this opinion in argument—the habit of arguing thus however, I have, entirely left off for more than five years—And I add here, I have always understood this same opinion to be held by several of the Christian denominations. The foregoing, is the whole truth, briefly stated, in relation to myself, upon this subject.

I do not think I could myself, be brought to support a man for office, whom I knew to be an open enemy of, and scoffer at, religion.—Leaving the higher matter of eternal consequences, between him and his Maker, I still do not think any man has the right thus to insult the feelings, and injure the morals, or the community in which he may live.—If, then, I was guilty of such conduct, I should blame no man who should condemn me for it; but I do blame those, whoever they may be, who falsely put such a charge in circulation against me.

A Lincoln.

July 31, 1846.

Interpretation

The importance of this statement bears no relation to its brevity. Coming four years after Lincoln's temperance address, it is perhaps the last time he allowed some public view of his general or philosophical thought and the first (and only) time he comes close to disclosing his mode of writing and the reason for it. He had been charged, as he put it, with being "an open scoffer at *Christianity*." He could have responded simply by saying that he fully believed in Christianity, that he certainly would never have scoffed at it, and that he could never himself support for office anyone who did. He might have cited the names of prominent people who could vouch for these assertions. This would have settled the matter, insofar as such a matter can be settled by the person maligned.

Instead, Lincoln takes an entirely different and most daring tack, complicating his defense by employing subtleties and equivocations and raising philosophical issues of the greatest moment that did not have to be raised at all. At the outset he concedes that he does not belong to any Christian church, but without saying why. He claims never to have denied the truth of Scriptures, which is not quite the same as a flat affirmation of Christian belief, and does he mean denied it *openly, publicly*? He says he has never "spoken with intentional disrespect of religion in general or of any denomination of Christians in particular," but what he speaks, or fails to speak, could be quite different from what he believes, or fails to believe. What *did* he believe? Why *didn't* he belong to any church?

The mystery deepens—Lincoln himself deepens it—by the introduction of a point not asserted by the accusatory rumors and wholly unnecessary to his defense against them. For the first time he tells us what he really believes, or better, what he was "inclined to believe" in early life, something he understands is called the "Doctrine of Necessity." The name sounds formidable. The word "doctrine" suggests a worked-out set of beliefs, principles or teachings from religion or philosophy. The word "necessity" is perfectly general, suggesting a kind of metaphysical doctrine that distinguishes necessity from such things as chance or purpose, and, by contrast, meaning sheer necessity or what just has to be.

Lincoln strays further from a straightforward defense by describing the content of this doctrine, and the content seems to be much more circumscribed than the name. It is "that the human mind is impelled to action, or held in rest by some power, over which the mind itself has no control." So the doctrine pertains solely to man, and, even then, to the human mind alone rather than to things universal, as its name suggests. What can this mean? And why is it introduced by Lincoln in the context of the accusation that he was an "open scoffer at *Christianity*?" Evidently he thinks of the doctrine as something like an alternative to Christianity and perhaps to all religion.

Lincoln gives no further help on the subject, except for adding that "in early life" he actually argued for the doctrine, but only with "one, two or three, but never publicly," and that he has "left off" so arguing "for more than five years." In short, he went from being very private or secretive about this activity to suspending it entirely—suspending the habit of so arguing, he says, which is not the same as ceasing to believe. But what could this doctrine mean, and why the need for such secrecy? How can the human mind be impelled to action or inaction by some power over which it has no control? The power is not identified, nor are we told whether mind means conscious or unconscious mind. The reference to its being "impelled to action or held in rest by some power over which the mind itself has no control" sounds very much like something out of a physics book, such as the law of inertia. The word "action" sounds closer to decision-making or conscious action, but Lincoln might be giving it a much larger scope and using it to mean change—change in ideas, including those, like reminiscing or ruminating, that are not directly tied to action in the ordinary sense. Thinking might be a term applying to both.

What is this power over which the mind, in its thinking, has no control? The very idea seems to fly in the face of ordinary experience. Does not our own mental experience tell us that we are free to think and act as we please? Is this not what we mean by "voluntary action," and is not our moral and legal thought based on this idea? Does it not also underlie the religious doctrine of freedom of the will? So the "doctrine of necessity"—which by now we see is a philosophical idea and not a religious one, as Lincoln uses it—is distinctly un-obvious and in fact defies what we all take for granted. Let us assume, to begin with, that the power causing the mind to act or not act must be either outside or inside the mind. If it is external to the mind, what could it be? Not simply the physical things outside us, because these—like scenery—do not compel the mind to act at all, even when they appeal to our desires or appetites. We see the apple and are tempted by it, but observing the wormholes we decide to wait. The apple itself had no compelling power over us. Nor is it likely Lincoln is referring to God, the highest possible external power, since in this context it would be odd not to mention God by name and since "the doctrine of necessity" has a decidedly un-religious or even anti-religious cast to it—which is probably why it had to be treated so secretively.

Our bodies are also external to our minds—even if our minds cannot exist and function without them. We immediately experience the difference between our mind and the body—let's say our leg—of which we (by our mind) are aware as an object. In many ways our bodies can cause us to act, but by by-passing or under-cutting the mind rather than causing the mind to act in a certain way. We come closest to acting without being directed by the mind—to being controlled by some other power, including bodily appetites, limbs, nerves, muscles—when we act instinctively, or impulsively, or by sheer habit, or by subconscious motives, or are forced by external pressure to act in ways we would not choose consciously and voluntarily. In these cases we ourselves feel that our mind has been by-passed, that it is not in the driver's seat. But Lincoln is talking about a power that causes the mind itself to act, so we must concentrate on our ordinary thinking, when we are not under these compulsive influences. Is not our conscious voluntary action caused by the mind, and isn't it perfectly clear that our minds are free to choose, and to will what we choose? What other power—not the external world, not God, not our bodies—could be the power over which the mind has no control that compels it to act or not act?

It may perhaps be objected that we have given insufficient consideration to external influences on the mind that come from other people—from parents, teachers, friends, books, society in general. Lincoln's position, as we interpret it, is far from denying such influences, some voluntary, some involuntary as among those that help form our character and thought. But the "doctrine of necessity," as he states it, says that the mind is impelled to action or inaction by "some power" over which it has no control. These words suggest a single power always at work, even when the mind is engaging in its most voluntary or deliberate actions, its most voluntary thinking. So we must look at the mind at the moment of decision, taking it as the existing product of its original nature and all prior influences on it. And when it seems most free, and is experienced by us as most free, is when the "doctrine of necessity" will have its clearest test case.

Here is what I think Lincoln argued "with one, two or three, but never publicly." When we make what we think are free conscious choices we do so (and overlook the fact that we do so) in a certain way because we have the particular mind we have, and over this the mind has no control. The mind does not give itself the natural power it possesses, or whatever overall characteristics it has at any given moment. The mind of Socrates chooses in a different way than the mind of Alcibiades, and at any given moment these minds cannot act differently: they have no control over their own mode of operation and its accompanying limitations. The same can be said of the perceptions, sensations, virtues and vices which enter into our choices, including the ones we consider most deliberate. For this reason a particular person can be expected to act the same way or make the same choice in the same set of circumstances (of course these are never perfectly the same). This is what we mean by a person's character or personality or motivation. It is what Shakespeare's plays show in every scene, and what every novelist dotes on in his plots. It is the reason Heraclitus said that character is destiny. Perhaps—and only perhaps—this is what Lincoln meant when he spoke of a power causing the mind to act or not act that the mind itself did not control.

There is another path to the same conclusion. Let us assume the opposite: that the mind is completely free to act or not act in any way it pleases. It would then be a real option for the profligate Alcibiades, at any moment, to become a Greek Mother Theresa working in the slums of Athens. The coward could become brave, the cruel sadist a gentle lamb, the wise man foolish and the foolish man wise, the dullard a poet and the poet a wordless dummy, all by the utter freedom of their minds. Furthermore, choice or decision would become inexplicable, since all the influences on a man, including his own mental powers, would be incapable of explaining whatever decision he comes to, since they could always be overruled by his freedom of choice. And what would motivate this freedom of choice? Either something already in him, or something completely novel. In the former case, we will be able to trace his choice to something in his character. In the latter, we could not: his action would be de novo, and for it he could hardly be held responsible or take credit. The phrase "I did it" would become meaningless, for the "I" would be an empty constantly changeable vacuum of motivation. It would end up being more comparable to sheer impulse than to an act of deliberation. We would have reduced the human being to either an empty suit or a bundle of muscles, of which his brain might be the weakest.

This view of the mind does not mean the human being is incapable of understanding, of discovering truth, of deliberate choosing and making wise decisions. Some things we *all* know, some deliberate actions we *all* engage in wisely and well. But some truth is more difficult to obtain, some falsehood more easily fallen into, some deliberations poorly conducted and decisions less than wisely come to—all by the necessities of our individual natures at a given moment in a given situation. By his nature man is equipped to do all these things, far beyond what any other animal can. In that sense he—and this goes for every man—is much freer than they can ever be. His freedom relative to the brutes is shown every time he ponders what to do and reviews three or four options in his mind, choosing one. It is shown every time he asks himself what causes something to happen and looks for the answer, sometimes finding it. These are beyond the capacity of other animals. But he is part of nature, and if he is in some sense also above it, it is not by being outside the flow of natural processes and forces, beyond cause and effect. His mind, with all its unique powers, is still a natural object. It does think, decide and act, but not as an independent self-subsistent entity. There we have the broader implications of the "doctrine of necessity"— the features that make it more than a view of man alone and turn it into a metaphysical doctrine with the generality its name suggests. The world as a whole is a mesh of natural necessities, without which there would be unintelligible gaps in the flow of causes and effects, and man is part of this world. It is impossible to exist without being subject to such necessities.

Lincoln says he was inclined to believe this "doctrine of necessity" in "early life." He does not say he no longer believes it, or, if he no longer does, what replaced it. He admits to having sometimes "tried to maintain this opinion in argument," but with very few people, and never publicly. Five years before (which is well beyond his early life) he completely dropped this "habit" of arguing—why he does not say. But again, neither does he say he no longer believes the argument true. In these few sentences, Lincoln shows how much he was aware, from the beginning, of the dangers of the philosophical quest. He had to know his opinion was threatening to religion and capable of arousing public ire. He had to know that it could spell instant death to the career of an ambitious public man. Five years before would have brought us back to 1841, when he was still in the Illinois legislature. As his political ambitions began to grow, we can imagine that there came a point when he would no longer risk even semi-private discussions with "one, two or three." In one final daring burst of concealed risk-taking, he wrote this *Handbill* to free himself from the charge of infidelity, at the same time that he gave indications verifying the charge more fully than those who made it could possibly have known.

Lincoln mentions, as if by afterthought, that "this same opinion" (the doctrine of necessity) is held by several of the Christian denominations. He must be thinking of the belief called "predestination," according to which all things that happen have been pre-ordained by an all-knowing and all-powerful God. He seems to be reaching out for traditional allies, but only a moment's thought is needed to see that the more important function of this remark is to make sure we observe the differences between traditional religion and the doctrine Lincoln has argued, in which God and all other elements of Christian belief have no place and go unmentioned. He also knows most Christian denominations have shied away from predestination in order to retain some place within God's overarching providence for human free will and responsibility—again, views Lincoln's doctrine modifies considerably.

Lincoln ends by saying he does not think he himself could be brought to support for office a man he knew to be "an open enemy of, and scoffer at, religion." Supporting such a scoffer would "insult the feelings, and injure the morals" of the community. Lincoln's use of the word "religion" rather than "Christianity" could not be accidental. It is religion society needs, not Christianity as such, and a person who realizes how indispensable religion is to society would not scoff at it. Lincoln has understood this for some time. Anyone so cautious as to cease discussing radical doctrines with even "one, two or three" people would be sure not to declare them publicly. He would never openly scoff—perhaps, out of respect for feelings, not scoff at all. By his mode of writing, Lincoln was able to avoid openly scoffing while raising issues that would encourage the kind of independent thought he might have deemed essential for American statesmanship. Consider what Lincoln said at the end of his *Perpetuation* speech, eight years earlier. To preserve our political institutions we need, most of all, "reason, cold, calculating, unimpassioned reason." Not only is reason needed to devise the instruments of our preservation—including a "political religion"—but to do so it must first understand the nature and needs of a society founded on reason. The political context in which our religions operate, that of a primarily secular liberal society, is not one they would have created on their own. That is why religion itself cannot provide the intellectual basis for American statesmanship, and why the statesman, for independence of mind, has to understand fully the rational alternative represented by the "doctrine of necessity."

Chapter 4

The War with Mexico, January 12, 1848

The war against Mexico had begun in May 1846, and Lincoln had barely taken his seat in the Thirtieth Congress when he delivered this attack on the president for wrongfully instigating it.

Text

Mr. Chairman

Some, if not all, the gentlemen on the other side of the House, who have addressed the committee within the last two days, have spoken rather complainingly, if I have rightly understood them, of the vote given a week or ten days ago, declaring that the war with Mexico was unnecessarily and unconstitutionally commenced by the President. I admit that such a vote should not be given, in mere party wantonness, and that the one given, is justly censurable, if it have no other or better foundation. I am one of those who joined in that vote; and I did so under my best impression of the *truth* of the case. How I got this impression, and how it may possibly be removed, I will now try to show. When the war began, it was my opinion that all those who, because of knowing too *little*, or because of knowing too *much*, could not conscientiously approve the conduct of the President, (in the beginning of it,) should, nevertheless, as good citizens and patriots, remain silent on that point, at least till the war should be ended. Some leading Democrats, including ex-President Van Buren, have taken this same view, as I understand them; and I adhered to it, and acted upon it, until since I took my seat here; and I think I should still adhere to it, were it not that the President and his friends will not allow it to be so. Besides, the continual effort of the President to argue every silent vote given for supplies into an endorsement of the justice and wisdom of his conduct; besides that singularly candid paragraph, in his late message, in which he tells us that Congress, with great unanimity, (only two in the Senate and fourteen in the House dissenting,) had declared that, "by the act of the Republic of Mexico a state of war exists between that

Government and the United States;" when the same journals that informed him
of this, also informed him that, when that declaration stood disconnected from
the question of supplies, sixty-seven in the House, and not fourteen, merely,
voted against it; besides this open attempt to prove by telling the *truth*, what he
could not prove by telling the *whole truth*, demanding of all who will not submit
to be misrepresented, in justice to themselves, to speak out; besides all this, one
of my colleagues [MR. RICHARDSON] at a very early day in the session, brought
in a set of resolutions, expressly endorsing the original justice of the war on the
part of the President. Upon these resolutions, when they shall be put on their
passage, I shall be *compelled* to vote; so that I can not be silent, if I would. Seeing this, I went about preparing myself to give the vote understandingly, when it
should come. I carefully examined the President's messages, to ascertain what
he himself had said and proved upon the point. The result of this examination
was to make the impression, that, taking for true, all the President states as facts,
he falls far short of proving his justification; and that the President would have
gone further with his proof, if it had not been for the small matter, that the *truth*
would not permit him. Under the impression thus made, I gave the vote before
mentioned. I propose now to give, concisely, the process of the examination I
made, and how I reached the conclusion I did.

The President, in his first message of May, 1846, declares that the soil was
ours on which hostilities were commenced by Mexico; and he repeats that declaration, almost in the same language, in each successive annual message—thus
showing that he esteems that point a highly essential one. In the importance of
that point, I entirely agree with the President. To my judgment, it is the *very
point*, upon which he should be justified, or condemned. In his message of December, 1846, it seems to have occurred to him, as is certainly true, that title,
ownership to soil or any thing else, is not a simple fact; but is a conclusion following one or more simple facts; and that it was incumbent upon him, to present
the facts from which he concluded the soil was ours on which the first blood of
the war was shed.

Accordingly, a little below the middle of page twelve, in the message last
referred to, he enters upon that task; forming an issue and introducing testimony,
extending the whole to a little below the middle of page fourteen. Now, I propose to try to show, that the whole of this—issue and evidence—is, from beginning to end, the sheerest deception. The issue, as he presents it, is in these
words: "But there are those who, conceding all this to be true, assume the
ground that the true western boundary of Texas is the Nueces, instead of the Rio
Grande; and that, therefore, in marching our army to the east bank of the latter
river, we passed the Texan line, and invaded the territory of Mexico." Now, this
issue is made up of two affirmatives and no negative. The main deception of it
is, that it assumes as true that *one* river or the *other* is necessarily the boundary,
and cheats the superficial thinker entirely out of the idea that *possibly* the boundary is somewhere *between* the two, and not actually at either. A further deception is, that it will let in *evidence* which a true issue would exclude. A true issue

made by the President, would be about as follows: "I say the soil *was ours* on which the first blood was shed; there are those who say it was not."

I now proceed to examine the President's evidence, as applicable to such an issue. When that evidence is analyzed, it is all included n the following propositions:

1. That the Rio Grande was the western boundary of Louisiana as we purchased it of France in 1803.

2. That the Republic of Texas always *claimed* the Rio Grande as her Western boundary.

3. That, by various acts, she had claimed it *on paper*.

4. That Santa Anna, in his treaty with Texas, recognized the Rio Grande, as her boundary.

5. That Texas *before*, and the United States *after* annexation, had *exercised* jurisdiction *beyond* the Nueces, *between* the two rivers.

6. That our Congress *understood* the boundary of Texas to extend beyond the Nueces.

Now for each of these in its turn:

His first item is, that the Rio Grande was the Western boundary of Louisiana, as we purchased it of France in 1803; and, seeming to expect this to be disputed, he argues over the amount of nearly a page to prove it true; at the end of which, he lets us know that, by the treaty of 1819, we sold to Spain the whole country, from the Rio Grande eastward to the Sabine. Now, admitting, for the present, that the Rio Grande was the boundary of Louisiana, what, under heaven, had that to do with the *present* boundary between us and Mexico? How, Mr. Chairman, the line that once divided your land from mine can *still* be the boundary between us *after* I have sold my land to you, is, to me, beyond all comprehension. And how any man, with an honest purpose only of proving the truth, could ever have *thought* of introducing such a fact to prove such an issue, is equally incomprehensible. The outrage upon common *right,* of seizing as our own what we have once sold, merely because it *was* ours *before* we sold it, is only equalled by the outrage on common *sense* of any attempt to justify it.

The President's next piece of evidence is, that "The Republic of Texas always *claimed* this river (Rio Grande) as her western boundary." That is not true, in fact. Texas *has* claimed it, but she has not *always* claimed it. There is, at least, one distinguished exception. Her state constitution—the Republic's most solemn, and well-considered act; that which may, without impropriety, be called her last will and testament, revoking all others—makes no such claim. But suppose she had always claimed it. Has not Mexico always claimed the contrary? So that there is but *claim* against *claim*, leaving nothing proved, until we get back of the claims, and find which has the better *foundation*.

Though not in the order in which the President presents his evidence, I now consider that class of his statements, which are, in substance, nothing more than that Texas has, by various acts of her Convention and Congress, claimed the Rio Grande as her boundary—*on paper*. I mean here what he says about the fixing

of the Rio Grande as her boundary, in her old constitution, (not her state constitution,) about forming congressional districts, counties &c. Now, all of this is
but naked *claim*; and what I have already said about claims is strictly applicable
to this. If I should claim your land by word of mouth, that certainly would not
make it mine; and if I were to claim it by a deed which I had made myself, and
with which you had had nothing to do, the claim would be quite the same, in
substance, or rather in utter nothingness.

I next consider the President's statement that Santa Anna, in his *treaty* with
Texas, recognised the Rio Grande, as the western boundary of Texas. Besides
the position so often taken that Santa Anna, while a prisoner of war—a captive—*could* not bind Mexico by a treaty, which I deem conclusive; besides this,
I wish to say something in relation to this treaty, so called by the President, with
Santa Anna. If any man would like to be amused by a sight of that *little* thing,
which the President calls by that *big* name, he can have it by turning to Niles'
Register volume 50, page 336. And if any one should suppose that Niles' Register is a curious repository of so mighty a document as a solemn treaty between
nations, I can only say that I learned, to a tolerable degree of certainty, by en-
quiry at the State Department, that the President himself never saw it anywhere
else. By the way, I believe I should not err if I were to declare, that during the
first ten years of the existence of that document, it was never by anybody *called*
a treaty; that it was never so called till the President, in his extremity, attempted,
by so calling it, to wring something from it in justification of himself in connection with the Mexican war. It has none of the distinguishing features of a treaty.
It does not call itself a treaty. Santa Anna does not therein assume to bind Mexico; he assumes only to act as the President, Commander-in-chief of the Mexican Army and Navy; stipulates that the then present hostilities should cease,
and that he would not *himself* take up arms, nor *influence* the Mexican people to
take up arms, against Texas, during the existence of the war of independence.
He did not recognise the independence of Texas; he did not assume to put an
end to the war but clearly indicated his expectation of its continuance; he did not
say one word about boundary, and most probably, never thought of it. It *is* stipulated therein that the Mexican forces should evacuate the territory of Texas,
passing to the other side of the Rio Grande; and in another article, it is stipulated
that to prevent collisions between the armies, the Texan army should not approach nearer than within five leagues—of *what* is not said—but clearly, from
the object stated, it is of the Rio Grande. Now, if this is a treaty, recognising the
Rio Grande, as the boundary of Texas, it contains the singular feauture, of stipulating that Texas shall not go within five leagues of *her own* boundary.

Next comes the evidence of Texas before annexation, and the United States
afterwards, *exercising* jurisdiction *beyond* the Nueces, and *between* the two rivers. This actual *exercise* of jurisdiction is the very class or quality of evidence
we want. It is excellent so far as it goes; but does it go far enough? He tells us it
went *beyond* the Nueces; but he does not tell us it went to the Rio Grande. He
tells us jurisdiction was exercised *between* the two rivers, but he does not tell us

it was exercised over *all* the territory between them. Some simple-minded people, think it *possible* to cross one river and go *beyond* it, without going *all the way* to the next; that jurisdiction may be exercised *between* two rivers without covering *all* the country between them. I know a man, not very unlike myself, who exercises jurisdiction over a piece of land between the Wabash and the Mississippi; and yet so far is this from being *all* there is between those rivers, that it is just one hundred and fifty two feet long by fifty wide, and no part of it much within a hundred miles of either. He has a neighbour between him and the Mississippi—that is, just across the street, in that direction—whom, I am sure, he could neither *persuade* nor *force* to give up his habitation; but which nevertheless he could certainly annex, if it were to be done, by merely standing on his own side of the street and *claiming* it, or even sitting down and writing a *deed* for it.

But next, the President tells us, the Congress of the United States *understood* the State of Texas they admitted into the Union to extend *beyond* the Nueces. Well, I suppose they did—I certainly so understood it—but how *far* beyond? That Congress did *not* understand it to extend clear to the Rio Grande, is quite certain by the fact of their joint resolutions for admission expressly leaving all questions of boundary to future adjustment. And, it may be added, that Texas herself, is proved to have had the same understanding of it that our Congress had, by the fact of the exact conformity of her new constitution, to those resolutions.

I am now through the whole of the President's evidence; and it is a singular fact, that if any one should declare the President sent the army into the midst of a settlement of Mexican people, who had never submitted, by consent or by force to the authority of Texas or of the United States, and that *there*, and *thereby*, the first blood of the war was shed, there is not one word in all the President has said, which would either admit or deny the declaration. In this strange omission chiefly consists the deception of the President's evidence—an omission which, it does seem to me, could scarcely have occurred but by design. My way of living leads me to be about the courts of justice; and there I have sometimes seen a good lawyer, struggling for his client's neck, in a desperate case, employing every artifice to work round, befog, and cover up with many words some position pressed upon him by the prosecution, which he *dared* not admit, and yet *could* not deny. Party bias may help to make it appear so; but, with all the allowance I can make for such bias, it still does appear to me, that just such, and from just such necessity, is the President's struggle in this case.

Some time after my colleague [MR. RICHARDSON] introduced the resolutions I have mentioned, I introduced a preamble, resolution, and interrogatories intended to draw the President out, if possible, on this hitherto untrodden ground. To show their relevancy, I propose to state my understanding of the true rule for ascertaining the boundary between Texas and Mexico. It is, that *wherever* Texas was *exercising* jurisdiction was hers; and *wherever* Mexico was exercising jurisdiction, was hers; and that *whatever* separated the actual exercise of jurisdiction of the one from that of the other, was the true boundary between them. If, as is probably true, Texas was exercising jurisdiction along the western bank of the Nueces, and Mexico was exercising it along the eastern bank of the Rio Grande, then *neither* river was the boundary; but the uninhabited country between the two was. The extent of our territory in that region depended, not on any *treaty-fixed* boundary, (for no treaty had attempted it,) but on revolution. Any people anywhere, being inclined and having the power, have the *right* to rise up and shake off the existing government, and form a new one that suits them better. This is a most valuable, amost sacred right—a right which, we hope and believe, is to liberate the world. Nor is this right confined to cases in which the whole people of an existing government may choose to exercise it. Any portion of such people that *can may* revolutionize, and make their *own*, of so much of the territory as they inhabit. More than this, a *majority* of any portion of such people may revolutionize, putting down a *minority*, intermingled with, or near about them, who may oppose their movements. Such minority was precisely the case of the Tories of our own revolution. It is a quality of revolutions not to go by *old* lines, or *old* laws; but to break up both, and make new ones. As to the country now in question, we bought it of France in 1803, and sold it to Spain in 1819, according to the President's statements. After this, all Mexico, including Texas, revolutionized against Spain; and still later, Texas revolutionized against Mexico. In my view, just so far as she carried her revolution, by obtaining the *actual*, willing or unwilling, submission of the people, *so far*, the country was hers, and no farther.

Now, sir, for the purpose of obtaining the very best evidence, as to whether Texas had actually carried her revolution to the place where the hostilities of the present war commenced, let the President answer the interrogatories I proposed, as before mentioned, or some other similar ones. Let him answer, fully, fairly, and candidly. Let him answer with *facts*, and not with arguments. Let him remember he sits where Washington sat; and, so remembering, let him answer as Washington would answer. As a nation *should* not, and the Almighty *will* not, be evaded, so let him attempt no evasion, no equivocation. And if, so answering, he can show that the soil was ours where the first blood of the war was shed—that it was not within an inhabited country, or, if within such, that the inhabitants had submitted themselves to the civil authority of Texas, or of the United States, and that the same is true of the site of Fort Brown—then I am with him for his justification. In that case, I shall be most happy to reverse the vote I gave the other day. I have a selfish motive for desiring that the President may do this; I expect to give some votes, in connection with the war, which, without his so doing, will be of doubtful propriety, in my own judgment, but which will be free from the doubt, if he does so. But if he *cannot* or *will not* do this—if, on any pretence, or no pretence, he shall refuse or omit it—then I shall be fully convinced, of what I more than suspect already, that he is deeply conscious of being in the wrong; that he feels the blood of this war, like the blood of Abel, is crying to Heaven against him; that he ordered General Taylor into the midst of a peaceful Mexican settlement, purposely to bring on war; that originally having some strong motive—what I will not stop now to give my opinion concerning—to involve the two countries in a war, and trusting to escape scrutiny by fixing the public gaze upon the exceeding brightness of military glory—that attractive rainbow that rises in showers of blood—that serpent's eye, that charms to destroy—he plunged into it, and has swept *on* and *on*, till, disappointed in his calculation of the ease with which Mexico might be subdued, he now finds himself he knows not where. How like the half-insane mumbling of a fever dream is the whole war part of his late message! At one time telling us that Mexico has nothing whatever that we can get but territory; at another, showing us how we can support the war by levying contributions on Mexico. At one time urging the national honor, the security of the future, the prevention of foreign interference, and even the good of Mexico herself, as among the objects of the war; at another, telling us that, "to reject indemnity, by refusing to accept a cession of territory, would be to abandon all our just demands, and to wage the war, bearing all its expenses, *without a purpose or definite object.*" So then, the national honor, security of the future, and everything but territorial indemnity, may be considered the *no-purposes* and *indefinite* objects of the war! But, having it now settled that territorial indemnity is the only object, we are urged to seize, by legislation here, all that he was content to take a few months ago, and the whole province of Lower California to boot, and to still carry on the war—to take *all* we are fighting for, and still *fight* on. Again, the President is resolved, under all circumstances, to have full territorial indemnity for the expenses of the war; but he forgets to tell us how we are to get the *excess* after those expenses shall have surpassed the value of the *whole* of the Mexican territory. So again, he insists that the separate national existence of Mexico shall be maintained; but he does not tell us *how* this can be done after we shall have taken *all* her territory. Lest the questions I here suggest be considered speculative merely, let me be indulged a moment in trying to show they are not.

The war has gone on some twenty months; for the expenses of which, together with an inconsiderable old score, the President now claims about one half of the Mexican territory; and that by far the better half, so far as concerns our ability to make anything out of it. *It* is comparatively uninhabited; so that we could establish land offices in it, and raise some money in that way. But the other half is already inhabited, as I understand it, tolerably densely for the nature of the country; and all its lands, or all that are valuable, already appropriated as private property. How then are we to make anything out of these lands with this encumbrance on them, or how remove the encumbrance? I suppose no one will say we should kill the people, or drive them out, or make slaves of them, or even confiscate their property? How, then can we make much out of this part of the territory? If the prosecution of the war has, in expenses, already equaled the *better* half of the country, how long its future prosecution will be in equaling the less valuable half is not a *speculative*, but a *practical* question, pressing closely upon us; and yet it is a question which the President seems to never have thought of.

As to the mode of terminating the war and securing peace, the President is equally wandering and indefinite. First, it is to be done by a more vigorous prosecution of the war in the vital parts of the enemy's country; and, after apparently, talking himself tired on this point, the President drops down into a half despairing tone, and tells us, that "with a people distracted and divided by contending factions, and a government subject to constant changes, by successive revolutions, *the continued success of our arms may fail to secure a satisfactory peace.*" Then he suggests the propriety of wheedling the Mexican people to desert the counsels of their own leaders, and, trusting in our protection, to set up a Government from which we can secure a satisfactory peace; telling us, that *"this may become the only mode of obtaining such a peace."* But soon he falls into doubt of this too, and then drops back on to the already half-abandoned ground of "more vigorous prosecution." All this shows that the President is in no wise satisfied with his own positions. First, he takes up one, and, in attempting to argue us *into* it, he argues himself *out* of it; then seizes another, and goes through the same process; and then, confused at being able to think of nothing new, he snatches up the old one again, which he has some time before cast off. His mind, tasked beyond its power, is running hither and thither, like some tortured creature on a burning surface, finding no position on which it can settle down, and be at ease.

Again, it is a singular omission in this message, that it no where intimates *when* the President expects the war to terminate. At its beginning, General Scott was, by this same President, driven into disfavor, if not disgrace, for intimating that peace could not be conquered in less than three or four months. But now, at the end of about twenty months, during which time our arms have given us the most splendid successes—every department, and every part, land and water, officers and privates, regulars and volunteers, doing all that men *could* do, and hundreds of things which it had ever before been thought men could *not* do; after all this, this same President gives us a long message without showing us that, *as to the end*, he himself has even an imaginary conception. As I have before said, he knows not where he is. He is a bewildered, confounded, and miserably-perplexed man. God grant he may be able to show there is not something about his conscious, more painful than all his mental perplexity!

Interpretation

Numbering himself among "good citizens and patriots," Lincoln was prepared, he says, to wait until the war with Mexico was over before expressing his objections to it. But several unfair interpretations of House votes by President Polk, together with the need for voting soon on a bill expressly endorsing the justice of the war, convinced him to end his silence. So the freshman Congressman dares to make a speech explaining his opposition to the war, with logic so powerful and words so strong as to leave an indelible impression on all who listened to it with any care.

We need not enter into all the details of the problem. Referring primarily to the President's messages of May and December, 1846, Lincoln's criticism comes down to this: that the President made territorial demands of Mexico that were not justified. For our purposes, it is Lincoln's manner of proof, his general principles and the language he uses that interest most. His legal training and aptitude for logical analysis are plain to see. Reducing the President's position to six propositions, he considers them one by one and concludes that the President knowingly and systematically obfuscated and has not said "one word" either admitting or denying that he "sent the army into the midst of a settlement of Mexican people, who had never submitted, by consent or by force to the authority of Texas or of the United States and that *there*, and *thereby*, the first blood of the war was shed. . . ."

The only question, as Lincoln saw it, was whether the contested area (between two rivers) became part of Texas when Texas revolted from Mexico and hence part of the United States when Texas joined the union. If it did, it is American; if not, it is Mexican. To justify coming to this point, he offers a very broad principle with three parts, stated one after the other: "Any people anywhere, being inclined and having the power, have the *right* to rise up and shake off the existing government, and form a new one that suits them better. This is a most valuable, a most sacred right—a right which, we hope and believe is to liberate the world." Lincoln shows how far this right extends by adding: "Nor is this right confined to cases in which the whole people of an existing government may choose to exercise it. Any portion of such people that *can may* revolutionize, and make their *own* of so much of the territory as they inhabit. But the right goes even further: "More than this, a *majority* of any portion of such people may revolutionize, putting down a *minority*, intermingled with, or near about them, who may oppose their movements." Applying this to the contested area, Lincoln says: "In my view, just so far as she (Texas) carried her revolution, by obtaining the *actual*, willing or unwilling, submission of the people, *so far* the country was hers, and no farther."

Lincoln has assumed here, without expressly stipulating, that a new government formed by a revolution of a people, or part of a people, will have the object of protecting them and their rights better. He does not anticipate popular revolutions in favor of despotism. He has no objection to the fact that Mexico "revolutionized" against Spain, and Texas against Mexico. But in view of what was to transpire later in this country, it may be asked how he could denounce the secession of the South, given this view of the right to revolution. If a people and also a part of a people have the right to "revolutionize"—"to rise up and shake off the existing government and form a new one that suits them better"—would that not apply to the South's right to secede and form a new government that "suits them better"?

There are two ways of responding. One is that the right to revolutionize must be understood to be rightful only when the revolution aims at better securing rights, and the South's object in seceding was to preserve slavery, not end it. This is the kind of consideration we may infer from Lincoln's expectation that this right will "liberate the world"—in other words, not continue or extend despotism in any form. The second is the approach Lincoln himself later took in arguing against secession. He contended that there were constitutional obligations of the component states to the Union and each other that modified their right to secede—i.e., their right to revolutionize. Together, these points show that Lincoln's general way of expressing the right to revolutionize in this speech on the Mexican War was in some need of qualification. In addition, by declaring the right of a people or part of a people to revolutionize, Lincoln ran the risk of encouraging inadvertently not only excessive political and social disintegration but revolutions made in the name of the people by ruthless organized minorities—a problem that had already shown itself in the French Revolution and was to show itself even more abundantly in the twentieth century. Are not such dangers inherent in every effort to state, abstractly, a simple "right to revolution"? In the Declaration of Independence the difficulty is avoided by stipulating a "long train of tyrannical abuses" as the sufficient justification for our own revolution against Great Britain.

It is also curious that Lincoln spoke of submitting "by consent or by force, to the authority of Texas or of the United States,. . ." as if force is a sufficient title to rule. Soon afterward he repeats this: "In my view, just so far as she carried her revolution, by obtaining the *actual*, willing or unwilling, submission of the people, *so far* the country was hers, and no farther." Unwilling submission seems as good as willing submission. How can this be? To have submitted to us, either people in the disputed area were already part of the territory of Texas (as the Tories were with us) or they were conquered by Texas. Through his set of interrogatories for the President, Lincoln wants to determine "whether Texas had actually carried her revolution to the place where the hostilities of the present war commenced. . . ." That area was either uninhabited, as Lincoln originally states, or inhabited, and the question, in the latter case, is whether "the inhabitants had submitted themselves to the civil authority of Texas, or of the United States." He thinks not.

Twice Lincoln assumes that submission obtained through force as well as through consent is a sufficient title to rule the inhabitants of the area. He does not carefully restrict his principle to minorities, like the Tories, already living within the area. Nor does he even insist that the conquest be just. Is this not inconsistent with the Declaration of Independence itself, according to which anything short of consent of the governed lacks legitimacy? And is there not also a glaring inconsistency between this and Lincoln's fierce condemnation of President Polk for engaging in what amounted to an unjust conquest? In the latter part of the seventeenth century, the right to conquest had been asserted by Thomas Hobbes as a basis, along with consent, for political legitimacy, but soon afterward John Locke insisted that even conquest in a just war yielded no right to keep the conquered territories. Nevertheless, by Lincoln's day, international law had accorded a solid position to the right of conquest—a situation that changed only after World War I.

In framing his argument against the war, Lincoln may have chosen to give the President's position as much leeway as possible, using generally accepted standards of international law, whether sound or not, to prove that the war is still unjust. He could do this consistently because that article of international law was meant to allow for already-existing conquests, not to encourage new wars and new conquests (even though that may have been its effect in some cases). From the American point of view—and this is Lincoln's own standard—to invade a Mexican settlement that does not belong to us, claim it for our own and wage an enlarged war over it is a simple exercise in despotism, and that's how Lincoln treats it. On examining President Polk's motives and avowed purposes, Lincoln uses the strongest rhetoric of the speech to condemn him as an unjust conqueror and even murderer. He suspects that the President is "deeply conscious of being in the wrong. . . ." He accuses him of using the baleful attractiveness of military glory to goad the country on. He ridicules the President's appeal to national honor and security, and especially his impossible demands for enormous indemnities. He casts a lurid light on the President's intellectual inability to show how he plans to end a war that has already lasted twenty months.

Lincoln had pledged to serve only one term, and a good thing too, since his stand on the Mexican War was very unpopular in Illinois. The speech had little direct effect one way or the other, but it trumpeted Lincoln's arrival on the national scene. For a freshman in the House to have given voice to such a speech, taking on the president in terms that could not be stronger, was a harbinger of things to come involving much greater issues. Lincoln was always willing to stand alone, but he was also anxious to find ways to persuade others of his views. The combination of independent and powerful thought with memorable expression suited to the occasion was always his hallmark. His political career and meteoric rise are hard to conceive without it.

A question has been raised as to whether Lincoln was guilty of gross exaggeration in condemning Polk did he do it for partisan Whig purposes, or simply to draw attention to himself? The vehemence of Lincoln's attack can be explained much more easily and directly. He did not want his country to do a great injustice—a country uniquely devoted to justice and human rights. He did not want to see it engage in the kind of war for gain and aggrandizement so common in history and so often undertaken by undemocratic regimes. And he may have had particular apprehension about acquiring land in warmer climes that might be conducive to slavery. As Lincoln saw it, the president was causing the country to violate its own principles, and for that he deserved severe censure. Nor, we suspect, did Lincoln mind, in the process, drawing attention to himself.

Chapter 5

The Eulogy on Henry Clay, July 6, 1852

Lincoln delivered this eulogy at the State House in Springfield as part of a memorial service for Clay.

Text

On the fourth day of July, 1776, the people of a few feeble and oppressed colonies of Great Britain, inhabiting a portion of the Atlantic coast of North America, publicly declared their national independence, and made their appeal to the justice of their cause, and to the God of battles, for the maintainance of that declaration. That people were few in numbers, and without resources, save only their own wise heads and stout hearts. Within the first year of that declared independence, and while its maintainance was yet problematical—while the bloody struggle between those resolute rebels, and their haughty would-be-masters, was still waging, of undistinguished parents, and in an obscure district of one of those colonies, Henry Clay was born. The infant nation, and the infant child began the race of life together. For three quarters of a century they have travelled hand in hand. They have been companions ever. The nation has passed its perils, and is free, prosperous, and powerful. The child has reached his manhood, his middle age, his old age, and is dead. In all that has concerned the nation the man ever sympathised; and now the nation mourns for the man.

The day after his death, one of the public Journals, opposed to him politically, held the following pathetic and beautiful language, which I adopt, partly because such high and exclusive eulogy, originating with a political friend, might offend good taste, but chiefly, because I could not, in any language of my own, so well express my thoughts—

"Alas! who can realize that Henry Clay is dead! Who can realize that never again that majestic form shall rise in the council-chambers of his country to beat back the storms of anarchy which may threaten, or pour the oil of peace upon the troubled billows as they rage and menace around? Who can realize, that the workings of that mighty mind have ceased—that the throbbings of that gallant heart are stilled—that the mighty sweep of that graceful arm will be felt no more, and the magic of that eloquent tongue, which spake as spake no other tongue besides, is hushed—hushed forever! Who can realize that freedom's champion—the champion of a civilized world, and of all tongues and kindreds and people, has indeed fallen! Alas, in those dark hours, which, as they come in the history of all nations, must come in ours—those hours of peril and dread which our land has experienced, and which she may be called to experience again—to whom now may her people look up for that counsel and advice, which only wisdom and experience and patriotism can give, and which only the undoubting confidence of a nation will receive? Perchance, in the whole circle of the great and gifted of our land, there remains but one on whose shoulders the mighty mantle of the departed statesman may fall—one, while we now write, is doubtless pouring his tears over the bier of his brother and his friend—brother, friend ever, yet in political sentiment, as far apart as party could make them. Ah, it is at times like these, that the petty distinctions of mere party disappear. We see only the great, the grand, the noble features of the departed statesman; and we do not even beg permission to bow at his feet and mingle our tears with those who have ever been his political adherents—we do [not?] beg this permission—we claim it as a right, though we feel it as a privilege. Henry Clay belonged to his country—to the world, mere party cannot claim men like him. His career has been national—his fame has filled the earth—his memory will endure to "the last syllable of recorded time."

"Henry Clay is dead!—He breathed his last on yesterday at twenty minutes after eleven, in his chamber at Washington. To those who followed his lead in public affairs, it more appropriately belongs to pronounce his eulogy, and pay specific honors to the memory of the illustrious dead—but all Americans may show the grief which his death inspires, for, his character and fame are national property. As on a question of liberty, he knew no North, no South, no East, no West, but only the Union, which held them all in its sacred circle, so now his countrymen will know no grief, that is not as wide-spread as the bounds of the confederacy. The career of Henry Clay was a public career. From his youth he has been devoted to the public service, at a period too, in the world's history justly regarded as a remarkable era in human affairs. He witnessed in the beginning the throes of the French Revolution. He saw the rise and fall of Napoleon. He was called upon to legislate for America, and direct her policy when all Europe was the battle-field of contending dynasties, and when the struggle for supremacy imperilled the rights of all neutral nations. His voice spoke war and peace in the contest with Great Britain.

"When Greece rose against the Turks and struck for liberty, his name was mingled with the battle-cry of freedom. When South America threw off the thraldom of Spain, his speeches were read at the head of her armies by Bolivar. His name has been, and will continue to be, hallowed in two hemispheres, for it is—

One of the few the immortal names
That were not born to die,

"To the ardent patriot and profound statesman, he added a quality possessed by few of the gifted on earth. His eloquence has not been surpassed. In the effective power to move the heart of man, Clay was without an equal, and the heaven born endowment, in the spirit of its origin, has been most conspicuously exhibited against intestine feud. On at least three important occasions, he has quelled our civil commotions, by a power and influence, which belonged to no other statesman of his age and times. And in our last internal discord, when this Union trembled to its center—in old age, he left the shades of private life and gave the death blow to fraternal strife, with the vigor of his earlier years in a series of Senatorial efforts, which in themselves would bring immortality, by challenging comparison with the efforts of any statesman in any age. He exorcised the demon which possessed the body politic, and gave peace to a distracted land. Alas! The achievement cost him his life! He sank day by day to the tomb—his pale, but noble brow, bound with a triple wreath, put there by a grateful country. May his ashes rest in peace, while his spirit goes to take its station among the great and good men who preceded him!"

While it is customary, and proper, upon occasions like the present, to give a brief sketch of the life of the deceased, in the case of Mr. Clay, it is less necessary than most others; for his biography has been written and re-written, and read and re-read, for the last twenty-five years; so that, with the exception of a few of the latest incidents of his life, all is as well known, as it can be. The short sketch which I give is, therefore, merely to maintain the connection of this discourse.

Henry Clay was born on the 12th of April 1777, in Hanover County, Virginia. Of his father, who died in the fourth or fifth year of Henry's age, little seems to be known, except that he was a respectable man, and a preacher of the Baptist persuasion. Mr. Clay's education, to the end of life, was comparatively limited. I say *"to the end of life,"* because I have understood that, from time to time, he added something to his education during the greater part of his whole life. Mr. Clay's lack of a more perfect early education, however it may be regretted generally, teaches at least one profitable lesson: it teaches that in this country, one can scarcely be so poor, but that, if he *will,* he *can* acquire sufficient education to get through the world respectably. In his twenty-third year Mr. Clay was licenced to practice law, and emigrated to Lexington, Kentucky. Here he commenced and continued the practice till the year 1803, when he was first elected to the Kentucky legislature. By successive elections he was continued in the Legislature till the latter part of 1806, when he was elected to fill a vacancy, of a single session, in the United States Senate. In 1807 he was again elected to the Kentucky House of Representatives, and by that body, chosen its Speaker. In 1808 he was re-elected to the same body. In 1809 he was again chosen to fill a vacancy of two years in the United States Senate. In 1811 he was elected to the

United States House of Representatives, and on the first day of taking his seat in that body, he was chosen its Speaker. In 1813 he was again elected Speaker. Early in 1814, being the period of our last British war, Mr. Clay was sent as commissioner, with others, to negotiate a treaty of peace, which treaty was concluded in the latter part of the same year. On his return from Europe he was again elected to the lower branch of Congress, and on taking his seat in December 1815 was called to his old post—the Speaker's, a position in which he was retained by successive elections, with one brief intermission, till the inauguration of John Q. Adams in March 1825. He was then appointed Secretary of State, and occupied that important station till the inauguration of Gen. Jackson in March 1829. After this he returned to Kentucky, resumed the practice of the law, and continued it till the autumn of 1831, when he was by the legislature of Kentucky, again placed in the United States Senate. By a re-election he continued in the Senate till he resigned his seat, and retired, in March 1848. In December 1849 he again took his seat in the Senate, which he again resigned only a few months before his death.

By the foregoing it is perceived that the period from the beginning of Mr. Clay's official life, in 1803, to the end of it in 1852, is but one year short of half a century; and that the sum of all the intervals in it, will not amount to ten years. But mere duration of time in office, constitutes the smallest part of Mr. Clay's history. Throughout that long period, he has constantly been the most loved, and most implicitly followed by friends, and the most dreaded by opponents, of all living American politicians. In all the great questions which have agitated the country, and particularly in those fearful crises, the Missouri question—the Nullification question, and the late slavery question, as connected with the newly acquired territory, involving and endangering the stability of the Union, his has been the leading and most conspicuous part. In 1824 he was first a candidate for the Presidency, and was defeated; and, although he was successively defeated for the same office in 1832 and in 1844, there has never been a moment since 1824 till after 1848 when a very large portion of the American people did not cling to him with an enthusiastic hope and purpose of still elevating him to the Presidency. With other men, to be defeated, was to be forgotten; but to him, defeat was but a trifling incident, neither changing him, or the world's estimate of him. Even those of both political parties who have been preferred to him for the highest office, have run far briefer courses than he, and left him, still shining high in the heavens of the political world. Jackson, Van Buren, Harrison, Polk, and Taylor, all rose *after,* and set long before him. The spell—the long enduring spell—with which the souls of men were bound to him, is a miracle. Who can compass it? It is probably true he owed his pre-eminence to no one quality, but to a fortunate combination of several. He was surpassingly eloquent; but many eloquent men fail utterly; and they are not, as a class, generally successful. His judgment was excellent; but many men of good judgment, live and die unnoticed.—His will was indomitable; but this quality often secures to its owner nothing better than a character for useless obstinacy. These then were Mr. Clay's leading qualities. No one of them is very uncommon; but all together are rarely combined in a single individual; and this is probably the reason why such men as Henry Clay are so rare in the world.

Mr. Clay's eloquence did not consist, as many fine specimens of eloquence do, of types and figures—of antithesis, and elegant arrangement of words and sentences; but rather of that deeply earnest and impassioned tone, and manner, which can proceed only from great sincerity, and thorough conviction, in the speaker of the justice and importance of his cause. This it is, that truly touches the chords of sympathy; and those who heard Mr. Clay never failed to be moved by it, or ever afterwards, forgot the impression. All his efforts were made for practical effect. He never spoke merely to be heard. He never delivered a Fourth of July oration, or an eulogy on an occasion like this. As a politician or states-man, no one was so habitually careful to avoid all sectional ground. Whatever he did, he did for the whole country. In the construction of his measures he ever carefully surveyed every part of the field, and duly weighed every conflicting interest. Feeling, as he did, and as the truth surely is, that the world's best hope depended on the continued Union of these States, he was ever jealous of, and watchful for, whatever might have the slightest tendency to separate them.

Mr. Clay's predominant sentiment, from first to last, was a deep devotion to the cause of human liberty—a strong sympathy with the oppressed everywhere, and an ardent wish for their elevation. With him, this was a primary and all con-trolling passion. Subsidiary to this was the conduct of his whole life. He loved his country partly because it was his own country, but mostly because it was a free country; and he burned with a zeal for its advancement, prosperity and glory, because he saw in such, the advancement, prosperity and glory, of human liberty, human right and human nature. He desired the prosperity of his coun-trymen partly because they were his countrymen, but chiefly to show to the world that freemen could be prosperous.

That his views and measures were always the wisest, needs not to be af-firmed; nor should it be, on this occasion, where so many, thinking differently, join in doing honor to his memory. A free people, in times of peace and quiet—when pressed by no common danger—naturally divide into parties. At such times the man who is of neither party, is not—cannot be, of any consequence. Mr. Clay, therefore, was of a party. Taking a prominent part, as he did, in all the great political questions of his country for the last half century, the wisdom of his course on many, is doubted and denied by a large portion of his countrymen; and of such it is not now proper to speak particularly.—But there are many oth-ers, about his course upon which, there is little or no disagreement amongst in-telligent and patriotic Americans. Of these last are the War of 1812, the Mis-souri question, Nullification, and the now recent compromise measures. In 1812 Mr. Clay, though not unknown, was still a young man. Whether we should go to war with Great Britain, being the question of the day, a minority opposed the declaration of war by Congress, while the majority, though apparently inclining to war, had, for years, wavered, and hesitated to act decisively. Meanwhile British aggressions multiplied, and grew more daring and aggravated. By Mr. Clay, more than any other man, the struggle was brought to a decision in Congress. The question, being now fully before Congress, came up, in a variety of ways, in rapid succession, on most of which occasions Mr. Clay spoke. Adding to all the logic, of which the subject was susceptible, that noble inspiration, which came to him as it came to no other, he aroused, and nerved, and inspired his friends, and confounded and bore-down all opposition. Several of his speeches, on these occasions, were reported, and are still extant; but the best of these all never was. During its delivery the reporters forgot their vocations, dropped their pens, and sat enchanted from near the beginning to quite the close. The speech now lives only in the memory of a few old men; and the enthusiasm with which they cherish their recollection of it is absolutely astonishing. The precise language of this speech we shall never know; but we do know—we cannot help knowing—that, with deep pathos, it pleaded the cause of the injured sailor—that it invoked the genius of the revolution—that it apostrophized the names of Otis, of Henry and of Washington—that it appealed to the interest, the pride, the honor and the glory of the nation—that it shamed and taunted the timidity of friends—that it scorned, and scouted, and withered the temerity of domestic foes—that it bearded and defied the British Lion—and rising, and swelling, and maddening in its course, it sounded the onset, till the charge, the shock, the steady struggle, and the glorious victory, all passed in vivid review before the entranced hearers.

Important and exciting as was the war question, of 1812, it never so alarmed the sagacious statesmen of the country for the safety of the republic, as afterwards did the Missouri question. This sprang from that unfortunate source of discord—negro slavery. When our Federal Constitution was adopted, we owned no territory beyond the limits or ownership of the States, except the territory North-West of the River Ohio, and east of the Mississippi. What has since been formed into the States of Maine, Kentucky, and Tennessee, was, I believe, within the limits of or owned by Massachusetts, Virginia, and North Carolina. As to the North Western Territory, provision had been made, even before the adoption of the Constitution, that slavery should never go there. On the admission of the States into the Union carved from the territory we owned before the constitution, no question—or at most, no considerable question—arose about slavery—those which were within the limits of or owned by the old states, following, respectively, the condition of the parent state, and those within the North West territory, following the previously made provision. But in 1803 we purchased Louisiana of the French; and it included with much more, what has since been formed into the State of Missouri. With regard to it, nothing had been done to forestall the question of slavery. When, therefore, in 1819, Missouri, having formed a State constitution, without excluding slavery, and with slavery already actually existing within its limits, knocked at the door of the Union for admission, almost the entire representation of the non-slave-holding states, objected. A fearful and angry struggle instantly followed. This alarmed thinking men, more than any previous question, because, unlike all the former, it divided the country by geographical lines. Other questions had their opposing partizans in all localities of the country and in almost every family; so that no division of the Union could follow such, without a separation of friends, to quite as great an extent, as that of opponents.—Not so with the Missouri question. On this a geographical line could be traced which, in the main, would separate opponents only. This was the danger. Mr. Jefferson, then in retirement, wrote:

"I had for a long time ceased to read newspapers, or to pay any attention to public affairs, confident they were in good hands, and content to be a passenger in our bark to the shore from which I am not distant. But this momentous question, like a fire bell in the night, awakened, and filled me with terror. I considered it at once as the knell of the Union. It is hushed, indeed, for the moment. But this is a reprieve only, not a final sentence. A geographical line, co-inciding with a marked principle, moral and political, once conceived, and held up to the angry passions of men, will never be obliterated, and every irritation will mark it deeper and deeper. I can say, with conscious truth, that there is not a man on earth who would sacrifice more than I would to relieve us from this heavy reproach, in any practicable way. The cession of that kind of property, for so it is misnamed, is a bagatelle which would not cost me a second thought, if, in that way, a general emancipation, and expatriation could be effected; and, gradually, and with due sacrifices I think it might be. But as it is, we have the wolf by the ears and we can neither hold him, nor safely let him go. Justice is in one scale, and self-preservation in the other."

Mr. Clay was in Congress, and, perceiving the danger, at once engaged his whole energies to avert it. It began, as I have said, in 1819; and it did not terminate till 1821. Missouri would not yield the point; and Congress—that is, a majority in Congress—by repeated votes, showed a determination to not admit the State unless it should yield. After several failures, and great labor on the part of Mr. Clay to so present the question that a majority could consent to the admission, it was, by a vote, rejected, and as all seemed to think, finally. A sullen gloom hung over the nation. All felt that the rejection of Missouri, was equivalent to a dissolution of the Union, because those states which already had, what Missouri was rejected for refusing to relinquish, would go with Missouri. All deprecated and deplored this, but none saw how to avert it. For the judgment of members to be convinced of the necessity of yielding, was not the whole difficulty; each had a constituency to meet, and to answer to. Mr. Clay, though worn down, and exhausted, was appealed to by members, to renew his efforts at compromise. He did so, and by some judicious modifications of his plan, coupled with laborious efforts with individual members, and his own over-mastering eloquence upon the floor, he finally secured the admission of the State. Brightly, and captivating as it had previously shown, it was now perceived that his great eloquence, was a mere embellishment, or, at most, but a helping hand to his inventive genius, and his devotion to his country in the day of her extreme peril.

After the settlement of the Missouri question, although a portion of the American people have differed with Mr. Clay, and a majority even, appear generally to have been opposed to him on questions of ordinary administration, he seems constantly to have been regarded by all, as *the* man for a crisis. Accordingly, in the days of Nullification, and more recently in the re-appearance of the slavery question, connected with our territory newly acquired of Mexico, the task of devising a mode of adjustment, seems to have been cast upon Mr. Clay, by common consent—and his performance of the task, in each case, was little else than, a literal fulfilment of the public expectation.

Mr. Clay's efforts in behalf of the South Americans, and afterwards, in behalf of the Greeks, in the times of their respective struggles for civil liberty are among the finest on record, upon the noblest of all themes; and bear ample corroboration of what I have said was his ruling passion—a love of liberty and right, unselfishly, and for their own sakes.

Having been led to allude to domestic slavery so frequently already, I am unwilling to close without referring more particularly to Mr. Clay's views and conduct in regard to it. He ever was on principle and in feeling, opposed to slavery. The very earliest, and one of the latest public efforts of his life, separated by a period of more than fifty years, were both made in favor of gradual emancipation of the slave in Kentucky. He did not perceive, that on a question of human right, the negroes were to be excepted from the human race. And yet Mr. Clay was the owner of slaves. Cast into life where slavery was already widely spread and deeply seated, he did not perceive, as I think no wise man has perceived, how it could be at *once* eradicated, without producing a greater evil, even to the cause of human liberty itself. His feeling and his judgment, therefore, ever led him to oppose both extremes of opinion on the subject. Those who would shiver into fragments the Union of these States; tear to tatters its now venerated constitution; and even burn the last copy of the Bible, rather than slavery should continue a single hour, together with all their more halting sympathisers, have received, and are receiving their just execration; and the name, and opinions, and influence of Mr. Clay, are fully, and, as I trust, effectually and enduringly, arrayed against them. But I would also, if I could, array his name, opinions, and influence against the opposite extreme—against a few, but an increasing number of men, who, for the sake of perpetuating slavery, are beginning to assail and to ridicule the white man's charter of freedom—the declaration that "all men are created free and equal." So far as I have learned, the first American, of any note, to do or attempt this, was the late John C. Calhoun; and if I mistake not, it soon after found its way into some of the messages of the Governors of South Carolina. We, however, look for, and are not much shocked by, political eccentricities and heresies in South Carolina. But, only last year, I saw with astonishment, what purported to be a letter of a very distinguished and influential clergyman of Virginia, copied, with apparent approbation, into a St. Louis news-paper, containing the following, to me, very unsatisfactory language—

"I am fully aware that there is a text in some Bibles that is not in mine. Professional abolitionists have made more use of it, than of any passage in the Bible. It came, however, as I trace it, from Saint Voltaire, and was baptized by Thomas Jefferson, and since almost universally regarded as canonical authority, '*All men are born free and equal.*'

"This is a genuine coin in the political currency of our generation. I am sorry to say that I have never seen two men of whom it is true. But I must admit I never saw the Siamese twins, and therefore will not dogmatically say that no man ever saw a proof of this sage aphorism."

This sounds strangely in republican America.—The like was not heard in the fresher days of the Republic. Let us contrast with it the language of that truly national man, whose life and death we now commemorate and lament. I quote from a speech of Mr. Clay delivered before the American Colonization Society in 1827:

"We are reproached with doing mischief by the agitation of this question. The society goes into no household to disturb its domestic tranquillity; it addresses itself to no slaves to weaken their obligations of obedience. It seeks to affect no man's property. It neither has the power nor the will to affect the property of any one contrary to his consent.—The execution of its scheme would augment instead of diminishing the value of the property left behind. The society, composed of free men, concerns itself only with the free. Collateral consequences we are not responsible for. It is not this society which has produced the great moral revolution which the age exhibits. What would they, who thus reproach us, have done? If they would repress all tendencies towards liberty, and ultimate emancipation, they must do more than put down the benevolent efforts of this society. They must go back to the era of our liberty and independence, and muzzle the cannon which thunders its annual joyous return. They must renew the slave trade with all its train of atrocities. They must suppress the workings of British philanthropy, seeking to meliorate the condition of the unfortunate West Indian slave. They must arrest the career of South American deliverance from thraldom. They must blow out the moral lights around us, and extinguish that greatest torch of all which America presents to a benighted world— pointing the way to their rights, their liberties, and their happiness. And when they have achieved those purposes their work will be yet incomplete. They must penetrate the human soul, and eradicate the light of reason and the love of liberty. Then, and not till then, when universal darkness and despair prevail, can you perpetuate slavery, and repress all sympathy, and all humane, and benevolent efforts among free men, in behalf of the unhappy portion of our race doomed to bondage."

The American Colonization Society was organized in 1816. Mr. Clay, though not its projector, was one of its earliest members; and he died, as for the many preceding years he had been, its President.—It was one of the most cherished objects of his direct care and consideration; and the association of his name with it has probably been its very greatest collateral support. He considered it no demerit in the society, that it tended to relieve slave-holders from the troublesome presence of the free negroes; but this was far from being its whole merit in his estimation. In the same speech from which I have quoted he says:

"There is a moral fitness in the idea of returning to Africa her children, whose ancestors have been torn from her by the ruthless hand of fraud and violence. Transplanted in a foreign land, they will carry back to their native soil the rich fruits of religion, civilization, law and liberty. May it not be one of the great designs of the Ruler of the universe, (whose ways are often inscrutable by short-sighted mortals,) thus to transform an original crime, into a signal blessing to that most unfortunate portion of the globe?"

This suggestion of the possible ultimate redemption of the African race and African continent, was made twenty-five years ago. Every succeeding year has added strength to the hope of its realization.—May it indeed be realized! Pharaoh's country was cursed with plagues, and his hosts were drowned in the Red Sea for striving to retain a captive people who had already served them more than four hundred years. May like disasters never befall us! If as the friends of colonization hope, the present and coming generations of our countrymen shall by any means, succeed in freeing our land from the dangerous presence of slavery; and, at the same time, in restoring a captive people to their long-lost father-land, with bright prospects for the future; and this too, so gradually, that neither races nor individuals shall have suffered by the change, it will indeed be a glorious consummation. And if, to such a consummation, the efforts of Mr. Clay shall have contributed, it will be what he most ardently wished, and none of his labors will have been more valuable to his country and his kind.

But Henry Clay is dead. His long and eventful life is closed. Our country is prosperous and powerful; but could it have been quite all it has been, and is, and is to be, without Henry Clay? Such a man the times have demanded, and such, in the providence of God was given us. But he is gone. Let us strive to deserve, as far as mortals may, the continued care of Divine Providence, trusting that, in future national emergencies, He will not fail to provide us the instruments of safety and security.

Interpretation

It is not often that a great man receives a eulogy from another great man—in this case, as it happens, an even greater man. Lincoln's carefully woven speech tells us why he thought Clay great, and from it we can infer the standard of greatness he applies. We also come to see some of the differences between the two men. Lincoln tells us Clay, who ran unsuccessfully for president three times, did not make eulogies, and here is Lincoln eulogizing Clay.

At the beginning, Lincoln relates Clay's life-span to that of the Union, and actually exaggerates the Union's success or health when he says, "The nation has passed its perils, and is free, prosperous, and powerful." As of 1852, two years after Clay's last great Compromise, it may have looked that way, but Lincoln knew better. He knew that the forces of disunity had hardly disappeared, as later shown by the quotation from Thomas Jefferson and his own description of recent pro-slavery expression. He proceeds to the speech's longest quotation by far from the eulogy of Clay given by a Journal opposed to him politically. Its language is truly remarkable. It celebrates Clay's "mighty mind," "gallant heart," and "eloquent tongue." It calls him "freedom's champion—the champion of a civilized world, and of all tongues and kindreds and people. . . ." And "His eloquence has not been surpassed. In the effective power to move the heart of man, Clay was without equal." This judgment of Clay's eloquence Lincoln himself corroborates toward the end of the speech when he cites a particularly striking example of Clay's rhetoric. The Journal eulogy concludes by stating that Clay "quelled our civil commotions" at least three times, and with his last effort, "He exorcised the demon which possessed the body politic, and gave peace to a distracted land." This time it is the Journal, even more than Lincoln, that overstates the case for Clay's accomplishments: the "civil commotions" may have been quieted, but they were hardly quelled.

Then we have from Lincoln himself a short sketch of Clay's life, with political accomplishments starting in 1803, when he was only twenty-six years old. His relative lack of education proves that "in this country, one can scarcely be so poor, but that, if he will, he can acquire sufficient education to get through the world respectably." Lincoln cites the many and various positions Clay held, starting with the Kentucky legislature and mounting to the U.S. House of Representatives (usually as Speaker) and Senate, with some time in between for a stint of diplomacy and service as Secretary of State, in all, a period of about forty years. Throughout, Lincoln tells us, he was the "most loved" and the "most feared" of all politicians of his time. He played the "most conspicuous part" in all the great issues, and "particularly in those fearful crises, the Missouri question—the Nullification question, and the late slavery question, as connected with the newly acquired territory (from the Mexican War), involving and endangering the stability of the Union. . . ." He ran for president three times and was defeated three times. But neither he nor "the world's estimate of him" ever changed: "The spell—the long-enduring spell—with which the souls of men were bound to him, is a miracle." His preeminence was owed, Lincoln tells us, to a combination of three qualities"—his eloquence, his excellent judgment, and his indomitable will—rarely found together in one man, so his spell over men would not quite be a miracle.

Lincoln turns first to Clay's eloquence. It is his "deeply earnest and impassioned tone" that truly touches the chords of sympathy" and moves his listeners unforgettably. But he never spoke at ordinary events, "never delivered a Fourth of July oration or a eulogy on an occasion like this one." He never took a merely sectional stance, always looked to the good of the "whole country," and felt—as is true, Lincoln says—that "the world's best hope depended on the continued Union of these States." Before turning to Clay's judgment or wisdom, Lincoln tells us that his "predominant sentiment" was his devotion to liberty and his sympathy for the oppressed. He loved his country, partly because it was his own but "mostly because it was a free country. . . ." Having participated in the great issues facing his country over a long period of time, there are bound to be disagreements as to the wisdom of his policies, but there is "little or no disagreement" about the role he played in many, including these four: "the War of 1812, the Missouri question, Nullification, and the more recent compromise measures." Lincoln adds the first of these to the three cited in the Journal eulogy, as if to indicate that Clay was prepared to seek war against external enemies as well as peace within the Union. Of the four, Lincoln dilates only on the first two. In his description of the heights of eloquence to which Clay reached in arguing for the War of 1812, Lincoln speaks of his best speech as unrecorded and then gives us a most masterful account of how that speech probably sounded.

With respect to the Missouri question, Lincoln presents the background leading up to the crisis, which, because it split the nation geographically over the issue of slavery, deeply threatened the Union. He quotes from Jefferson's letter likening "this momentous question" to a "firebell in the night." "All felt," Lincoln tells us, "that the rejection of Missouri, was equivalent to a dissolution of the Union, because those states which already had, what Missouri was rejected for refusing to relinquish, would go with Missouri." Lincoln does not state the compromise plan with which Clay finally won the day, and, while paying tribute to his "inventive genius," falls short of commending its wisdom. And we must remember the line Lincoln also quotes from Jefferson: "But this is a reprieve only, not a final sentence." The problem of slavery will not go away.

Instead of treating the other two of Clay's greatest accomplishments—Nullification and the "now recent compromise measures" of 1850—Lincoln mentions them again, briefly, and goes on to refer to Clay's efforts abroad in behalf of liberty in South America and Greece as "among the finest on record, upon the noblest of all themes," testifying once more to "his ruling Passion—a love of liberty, and right, unselfishly, and for their own sakes." His final extended topic becomes Clay's attitude toward slavery. Since Lincoln had introduced the four accomplishments by saying how fully the country was behind them, and since the two omitted topics—the one by the very nature of the nullification idea, the other by its recent urgency—at least equal the Missouri question (and exceed the war of 1812) in importance, we have to wonder about their omission. In re-examining the passage in question we see that Lincoln had said about Clay, in introducing them, "That his views and measures were always the wisest, needs not to be affirmed"; and while granting that the wisdom of many "is doubted and denied by a large part of his countrymen," there are many others, including the four he specifies, on which "there is little or no disagreement amongst intelligent and patriotic Americans." Now this lack of disagreement isn't quite the same thing as affirming their wisdom. Those "intelligent and patriotic Americans"—and Lincoln doesn't say he was one of them—could be wrong. This may be a little indication that he avoided two of the four major topics because he could not enter into them without criticizing Clay and showing the shortcomings of compromise itself. We know that when Lincoln was in Congress he voted time and again against allowing slavery in any of the territories obtained from Mexico, and this by itself would make him leery of the territorial compromises of 1850. As for nullification, an issue settled as far back as 1835, when Lincoln was still in the Illinois legislature, we can infer his likely position on it from the stand he later took on secession. The same principle is at issue in both, and Lincoln's opposition to secession allowed of no concession or compromise: the very existence of the Federal Union was at stake. The same unwillingness to compromise held for his opposition to the extension of slavery into the territories.

A eulogy has its own demands, and Lincoln did his job well. He gives us an open and full idea of Clay's greatness and a much less obvious idea of his limitations—from which we can also gather a better appreciation of Lincoln's own greatness. The last part of the eulogy deals with Clay's "views and conduct" regarding slavery, which "on principle and in feeling" he always opposed. Clay tried to bring about the "gradual emancipation of the slave in Kentucky" in his very first "public effort," and in one of his last as well. He owned slaves, and, seeing how "widely spread and deeply seated" the institution was, could perceive no way, "as I think no wise man has perceived," of eradicating it at *once* without at the same time "producing a greater evil, even to the cause of human liberty itself." For that reason, "His feeling and his judgment," led him to oppose the two extremes of abolitionism (Lincoln does not use the term) and hardened pro-slavery sentiment. Here is where Lincoln and Clay are closest to each other.

Lincoln has harsh words for the abolitionists, who "together with all their more halting sympathizers, have received, and are receiving their just execration," and Clay's views are helping in this cause. But Lincoln, talking for himself now, says he "would also, if I could, array his name, opinions, and influence against the opposite extreme," the increasing number of men (Lincoln traces their origin to John C. Calhoun) who assault the principle of the equality of all men in order to "perpetuate slavery." Lincoln does not say that Clay himself confronted these men, and perhaps implies that he didn't, if Lincoln has to do the arraying for him. What he does is quote a long wonderful passage from an early speech of Clay's in 1827, defending the American Colonization Society against attack. This is how Lincoln does the arraying. Falling just short of citing the Declaration of Independence for our principles of equality and liberty, Clay nevertheless gives a truly eloquent defense of the "great moral revolution which the age exhibits," tracing it to "the light of reason and the love of liberty, and broadly attacking those who would "perpetuate slavery, and repress all sympathy, and all humane, and benevolent efforts among free men, in behalf of the unhappy portion of our race doomed to bondage."

Clay had been one of the earliest members of the American Colonization Society and was its president when he died. The society looked to the gradual voluntary emancipation of the blacks by their owners (he had worked for such a system in Kentucky) and helping them return to Africa, bringing with them "the rich fruits of religion, civilization, law and liberty," and thus transforming an "original crime," a crime of "fraud and violence," into a "signal blessing to that most unfortunate portion of the globe." But Clay's work for emancipation in Kentucky began even before 1802, according to Lincoln, and that was years before the society was formed in 1816 and before he joined it soon afterward. For all those years Clay must have believed in a gradual emancipation by which the freed slave remained here in American society, and that presupposition Lincoln never criticizes, even though Clay, possibly out of desperation, turns to colonization as the solution for the freed black. In other words, if, for whatever reason, colonization proves impracticable, the idea of gradual emancipation, joined with some kind of integration here, on these shores, remained a possible alternative.

Lincoln speaks optimistically of the continual strengthening of the colonization idea. Hoping for its realization, he cites the fate of Pharaoh's Egypt when it refused to free a captive people: "May like disasters never befall us!" He says it would be a "glorious consummation" were our countrymen to succeed "by any means" in "freeing our land from the dangerous presence of slavery," doing it "so gradually that neither races nor individuals shall have suffered by the change," and bringing about the "possible ultimate redemption of the African race and African continent." If Henry Clay's efforts "shall have contributed to this consummation," none of his accomplishments would prove more valuable "to his country and kind." Lincoln fails to mention that it was by a divine miracle that Egypt was punished in the Bible, and by referring to the "dangerous presence of slavery" he could mean either a danger coming from God, from a civil war about it, or (more likely from the Biblical example) from the slaves themselves—in other words, a veiled warning. Whether in this speech, in 1852, Lincoln was the confirmed believer in colonization he seems to be, despite its obvious difficulties, is hard to know. He does not call himself a member of the society. Even during his presidency he spoke of colonization as the solution, but on other occasions, usually less openly, he indicated his view that gradual emancipation and integration, on these shores, can work. There are clear signs that he even thought the sudden overall non-gradual emancipation he himself proc-laimed during the Civil War could be made to work here, without the benefit of colonization.

II. Pre-Civil War Speeches

Chapter 6

The Repeal of the Missouri Compromise, October 16, 1854

After Senator Stephen Douglashad spoken for three hours in the afternoon, Lincoln gave this long speech—by pre-arrangement with Douglas—that evening. Lincoln had also agreed, reluctantly, to Judge Douglas' having a final hour to respond to him, but for reasons "not wholly unselfish." Fearing that the Democrats would leave after hearing the Judge's main speech, he told them that "by giving him the close, I felt confident you would stay for the fun of hearing him skin me." The encounter was noteworthy, since Judge Douglas was the primary force behind Congress' repeal of the Missouri Compromise earlier that year.

Text

The repeal of the Missouri Compromise, and the propriety of its restoration, constitute the subject of what I am about to say.

As I desire to present my own connected view of this subject, my remarks will not be, specifically, an answer to Judge Douglas; yet, as I proceed, the main points he has presented will arise, and will receive such respectful attention as I may be able to give them.

I wish further to say, that I do not propose to question the patriotism, or to assail the motives of any man, or class of men; but rather to strictly confine myself to the naked merits of the question.

I also wish to be no less than National in all the positions I may take; and whenever I take ground which others have thought, or may think, narrow, sectional and dangerous to the Union, I hope to give a reason, which will appear sufficient, at least to some, why I think differently.

And, as this subject is no other, than part and parcel of the larger general question of domestic-slavery, I wish to MAKE and to KEEP the distinction between the EXISTING institution, and the EXTENSION of it, so broad, and so clear, that no honest man can misunderstand me, and no dishonest one, successfully misrepresent me.

In order to [get?] a clear understanding of what the Missouri Compromise is, a short history of the preceding kindred subjects will perhaps be proper. When we established our independence, we did not own, or claim, the country to which this compromise applies. Indeed, strictly speaking, the confederacy then owned no country at all; the States respectively owned the country within their limits; and some of them owned territory beyond their strict State limits. Virginia thus owned the North-Western territory—the country out of which the principal part of Ohio, all Indiana, all Illinois, all Michigan and all Wisconsin, have since been formed. She also owned (perhaps within her then limits) what has since been formed into the State of Kentucky. North Carolina thus owned what is now the State of Tennessee; and South Carolina and Georgia, in separate parts, owned what are now Mississippi and Alabama. Connecticut, I think, owned the little remaining part of Ohio—being the same where they now send Giddings to Congress, and beat all creation at making cheese. These territories, together with the States themselves, constituted all the country over which the confederacy then claimed any sort of jurisdiction. We were then living under the Articles of Confederation, which were superceded by the Constitution several years afterwards. The question of ceding these territories to the general government was set on foot. Mr. Jefferson, the author of the Declaration of Independence, and otherwise a chief actor in the revolution; then a delegate in Congress; afterwards twice President; who was, is, and perhaps will continue to be, the most distinguished politician of our history; a Virginian by birth and continued residence, and withal, a slave-holder; conceived the idea of taking that occasion, to prevent slavery ever going into the north-western territory. He prevailed on the Virginia Legislature to adopt his views, and to cede the territory, making the prohibition of slavery therein, a condition of the deed. ["'Mr. Lincoln afterward authorized the correction of the error into which the report here falls, with regard to the prohibition being made a condition of the deed. It was not a condition.'"—Nicholay and Hay, *Complete Works of Abraham Lincoln*, Vol. II, p 194.] Congress accepted the cession, with the condition; and in the first Ordinance (which the acts of Congress were then called) for the government of the territory, provided that slavery should never be permitted therein. This is the famed ordinance of '87 so often spoken of. Thenceforward, for sixty-one years, and until in 1848, the last scrap of this territory came into the Union as the State of Wisconsin, all parties acted in quiet obedience to this ordinance. It is now what Jefferson foresaw and intended—the happy home of teeming millions of free, white, prosperous people, and no slave amongst them.

Thus, with the author of the declaration of Independence, the policy of prohibiting slavery in new territory originated. Thus, away back of the constitution, in the pure fresh, free breath of the revolution, the State of Virginia, and the National congress put that policy in practice.—Thus through sixty odd of the best years of the republic did that policy steadily work to its great and beneficent end. And thus, in those five states, and five millions of free, enterprising people, we have before us the rich fruits of this policy. But now new light breaks upon us.—Now congress declares this ought never to have been; and the like of it, must never be again.—The sacred right of self government is grossly violated by it! We even find some men, who drew their first breath, and every other breath of their lives, under this very restriction, now live in dread of absolute suffocation, if they should be restricted in the "sacred right" of taking slaves to Nebraska. That perfect liberty they sigh for—the liberty of making slaves of other people—Jefferson never thought of; their own father never thought of; they never thought of themselves, a year ago. How fortunate for them, they did not sooner become sensible of their great misery! Oh, how difficult it is to treat with respect, such assaults upon all we have ever really held sacred.

But to return to history. In 1803 we purchased what was then called Louisiana, of France. It included the now states of Louisiana, Arkansas, Missouri, and Iowa; also the territory of Minnesota, and the present bone of contention, Kansas and Nebraska. Slavery already existed among the French at New Orleans; and, to some extent, at St. Louis. In 1812 Louisiana came into the Union as a slave state, without controversy. In 1818 or '19, Missouri showed signs of a wish to come in with slavery. This was resisted by northern members of Congress; and thus began the first great slavery agitation in the nation. This controversy lasted several months, and became very angry and exciting; the House of Representatives voting steadily for the prohibition of slavery in Missouri, and the Senate voting as steadily against it. Threats of breaking up the Union were freely made; and the ablest public men of the day became seriously alarmed. At length a compromise was made, in which, like all compromises, both sides yielded something. It was a law passed on the 6th day of March, 1820, providing that Missouri might come into the Union *with* slavery, but that in all the remaining part of the territory purchased of France, which lies north of 36 degrees and 30 minutes north latitude, slavery should never be permitted. This provision of law, *is the Missouri Compromise*. In excluding slavery North of the line, the same language is employed as in the Ordinance of '87. It directly applied to Iowa, Minnesota, and to the present bone of contention, Kansas and Nebraska. Whether there should or should not, be slavery south of that line, nothing was said in the law; but Arkansas constituted the principal remaining part, south of the line; and it has since been admitted as a slave state without serious controversy. More recently, Iowa, north of the line, came in as a free state without controversy. Still later, Minnesota, north of the line, had a territorial organization without controversy. Texas principally south of the line, and West of Arkansas; though originally within the purchase from France, had, in 1819, been traded off to Spain, in our treaty for the acquisition of Florida. It had thus become a part of Mexico. Mexico revolutionized and became independent of Spain. American citizens began settling rapidly, with their slaves in the southern part of Texas. Soon they revolutionized against Mexico, and established an independent government of their own, adopting a constitution, with slavery, strongly resembling the constitutions of our slave states. By still another rapid move, Texas, claiming a boundary much further West, than when we parted with her in 1819, was brought back to the United States, and admitted into the Union as a slave state. There then was little or no settlement in the northern part of Texas, a considerable portion of which lay north of the Missouri line; and in the resolutions admitting her into the Union, the Missouri restriction was expressly extended westward across her territory. This was in 1845, only nine years ago.

Thus originated the Missouri Compromise; and thus has it been respected down to 1845.—And even four years later, in 1849, our distinguished Senator, in a public address, held the following language in relation to it:

"The Missouri Compromise had been in practical operation for about a quarter of a century, and had received the sanction and approbation of men of all parties in every section of the Union. It had allayed all sectional jealousies and irritations growing out of this vexed question, and harmonized and tranquilized the whole country. It had given to Henry Clay, as its prominent champion, the proud sobriquet of the "*Great Pacificator*" and by that title and for that service, his political friends had repeatedly appealed to the people to rally under his standard, as a presidential candidate, as the man who had exhibited the patriotism and the power to suppress, an unholy and treasonable agitation, and preserve the Union. He was not aware that any man or any party from any section of the Union, had ever urged as an objection to Mr. Clay, that he was the great champion of the Missouri Compromise. On the contrary, the effort was made by the opponents of Mr. Clay, to prove that he was not entitled to the exclusive merit of that great patriotic measure, and that the honor was equally due to others as well as to him, for securing its adoption—that it had its origin in the hearts of all patriotic men, who desired to preserve and perpetuate the blessings of our glorious Union—an origin akin that of the constitution of the United States, conceived in the same spirit of fraternal affection, and calculated to remove forever, the only danger, which seemed to threaten, at some distant day, to sever the social bond of union. All the evidences of public opinion at that day, seemed to indicate that this Compromise had been canonized in the hearts of the American people, as a sacred thing which no ruthless hand would ever be reckless enough to disturb."

I do not read this extract to involve Judge Douglas in an inconsistency.—If he afterwards thought he had been wrong, it was right for him to change—I bring this forward merely to show the high estimate placed on the Missouri Compromise by all parties up to so late as the year 1849.

But, going back a little, in point of time, our war with Mexico broke out in 1846. When Congress was about adjourning that session, President Polk asked them to place two millions of dollars under his control, to be used by him in the recess, if found practicable and expedient, in negotiating a treaty of peace with Mexico, and acquiring some part of her territory.—A bill was duly got up, for the purpose, and was progressing swimmingly, in the House of Representatives, when a member by the name of David Wilmot, a democrat from Pennsylvania, moved as an amendment "Provided that in any territory thus acquired, there shall never be slavery."

This is the origin of the far-famed "Wilmot Proviso." It created a great flutter; but it stuck like wax, was voted into the bill, and the bill passed with it through the House. The Senate, however, adjourned without final action on it and so both appropriation and proviso were lost, for the time.—The war continued, and at the next session, the president renewed his request for the appropriation, enlarging the amount, I think, to three million. Again came the proviso; and defeated the measure.—Congress adjourned again, and the war went on. In Dec. 1847, the new congress assembled.—I was in the lower House that term.—The "Wilmot Proviso" or the principle of it, was constantly coming up in some shape or other, and I think I may venture to say I voted for it at least forty times; during the short term I was there. The Senate, however, held it in check, and it never became law. In the spring of 1848 a treaty of peace was made with Mexico; by which we obtained that portion of her country which now constitutes the territories of New Mexico and Utah, and the now state of California. By this treaty the Wilmot Proviso was defeated, as so far as it was intended to be, a condition of the acquisition of territory. Its friends however, were still determined to find some way to restrain slavery from getting into the new country. This new acquisition lay directly West of our old purchase from France, and extended west to the Pacific ocean—and was so situated that if the Missouri line should be extended straight West, the new country would be divided by such extended line, leaving some North and some South of it. On Judge Douglas' motion a bill, or provision of a bill, passed the Senate to so extend the Missouri line. The Proviso men in the House, including myself, voted it down, because by implication, it gave up the Southern part to slavery, while we were bent on having it all free.

In the fall of 1848 the gold mines were discovered in California. This attracted people to it with unprecedented rapidity, so that on, or soon after, the meeting of the new congress in Dec., 1849, she already had a population of nearly a hundred thousand, had called a convention, formed a state constitution, excluding slavery, and was knocking for admission into the Union.—The Proviso men, of course were for letting her in, but the Senate, always true to the other side would not consent to her admission. And there California stood, kept *out* of the Union, because she would not let slavery *into* her borders. Under all the circumstances perhaps this was not wrong. There were other points of dispute, connected with the general question of slavery, which equally needed adjustment. The South clamored for a more efficient fugitive slave law. The North clamored for the abolition of a peculiar species of slave trade in the District of Columbia, in connection with which, in view from the windows of the capitol, a sort of negro-livery stable, where droves of negroes were collected, temporarily kept, and finally taken to Southern markets, precisely like droves of horses, had been openly maintained for fifty years. Utah and New Mexico needed territorial governments; and whether slavery should or should not be prohibited within them, was another question. The indefinite Western boundary of Texas was to be settled. She was received a slave state; and consequently the farther West the slavery men could push her boundary, the more slave country they secured. And the farther East the slavery opponents could thrust the boundary back, the less slave ground was secured. Thus this was just as clearly a slavery question as any of the others.

These points all needed adjustment; and they were all held up, perhaps wisely to make them help to adjust one another. The Union, now, as in 1820, was thought to be in danger; and devotion to the Union rightfully inclined men to yield somewhat, in points where nothing else could have so inclined them. A compromise was finally effected. The South got their new fugitive-slave law; and the North got California, (the far best part of our acquisition from Mexico,) as a free State. The South got a provision that New Mexico and Utah, *when admitted as States*, may come in *with* or *without* slavery as they may then choose; and the North got the slave-trade abolished in the District of Columbia. The North got the western boundary of Texas, thence further back eastward than the South desired; but, in turn, they gave Texas ten millions of dollars, with which to pay her old debts. This is the Compromise of 1850.

Preceding the Presidential election of 1852, each of the great political parties, democrats and whigs, met in convention, and adopted resolutions endorsing the compromise of '50; as a "finality," a final settlement, so far as these parties could make it so, of all slavery agitation. Previous to this, in 1851, the Illinois Legislature had indorsed it.

During this long period of time Nebraska had remained, substantially an uninhabited country, but now emigration to, and settlement within it began to take place. It is about one third as large as the present United States, and its importance so long overlooked, begins to come into view. The restriction of slavery by the Missouri Compromise directly applies to it; in fact, was first made, and has since been maintained, expressly for it. In 1853, a bill to give it a territorial government passed the House of Representatives, and, in the hands of Judge Douglas, failed of passing the Senate only for want of time. This bill contained no repeal of the Missouri Compromise. Indeed, when it was assailed because it did not contain such repeal, Judge Douglas defended it in its existing form. On January 4th, 1854, Judge Douglas introduces a new bill to give Nebraska territorial government. He accompanies this bill with a report, in which last, he expressly recommends that the Missouri Compromise shall neither be affirmed nor repealed.

Before long the bill is so modified as to make two territories instead of one; calling the Southern one Kansas.

Also, about a month after the introduction of the bill, on the judge's own motion, it is so amended as to declare the Missouri Compromise inoperative and void; and, substantially, that the People who go and settle there may establish slavery, or exclude it, as they may see fit. In this shape the bill passed both branches of congress, and became a law.

This is the *repeal* of the Missouri Compromise. The foregoing history may not be precisely accurate in every particular; but I am sure it is sufficiently so, for all the uses I shall attempt to make of it, and in it, we have before us, the chief material enabling us to correctly judge whether the repeal of the Missouri Compromise is right or wrong.

I think, and shall try to show, that it is wrong; wrong in its direct effect, letting slavery into Kansas and Nebraska—and wrong in its prospective principle, allowing it to spread to every other part of the wide world, where men can be found inclined to take it.

This *declared* indifference, but as I must think, covert *real zeal* for the spread of slavery, I can not but hate. I hate it because of the monstrous injustice of slavery itself. I hate it because it deprives our republican example of its just influence in the world,—enables the enemies of free institutions, with plausibility, to taunt us as hypocrites—causes the real friends of freedom to doubt our sincerity, and especially because it forces so many really good men amongst ourselves into an open war with the very fundamental principles of civil liberty—criticizing the Declaration of Independence, and insisting that there is no right principle of action but *self-interest*.

Before proceeding, let me say I think I have no prejudice against the Southern people. They are just what we would be in their situation. If slavery did not now exist amongst them, they would not introduce it. If it did now exist amongst us, we should not instantly give it up.—This I believe of the masses north and south.—Doubtless there are individuals, on both sides, who would not hold slaves under any circumstances; and others who would gladly introduce slavery anew, if it were out of existence. We know that some southern men do free their slaves, go north, and become tip-top abolitionists; while some northern ones go south, and become most cruel slave-masters.

When southern people tell us they are no more responsible for the origin of slavery, than we; I acknowledge the fact. When it is said that the institution exists; and that it is very difficult to get rid of it, in any satisfactory way, I can understand and appreciate the saying. I surely will not blame them for not doing what I should not know how to do myself. If all earthly power were given me, I should not know what to do, as to the existing institution. My first impulse would be to free all the slaves, and send them to Liberia,—to their own native land. But a moment's reflection would convince me, that whatever of high hope, (as I think there is) there may be in this, in the long run, its sudden execution is impossible. If they were all landed there in a day, they would all perish in the next ten days; and there are not surplus shipping and surplus money enough in the world to carry them there in many times ten days. What then? Free them all, and keep them among us as underlings? Is it quite certain that this betters their condition? I think I would not hold one in slavery, at any rate; yet the point is not clear enough for me to denounce people upon. What next? Free them, and make them politically and socially, our equals? My own feelings will not admit of this; and if mine would, we well know that those of the great mass of white people will not. Whether this feeling accords with justice and sound judgment, is not the sole question, if indeed, it is any part of it. A universal feeling, whether well or ill-founded, can not be safely disregarded. We can not, then, make them equals. It does seem to me that systems of gradual emancipation might be adopted; but for their tardiness in this, I will not undertake to judge our brethren of the south.

When they remind us of their constitutional rights, I acknowledge them, not grudgingly, but fully, and fairly; and I would give them any legislation for the reclaiming of their fugitives, which should not, in its stringency, be more likely to carry a free man into slavery, than our ordinary criminal laws are to hang an innocent one.

But all this, to my judgment, furnishes no more excuse for permitting slavery to go into our own free territory, than it would for reviving the African slave trade by law. The law which forbids the bringing of slaves *from* Africa; and that which has so long forbid the taking them *to* Nebraska, can hardly be distinguished on any moral principle; and the repeal of the former could find quite as plausible excuses as that of the latter.

The arguments by which the repeal of the Missouri Compromise is sought to be justified, are these:

First, that the Nebraska country needed a territorial government.

Second, that in various ways, the public had repudiated it, and demanded the repeal; and therefore should not now complain of it.

And lastly, that the repeal establishes a principle, which is intrinsically right.

I will attempt an answer to each of them in its turn.

First, then, if that country was in need of a territorial organization, could it not have had it as well without as with the repeal? Iowa and Minnesota, to both of which the Missouri restriction applied, had, without its repeal, each in succession, territorial organizations. And even, the year before, a bill for Nebraska itself, was within an ace of passing, without the repealing clause; and this in the hands of the same men who are now the champions of repeal. Why no necessity then for the repeal? But still later, when this very bill was first brought in, it contained no repeal. But, say they, because the public had demanded, or rather commanded the repeal, the repeal was to accompany the organization, whenever that should occur.

Now I deny that the public ever demanded any such thing—ever repudiated the Missouri Compromise—ever commanded its repeal. I deny it, and call for the proof. It is not contended, I believe, that any such command has ever been given in express terms. It is only said that it was done *in principle*. The support of the Wilmot Proviso, is the first fact mentioned, to prove that the Missouri restriction was repudiated in *principle*, and the second is, the refusal to extend the Missouri line over the country acquired from Mexico. These are near enough alike to be treated together. The one was to exclude the chances of slavery from the *whole* new acquisition by the lump; and the other was to reject a division of it, by which one *half* was to be given up to those chances. Now whether this was a repudiation of the Missouri line, in *principle*, depends upon whether the Missouri law contained any *principle* requiring the line to be extended over the country acquired from Mexico. I contend it did not. I insist that it contained no general principle, but that it was, in every sense, specific. That its terms limit it to the country purchased from France, is undenied and undeniable. It could have no principle beyond the intention of those who made it. They did not intend to extend the line to country which they did not own. If they intended to extend it, in the event of acquiring additional territory, why did they not say so? It was just as easy to say, that "in all the country west of the Mississippi, which we now own, or *may hereafter acquire* there shall never be slavery," as to say, what they did say; and they would have said it if they had meant it. An intention to extend the law is not only not mentioned in the law, but is not mentioned in any contemporaneous history. Both the law itself, and the history of the times are a blank as to any *principle* of extension; and by neither the known rules for construing statutes and contracts, nor by common sense, can any such *principle* be inferred.

Another fact showing the *specific* character of the Missouri law—showing that it intended no more than it expressed—showing that the line was not intended as a universal dividing line between free and slave territory, present and prospective—north of which slavery could never go—is the fact that by that very law, Missouri came in as a slave state, *north* of the line. If that law contained any prospective *principle*, the whole law must be looked to in order to ascertain what the *principle* was. And by this rule, the south could fairly contend that inasmuch as they got one slave state north of the line at the inception of the law, they have the right to have another given them *north* of it occasionally—now and then in the indefinite westward extension of the line. This demonstrates the absurdity of attempting to deduce a prospective principle from the Missouri Compromise line.

When we voted for the Wilmot Proviso, we were voting to keep slavery *out* of the whole Missouri [Mexican?] acquisition; and little did we think we were thereby voting, to let it *into* Nebraska, laying several hundred miles distant. When we voted against extending the Missouri line, little did we think we were voting to destroy the old line, then of near thirty years standing. To argue that we thus repudiated the Missouri Compromise is no less absurd than it would be to argue that because we have, so far, forborne to acquire Cuba, we have thereby, *in principle*, repudiated our former acquisitions, and determined to throw them out of the Union! No less absurd than it would be to say that because I may have refused to build an addition to my house, I thereby have decided to destroy the existing house! And if I catch you setting fire to my house, you will turn upon me and say I INSTRUCTED you to do it! The most conclusive argument, however, that, while voting for the Wilmot Proviso, and while voting against the EXTENSION of the Missouri line, we never thought of disturbing the original Missouri Compromise, is found in the facts, that there was then, and still is, an unorganized tract of fine country, nearly as large as the state of Missouri, lying immediately west of Arkansas, and south of the Missouri Compromise line; and that we never attempted to prohibit slavery as to it. I wish particular attention to this. It adjoins the original Missouri Compromise line, by its northern boundary; and consequently is part of the country, into which, by implication, slavery was permitted to go, by that compromise. There it has lain open ever since, and there it still lies. And yet no effort has been made at any time to wrest it from the south. In all our struggles to prohibit slavery within our Mexican acquisitions, we never so much as lifted a finger to prohibit it, as to this tract. Is not this entirely conclusive that at all times, we have held the Missouri Compromise as a sacred thing; even when against ourselves, as well as when for us?

Senator Douglas sometimes says the Missouri line itself was, *in principle*, only an extension of the line of the ordinance of '87—that is to say, an extension of the Ohio River. I think this is weak enough on its face. I will remark, however that, as a glance at the map will show, the Missouri line is a long way farther South than the Ohio; and that if our Senator, in proposing his extension, had stuck to the *principle* of jogging southward, perhaps it might not have been voted down so readily.

But next it is said that the compromises of '50 and the ratification of them by both political parties, in '52, established a *new principle*, which required the repeal of the Missouri Compromise. This again I deny. I deny it, and demand the proof. I have already stated fully what the compromises of '50 are. The particular part of those measures, for which the virtual repeal of the Missouri Compromise is sought to be inferred (for it is admitted they contain nothing about it, in express terms) is the provision in the Utah and New Mexico laws, which permits them when they seek admission into the Union as States, to come in with or without slavery as they shall then see fit. Now I insist this provision was made for Utah and New Mexico, and for no other place whatever. It had no more direct reference to Nebraska than it had to the territories of the moon. But, say they, it had reference to Nebraska, *in principle*. Let us see. The North consented to this provision, not because they considered it right in itself; but because they were compensated—paid for it. They, at the same time, got California into the Union as a free State. This was far the best part of all they had struggled for by the Wilmot Proviso. They also got the area of slavery somewhat narrowed in the settlement of the boundary of Texas. Also, they got the slave trade abolished in the District of Columbia. For all these desirable objects the North could afford to yield something; and they did yield to the South the Utah and New Mexico provision. I do not mean that the whole North, or even a majority, yielded, when the law passed; but enough yielded, when added to the vote of the South, to carry the measure. Now can it be pretended that the *principle* of this arrangement requires us to permit the same provision to be applied to Nebraska, *without any equivalent at all?* Give us another free State; press the boundary of Texas still further back, give us another step toward the destruction of slavery in the District, and you present us a similar case. But ask us not to repeat, for nothing, what you paid for in the first instance. If you wish the thing again, pay again. That is the *principle* of the compromises of '50, if indeed they had any principles beyond their specific terms—it was the system of equivalents.

Again, if Congress, at that time, intended that all future territories should, when admitted as States, come in with or without slavery, at their own option, why did it not say so? With such an universal provision, all know the bills could not have passed. Did they, then—could they—establish a *principle* contrary to their own intention? Still further, if they intended to establish the principle that wherever Congress had control, it should be left to the people to do as they thought fit with slavery why did they not authorize the people of the District of Columbia at their adoption to abolish slavery within these limits? I personally know that this has not been left undone, because it was unthought of. It was frequently spoken of by members of Congress and by citizens of Washington six years ago; and I heard no one express a doubt that a system of gradual emancipation, with compensation to owners, would meet the approbation of a large majority of the white people of the District. But without the action of Congress they could say nothing; and Congress said "no." In the measures of 1850 Congress had the subject of slavery in the District expressly in hand. If they were then establishing the *principle* of allowing the people to do as they please with slavery, why did they not apply the *principle* to that people?

Again, it is claimed that by the Resolutions of the Illinois Legislature, passed in 1851, the repeal of the Missouri Compromise was demanded. This I deny also. Whatever may be worked out by a criticism of the language of those resolutions, the people have never understood them as being any more than an endorsement of the compromises of 1850; and a release of our Senators from voting for the Wilmot Proviso. The whole people are living witnesses, that this only, was their view. Finally, it is asked "If we did not mean to apply the Utah and New Mexico provision, to all future territories, what did we mean, when we, in 1852, endorsed the compromises of '50?"

For myself, I can answer this question most easily. I meant not to ask a repeal, or modification of the fugitive slave law. I meant not to ask for the abolition of slavery in the District of Columbia. I meant not to resist the admission of Utah and New Mexico, even should they ask to come in as slave States. I meant nothing about additional territories, because, as I understood, we then had no territory whose character as to slavery was not already settled. As to Nebraska, I regarded its character as being fixed, by the Missouri Compromise, for thirty years—as unalterably fixed as that of my own home in Illinois. As to new acquisitions I said "sufficient unto the day is the evil thereof." When we make new acquaintances, [acquisitions?] we will, as heretofore, try to manage them some how. That is my answer. That is what I meant and said; and I appeal to the people to say, each for himself, whether that was not also the universal meaning of the free States.

And now, in turn, let me ask a few questions. If by any, or all these matters, the repeal of the Missouri Compromise was commanded, why was not the command sooner obeyed? Why was the repeal omitted in the Nebraska bill of 1853?—Why was it omitted in the original bill of 1854? Why, in the accompanying report, was such a repeal characterized as a *departure* from the course pursued in 1850? and its continued omission recommended?

I am aware Judge Douglas now argues that the subsequent express repeal is no substantial alteration of the bill. This argument seems wonderful to me. It is as if one should argue that white and black are not different. He admits, however, that there is a literal change in the bill; and that he made the change in deference to other Senators, who would not support the bill without. This proves that those other Senators thought the change a substantial one; and that the Judge thought their opinions worth deferring to. His own opinions, therefore, seem not to rest on a very firm basis even in his own mind—and I suppose the world believes, and will continue to believe, that precisely on the substance of that change this whole agitation has arisen.

I conclude then, that the public never demanded the repeal of the Missouri Compromise.

I now come to consider whether the repeal, with its avowed principle, is intrinsically right. I insist that it is not. Take the particular case. A controversy had arisen between the advocates and opponents of slavery, in relation to its establishment within the country we had purchased of France. The southern, and then best part of the purchase, was already in as a slave state. The controversy was settled by also letting Missouri in as a slave State; but with the agreement that within all the remaining part of the purchase, north of a certain line, there should never be slavery. As to what was to be done with the remaining part south of the line, nothing was said; but perhaps the fair implication was, that it should come in with slavery if it should so choose. The southern part, except a portion heretofore mentioned, afterwards did come in with slavery, as the State of Arkansas. All these many years since 1820, the Northern part had remained a wilderness. At length settlements began in it also. In due course, Iowa, came in as a free State, and Minnesota was given a territorial government, without removing the slavery restriction. Finally the sole remaining part, north of the line, Kansas and Nebraska, was to be organized; and it is proposed, and carried, to blot out the old dividing line of thirty-four years standing, and to open the whole of that country to the introduction of slavery. Now, this, to my mind, is manifestly unjust. After an angry and dangerous controversy, the parties made friends by dividing the bone of contention. The one party first appropriates her own share, beyond all power to be disturbed in the possession of it; and then seizes the share of the other party. It is as if two starving men had divided their only loaf; the one had hastily swallowed his half, and then grabbed the other half just as he was putting it to his mouth!

Let me here drop the main argument, to notice what I consider rather an inferior matter. It is argued that slavery will not go to Kansas and Nebraska, *in any event*. This is a *palliation*—a *lullaby*. I have some hope that it will not; but let us not be too confident. As to climate, a glance at the map shows that there are five slave States—Delaware, Maryland, Virginia, Kentucky, and Missouri—and also the District of Columbia, all north of the Missouri compromise line. The census returns of 1850 show that, within these, there are 867,276 slaves—being more than one-fourth of all the slaves in the nation.

It is not climate, then, that will keep slavery out of these territories. Is there any thing in the peculiar nature of the country? Missouri adjoins these territories, by her entire western boundary, and slavery is already within every one of her western counties. I have even heard it said that there are more slaves, in proportion to whites, in the northwestern county of Missouri, than within any county of the State. Slavery pressed entirely up to the old western boundary of the State, and when, rather recently, a part of that boundary, at the north-west was moved out a little farther west, slavery followed on quite up to the new line. Now, when the restriction is removed, what is to prevent it from going still further? Climate will not.—No peculiarity of the country will—nothing in *nature* will. Will the disposition of the people prevent it? Those nearest the scene, are all in favor of the extension. The yankees, who are opposed to it may be more numerous; but in military phrase, the battle-field is too far from *their* base of operations.

But it is said, there now is *no* law in Nebraska on the subject of slavery; and that, in such case, taking a slave there, operates his freedom. That is good book-law; but is not the rule of actual practice. Wherever slavery is, it has been first introduced without law. The oldest laws we find concerning it, are not laws introducing it; but *regulating* it, as an already existing thing. A white man takes his slave to Nebraska now; who will inform the negro that he is free? Who will take him before court to test the question of his freedom? In ignorance of his legal emancipation, he is kept chopping, splitting and plowing. Others are brought, and move on in the same track. At last, if ever the time for voting comes, on the question of slavery, the institution already in fact exists in the country, and cannot well be removed. The facts of its presence, and the difficulty of its removal will carry the vote in its favor. Keep it out until a vote is taken, and a vote in favor of it, can not be got in any population of forty thousand, on earth, who have been drawn together by the ordinary motives of emigration and settlement. To get slaves into the country simultaneously with the whites, in the incipient stages of settlement, is the precise stake played for, and won in this Nebraska measure.

The question is asked us, "If slaves will go in, notwithstanding the general principle of law liberates them, why would they not equally go in against positive statute law?—go in, even if the Missouri restriction were maintained?" I answer, because it takes a much bolder man to venture in, with his property, in the latter case, than in the former—because the positive congressional enactment is known to, and respected by all, or nearly all; whereas the negative principle that *no* law is free law, is not much known except among lawyers. We have some experience of this practical difference. In spite of the Ordinance of '87, a few negroes were brought into Illinois, and held in a state of quasi slavery; not enough, however to carry a vote of the people in favor of the institution when they came to form a constitution. But in the adjoining Missouri country, where there was no ordinance of '87—was no restriction—they were carried ten times, nay a hundred times, as fast, and actually made a slave State. This is fact—naked fact.

Another LULLABY argument is, that taking slaves to new countries does not increase their number—does not make any one slave who otherwise would be free. There is some truth in this, and I am glad of it, but it [is] not WHOLLY true. The African slave trade is not yet effectually suppressed; and if we make a reasonable deduction for the white people amongst us, who are foreigners, and the descendants of foreigners, arriving here since 1808, we shall find the increase of the black population out-running that of the white, to an extent unaccountable, except by supposing that some of them too, have been coming from Africa. If this be so, the opening of new countries to the institution, increases the demand for, and augments the price of slaves, and so does, in fact, make slaves of freemen by causing them to be brought from Africa, and sold into bondage.

But, however this may be, we know the opening of new countries to slavery, tends to the perpetuation of the institution, and so does KEEP men in slavery who otherwise would be free. This result we do not KEEP like favoring, and we are under no legal obligation to suppress our feelings in this respect.

Equal justice to the south, it is said, requires us to consent to the extending of slavery to new countries. That is to say, inasmuch as you do not object to my taking my hog to Nebraska, therefore I must not object to you taking your slave. Now, I admit this is perfectly logical, if there is no difference between hogs and negroes. But while you thus require me to deny the humanity of the negro, I wish to ask whether you of the south yourselves, have ever been willing to do as much? It is kindly provided that of all those who come into the world, only a small percentage are natural tyrants. That percentage is no larger in the slave States than in the free. The great majority, south as well as north, have human sympathies, of which they can no more divest themselves than they can of their sensibility to physical pain. These sympathies in the bosoms of the southern people, manifest in many ways, their sense of the wrong of slavery, and their consciousness that, after all, there is humanity in the negro. If they deny this, let me address them a few plain questions. In 1820 you joined the north, almost unanimously, in declaring the African slave trade piracy, and in annexing to it the punishment of death. Why did you do this? If you did not feel that it was wrong, why did you join in providing that men should be hung for it? The pratice was no more than bringing wild negroes from Africa, to sell to such as would buy them. But you never thought of hanging men for catching and selling wild horses, wild buffaloes or wild bears.

Again, you have amongst you, a sneaking individual, of the class of native tyrants, known as the "SLAVE-DEALER." He watches your necessities, and crawls up to buy your slave, at a speculating price. If you cannot help it, you sell to him; but if you can help it, you drive him from your door. You despise him utterly. You do not recognize him as a friend, or even as an honest man. Your children must not play with his; they may rollick freely with the little negroes, but not with the "slave-dealers" children. If you are obliged to deal with him, you try to get through the job without so much as touching him. It is common with you to join hands with the men you meet; but with the slave-dealer you avoid the ceremony—instinctively shrinking from the snaky contact. If he grows rich and retires from business, you still remember him, and still keep up the ban of non-intercourse upon him and his family. Now why is this? You do not so treat the man who deals in corn, cattle or tobacco.

And yet again; there are in the United States and territories, including the District of Columbia, 433,643 free blacks. At $500 per head they are worth over two hundred millions of dollars. How comes this vast amount of property to be running about without owners? We do not see free horses or free cattle running at large. How is this? All these free blacks are the descendants of slaves, or have been slaves themselves, and they would be slaves now, but for SOMETHING which has operated on their white owners, inducing them, at vast pecuniary sacrifices, to liberate them. What is that SOMETHING? Is there any mistaking it? In all these cases it is your sense of justice, and human sympathy, continually telling you, that the poor negro has some natural right to himself—that those who deny it, and make mere merchandise of him, deserve kickings, contempt and death.

And now, why will you ask us to deny the humanity of the slave? and estimate him only as the equal of the hog? Why ask us to do what you will not do yourselves? Why ask us to do for *nothing*, what two hundred million of dollars could not induce you to do?

But one great argument in the support of the repeal of the Missouri Compromise, is still to come. That argument is "the sacred right of self government." It seems our distinguished Senator has found great difficulty in getting his antagonists, even in the Senate to meet him fairly on this argument—some poet has said:

"Fools rush in where angels fear to tread."

At the hazzard [*sic*] of being thought one of the fools of this quotation, I meet that argument—I rush in, I take that bull by the horns.

I trust I understand, and truly estimate the right of self-government. My faith in the proposition that each man should do precisely as he pleases with all which is exclusively his own, lies at the foundation of the sense of justice there is in me. I extend the principles to communities of men, as well as to individuals. I so extend it, because it is politically wise, as well as naturally just; politically wise, in saving us from broils about matters which do not concern us. Here, or at Washington, I would not trouble myself with the oyster laws of Virginia, or the cranberry laws of Indiana.

The doctrine of self-government is right—absolutely and eternally right—but it has no just application, as here attempted. Or perhaps I should rather say that whether it has such just application depends upon whether a negro is *not* or *is* a man. If he is not a man, why in that case, he who is a man may, as a matter of self-government, do just as he pleases with him. But if the negro is a man, is it not to that extent, a total destruction of self-government, to say that he too shall not govern *himself?* When the white man governs himself that is self-government; but when he governs himself, and also governs *another* man, that is *more* than self-government—that is despotism. If the negro is a *man*, why then my ancient faith teaches me that "all men are created equal;" and that there can be no moral right in connection with one man's making a slave of another.

Judge Douglas frequently, with bitter irony and sarcasm, paraphrases our argument by saying "The white people of Nebraska are good enough to govern themselves, *but they are not good enough to govern a few miserable negroes!*"

Well I doubt not that the people of Nebraska are, and will continue to be as good as the average of people elsewhere. I do not say the contrary. What I do say is, that no man is good enough to govern another man, *without that other's consent.* I say this is the leading principle—the sheet anchor of American republicanism. Our Declaration of Independence says:

"We hold these truths to be self evident: that all men are created equal; that they are endowed by their Creator with certain inalienable rights; that among these are life, liberty and the pursuit of happiness. That to secure these rights, governments are instituted among men, DERIVING THEIR JUST POWERS FROM THE CONSENT OF THE GOVERNED."

I have quoted so much at this time merely to show that according to our ancient faith, the just powers of governments are derived from the consent of the governed. Now the relation of masters and slaves is, PROTANTO, a total violation of this principle. That master not only governs the slave without his consent; but he governs him by a set of rules altogether different from those which he prescribes for himself. Allow ALL the governed an equal voice in the government, and that, and that only is self government.

Let it not be said I am contending for the establishment of political and social equality between the whites and blacks. I have already said the contrary. I am not now combating the argument of NECESSITY, arising from the fact that the blacks are already amongst us; but I am combating what is set up as MORAL argument for allowing them to be taken where they have never yet been—arguing against the EXTENSION of a bad thing, which where it already exists, we must of necessity, manage as we best can.

In support of his application of the doctrine of self-government, Senator Douglas has sought to bring to his aid the opinions and examples of our revolutionary fathers. I am glad he has done this. I love the sentiments of those old-time men; and shall be most happy to abide by their opinions. He shows us that when it was in contemplation for the colonies to break off from Great Britain, and set up a new government for themselves, several of the states instructed their delegates to go for the measure PROVIDED EACH STATE SHOULD BE ALLOWED TO REGULATE ITS DOMESTIC CONCERNS IN ITS OWN WAY. I do not quote; but this in substance. This was right. I see nothing objectionable in it. I also think it probable that it had some reference to the existence of slavery amongst them. I will not deny that it had. But had it, in any reference to the carrying of slavery into NEW COUNTRIES? That is the question; and we will let the fathers themselves answer it.

This same generation of men, and mostly the same individuals of the generation, who declared this principle—who declared independence—who fought the war of the revolution through—who afterwards made the constitution under which we still live—these same men passed the ordinance of '87, declaring that slavery should never go to the north-west territory. I have no doubt Judge Douglas thinks they were very inconsistent in this. It is a question of discrimination between them and him. But there is not an inch of ground left for his claiming that their opinions—their example—their authority—are on his side in this controversy.

Again, is not Nebraska, while a territory, a part of us? Do we not own the country? And if we surrender the control of it, do we not surrender the right of self-government? It is part of ourselves. If you say we shall not control it because it is ONLY part, the same is true of every other part; and when all the parts are gone, what has become of the whole? What is then left of us? What use for the general government, when there is nothing left for it [to] govern?

But you say this question should be left to the people of Nebraska, because they are more particularly interested. If this be the rule, you must leave it to each individual to say for himself whether he will have slaves. What better moral right have thirty-one citizens of Nebraska to say, that the thirty-second shall not hold slaves, than the people of the thirty-one States have to say that slavery shall not go into the thirty-second State at all?

But if it is a sacred right for the people of Nebraska to take and hold slaves there, it is equally their sacred right to buy them where they can buy them cheapest; and that undoubtedly will be on the coast of Africa; provided you will consent to not hang them for going there to buy them. You must remove this restriction too, from the sacred right of self-government. I am aware you say that taking slaves from the States to Nebraska, does not make slaves of freemen; but the African slave-trader can say just as much. He does not catch free negroes and bring them here. He finds them already slaves in the hands of their black captors, and he honestly buys them at the rate of about a red cotton handkerchief a head. This is very cheap, and it is a great abridgement of the sacred right of self-government to hang men for engaging in this profitable trade!

Another important objection to this application of the right of self-government, is that it enables the first FEW, to deprive the succeeding MANY, of a free exercise of the right of self-government. The first few may get slavery IN, and the subsequent many cannot easily get it OUT. How common is the remark now in the slave States—"If we were only clear of our slaves, how much better it would be for us." They are actually deprived of the privilege of governing themselves as they would, by the action of a very few, in the beginning. The same thing was true of the whole nation at the time our constitution was formed.

Whether slavery shall go into Nebraska, or other new territories, is not a matter of exclusive concern to the people who may go there. The whole nation is interested that the best use shall be made of these territories. We want them for the homes of free white people. This they cannot be, to any considerable extent, if slavery shall be planted within them. Slave States are places for poor white people to remove FROM; not to remove TO. New free States are the places for poor people to go to and better their condition. For this use, the nation needs these territories.

Still further; there are constitutional relations between the slave and free States, which are degrading to the latter. We are under legal obligations to catch and return their runaway slaves to them—a sort of dirty, disagreeable job, which I believe, as a general rule the slave-holders will not perform for one another. Then again, in the control of the government—the management of the partnership affairs—they have greatly the advantage of us. By the constitution, each State has two Senators—each has a number of Representatives; in proportion to the number of its people—and each has a number of presidential electors, equal to the whole number of its Senators and Representatives together. But in ascertaining the number of the people, for this purpose, five slaves are counted as being equal to three whites. The slaves do not vote; they are only counted and so used, as to swell the influence of the white people's votes. The practical effect of this is more aptly shown by a comparison of the States of South Carolina and Maine. South Carolina has six representatives, and so has Maine; South Carolina has eight presidential electors, and so has Maine. This is precise equality so far; and, of course they are equal in Senators, each having two. Thus in the control of the government, the two States are equals precisely. But how are they in the number of their white people? Maine has 581,813—while South Carolina has 274,567. Maine has twice as many as South Carolina, and 32,679 over. Thus each white man in South Carolina is more than the double of any man in Maine. This is all because South Carolina, besides her free people, has 384,984 slaves. The South Carolinian has precisely the same advantage over the white man in every other free State, as well as in Maine. He is more than the double of any one of us in this crowd. The same advantage, but not to the same extent, is held by all the citizens of the slave States, over those of the free; and it is an absolute truth, without an exception, that there is no voter in any slave State, but who has more legal power in the government, than any voter in any free State. There is no instance of exact equality; and the disadvantage is against us the whole chapter through. This principle, in the aggregate, gives the slave States, in the present Congress, twenty additional representatives—being seven more than the whole majority by which they passed the Nebraska bill.

Now all this is manifestly unfair; yet I do not mention it to complain of it, in so far as it is already settled. It is in the constitution; and I do not, for that cause, or any other cause, propose to destroy, or alter, or disregard the constitution. I stand to it, fairly, fully, and firmly.

But when I am told I must leave it altogether to OTHER PEOPLE to say whether new partners are to be bred up and brought into the firm, on the same degrading terms against me. I respectfully demur. I insist, that whether I shall be a whole man, or only, the half of one, in comparison with others, is a question in which I am somewhat concerned; and one which no other man can have a sacred right of deciding for me. If I am wrong in this—if it really be a sacred right of self-government, in the man who shall go to Nebraska, to decide whether he will be the EQUAL of me or the DOUBLE of me, then after he shall have exercised that right, and thereby shall have reduced me to a still smaller fraction of a man than I already am, I should like for some gentleman deeply skilled in the mysteries of sacred rights, to provide himself with a microscope, and peep about, and find out, if he can, what has become of my sacred rights! They will surely be too small for detection with the naked eye.

Finally, I insist, that if there is ANY THING which it is the duty of the WHOLE PEOPLE to never entrust to any hands but their own, that thing is the preservation and perpetuity, of their own liberties, and institutions. And if they shall think, as I do, that the extension of slavery endangers them, more than any, or all other causes, how recreant to themselves, if they submit the question, and with it, the fate of their country, to a mere hand-full of men, bent only on temporary self-interest. If this question of slavery extension were an insignificant one—one having no power to do harm—it might be shuffled aside in this way. But being, as it is, the great Behemoth of danger, shall the strong gripe of the nation be loosened upon him, to entrust him to the hands of such feeble keepers?

I have done with this mighty argument, of self-government. Go, sacred thing! Go in peace.

But Nebraska is urged as a great Union-saving measure. Well I too, go for saving the Union. Much as I hate slavery, I would consent to the extension of it rather than see the Union dissolved, just as I would consent to any GREAT evil, to avoid a GREATER one. But when I go to Union saving, I must believe, at least, that the means I employ has some adaptation to the end. To my mind, Nebraska has no such adaptation.

"It hath no relish of salvation in it."

It is an aggravation, rather, of the only one thing which ever endangers the Union. When it came upon us, all was peace and quiet. The nation was looking to the forming of new bonds of Union; and a long course of peace and prosperity seemed to lie before us. In the whole range of possibility, there scarcely appears to me to have been any thing, out of which the slavery agitation could have been revived, except the very project of repealing the Missouri compromise.—Every inch of territory we owned, already had a definite settlement of the slavery question, and by which, all parties were pledged to abide. Indeed, there was no uninhabited country on the continent, which we could acquire; if we except some extreme northern regions, which are wholly out of the question. In this state of case, the genius of Discord himself, could scarcely have invented a way of again setting us by the ears, but by turning back and destroying the peace measures of the past. The councils of that genius seem to have prevailed, the Missouri compromise was repealed; and here we are, in the midst of a new slavery agitation, such, I think, as we have never seen before. Who is responsible for this? Is it those who resist the measure; or those who, causelessly, brought it forward, and pressed it through, having reason to know, and, in fact, knowing it must and would be so resisted? It could not but be expected by its author, that it would be looked upon as a measure for the extension of slavery, aggravated by a gross breach of faith. Argue as you will, and long as you will, this is the naked FRONT and ASPECT, of the measure. And in this aspect, it could not but produce agitation. Slavery is founded in the selfishness of man's nature—opposition to it, is [*sic*] his love of justice. These principles are an eternal antagonism; and when brought into collision so fiercely, as slavery extension brings them, shocks, and throes, and convulsions must ceaselessly follow. Repeal the Missouri Compromise—repeal all compromises—repeal the declaration of independence—repeal all past history, you still can not repeal human nature. It still will be the abundance of man's heart, that slavery extension is wrong; and out of the abundance of his heart, his mouth will continue to speak.

The structure, too, of the Nebraska bill is very peculiar. The people are to decide the question of slavery for themselves; but WHEN they are to decide; or HOW they are to decide; or whether, when the question is once decided, it is to remain so, or is it to be subject to an indefinite succession of new trials, the law does not say. Is it to be decided by the first dozen settlers who arrive there? or is it to await the arrival of a hundred? Is it to be decided by a vote of the people? or a vote of the legislature? or, indeed by a vote of any sort? To these questions, the law gives no answer. There is a mystery about this; for when a member proposed to give the legislature express authority to exclude slavery, it was hooted down by the friends of the bill. This fact is worth remembering. Some yankees, in the east, are sending emigrants to Nebraska, to exclude slavery from it; and, so far as I can judge, they expect the question to be decided by voting, in some way or other. But the Missourians are awake too. They are within a stone's throw of the contested ground. They hold meetings, and pass resolutions, in which not the slightest allusion to voting is made. They resolve that slavery already exists in the territory; that more shall go there; that they, remaining in Missouri will protect it; and that abolitionists shall be hung, or driven away. Through all this, bowie-knives and six-shooters are seen plainly enough; but never a glimpse of the ballot-box. And, really, what is to be the result of this? Each party WITHIN, having numerous and determined backers WITHOUT, is it not probable that the contest will come to blows, and bloodshed? Could there be a more apt invention to bring about collision and violence, on the slavery question, than this Nebraska project is? I do not charge, or believe, that such was intended by Congress; but if they had literally formed a ring, and placed champions within it to fight out the controversy, the fight could be no more likely to come off, than it is. And if this fight should begin, is it likely to take a very peaceful, Union-saving turn? Will not the first drop of blood so shed, be the real knell of the Union?

The Missouri Compromise ought to be restored. For the sake of the Union, it ought to be restored. We ought to elect a House of Representatives which will vote its restoration. If by any means, we omit to do this, what follows?—Slavery may or may not be established in Nebraska. But whether it be or not, we shall have repudiated—discarded from the councils of the Nation—the SPIRIT OF COMPROMISE; for who after this will ever trust in a national compromise? The spirit of mutual concession—that spirit which first gave us the constitution, and which has thrice saved the Union—we shall have strangled and cast from us forever. And what shall we have in lieu of it? The South flushed with triumph and tempted to excesses; the North, betrayed, as they believe, brooding on wrong and burning for revenge. One side will provoke; the other resent. The one will taunt, the other defy; one agrees [aggresses?], the other retaliates. Already a few in the North, defy all constitutional restraints, resist the execution of the fugitive slave law, and even menace the institution of slavery in the states where it exists.

Already a few in the South, claim the constitutional right to take and to hold slaves in the free states—demand the revival of the slave trade; and demand a treaty with Great Britain by which fugitive slaves may be reclaimed from Canada. As yet they are but few on either side. It is a grave question for the lovers of the Union, whether the final destruction of the Missouri Compromise, and with it the spirit of all compromise will or will not embolden and embitter each of these, and fatally increase the numbers of both.

But restore the compromise, and what then? We thereby restore the national faith, the national confidence, the national feeling of brotherhood. We thereby reinstate the spirit of concession and compromise—that spirit which has never failed us in past perils, and which may be safely trusted for all the future. The south ought to join in doing this. The peace of the nation is as dear to them as to us. In memories of the past and hopes of the future, they share as largely as we. It would be on their part, a great act—great in its spirit, and great in its effect. It would be worth to the nation a hundred years' purchase of peace and prosperity. And what of sacrifice would they make? They only surrender to us, what they gave us for a consideration long, long ago; what they have not now, asked for, struggled or cared for; what has been thrust upon them, not less to their own astonishment than to ours.

But it is said we cannot restore it; that though we elect every member of the lower house, the Senate is still against us. It is quite true, that of the Senators who passed the Nebraska bill, a majority of the whole Senate will retain their seats in spite of the elections of this and the next year. But if at these elections, their several constituencies shall clearly express their will against Nebraska, will these senators disregard their will? Will they neither obey, nor make room for those who will?

But even if we fail to technically restore the compromise, it is still a great point to carry a popular vote in favor of the restoration. The moral weight of such a vote can not be estimated too highly. The authors of Nebraska are not at all satisfied with the destruction of the compromise—an endorsement of this PRINCIPLE, they proclaim to be the great object. With them, Nebraska alone is a small matter—to establish a principle, for FUTURE USE, is what they particularly desire.

That future use is to be the planting of slavery wherever in the wide world, local and unorganized opposition can not prevent it. Now if you wish to give them this endorsement—if you wish to establish this principle—do so. I shall regret it; but it is your right. On the contrary if you are opposed to the principle—intend to give it no such endorsement—let no wheedling, no sophistry, divert you from throwing a direct vote against it.

Some men, mostly whigs, who condemn the repeal of the Missouri Compromise, nevertheless hesitate to go for its restoration, lest they be thrown in company with the abolitionist. Will they allow me as an old whig to tell them good humoredly, that I think this is very silly? Stand with anybody that stands RIGHT. Stand with him while he is right and PART with him when he goes wrong. Stand WITH the abolitionist in restoring the Missouri Compromise; and stand AGAINST him when he attempts to repeal the fugitive slave law. In the latter case you stand with the southern disunionist. What of that? you are still right. In both cases you are right. In both cases you expose the dangerous extremes. In both you stand on middle ground and hold the ship level and steady. In both you are national and nothing less than national. This is good old whig ground. To desert such ground, because of any company, is to be less than a whig—less than a man—less than an American.

I particularly object to the NEW position which the avowed principle of this Nebraska law gives to slavery in the body politic. I object to it because it assumes that there CAN be MORAL RIGHT in the enslaving of one man by another. I object to it as a dangerous dalliance for a few [free?] people—a sad evidence that, feeling prosperity we forget right—that liberty, as a principle, we have ceased to revere. I object to it because the fathers of the republic eschewed, and rejected it. The argument of "Necessity" was the only argument they ever admitted in favor of slavery; and so far, and so far only as it carried them, did they ever go. They found the institution existing among us, which they could not help; and they cast blame upon the British King for having permitted its introduction. BEFORE the constitution, they prohibited its introduction into the northwestern Territory—the only country we owned, then free from it. AT the framing and adoption of the constitution, they forbore to so much as mention the word "slave" or "slavery" in the whole instrument. In the provision for the recovery of fugitives, the slave is spoken of as a "PERSON HELD TO SERVICE OR LABOR." In that prohibiting the abolition of the African slave trade for twenty years, that trade is spoken of as "The migration or importation of such persons as any of the States NOW EXISTING, shall think proper to admit," &c. These are the only provisions alluding to slavery. Thus, the thing is hid away, in the constitution, just as an afflicted man hides away a wen or a cancer, which he dares not cut out at once, lest he bleed to death; with the promise, nevertheless, that the cutting may begin at the end of a given time. Less than this our fathers COULD not do; and NOW (more) they WOULD not do. Necessity drove them so far, and farther, they would not go. But this is not all. The earliest Congress, under the constitution, took the same view of slavery. They hedged and hemmed it in to the narrowest limits of necessity.

In 1794, they prohibited an out-going slave-trade—that is, the taking of slaves FROM the United States to sell.

In 1798, they prohibited the bringing of slaves from Africa, INTO the Mississippi Territory—this territory then comprising what are now the States of Mississippi and Alabama. This was TEN YEARS before they had the authority to do the same thing as to the States existing at the adoption of the constitution.

In 1800 they prohibited AMERICAN CITIZENS from trading in slaves between foreign countries—as, for instance, from Africa to Brazil.

In 1803 they passed a law in aid of one or two State laws, in restraint of the internal slave trade.

In 1807, in apparent hot haste, they passed the law, nearly a year in advance to take effect the first day of 1808—the very first day the constitution would permit—prohibiting the African slave trade by heavy pecuniary and corporal penalties.

In 1820, finding these provisions ineffectual, they declared the trade piracy, and annexed to it, the extreme penalty of death. While all this was passing in the general government, five or six of the original slave States had adopted systems of gradual emancipation; and by which the institution was rapidly becoming extinct within these limits.

Thus we see, the plain unmistakable spirit of that age, towards slavery, was hostility to the PRINCIPLE, and toleration, ONLY BY NECESSITY.

But NOW it is to be transformed into a "sacred right." Nebraska brings it forth, places it on the high road to extension and perpetuity; and, with a pat on its back, says to it, "Go, and God speed you." Henceforth it is to be the chief jewel of the nation—the very figure-head of the ship of State. Little by little, but steadily as man's march to the grave, we have been giving up the OLD for the NEW faith. Near eighty years ago we began by declaring that all men are created equal; but now from that beginning we have run down to the other declaration, that for SOME men to enslave OTHERS is a "sacred right of self-government." These principles can not stand together. They are as opposite as God and mammon; and whoever holds to the one, must despise the other. When Pettit, in connection with his support of the Nebraska bill, called the Declaration of Indepen-

dence "a self-evident lie" he only did what consistency and candor require all
other Nebraska men to do. Of the forty odd Nebraska Senators who sat present
and heard him, no one rebuked him. Nor am I apprized that any Nebraska newspaper, or any Nebraska orator, in the whole nation, has ever yet rebuked him. If
this had been said among Marion's men, Southerners though they were, what
would have become of the man who said it? If this had been said to the men who
captured Andre, the man who said it, would probably have been hung sooner
than Andre was. If it had been said in old Independence Hall, seventy-eight
years ago, the very door-keeper would have throttled the man, and thrust him
into the street.

Let no one be deceived. The spirit of seventy-six and the spirit of Nebraska,
are utter antagonisms; and the former is being rapidly displaced by the latter.

Fellow countrymen—Americans south, as well as north, shall we make no
effort to arrest this? Already the liberal party throughout the world, express the
apprehension "that the one retrograde institution in America, is undermining the
principles of progress, and fatally violating the noblest political system the
world ever saw." This is not the taunt of enemies, but the warning of friends. Is
it quite safe to disregard it—to despise it? Is there no danger to liberty itself, in
discarding the earliest practice, and first precept of our ancient faith? In our
greedy chase to make profit of the negro, let us beware, lest we "cancel and tear
to pieces" even the white man's charter of freedom.

Our republican robe is soiled, and trailed in the dust. Let us repurify it. Let
us turn and wash it white, in the spirit, if not the blood, of the Revolution. Let us
turn slavery from its claims of "moral right," back upon its existing legal rights,
and its arguments of "necessity." Let us return it to the position our fathers gave
it; and there let it rest in peace. Let us re-adopt the Declaration of Independence,
and with it, the practices, and policy, which harmonize with it. Let north and
south—let all Americans—let all lovers of liberty everywhere—join in the great
and good work. If we do this, we shall not only have saved the Union; but we
shall have so saved it, as to make, and to keep it, forever worthy of the saving.
We shall have so saved it, that the succeeding millions of free happy people, the
world over, shall rise up, and call us blessed, to the latest generations.

At Springfield, twelve days ago, where I had spoken substantially as I have
here, Judge Douglas replied to me—and as he is to reply to me here, I shall attempt to anticipate him, by noticing some of the points he made there.

He commenced by stating I had assumed all the way through, that the principle of the Nebraska bill, would have the effect of extending slavery. He denied
that this was INTENDED, or that this EFFECT would follow.

I will not re-open the argument upon this point. That such was the intention,
the world believed at the start, and will continue to believe. This was the COUN-
TENANCE of the thing; and, both friends and enemies, instantly recognized it as
such. That countenance can not now be changed by argument. You can as easily
argue the color out of the negroes' skin. Like the "bloody hand" you may wash
it, and wash it, the red witness of guilt still sticks, and stares horribly at you.

Next he says, congressional intervention never prevented slavery any where—that it did not prevent it in the north west territory, now (nor) in Illinois—that in fact, Illinois came into the Union as a slave State—that the principle of the Nebraska bill expelled it from Illinois, from several old States, from every where.

Now this is mere quibbling all the way through. If the ordinance of '87 did not keep slavery out of the north west territory, how happens it that the north west shore of the Ohio river is entirely free from it; while the south east shore, less than a mile distant, along nearly the whole length of the river, is entirely covered with it?

If that ordinance did not keep it out of Illinois, what was it that made the difference between Illinois and Missouri? They lie side by side, the Mississippi river only dividing them; while their early settlements were within the same latitude. Between 1810 and 1820 the number of slaves in Missouri INCREASED 7,211; while in Illinois, in the same ten years, they DECREASED 51. This appears by the census returns. During nearly all of that ten years, both were territories—not States. During this time, the ordinance forbid slavery to go into Illinois; and NOTHING forbid it to go into Missouri. It DID go into Missouri, and did NOT go into Illinois. That is the fact. Can any one doubt as to the reason of it?

But, he says, Illinois came into the Union as a slave State. Silence, perhaps, would be the best answer to this flat contradiction of the known history of the country. What are the facts upon which this bold assertion is based? When we first acquired the country, as far back as 1787, there were some slaves within it, held by the French inhabitants at Kaskaskia. The territorial legislation, admitted a few negroes, from the slave States, as indentured servants. One year after the adoption of the first State constitution the whole number of them was—what do you think? just 117—while the aggregate free population was 55,094—about 470 to one. Upon this state of facts, the people framed their constitution prohibiting the further introduction of slavery, with a sort of guaranty to the owners of the few indentured servants, giving freedom to their children to be born thereafter, and making no mention whatever, of any supposed slave for life. Out of this small matter, the Judge manufactures his argument that Illinois came into the Union as a slave State. Let the facts be the answer to the argument.

The principles of the Nebraska bill, he says, expelled slavery from Illinois? The principle of that bill first planted it here—that is, it first came, because there was no law to prevent it—first came before we owned the country; and finding it here, and having the ordinance of '87 to prevent its increasing, our people struggled along, and finally got rid of it as best they could.

But the principle of the Nebraska bill abolished slavery in several of the old States. Well, it is true that several of the old States, in the last quarter of the last century, did adopt systems of gradual emancipation, by which the institution has finally become extinct within their limits; but it MAY or MAY NOT be true that the principle of the Nebraska bill was the cause that led to the adoption of these measures. It is now more than fifty years, since the last of these States adopted

its system of emancipation. If Nebraska bill is the real author of these benevolent works, it is rather deplorable, that he has, for so long a time, ceased working
all together. Is there not some reason to suspect that it was the principle of the
REVOLUTION, and not the principle of Nebraska bill, that led to emancipation in
these old States? Leave it to the people of those old emancipating States, and I
am quite sure they will decide, that neither that, nor any other good thing, ever
did, or ever will come of Nebraska bill.

In the course of my main argument, Judge Douglas interrupted me to say,
that the principle of the Nebraska bill was very old; that it originated when God
made man and placed good and evil before him, allowing him to choose for
himself, being responsible for the choice he should make. At the time I thought
this was merely playful; and I answered it accordingly. But in his reply to me he
renewed it, as a serious argument. In seriousness then, the facts of this proposition are not true as stated. God did not place good and evil before man, telling
him to make his choice. On the contrary, he did tell him there was one tree, of
the fruit of which, he should not eat, upon pain of certain death. I should scarcely wish so strong a prohibition against slavery in Nebraska.

But this argument strikes me as not a little remarkable in another particular—in its strong resemblance to the old argument for the 'Divine right of
Kings.' By the latter, the King is to do just as he pleases with his white subjects,
being responsible to God alone. By the former the white man is to do just as he
pleases with his black slaves, being responsible to God alone. The two things are
precisely alike; and it is but natural that they should find similar arguments to
sustain them.

I had argued, that the application of the principle of self-government, as
contended for, would require the revival of the African slave trade—that no argument could be made in favor of a man's right to take slaves to Nebraska,
which could not be equally well made in favor of his right to bring them from
the coast of Africa. The Judge replied, that the constitution requires the suppression of the foreign slave trade; but does not require the prohibition of slavery in
the territories. That is a mistake, in point of fact. The constitution does NOT require the action of Congress in either case; and it does AUTHORIZE it in both.
And so, there is still no difference between the cases.

In regard to what I had said, the advantage the slave States have over the
free, in the matter of representation, the Judge replied that we, in the free States,
count five free negroes as five white people, while in the slave States, they count
five slaves as three whites only; and that the advantage, at last, was on the side
of the free States.

Now, in the slave States, they count free negroes just as we do; and it so
happens that besides their slaves, they have as many free negroes as we have,
and thirty-three thousand over. Thus their free negroes more than balance ours;
and their advantage over us, in consequence of their slaves, still remains as I
stated it.

In reply to my argument, that the compromise measures of 1850, were a system of equivalents; and that the provisions of no one of them could fairly be carried to other subjects, without its corresponding equivalent being carried with it, the Judge denied out-right, that these measures had any connection with, or dependence upon, each other. This is mere desperation. If they have no connection, why are they always spoken of in connection? Why has he so spoken of them, a thousand times? Why has he constantly called them a SERIES of measures? Why does everybody call them a compromise? Why was California kept out of the Union, six or seven months, if it was not because of its connection with the other measures? Webster's leading definition of the verb "to compromise" is "to adjust and settle a difference, by mutual agreement with concessions of claims by the parties." This conveys precisely the popular understanding of the word compromise. We knew, before the Judge told us, that these measures passed separately, and in distinct bills; and that no two of them were passed by the votes of precisely the same members. But we also know, and so does he know, that no one of them could have passed both branches of Congress but for the understanding that the others were to pass also. Upon this understanding each got votes, which it could have got in no other way. It is this fact, which gives to the measures their true character; and it is the universal knowledge of this fact, that has given them the name of compromise so expressive of that true character.

I had asked "If in carrying the provisions of the Utah and New Mexico laws to Nebraska, you could clear away other objection, how can you leave Nebraska "perfectly free" to introduce slavery BEFORE she forms a constitution—during her territorial government?—while the Utah and New Mexico laws only authorize it WHEN they form constitutions, and are admitted into the Union?" To this Judge Douglas answered that the Utah and New Mexico laws, also authorized it BEFORE; and to prove this, he read from one of their laws, as follows: "That the legislative power of said territory shall extend to all rightful subjects of legislation consistent with the constitution of the United States and the provisions of this act."

Now it is perceived from the reading of this, that there is nothing express upon the subject; but that the authority is sought to be implied merely, for the general provision of "all rightful subjects of legislation." In reply to this, I insist, as a legal rule of construction, as well as the plain popular view of the matter, that the EXPRESS provision for Utah and New Mexico coming in with slavery if they choose, when they shall form constitutions, is an EXCLUSION of all implied authority on the same subject—that Congress, having the subject distinctly in their minds, when they made the express provision, they therein expressed their WHOLE meaning on that subject.

The Judge rather insinuated that I had found it convenient to forget the Washington territorial law passed in 1853. This was a division of Oregon, organizing the northern part, as the territory of Washington. He asserted that, by this act, the ordinance of '87 theretofore existing in Oregon, was repealed; that nearly all the members of Congress voted for it, beginning in the H.R., with Charles Allen of Massachusetts, and ending with Richard Yates, of Illinois; and that he could not understand how those who now oppose the Nebraska bill, so voted then, unless it was because it was then too soon after both the great political parties had ratified the compromises of 1850, and the ratification therefore too fresh, to be then repudiated.

Now I had seen the Washington act before; and I have carefully examined it since; and I aver that there is no repeal of the ordinance of '87, or of any prohibition of slavery, in it. In express terms, there is absolutely nothing in the whole law upon the subject—in fact, nothing to lead a reader to THINK of the subject. To my judgment, it is equally free from everything from which such repeal can be legally implied; but however this may be, are men now to be entrapped by a legal implication, extracted from covert language, introduced perhaps, for the very purpose of entrapping them? I sincerely wish every man could read this law quite through, carefully watching every sentence, and every line, for a repeal of the ordinance of '87 or anything equivalent to it.

Another point on the Washington act. If it was intended to be modeled after the Utah and New Mexico acts, as Judge Douglas, insists, why was it not inserted in it, as in them, that Washington was to come in with or without slavery as she may choose at the adoption of her constitution? It has no such provision in it; and I defy the ingenuity of man to give a reason for the omission, other than that it was not intended to follow the Utah and New Mexico laws in regard to the question of slavery.

The Washington act not only differs vitally from the Utah and New Mexico acts; but the Nebraska act differs vitally from both. By the latter act the people are left "perfectly free" to regulate their own domestic concerns, &c.; but in all the former, all their laws are to be submitted to Congress, and if disapproved are to be null. The Washington act goes even further; it absolutely prohibits the territorial legislation [legislature?], by very strong and guarded language, from establishing banks, or borrowing money on the faith of the territory. Is this the sacred right of self-government we hear vaunted so much? No sir, the Nebraska bill finds no model in the acts of '50 or the Washington act. It finds no model in any law from Adam till today. As Phillips says of Napoleon, the Nebraska act is grand, gloomy, and peculiar; wrapped in the solitude of its own originality; without a model, and without a shadow upon the earth.

In the course of his reply, Senator Douglas remarked, in substance, that he had always considered this government was made for the white people and not for the negroes. Why, in point of mere fact, I think so too. But in this remark of the Judge, there is a significance, which I think is the key to the great mistake (if there is any such mistake) which he has made in this Nebraska measure. It shows that the Judge has no very vivid impression that the negro is a human; and consequently has no idea that there can be any moral question in legislating about him. In his view, the question of whether a new country shall be slave or free, is a matter of as utter indifference, as it is whether his neighbor shall plant his farm with tobacco, or stock it with horned cattle. Now, whether this view is right or wrong, it is very certain that the great mass of mankind take a totally different view. They consider slavery a great moral wrong; and their feelings against it, is not evanescent, but eternal. It lies at the very foundation of their sense of justice; and it cannot be trifled with. It is a great and durable element of popular action, and, I think, no statesman can safely disregard it.

Our Senator also objects that those who oppose him in this measure do not entirely agree with one another. He reminds me that in my firm adherence to the constitutional rights of the slave States, I differ widely from others who are co-operating with me in opposing the Nebraska bill; and he says it is not quite fair to oppose him in this variety of ways. He should remember that he took us by surprise—astounded us—by this measure. We were thunderstruck and stunned; and we reeled and fell in utter confusion. But we rose each fighting, grasping whatever he could first reach—a scythe—a pitchfork—a chopping axe, or a butcher's cleaver. We struck in the direction of the sound; and we are rapidly closing in upon him. He must not think to divert us from our purpose, by show-ing us that our drill, our dress, and our weapons, are not entirely perfect and uniform. When the storm shall be past, he shall find us still Americans; no less devoted to the continued Union and prosperity of the country than heretofore.

Finally, the Judge invokes against me, the memory of Clay and of Webster. They were great men; and men of great deeds. But where have I assailed them? For what is it, that their life-long enemy, shall now make profit, by assuming to defend them against me, their life-long friend? I go against the repeal of the Missouri Compromise; did they ever go for it? They went for the compromise of 1850; did I ever go against them? They were greatly devoted to the Union; to the small measure of my ability, was I ever less so? Clay and Webster were dead before this question arose; by what authority shall our Senator say they would espouse his side of it, if alive? Mr. Clay was the leading spirit in making the Missouri Compromise; is it very credible that if now alive, he would take the lead in the breaking of it? The truth is that some support from whigs is now a necessity with the Judge, and for this it is, that the names of Clay and Webster are now invoked. His old friends have deserted him in such numbers as to leave too few to live by. He came to his own, and his own received him not, and Lo! he turns unto the Gentiles.

A word now as to the Judge's desperate assumption that the compromises of '50 had no connection with one another; that Illinois came into the Union as a slave state, and some other similar ones. This is no other than a bold denial of the history of the country. If we do not know that the compromises of '50 were dependent on each other; if we do not know that Illinois came into the Union as a free state—we do not know any thing. If we do not know these things, we do not know that we ever had a revolutionary war, or such a chief as Washington. To deny these things is to deny our national axioms, or dogmas, at least; and it puts an end to all argument. If a man will stand up and assert, and repeat, and re-assert, that two and two do not make four, I know nothing in the power of argument that can stop him. I think I can answer the Judge so long as he sticks to the premises; but when he flies from them, I cannot work an argument into the consistency of a maternal gag, and actually close his mouth with it. In such a case I can only commend him to the seventy thousand answers just in from Pennsylvania, Ohio and Indiana.

Interpretation

Lincoln argues for the restoration of the Missouri Compromise, the repeal of which Douglas had just masterminded in Congress. The simple historical account with which he begins reaches back to Thomas Jefferson, the author of the Declaration of Independence, a slave-holder himself and, in Lincoln's judgment, "the most distinguished politician of our history." Jefferson conceived the idea of having Virginia cede its Northwest Territory to the new nation, with the expectation that slavery would be banned from it (Lincoln erred in saying Virginia made this prohibition a condition of the gift and afterward authorized the text to be corrected). And so it happened, first under the Articles of Confederation, then re-affirmed under the new Constitution. This act of Congress eventually allowed the Territory to become "the happy home of teeming millions of free, white, prosperous people, and no slave among them." But now this old anti-slavery principle has been renounced (by Douglas and the present Congress) in favor of the pretended right of white men to take slaves into the various territories and establish slavery there.

The Missouri Compromise of 1820, Lincoln tells us, was meant to deal with the question of slavery in the territory of the Louisiana Purchase and nowhere else. It allowed Missouri to enter the Union with slavery but forbade slavery north of the line drawn westward, within that territory, from its southern boundary. Even as late as 1849 this compromise won the unconditional plaudits of Senator Douglas himself, whose impressive words Lincoln quotes. Difficulties had begun a few years before, however, during the Mexican War. At that time the so-called Wilmot Proviso was introduced again and again in the House, with Lincoln's constant support, only to be defeated in the Senate. Its intent was to acquire no new territory from Mexico unless slavery was banned in it. As it happened, new territory—New Mexico, Utah and the state of California—was acquired without that ban, but the question of the disposition of slavery in those areas remained. It was only settled by the several articles of the Compromise of 1850. Four years later the present difficulties began, with Senator Douglas first upholding and then discarding the Missouri Compromise in his effort to deal with Kansas and Nebraska. He ended by allowing these two territories (both north of the old "Missouri" line) to decide whether to have slavery or not, in the process expressly repealing the Missouri Compromise, which would have flatly banned slavery there. He called this "popular sovereignty."

With the stage now set for the current discussion, Lincoln cites the Declaration of Independence and says he "can not but hate" the seeming indifference to slavery which in fact is a "covert *real* zeal" for spreading it. Thus begins a section of his speech so important in his eyes that he repeated it verbatim a few years later in his first debate with Douglas. Lincoln displays an unusual understanding of human nature and of the interests generated by slavery: he does not blame the South for being reluctant to give up slavery, or for not knowing what to do about slavery. He is much harsher on Douglas and his principle of white popular sovereignty than on the South. He even admits to having no solution to the slavery problem itself. To show as much, he assesses the four available alternatives: 1) freeing all the slaves and sending them to Liberia; 2) freeing them and keeping them as "underlings"; 3) freeing them and making them "politically and socially our equals"; 4) gradual emancipation.

His "first impulse" would be to free the slaves and send them back to their native land, but "a moment's reflection" tells him it would fail quickly, although there is hope for it "in the long run." The second option—freeing them but without allowing further equality—does not represent much of an improvement for the blacks, although Lincoln adds that he "would not hold one in slavery, at any rate." The third alternative is the most radical: free them suddenly and make them equal. His own feelings will not admit of this, but if they would, those of most white people will not. Can Lincoln have feelings different from those of most whites? He thinks of that possibility, and then complicates the matter by detracting from the importance of "feelings" as such, distinguishing them from the dictates of "justice and sound judgment." Objective justice and objective judgment, not feelings, Lincoln implies, should really decide the matter, and Lincoln's way of putting this suggests that the judgment of blacks by most whites might be unjust and unsound. But he immediately adds that justice and right judgment may have no place in the question at all, for what he now calls, with some exaggeration, a "universal feeling" on the part of the whites, "can not be safely disregarded." Power lies with those feelings. So the alternative combining full emancipation and equalization is out. About the last option—gradual emancipation—Lincoln has nothing adverse to say, a point as momentous as easily overlooked. He ends by asserting the kinship between the law stopping the importation of slaves (allowed for in the Constitution itself) and the prohibition on slavery in Kansas and Nebraska that was assured by the Missouri Compromise up till the time of its repeal. These were part of the same condemnatory policy with regard to slavery.

It is amazing that Lincoln, over the next few years, was able to win so much support in the North for a position that combined keeping slavery out of the territories (in anticipation of its eventual demise) with the candid admission that he had no solution to the aftermath of emancipation. What he relied on in the people was an amalgam of belief and hope: belief in the principles of the Declaration of Independence, calling for the recognition of the negro's humanity and rights, and hope that somewhere along the way would emerge the outlines of a solution not yet seen, or perhaps not yet capable of being discussed. From the above list, gradual emancipation seemed to offer the best prospects, but joined with what? With colonization, or with some form of assimilation? Were the freed blacks to be sent abroad or to remain here? Would they want to leave? This difficulty in Lincoln's position, so apparent from his own analysis, must have made many in the South more convinced than ever that freeing the slaves would be a terrible mistake.

In the body of the speech, Lincoln takes up one by one the arguments used to justify the repeal of the Missouri Compromise. He denies that the public (i.e., Congress) intended by the Compromise of 1850 to establish a principle of self-determination applicable to Kansas and Nebraska and requiring the repeal of the Compromise. He refuses to accept the claim—the "lullaby" argument, he calls it—that climate by itself will keep slavery confined to the South, citing the fact that five of the slave states and the District of Columbia, containing more than a quarter of all the slaves in the nation, are already north of the Missouri Compromise line. He also adduces evidence to prove that Southerners themselves realize slavery is wrong. Did they not almost unanimously join the North in stopping the African slave trade? Do they not detest the slave-traders in their midst? How can we account for the existence of almost half a million free blacks in the country if they had not at some time been emancipated by sympathetic owners—owners who knew they had been violating the negro's "natural right to himself"?

For the sake of dealing with Douglas' appeal to "the sacred right of self-government," Lincoln clarifies his own attitude toward self-government: "My faith in the proposition that each man should do precisely as he pleases with all which is exclusively his own, lies at the foundation of the sense of justice that is in me." This principle, so important to Lincoln's thought, applies to communities of men as well as to individuals. Its application to the treatment of blacks by whites completely depends on whether the black is a man or not. If he is, "why then my ancient faith teaches me that 'all men are created equal,' and that there can be no moral right in connection with one man's making a slave of another." Repeating the word "faith" here shows Lincoln's willingness to use elements of Biblical religion for the rational "truths" of the Declaration (even in its references to God). Now, almost eighty years later, those principles, so new and novel in 1776, might be considered "ancient." They may even have for many the status of a faith, something they have not reasoned. Perhaps the principles are strengthened, rather than weakened, thereby. Again, in using the term "faith" Lincoln undoubtedly calls upon the spirit of Biblical religion to infuse and shore up what is, instrinsically, the product of nothing but reason.

At this point Lincoln does not hesitate to quote from the Declaration, the "sheet-anchor of American republicanism." And his conclusion: "Allow ALL the governed an equal voice in the government, and that, and that only, is self-government." This sounds like a broad political conclusion rather than one dealing with slavery alone, and as such it implies the need for granting full citizenship to the blacks. Lincoln must therefore leap in quickly with a qualifier: "Let it not be said I am contending for the establishment of political and social equality between the whites and the blacks." He is not now combating the "argument of NECESSITY"—caused by the blacks already being here among us, which might be used to keep them in slavery. What he is opposing is the MORAL argument for bringing slavery to areas where it does not yet exist. Even so, the implication of his argument remains that freed blacks have a right to become citizens and participate in self-government. This—again by implication—is the only self-government worthy of the name, not Douglas' "popular sovereignty." Here we have a most radical message contained within a speech that tries to look traditional and conventional. It may set the goal toward which Lincoln, however slowly, would attempt to move the country.

Lincoln welcomes Douglas' reverting to the opinions of our "revolutionary fathers": "I love the sentiments of those old-time men; and shall be most happy to abide by their opinions." He admits they were willing to guarantee the continuance of slavery in the states where it was already existed, but, again, the Northwest Ordinance proves that they would not admit it into new territories. Lincoln adds several other arguments against granting Douglas' right of "popular sovereignty" to the people of Nebraska. His final point, one of his best, derives from the constitutional provision counting five slaves as equal to three whites for the purpose of allocating representation in Congress. Following Douglas' principle, a handful of white men in Nebraska, led only by self-interest in wanting slavery, can with the help of this constitutional provision add to the influence of slave states and decrease the influence of free states in the House of Representatives.

Lincoln then turns to an argument for repealing the Missouri Compromise that did not appear among those he said he would treat. It is that the new policy will save the Union. But in fact this policy has engendered a renewed desire to spread slavery and led to a flaring up of the most intense discord. "Slavery is founded in the selfishness of man's nature—opposition to it, in his love of justice. These principles are an eternal antagonism." So the thrust for slavery arouses a thrust against it. Furthermore, renouncing the Missouri Compromise is likely to kill the "SPIRIT OF COMPROMISE" itself on which the nation was originated and by which it has several times since been held together. He calls for joining with abolitionists in an effort to restore the Compromise, even if they must differ with the abolitionist attempt to repeal the fugitive slave law.

Lincoln insists that Douglas' new principle, with its assumption that "there can be MORAL RIGHT in the enslaving of one man by another," is essentially different from what the fathers of the republic believed. They were willing to concede to the necessity imposed by existing slavery, but with the understanding that slavery was wrong. In support of this claim, Lincoln adduces the interesting fact that the word "slavery" never appears in the Constitution, despite several undoubted references to it. It is "hidden away in the Constitution, just as an afflicted man hides away a wen or a cancer." The founders, looking forward to its ultimate extinction, did not want to mar their document by mentioning its existence. Lincoln goes on to list the many acts of Congress between 1794 and 1820 evincing a manifest desire to end the slave trade. At the same time, "five or six of the original slave states adopted systems of gradual emancipation." Living then, one might have concluded that slavery was indeed on its way out!

Having predicted, with great accuracy, the bloody violence about to break out between pro-slavery and anti-slavery forces in the Nebraska territory, Lincoln ends this section of his speech by returning to the Declaration of Independence and what has happened to it. He is shocked that a Nebraskan named Pettit—apparently a member of the Nebraskan territorial senate—called the Declaration "a self-evident lie" and received no rebuke for doing so. He asks what Marion's men—Southerners who fought so hard for our independence—would have done to such a man, and imagines that the men who captured the spy Andre, also in the revolution, would have hung such a man before they hung Andre himself. The very doorkeeper of old Independence Hall, in 1776, would have throttled such a man. These examples show the importance Lincoln attributed to the lasting vigor of the Declaration in the public mind. To renounce it is to become an enemy of the revolution and the country.

By reminding his contemporaries of the spirit in which the Declaration was originally held, Lincoln intends to revive that spirit and the moral indignation attendant on it. The "spirit of Nebraska" is driving out the spirit of the Declaration, our "ancient faith." The source of the danger is not simply the South but "our greedy chase to make profit of the negro." The consequence can be that we "cancel and tear to pieces" the white man's charter of freedom as well. The quotation is from a speech by Shakespeare's Macbeth as he welcomes the night in which he will have his friend Banquo murdered (*Macbeth*, III, 2:48). Lincoln calls upon his countrymen to return to the Declaration and the policies in harmony with it. This is the only true way of saving the union, and making it "forever worthy of the saving."

The last part of the Peoria address is devoted to considering some thirteen points made by Douglas on a previous occasion and now dealt with by Lincoln. We shall only remark upon a few of these. In discussing the fifth point, Lincoln mentions a fact that is little known today: that the South in his day contained 33,000 more *free* blacks than the North. In the tenth point, he maintains that Douglas' principle of popular sovereignty assumes there is no moral question in deciding about the black's status, slave or free. Lincoln contends, however, that the great mass of mankind considers slavery "a great moral wrong," and their feeling against it "lies at the very foundation of their sense of justice." He ends with a severe censure of Douglas' ignorance of facts concerning the compromises of 1850 that are as elementary as the fact that we had a revolutionary war and a leader named Washington—things he refers to as our "national axioms, or dogmas, at least."

Why this peculiar closing language? What accounts for Douglas' ignorance of simple historical facts, and how can facts about the revolution be either axioms or dogmas? An axiom is best known as a term from geometry, referring to a statement true in itself that is used to assist demonstrations. A dogma is an article of religious belief or faith. But can these words apply to facts? For one thing, it follows from his statement that the compromises of 1850 do not have the same status as the revolution itself: they are neither national axioms nor dogmas, and we can see why: as compromises between freedom and slavery, they lack internal consistency. But the facts concerning these compromises are clear enough: how can Douglas misunderstand them? Perhaps Lincoln points to the answer with his examples of the revolutionary war and Washington. What makes these facts significant are the principles that animated them, and these principles derive from the Declaration of Independence, with which the revolution began. In these principles resides the larger meaning of the revolutionary war and Washington's leadership before and after it—more fundamental, as a declaration of equality and freedom, than the Constitution itself.

Principles can be national axioms or dogmas, even if facts as such cannot. But which of the two are the principles of the revolution? Are they matters of science and reason, on the one hand, or religion and faith, on the other? It is true that Lincoln's use of the qualifier "at least" gives the impression that dogmas are not quite as good as axioms, and from the point of view of knowledge (strictly speaking) they are not. But the two are not hostile to each other politically. The philosophers among us hold these principles as rational knowledge, the rest of us as matters we trust to be true without knowing them to be. As alternative modes of belief, the two combine to hold the country together. So, by extension, Douglas' ignorance of the facts of the compromises of 1850 may be rooted in his misunderstanding of the Declaration of Independence, which would also render him incapable of appreciating the facts of the revolution—facts deeper than those of the compromises of 1850—as either axioms or dogmas.

Chapter 7

The Dred Scott Decision, June 26, 1857

This is Lincoln's response, in Springfield, Illinois, to a speech Judge Douglas had given there two weeks earlier. Back in March, the Supreme Court had issued its decision in the Dred Scott case. Scott was a slave whose master had stayed with him in areas (Illinois and Minnesota Territory) designated as free by the Missouri Compromise, and who therefore sued for his freedom in the federal courts. The Court, speaking through Chief Justice Roger B. Taney, declared that negroes could not be citizens and could not sue in federal courts, and that slavery could not be kept out of the territories by Congress, in effect rejecting as unconstitutional the Missouri Compromise Congress itself had repealed in 1854.

Text

Fellow-citizens:—

I am here to-night, partly by the invitation of some of you, and partly by my own inclination. Two weeks ago Judge Douglas spoke here on the several subjects of Kansas, the *Dred Scott* decision, and Utah. I listened to the speech at the time, and have read the report of it since. It was intended to controvert opinions which I think just, and to assail (politically, not personally,) those men who, in common with me, entertain those opinions. For this reason I wished then, and still wish, to make some answer to it, which I now take the opportunity of doing.

I begin with Utah. If it prove to be true, as is probable, that the people of Utah are in open rebellion to the United States, then Judge Douglas is in favor of repealing their territorial organization, and attaching them to the adjoining States for judicial purposes. I say, too, if they are in rebellion, they ought to be somehow coerced to obedience; and I am not now prepared to admit or deny that the Judge's mode of coercing them is not as good as any. The Republicans can fall in with it without taking back anything they have ever said. To be sure, it would be a considerable backing down by Judge Douglas from his much vaunted doctrine of self-government for the territories; but this is only additional proof of what was very plain from the beginning, that that doctrine was a mere deceitful pretense for the benefit of slavery. Those who could not see that much in the Nebraska act itself, which forced Governors, and Secretaries, and Judges on the people of the territories, without their choice or consent, could not be made to see, though one should rise from the dead to testify.

But in all this, it is very plain the Judge evades the only question the Republicans have ever pressed upon the Democracy in regard to Utah. That question the Judge well knows to be this: "If the people of Utah shall peacefully form a State Constitution tolerating polygamy, will the Democracy admit them into the Union?" There is nothing in the United States Constitution or law against polygamy; and why is it not a part of the Judge's "sacred right of self-government" for that people to have it, or rather to *keep* it, if they choose? These questions, so far as I know, the Judge never answers. It might involve the Democracy to answer them either way, and they go unanswered.

As to Kansas. The substance of the Judge's speech on Kansas is an effort to put the free State men in the wrong for not voting at the election of delegates to the Constitutional Convention. He says: *"There is every reason to hope and believe that the law will be fairly interpreted and impartially executed, so as to insure to every bona fide inhabitant the free and quiet exercise of the elective franchise."*

It appears extraordinary that Judge Douglas should make such a statement. He knows that, by the law, no one can vote who has not been registered; and he knows that the free State men place their refusal to vote on the ground that but few of them have been registered. It is *possible* this is not true, but Judge Douglas knows it is asserted to be true in letters, newspapers and public speeches, and borne by every mail, and blown by every breeze to the eyes and ears of the world. He knows it is boldly declared that the people of many whole counties, and many whole neighborhoods in others, are left unregistered; yet, he does not venture to contradict the declaration, nor to point out how they *can* vote without being registered; but he just slips along, not seeming to know there is any such question of fact, and complacently declares: "There is every reason to hope and believe that the law will be fairly and impartially executed, so as to insure to every *bona fide* inhabitant the free and quiet exercise of the elective franchise."

I readily agree that if all had a chance to vote, they ought to have voted. If, on the contrary, as they allege, and Judge Douglas ventures not to particularly contradict, few only of the free State men had a chance to vote, they were perfectly right in staying from the polls in a body.

By the way since the Judge spoke, the Kansas election has come off. The Judge expressed his confidence that all the Democrats in Kansas would do their duty—including "free state Democrats" of course. The returns received here as yet are very incomplete; but so far as they go, they indicate that only about one sixth of the registered voters, have really voted; and this too, when not more, perhaps, than one half of the rightful voters have been registered, thus showing the thing to have been altogether the most exquisite farce ever enacted. I am watching with considerable interest, to ascertain what figure "the free state Democrats" cut in the concern. Of course they voted—all democrats do their duty—and of course they did not vote for slave-state candidates. We soon shall know how many delegates *they* elected, how many candidates they had, pledged for a free state; and how many votes were cast for them.

Allow me to barely whisper my suspicion that there were no such things in Kansas "as free state Democrats"—that they were altogether mythical, good only to figure in newspapers and speeches in the free states. If there should prove to be one real living free state Democrat in Kansas, I suggest that it might be well to catch him, and stuff and preserve his skin, as an interesting specimen of that soon to be extinct variety of the genus, Democrat.

And now as to the *Dred Scott* decision. That decision declares two propositions—first, that a negro cannot sue in the U.S. Courts; and secondly, that Congress cannot prohibit slavery in the Territories. It was made by a divided court—dividing differently on the different points. Judge Douglas does not discuss the merits of the decision; and, in that respect, I shall follow his example, believing I could no more improve on McLean and Curtis, than he could on Taney.

He denounces all who question the correctness of that decision, as offering violent resistance to it. But who resists it? Who has, in spite of the decision, declared Dred Scott free, and resisted the authority of his master over him?

Judicial decisions have two uses—first, to absolutely determine the case decided, and secondly, to indicate to the public how other similar cases will be decided when they arise. For the latter use, they are called "precedents" and "authorities."

We believe, as much as Judge Douglas, (perhaps more) in obedience to, and respect for the judicial department of government. We think its decisions on Constitutional questions, when fully settled, should control, not only the particular cases decided, but the general policy of the country, subject to be disturbed only by amendments of the Constitution as provided in that instrument itself. More than this would be revolution. But we think the *Dred Scott* decision is erroneous. We know the court that made it, has often over-ruled its own decisions, and we shall do what we can to have it to over-rule this. We offer no *resistance* to it.

Judicial decisions are of greater or less authority as precedents, according to circumstances. That this should be so, accords both with common sense, and the customary understanding of the legal profession.

If this important decision had been made by the unanimous concurrence of the judges, and without any apparent partisan bias, and in accordance with legal public expectation, and with the steady practice of the departments throughout our history, and had been in no part, based on assumed historical facts which are not really true; or, if wanting in some of these, it had been before the court more than once, and had there been affirmed and re-affirmed through a course of years, it then might be, perhaps would be, factious, nay, even revolutionary, to not acquiesce in it as a precedent.

But when, as it is true we find it wanting in all these claims to the public confidence, it is not resistance, it is not factious, it is not even disrespectful, to treat it as not having yet quite established a settled doctrine for the country. But Judge Douglas considers this view awful. Hear him:

"The courts are the tribunals prescribed by the Constitution and created by the authority of the people to determine, expound and enforce the law. Hence, whoever resists the final decision of the highest judicial tribunal, aims a deadly blow to our whole Republican system of government—a blow, which if successful would place all our rights and liberties at the mercy of passion, anarchy and violence. I repeat, therefore, that if resistance to the decisions of the Supreme Court of the United States, in a matter like the points decided in the Dred Scott case, clearly within their jurisdiction as defined by the Constitution, shall be forced upon the country as a political issue, it will become a distinct and naked issue between the friends and the enemies of the Constitution—the friends and the enemies of the supremacy of the laws."

Why this same Supreme court once decided a national bank to be constitutional; but Gen. Jackson, as President of the United States, disregarded the decision, and vetoed a bill for a re-charter, partly on constitutional ground, declaring that each public functionary must support the Constitution, *"as he understands it."* But hear the General's own words. Here they are, taken from his veto message:

"It is maintained by the advocates of the bank, that its constitutionality, in all its features, ought to be considered as settled by precedent, and by the decision of the Supreme Court. To this conclusion I cannot assent. Mere precedent is a dangerous source of authority, and should not be regarded as deciding questions of constitutional power, except where the acquiescence of the people and the States can be considered as well settled. So far from this being the case on this subject, an argument against the bank might be based on precedent. One Congress in 1791, decided in favor of a bank; another in 1811, decided against it. One Congress in 1815 decided against a bank; another in 1816 decided in its favor. Prior to the present Congress, therefore the precedents drawn from that source were equal. If we resort to the States, the expressions of legislative, judicial and executive opinions against the bank have been probably to those in its favor as four to one. There is nothing in precedent, therefore, which if its authority were admitted, ought to weigh in favor of the act before me."

I drop the quotations merely to remark that all there ever was, in the way of precedent up to the *Dred Scott* decision, on the points therein decided, had been against that decision. But hear Gen. Jackson further—

"If the opinion of the Supreme court covered the whole ground of this act, it ought not to control the co-ordinate authorities of this Government. The Congress, the executive and the court, must each for itself be guided by its own opinion of the Constitution. Each public officer, who takes an oath to support the

Constitution, swears that he will support it as he understands it, and not as it is understood by others."

Again and again have I heard Judge Douglas denounce that bank decision, and applaud Gen. Jackson for disregarding it. It would be interesting for him to look over his recent speech, and see how exactly his fierce philippics against us for resisting Supreme Court decisions, fall upon his own head. It will call to his mind a long and fierce political war in this country, upon an issue which, in his own language, and, of course, in his own changeless estimation, was "a distinct and naked issue between the friends and the enemies of the Constitution," and in which war he fought in the ranks of the enemies of the Constitution.

I have said, in substance, that the *Dred Scott* decision was, in part, based on assumed historical facts which were not really true; and I ought not to leave the subject without giving some reasons for saying this; I therefore give an instance or two, which I think fully sustain me. Chief Justice Taney, in delivering the opinion of the majority of the Court, insists at great length that negroes were no part of the people who made, or for whom was made, the Declaration of Independence, or the Constitution of the United States.

On the contrary, Judge Curtis, in his dissenting opinion, shows that in five of the then thirteen states, to wit, New Hampshire, Massachusetts, New York, New Jersey and North Carolina, free negroes were voters, and, in proportion to their numbers, had the same part in making the Constitution that the white people had. He shows this with so much particularity as to leave no doubt of its truth; and, as a sort of conclusion on that point, holds the following language:

"The Constitution was ordained and established by the people of the United States, through the action, in each State, of those persons who were qualified by its laws to act thereon in behalf of themselves and all other citizens of the State. In some of the States, as we have seen, colored persons were among those qualified by law to act on the subject. These colored persons were not only included in the body of 'the people of the United States,' by whom the Constitution was ordained and established; but in at least five of the States they had the power to act, and, doubtless, did act, by their suffrages, upon the question of its adoption."

Again, Chief Justice Taney says: "It is difficult, at this day to realize the state of public opinion in relation to that unfortunate race, which prevailed in the civilized and enlightened portions of the world at the time of the Declaration of Independence, and when the Constitution of the United States was framed and adopted." And again, after quoting from the Declaration, he says: "The general words above quoted would seem to include the whole human family, and if they were used in a similar instrument at this day, would be so understood."

In these the Chief Justice does not directly assert, but plainly assumes, as a fact, that the public estimate of the black man is more favorable *now* than it was in the days of the Revolution. This assumption is a mistake. In some trifling particulars, the condition of that race has been ameliorated; but, as a whole, in this country, the change between then and now is decidedly the other way; and their ultimate destiny has never appeared so hopeless as in the last three or four years. In two of the five States—New Jersey and North Carolina—that then gave the free negro the right of voting, the right has since been taken away; and in a third—New York—it has been greatly abridged; while it has not been extended, so far as I know, to a single additional State, though the number of the States has more than doubled. In those days, as I understand, masters could, at their own pleasure, emancipate their slaves; but since then, such legal restraints have been made upon emancipation, as to amount almost to prohibition. In those days, Legislatures held the unquestioned power to abolish slavery in their respective States; but now it is becoming quite fashionable for State Constitutions to withhold that power from the Legislatures. In those days, by common consent, the spread of the black man's bondage to new countries was prohibited; but now, Congress decides that it *will* not continue the prohibition, and the Supreme Court decides that it *could* not if it would. In those days, our Declaration of Independence was held sacred by all, and thought to include all; but now, to aid in making the bondage of the negro universal and eternal, it is assailed, and sneered at, and construed, and hawked at, and torn, till, if its framers could rise from their graves, they could not at all recognize it. All the powers of earth seem rapidly combining against him. Mammon is after him; ambition follows, and philosophy follows, and the Theology of the day is fast joining the cry. They have him in his prison house; they have searched his person, and left no prying instrument with him. One after another they have closed the heavy iron doors upon him, and now they have him, as it were, bolted in with a lock of a hundred keys, which can never be unlocked without the concurrence of every key; the keys in the hands of a hundred different men, and they scattered to a hundred different and distant places; and they stand musing as to what invention, in all the dominions of mind and matter, can be produced to make the impossibility of his escape more complete than it is.

It is grossly incorrect to say or assume, that the public estimate of the negro is more favorable now than it was at the origin of the government.

Three years and a half ago, Judge Douglas brought forward his famous Nebraska bill. The country was at once in a blaze. He scorned all opposition, and carried it through Congress. Since then he has seen himself superseded in a Presidential nomination, by one indorsing the general doctrine of his measure, but at the same time standing clear of the odium of its untimely agitation, and its gross breach of national faith; and he has seen that successful rival Constitutionally elected, not by the strength of friends, but by the division of adversaries, being in a popular minority of nearly four hundred thousand votes. He has seen his chief aids in his own State, Shields and Richardson, politically speaking, successively tried, convicted, and executed, for an offense not their own, but his. And now he sees his own case, standing next on the docket for trial.

There is a natural disgust in the minds of nearly all white people, to the idea of an indiscriminate amalgamation of the white and black races; and Judge Douglas evidently is basing his chief hope, upon the chances of being able to appropriate the benefit of this disgust to himself. If he can, by much drumming and repeating, fasten the odium of that idea upon his adversaries, he thinks he can struggle through the storm. He therefore clings to this hope, as a drowning man to the last plank. He makes an occasion for lugging it in from the opposition to the *Dred Scott* decision. He finds the Republicans insisting that the Declaration of Independence includes ALL men, black as well as white; and forthwith he boldly denies that it includes negroes at all, and proceeds to argue gravely that all who contend it does, do so only because they want to vote, and eat, and sleep, and marry with negroes! He will have it that they cannot be consistent else. Now I protest against that counterfeit logic which concludes that, because I do not want a black woman for a *slave* I must necessarily want her for a *wife*. I need not have her for either, I can just leave her alone. In some respects she certainly is not my equal; but in her natural right to eat the bread she earns with her own hands without asking leave of any one else, she is my equal, and the equal of all others.

Chief Justice Taney, in his opinion in the Dred Scott case, admits that the language of the Declaration is broad enough to include the whole human family, but he and Judge Douglas argue that the authors of that instrument did not intend to include negroes, by the fact that they did not at once, actually place them on an equality with the whites. Now this grave argument comes to just nothing at all, by the other fact, that they did not at once, *or ever afterwards*, actually place all white people on an equality with one or another. And this is the staple argument of both the Chief Justice and the Senator, for doing this obvious violence to the plain unmistakable language of the Declaration. I think the authors of that notable instrument intended to include *all* men, but they did not intend to declare all men equal *in all respects*. They did not mean to say all were equal in color, size, intellect, moral developments, or social capacity. They defined with tolerable distinctness, in what respects they did consider all men created equal—equal in "certain inalienable rights, among which are life, liberty, and the pursuit of happiness." This they said, and this meant. They did not mean to assert the obvious untruth, that all were then actually enjoying that equality, nor yet, that they were about to confer it immediately upon them. In fact they had no power to confer such a boon. They meant simply to declare the *right*, so that the *enforcement* of it might follow as fast as circumstances should permit. They meant to set up a standard maxim for free society, which should be familiar to all, and revered by all; constantly looked to, constantly labored for, and even though never perfectly attained, constantly approximated, and thereby constantly spreading and deepening its influence, and augmenting the happiness and value of life to all people of all colors everywhere. The assertion that "all men are created equal" was of no practical use in effecting our separation from Great Britain; and it was placed in the Declaration, nor for that, but for future use. Its authors meant it to be, thank God, it is now proving itself, a stumbling block to those who in after times might seek to turn a free people back into the hateful paths of despotism. They knew the proneness of prosperity to breed tyrants, and they meant when such should re-appear in this fair land and commence their vocation they should find left for them at least one hard nut to crack.

I have now briefly expressed my view of the *meaning* and *objects* of that part of the Declaration of Independence which declares that "all men are created equal."

Now let us hear Judge Douglas' view of the same subject, as I find it in the printed report of his late speech. Here it is:

"No man can vindicate the character, motives and conduct of the signers of the Declaration of Independence except upon the hypothesis that they referred to the white race alone, and not to the African, when they declared all men to have been created equal—that they were speaking of British subjects on this continent being equal to British subjects born and residing in Great Britain—that they were entitled to the same inalienable rights, and among them were enumerated life, liberty and the pursuit of happiness. The Declaration was adopted for the purpose of justifying the colonists in the eyes of the civilized world in withdrawing their allegiance from the British crown, and dissolving their connection with the mother country."

My good friends, read that carefully over some leisure hour, and ponder well upon it—see what a mere wreck—mangled ruin—it makes of our once glorious Declaration.

"They were speaking of British subjects on this continent being equal to British subjects born and residing in Great Britain!" Why, according to this, not only negroes but white people outside of Great Britain and America are not spoken of in that instrument. The English, Irish and Scotch, along with white Americans, were included to be sure, but the French, Germans and other white people of the world are all gone to pot along with the Judge's inferior races.

I had thought the Declaration promised something better than the condition of British subjects; but no, it only meant that we should be *equal* to them in their own oppressed and *unequal* condition. According to that, it gave no promise that having kicked off the King and Lords of Great Britain, we should not at once be saddled with a King and Lords of our own.

I had thought the Declaration contemplated the progressive improvement in the condition of all men everywhere; but no, it merely "was adopted for the purpose of justifying the colonists in the eyes of the civilized world in withdrawing their allegiance from the British crown, and dissolving their connection with the mother country." Why, that object having been effected some eighty years ago, the Declaration is of no practical use now—mere rubbish—old wadding left to rot on the battle-field after the victory is won.

I understand you are preparing to celebrate the "Fourth," tomorrow week. What for? The doings of that day had no reference to the present; and quite half of you are not even descendants of those who were referred to at that day. But I suppose you will celebrate; and will even go so far as to read the Declaration. Suppose after you read it once in the old fashioned way, you read it once more with Judge Douglas' version. It will then run thus: "We hold these truths to be self-evident that all British subjects who were on this continent eighty-one years ago, were created equal to all British subjects born and then residing in Great Britain."

And now I appeal to all—to Democrats as well as others,—are you really willing that the Declaration shall be thus frittered away?—thus left no more at most, than an interesting memorial of the dead past? thus shorn of its vitality, and practical value; and left without the *germ* or even the *suggestion* of the individual rights of man in it?

But Judge Douglas is especially horrified at the thought of the mixing blood by the white and black races: agreed for once—a thousand times agreed. There are white men enough to marry all the white women, and black men enough to marry all the black women; and so let them be married. On this point we fully agree with the Judge; and when he shall show that his policy is better adapted to prevent amalgamation than ours we shall drop ours, and adopt his. Let us see. In 1850 there were in the United States, 405,751, mulattoes. Very few of these are the offspring of whites and *free* blacks; nearly all have sprung from black *slaves* and white masters. A separation of the races is the only perfect preventive of amalgamation but as an immediate separation is impossible the next best thing is to *keep* them apart *where* they are not already together. If white and black people never get together in Kansas, they will never mix blood in Kansas. That is at least one self-evident truth. A few free colored persons may get into the free States, in any event; but their number is too insignificant to amount to much in the way of mixing blood. In 1850 there were in the free states, 56,649 mulattoes; but for the most part they were not born there—they came from the slave States, ready made up. In the same year the slave States had 348,874 mulattoes all of home production. The proportion of free mulattoes to free blacks—the only colored classes in the free states—is much greater in the slave than in the free states. It is worthy of note too, that among the free states those which make the colored man the nearest to equal the white, have, proportionably the fewest mulattoes the least of amalgamation. In New Hampshire, the State which goes farthest towards equality between the races, there are just 184 Mulattoes while there are in Virginia—how many do you think?—79,775, being 23,126 more than in all the free States together.

These statistics show that slavery is the greatest source of amalgamation; and next to it, not the elevation, but the degeneration of the free blacks. Yet Judge Douglas dreads the slightest restraints on the spread of slavery, and the slightest human recognition of the negro, as tending horribly to amalgamation.

This very Dred Scott case affords a strong test as to which party most favors amalgamation, the Republicans or the dear Union-saving Democracy. Dred Scott, his wife and two daughters were all involved in the suit. We desired the court to have held that they were citizens so far at least as to entitle them to a hearing as to whether they were free or not; and then, also, that they were in fact and in law really free. Could we have had our way, the chances of these black girls, ever mixing their blood with that of white people, would have been diminished at least to the extent that it could not have been without their consent. But Judge Douglas is delighted to have them decided to be slaves, and not human enough to have a hearing, even if they were free, and thus left subject to the forced concubinage of their masters, and liable to become the mothers of mulattoes in spite of themselves—the very state of case that produces nine tenths of all the mulattoes—all the mixing of blood in the nation.

Of course, I state this case as an illustration only, not meaning to say or intimate that the master of Dred Scott and his family, or any more than a percentage of masters generally, are inclined to exercise this particular power which they hold over their female slaves.

I have said that the separation of the races is the only perfect preventive of amalgamation. I have no right to say all the members of the Republican party are in favor of this, nor to say that as a party they are in favor of it. There is nothing in their platform directly on the subject. But I can say a very large proportion of its members are for it, and that the chief plank in their platform— opposition to the spread of slavery—is most favorable to that separation.

Such separation, if ever effected at all, must be effected by colonization; and no political party, as such, is now doing anything directly for colonization. Party operations at present only favor or retard colonization incidentally. The enterprise is a difficult one; but "when there is a will there is a way," and what colonization needs most is a hearty will. Will springs from the two elements of moral sense and self-interest. Let us be brought to believe it is morally right, and, at the same time, favorable to, or, at least, not against, our interest, to transfer the African to his native clime, and we shall find a way to do it, however great the task may be. The children of Israel, to such numbers as to include four hundred thousand fighting men, went out of Egyptian bondage in a body.

How differently the respective courses of the Democratic and Republican parties incidentally bear on the question of forming a will—a public sentiment— for colonization, is easy to see. The Republicans inculcate, with whatever of ability they can, that the negro is a man; that his bondage is cruelly wrong, and that the field of his oppression ought not to be enlarged. The Democrats deny his manhood; deny, or dwarf to insignificance, the wrong of his bondage;—so far as possible, crush all sympathy for him, and cultivate and excite hatred and disgust against him; compliment themselves as Union-savers for doing so; and call the indefinite outspreading of his bondage "a sacred right of self-government."

The plainest print cannot be read through a gold eagle; and it will be ever hard to find many men who will send a slave to Liberia, and pay his passage while they can send him to a new country, Kansas for instance, and sell him for fifteen hundred dollars, and the rise.

Interpretation

Judge Stephen Douglashad defended both his own principle of popular sovereignty and the Supreme Court's decision in the Dred Scott case. Lincoln begins with a severe criticism of popular sovereignty as applied to the Utah Mormons and the elections in Kansas. But his main fire is reserved for the *Dred Scott* decision and Douglas' support of it. "That decision declares two propositions—first, that a negro cannot sue in the U.S. Courts; and secondly, that Congress cannot prohibit slavery in the Territories."

While agreeing that it would be wrong to offer resistance to the decision—a charge Douglas had made against him—Lincoln nevertheless denies that questioning the decision amounts to resisting it. He is willing to admit that "fully settled" decisions on constitutional questions deserve to control not only the particular case at issue but the "general policy of the country," subject only to amendments to the Constitution. But the ability of a decision to serve as a general precedent or authority depends on what perhaps can be called its aggregate weightiness. Lincoln lists four attributes that contribute to this: unanimity on the Court, absence of apparent partisan bias, accord "with legal public expectation, and with the steady past practice of the departments throughout our history," and, finally, no dependence on "assumed historical facts which are not really true." Should a decision lack some of these, it could still be considered an authority or precedent if the issue appeared before the Court several times and the decision was re-affirmed "over a number of years." Only then might it be, "perhaps would be, factious, nay, even revolutionary, not to acquiesce in it as a precedent."

We should pause to ask why Lincoln still ends with some qualification here—his "might be," and "perhaps would be"—regarding authoritativeness. What more can he want? Perhaps he has in mind a consideration like this: How compelling can a decision be if, for example, one of its props is a false historical fact? What if this "fact" has been sustained or overlooked out of partisan bias continuing through all the re-affirming decisions? Would not the decision still remain somewhat unsettled because of this? And how often, and through how many years, must the decision be re-affirmed? Lincoln's hesitation might come from the thought that it is not possible to state an absolute principle defining when a Supreme Court decision becomes a binding authoritative precedent.

Applying this now to the Dred Scott case, when a decision is lacking in not one but all the listed claims to the public confidence, "it is not resistance, it is not factious, it is not even disrespectful, to treat it as not having quite established a settled doctrine for the country." This is Lincoln's forceful answer to Douglas' charge that Lincoln's "resistance" to the Court's decisions is a blow against the republic. In support of his position, Lincoln cites President Jackson's statement opposing the Supreme Court when it upheld the constitutionality of a national bank. Jackson went so far as to insist that each public officer must follow the

Constitution not as the Supreme Court but as he himself understands it. "Again
and again" Lincoln says, he has "heard Judge Douglas denounce the Court's
bank decision and applaud Gen. Jackson for disregarding it. "

Turning to the substance of the *Dred Scott* decision, Lincoln questions
Chief Justice 's claim that "negroes were no part of the people who made, or for
whom was made, the Declaration of Independence, or the Constitution of the
United States." Regarding the Constitution, Lincoln cites Justice Curtis' dissent
for the role blacks played in its promulgation or adoption. When Taney assumes
that the status of blacks is now better than it was at the beginning of the country,
Lincoln again denies the point: "their ultimate destiny has never appeared so
hopeless as in the last three or four years." In this marvelous paragraph, the facts
he adduces are brought to a moving peroration. Especially because of the dis-
memberment to which the Declaration has been subjected, the black is much
more a prisoner now than he was then. He has lost, not gained, much ground
politically.

The relation between the races is at the heart of the controversy. "There is a
natural disgust in the minds of nearly all white people, to the idea of an indiscriminate amalgamation of the white and black races." Lincoln says, and Judge
Douglas' whole effort politically is to accuse his adversaries of supporting that
amalgamation. Douglas, agreeing with Taney, denies that the Declaration included the black at all, and maintains that all those who interpret the Declaration
as if it does seek that amalgamation. Lincoln's answer became famous: "Now I
protest against that counterfeit logic which concludes that, because I do not want
a black woman for a slave I must necessarily want her for a wife. I need not
have her for either, I can just leave her alone. In some respects she is certainly
not my equal; but in her natural right to eat the bread she earns with her own
hands without asking leave of any one else, she is my equal, and the equal of all
others."

Lincoln does not say he shares the "natural" disgust whites feel at the idea
of "indiscriminate amalgamation" of the races. Not all but "nearly all" whites
feel this disgust—he does not explain the "nearly," or say whether these few
exceptions are better or worse than the majority, or whether he numbers himself
among them. He does not say whether a discriminate rather than an indiscriminate amalgamation of the races is possible, or how it might be accomplished.
Still, we must deal with the stubborn fact that most whites do not want to mix
reproductively with blacks—a feeling that Douglas has appealed to demagogi-
cally again and again. Lincoln was courageous indeed to speak up for not only
the black male but the black woman in her natural right not to be a slave and to
accumulate property, and to do so here, not elsewhere. To go further in the direction of political and social equality (rather than providing the slight indications he does) would clearly have left him open to even greater attack from
Douglas and destroyed him politically, ending his usefulness to the nation.

What did the Declaration mean by equality, and what conclusions follow
from it? Was the interpretation given by Taney and Douglas correct? The au-

thors of the Declaration, Lincoln says, did not mean that men were equal in all respects but only in "certain inalienable rights, among which are life, liberty and the pursuit of happiness." In other respects, men can vary considerably, but not in this one. The authors did not expect or intend these rights to be applied immediately, but only "as fast as circumstances should permit. They meant to set up a standard maxim for free society." They were to be held aloft and striven toward. In this way they not only promise an improvement in life to "all people of all colors everywhere," but can help keep free societies from being lured back into despotism (as was then happening here through the slave issue).

It cannot be said that Lincoln gives a perfect historical explanation of what the inalienable rights of man meant in the Declaration. Are they rights that can be proclaimed and acted on without delay by the oppressed everywhere? Can American blacks rebel to secure their own rights? Does not Lincoln have to conceal the final step in the Declaration's logic, which calls for revolution after a long train of abuses shows no sign of abating? In his speech on the Mexican War, Lincoln had spoken of the right of oppressed nations to "revolutionize"— to wrest their liberties from despotic rulers, by violence, if necessary. Certainly he knew of the explosive force contained in the principle of rights, especially the right to liberty, which, in addition to the right not to be a slave included the right not to live under political despotism—i.e., to be governed only by rulers to whom one has consented. This political dynamite Lincoln had to find a way of defusing, while not surrendering the principle of personal freedom itself. He accomplishes this by transforming rights capable of being immediately demanded into rights understood as goals, the achievement of which had to depend on circumstances. In this way even long enduring slavery could be justified, because an armed struggle to end it might threaten the very freedom into which the slave would at some future point be initiated. By this means Lincoln made the principle of natural rights more responsible, more prudent than it originally was.

Having given his own view of the Declaration, Lincoln turns to Judge Douglas'. Inference by devastating inference, he shows that Douglas reduces the Declaration to this statement: "We hold these truths to be self-evident, that all British subjects who were on this continent eighty-one years ago, were created equal to all British subjects born and *then* residing in Great Britain." Lincoln asks his audience whether they are willing to accept this fate for the "individual rights of man" celebrated in that document.

He turns, finally, to the question of the "mixing of blood by the white and black races" that so horrifies Judge Douglas. Using 1850 statistics, Lincoln readily shows that most the country's mulattoes are the product not of freedom but of the "forced concubinage" afforded by slavery. He suggests that the only perfect preventative of amalgamation is the "separation of races," which, "if ever effected at all, must be effected by colonization." With neither party doing anything directly for colonization, Lincoln calls the enterprise difficult but possible. What it needs is a "hearty will," for which he finds a Biblical example: "The children of Israel, to such numbers as to include four hundred thousand fighting men, went out of Egyptian bondage in a body."

This example is remarkable on several counts. First, in the Bible it took divine guidance every step of the way—not just a "hearty will"—to get the Israelites out of Egypt. In addition, they left by marching as a body into adjacent lands, and, when they came to it, crossing the Red Sea with the help of a divine miracle. They did not have to be repatriated across vast seas or oceans in small numbers, ship by ship, as would have to happen with American blacks. Again, does the example not have a frightening aspect, if the black slaves of America are likened to an Israelite army that, under Moses' leadership, liberated the children of Israel from the Egyptians? Was this a veiled warning of slave insurrections by Lincoln? Finally, in what seems to be a trivial detail, Lincoln, who knew his Bible so well, is mistaken in the numbers he uses for the Israelite army, which should have been 600,000 (Exodus 12:37; Numbers 1:46) rather than 400,000. What he meant by this inaccuracy—whether, in addition, to its other impracticalities he wanted to cast doubt on the truthfulness of the Biblical example itself—we have no idea.

The speech ends by distinguishing the two parties with respect to preparations for colonization. The Republicans teach that slavery for the black is wrong and not to be extended, whereas the Democrats deny that his bondage is wrong and "cultivate and excite hatred and disgust against him." Earlier Lincoln had spoken of "a natural disgust in the minds of nearly all white people" at the idea of mixing the races, but here we learn that part of white antipathy to this mixing is not natural but politically cultivated. Linked with Douglas' idea of "popular sovereignty"—the "sacred right of self-government" whereby whites decide whether to allow the slavery of blacks or not—this racial antipathy is also fed by greed. Thus, the profits anticipated from the sale of slaves in the territories constitute another great obstacle in the way of emancipation and colonization. Lincoln could not have put it more memorably: "the plainest print cannot be read through a gold eagle."

Chapter 8

The House Divided Speech, June 16, 1858

The Illinois Republican Convention, meeting in Springfield, had nominated Lincoln for the seat in the United States Senate held by Judge Douglas. This is Lincoln's acceptance speech.

Text

If we could first know *where* we are, and *whither* we are tending, we could then better judge *what* to do, and *how* to do it.

We are now far into the *fifth* year, since a policy was initiated, with the *avowed* object, and *confident* promise, of putting an end to slavery agitation.

Under the operation of that policy, that agitation has not only, *not ceased*, but has *constantly augmented.*

In *my* opinion, it *will* not cease, until a *crisis* shall have been reached, and passed.

"A house divided against itself cannot stand."

I believe this government cannot endure, permanently half *slave* and half *free.*

I do not expect the Union to be *dissolved*—I do not expect the house to *fall*—but I *do* expect it will cease to be divided.

It will become *all* one thing or *all* the other.

Either the *opponents* of slavery, will arrest the further spread of it, and place it where the public mind shall rest in the belief that it is in the course of ultimate extinction; or its *advocates* will push it forward, till it shall become alike lawful in *all* the States, *old* as well as *new*—*North* as well as *South.*

Have we no *tendency* to the latter condition?

Let any one who doubts, carefully contemplate that now almost complete legal combination—piece of *machinery* so to speak—compounded of the Nebraska doctrine, and the *Dred Scott* decision. Let him consider not only *what*

137

work the machinery is adapted to do, and *how well* adapted; but also, let him study the *history* of its construction, and trace, if he can, or rather *fail,* if he can, to trace the evidence of design and concert of action, among its chief bosses, from the beginning.

The new year of 1854 found slavery excluded from more than half the States by State Constitutions, and from most of the national territory by congressional prohibition.

Four days later, commenced the struggle, which ended in repealing that congressional prohibition.

This opened all the national territory to slavery, and was the first point gained.

But, so far, *Congress* only, had acted; and an *indorsement* by the people, *real* or *apparent,* was indispensable, to *save* the point already gained, and give chance for more.

This necessity had not been overlooked; but had been provided for, as well as might be, in the notable argument of "squatter sovereignty," otherwise called *"sacred right of self government,"* which latter phrase, though expressive of the only rightful basis of any government, was so perverted in this attempted use of it as to amount to just this: That if any *one* man, choose to enslave *another,* no *third* man shall be allowed to object.

That argument was incorporated into the Nebraska bill itself, in the language which follows: *"It being the true intent and meaning of this act not to legislate slavery into any Territory or state, nor to exclude it therefrom; but to leave the people thereof perfectly free to form and regulate their domestic institutions in their own way, subject only to the Constitution of the United States."*

Then opened the roar of loose declamation in favor of "Squatter Sovereignty," and "Sacred right of self-government."

"But," said opposition members, "let us be more *specific*—let us *amend* the bill so as to expressly declare that the people of the territory *may* exclude slavery." "Not we," said the friends of the measure; and down they voted the amendment.

While the Nebraska bill was passing through congress, a *law case* involving the question of a negro's freedom, by reason of his owner having voluntarily taken him first into a free state and then a territory covered by the congressional prohibition, and held him as a slave, for a long time in each, was passing through the U.S. Circuit Court for the District of Missouri; and both Nebraska bill and law suit were brought to a decision in the same month of May, 1854. The negro's name was "Dred Scott," which name now designates the decision finally made in the case.

Before the *then* next Presidential election, the law case came *to,* and was argued *in,* the Supreme Court of the United States; but the *decision* of it was deferred until *after* the election. Still, *before* the election, Senator Trumbull, on the floor of the Senate, requests the leading advocate of the Nebraska bill to state *his opinion* whether the people of a territory can constitutionally exclude slavery from their limits; and the latter answers: "That is a question for the Supreme Court."

The election came. Mr. Buchanan was elected, and the *indorsement,* such as it was, secured. That was the *second* point gained. The indorsement, however, fell short of a clear popular majority by nearly four hundred thousand votes, and so, perhaps, was not overwhelmingly reliable and satisfactory.

The *outgoing* President, in his last annual message, as impressively as possible, *echoed back* upon the people the *weight* and *authority* of the indorsement.

The Supreme Court met again; *did not* announce their decision, but ordered a re-argument.

The Presidential inauguration came, and still no decision of the court; but the *incoming* President, in his inaugural address, fervently exhorted the people to abide by the forthcoming decision, *whatever it might be.*

Then, in a few days, came the decision.

The reputed author of the Nebraska bill finds an early occasion to make a speech at this capital indorsing the Dred Scott decision, and vehemently denouncing all opposition to it.

The new President, too, seizes the early occasion of the Silliman letter to *indorse* and strongly *construe* that decision, and to express his *astonishment* that any different view had ever been entertained.

At length a squabble springs up between the President and the author of the Nebraska bill, on the *mere* question of *fact,* whether the Lecompton constitution was or was not, in any just sense, made by the people of Kansas; and in that quarrel the latter declares that all he wants is a fair vote for the people, and that he *cares* not whether slavery be voted *down* or voted *up.* I do not understand his declaration that he cares not whether slavery be voted down or voted up, to be intended by him other than as an *apt definition* of the *policy* he would impress upon the public mind—the *principle* for which he declares he has suffered much, and is ready to suffer to the end.

And well may he cling to that principle. If he has any parental feeling, well may he cling to it. That principle, is the only shred left of his original Nebraska doctrine. Under the *Dred Scott* decision, "squatter sovereignty" squatted out of existence, tumbled down like temporary scaffolding—like the mould at the foundry served through one blast and fell back into loose sand—helped to carry an election, and then was kicked to the winds. His late *joint* struggle with the Republicans, against the Lecompton Constitution, involves nothing of the original Nebraska doctrine. That struggle was made on a point, the right of a people to make their own constitution, upon which he and the Republicans have never differed.

The several points of the *Dred Scott* decision, in connection with Senator Douglas's "care-not" policy, constitute the piece of machinery, in its *present* state of advancement.

The *working* points of that machinery are:

First, that no negro slave, imported as such from Africa, and no descendant of such slave, can ever be a *citizen* of any State, in the sense of that term as used in the Constitution of the United States.

This point is made in order to deprive the negro, in every possible event, of the benefit of that provision of the United States Constitution, which declares that—

"the citizens of each State shall be entitled to all privileges and immunities of citizens in the several States."

Secondly, that "subject to the Constitution of the United States," neither *Congress* nor a *Territorial legislature* can exclude slavery from any United States Territory.

This point is made in order that individual men may *fill up* the Territories with slaves, without danger of losing them as property, and thus enhance the chances of *permanency* to the institution through all the future.

Thirdly, that whether the holding a negro in actual slavery in a free State makes him free, as against the holder, the United States courts will not decide, but will leave to be decided by the courts of any slave State the negro may be forced into by the master.

This point is made, not to be pressed *immediately*; but, if acquiesced in for a while, and apparently *indorsed* by the people at an election, *then* to sustain the logical conclusion that what Dred Scott's master might lawfully do with Dred Scott, in the free State of Illinois, every other master may lawfully do with any other *one*, or one *thousand* slaves, in Illinois, or in any other free State.

Auxiliary to all this, and working hand in hand with it, the Nebraska doctrine, or what is left of it, is to *educate* and *mould* public opinion, at least *Northern* public opinion, not to *care* whether slavery is voted *down* or voted *up*.

This shows exactly where we now *are*; and *partially*, also, whither we are tending.

It will throw additional light on the latter, to go back, and run the mind over the string of historical facts already stated. Several things will *now* appear less *dark* and mysterious than they did when they were transpiring. The people were to be left "perfectly free," subject only to the Constitution. What the *Constitution* had to do with it, outsiders could not *then* see. Plainly enough *now*, it was an exactly fitted *niche*, for the *Dred Scott* decision to afterward come in, and declare that *perfect freedom* of the people to be just no freedom at all.

Why was the amendment, expressly declaring the right of the people to exclude slavery, voted down? Plainly enough *now*, the adoption of it would have spoiled the niche for the *Dred Scott* decision.

Why was the court decision held up? Why, even a Senator's individual opinion withheld, till *after* the Presidential election? Plainly enough *now*, the speaking out *then* would have damaged the *"perfectly free"* argument upon which the election was to be carried.

Why the *outgoing* President's felicitation on the indorsement? Why the delay of a re-argument? Why the incoming President's *advance* exhortation in favor of the decision?

These things *look* like the cautious *patting* and *petting* of a spirited horse, preparatory to mounting him, when it is dreaded that he may give the rider a fall.

And why the hasty after-indorsements of the decision by the President and others?

We cannot absolutely *know* that all these exact adaptations are the result of preconcert. But when we see a lot of framed timbers, different portions of which we know have been gotten out at different times and places, and by different workmen—Stephen, Franklin, Roger, and James, for instance—and when we see these timbers joined together, and see they exactly make the frame of a house or a mill, all the tenons and mortices exactly fitting, and all the lengths and proportions of the different pieces exactly adapted to their respective places, and not a piece too many or too few—not omitting even scaffolding—or, if a single piece be lacking, we see the place in the frame exactly fitted and prepared yet to bring such piece in—in *such* a case we find it impossible not to *believe* that Stephen and Franklin and Roger and James all understood one another from the beginning, and all worked upon a common *plan* or *draft* drawn up before the first lick was struck.

It should not be overlooked that, by the Nebraska bill, the people of a *State*, as well as a *Territory*, were to be left *"perfectly free"* *"subject only to the Constitution."*

Why mention a *State*? They were legislating for *territories*, and not *for* or *about* States. Certainly the people of a *State* are and *ought* to be subject to the Constitution of the United States; but why is mention of this *lugged* into this merely *territorial* law? Why are the people of a *territory* and the people of a *state* therein *lumped* together, and their relation to the Constitution therein treated as being *precisely* the same?

While the opinion of the Court, by Chief Justice Taney, , in the Dred Scott case and the separate opinions of all the concurring judges, expressly declare that the Constitution of the United States neither permits Congress nor a Territorial legislature to exclude slavery from any United States Territory, they all *omit* to declare whether or not the same Constitution permits a State, or the people of a State, to exclude it.

Possibly this is a mere *omission*; but who can be *quite* sure, if McLean or Curtis had sought to get into the opinion a declaration of unlimited power in the people of a state to exclude slavery from their limits, just as Chase and Mace sought to get such declaration, in behalf of the people of a Territory, into the Nebraska bill—I ask, who can be quite *sure* that it would not have been voted down in the one case, as it had been in the other?

The nearest approach to the point of declaring the power of a State over slavery, is made by Judge Nelson. He approaches it more than once, using the precise idea, and *almost* the language, too, of the Nebraska Act. On one occasion, his exact language is, "except in cases where the power is restrained by the Constitution of the United States, the law of the State is supreme over the subject of slavery within its jurisdiction."

In what *cases* the power of the *states* is so restrained by the United States Constitution is left an *open* question, precisely [*sic*]as the same question, as to the restraint on the power of the *territories*, was left open in the Nebraska act. Put *that* and *that* together, and we have another nice little niche, which we may, ere long, see filled with another Supreme Court decision, declaring that the Constitution of the United States does not permit a state to exclude slavery from its limits.

And this may especially be expected if the doctrine of "care not whether slavery be voted *down* or voted *up*," shall gain upon the public mind sufficiently to give promise that such a decision can be maintained when made.

Such a decision is all that slavery now lacks of being alike lawful in all the States.

Welcome, or unwelcome, such decision *is* probably coming, and will soon be upon us, unless the power of the present political dynasty shall be met and overthrown. We shall *lie down* pleasantly dreaming that the people of *Missouri* are on the verge of making their State *free*, and we shall awake to the *reality* instead, that the *Supreme* Court has made *Illinois* a *slave* State.

To meet and overthrow the power of that dynasty is the work now before all those who would prevent that consummation.

This is *what* we have to do.

But *how* can we best do it?

There are those who denounce us *openly* to their *own* friends and yet whisper *us softly*, that *Senator Douglas* is the *aptest* instrument there is, with which to effect that object. *They* do *not* tell us, nor has *he* told us, that he *wishes* any such object to be effected. They wish us to *infer* all from the fact that he now has a little quarrel with the present head of the dynasty; and that he has regularly voted with us on a single point, upon which he and we have never differed.

They remind us that *he* is a *great* man, and that the largest of *us* are very small ones. Let this be granted. But "a *living dog* is better than a *dead lion*." Judge Douglas, if not a *dead* lion *for this work*, is at least a *caged* and *toothless* one. How can he oppose the advances of slavery? He don't *care* anything about it. His avowed *mission* is *impressing* the "public heart" to *care* nothing about it.

A leading Douglas Democratic newspaper thinks Douglas's superior talent will be needed to resist the revival of the African slave trade.

Does Douglas believe an effort to revive that trade is approaching? He has not said so. Does he *really* think so? But if it is, how can he resist it? For years he has labored to prove it a *sacred right* of white men to take negro slaves into the new territories. Can he possibly show that it is *less* a sacred right to *buy* them where they can be bought cheapest? And unquestionably they can be bought *cheaper* in *Africa* than in *Virginia*.

He has done all in his power to reduce the whole question of slavery to one of a mere *right of property*; and as such, how can *he* oppose the foreign slave trade—how can he refuse that trade in that "property" shall be "perfectly free"—unless he does it as a *protection* to the home production? And as the home *producers* will probably not ask the protection, he will be wholly without a ground of opposition.

Senator Douglas holds, we know, that a man may rightfully be *wiser today* than he was *yesterday*—that he may rightfully *change* when he finds himself wrong.

But can we, for that reason, run ahead, and *infer* that he *will* make any particular change, of which he, himself, has given no intimation? Can we *safely* base our action upon any such *vague* inference?

Now, as ever, I wish to not misrepresent Judge Douglas's *position*, question his *motives*, or do aught that can be personally offensive to him.

Whenever, *if ever*, he and we can come together on *principle* so that *our great cause* may have assistance from *his great ability*, I hope to have interposed no adventitious obstacle.

But clearly, he is not *now* with us—he does not *pretend* to be—he does not *promise* to *ever* be.

Our cause, then, must be intrusted to, and conducted by, its own undoubted friends—those whose hands are free, whose hearts are in the work—who *do care* for the result.

Two years ago the Republicans of the nation mustered over thirteen hundred thousand strong.

We did this under the single impulse of resistance to a common danger, with every external circumstance against us.

Of *strange, discordant*, and even *hostile* elements, we gathered from the four winds, and *formed* and fought the battle through, under the constant hot fire of a disciplined, proud, and pampered enemy.

Did we brave all *then* to *falter* now?—now—when that same enemy is *wavering*, dissevered, and belligerent?

The result is not doubtful. We shall not fail—if we stand firm, we shall not fail.

Wise counsels may *accelerate*, or *mistakes delay* it, but, sooner or later, the victory is *sure* to come.

Interpretation

With something like the blast of a trumpet, the new Republican candidate for the U.S. Senate announces that the constitutional compromise over slavery developed by the founding fathers cannot continue: the country has to go fully toward freedom or fully toward slavery. "A house divided against itself cannot stand." The quotation is from the Gospel According to St. Matthew, 12:25, where Jesus denies that he casts out demons "only by Beelzebub, the prince of demons," since that would show Beelzebub to be divided against himself. It is rather by the Spirit of God that he casts demons out.

Casting out the demon of slavery is another story. As Lincoln sees it, the nation is in crisis, brought about by a combination of Judge Douglas' Kansas-Nebraska Act of 1854 and the Supreme Court's *Dred Scott* decision of 1857. The former, far from ending the agitation over slavery, as promised, has resulted in its being "constantly augmented." Beyond these, action by the president himself has added to Lincoln's conviction that all were parts of a complex conspiracy. How else could the apparently unrelated actions dovetail so well? In the *Dred Scott* decision, Chief Justice Taney had made three rulings: 1) no "negro slave" can ever "be a citizen of any State"; 2) "neither *Congress* nor a *Territorial Legislature* can exclude slavery from any United States Territory"; 3) the decision as to whether a black slave is made free by being taken by his master into a free state will be left to the state courts in slave states. This last opens up the possibility that large quantities of slaves can be brought into free states by their slave masters, without legal hindrance. Note that the first two provisions directly violate Douglas' notion of "popular sovereignty," since they strip from the people the right to exclude slavery from the territories and allow blacks to become citizens. To complete this plot, all that is needed is "another Supreme Court decision, declaring that the Constitution of the United States does not permit a state to exclude slavery from its limits."

With this wave of changes strengthening slavery and the slave states in a possibly decisive way, Lincoln sees that moving back to the Constitution's original compromise is no longer possible. Hence his conclusion: "I believe this government cannot endure, permanently half *slave* and half *free*. I do not expect the Union to be *dissolved*—I do not expect the house to *fall*—but I do expect it will cease to be divided. It will become *all* one thing, or *all* the other." Bear in mind that the forces for freedom had received powerful setbacks from both Congress and the Supreme Court, assisted as well by the president, and were now drastically on the defensive. Lincoln had to rally the defenders of freedom: he had to make sure they understood the stark reality of their situation. And he had to call for concerted action.

To "meet and overthrow the power" of the "present political dynasty" is the object the Republicans must set themselves. For this purpose Lincoln thinks Judge Douglas of little use: "How can he oppose the advances of slavery? He don't *care* anything about it. His avowed *mission is impressing* the 'public heart' to *care* nothing about it." They must depend on their true friends. Two years before, the Republicans of the nation had garnered 1,300,000 votes, binding together "*strange, discordant* and even, *hostile* elements"—here the language takes on a military cast—to fight against "a disciplined, proud, and pampered enemy." They won't fail: "sooner or later the victory is *sure* to come."

This is a trumpet blast to political battle—to fight against the Democratic "dynasty" and, by votes, wrest from it control of all three branches of the national government. It meant that the compromises originally created by the founders and extended by Henry Clay were no longer viable. It meant that Lincoln's earlier calls for a return to the situation preceding the Kansas and Nebraska Acts no longer applied. Lincoln believed the founders had hoped their compromise would ultimately see slavery disappear. Instead, the forces and supporters of slavery now seem to have gained the ascendancy. The South could not detect in this talk any indication that Lincoln had joined the Abolitionist cause and would have recourse to extra-constitutional means to end slavery. But he clearly wanted to upset by legal means all the gains they had made—also by legal means. They had the highest court in the land for them: were the Republicans going to evade its mandates? What if this new champion, so dedicated to ending slavery, came to preside over the Union: would the South be willing to stand and fight politically? Instead, what it did was to secede and form its own nation, thus proving Lincoln expressed himself too hopefully when he said, "I do not expect the house to fall." It took a bloody civil war to put that house together again. No doubt Lincoln's blast in this speech helped strengthen secessionist sentiments in the South. No doubt, as well, he had no alternative but to make it.

Chapter 9

The First Lincoln-Douglas Debate, August 21, 1858

In a series of seven debates jointly agreed upon, Judge Douglas and Lincoln vied with each other all around Illinois as nominees of their parties for the seat in the Senate Douglas had occupied. The first debate took place in Ottawa and the last in Alton, on October 15.

Text

Mr. Douglas' Opening Speech

Ladies and gentlemen:

I appear before you to-day for the purpose of discussing the leading political topics which now agitate the public mind. By an arrangement between Mr. Lincoln and myself, we are present here to-day for the purpose of having a joint discussion, as the representatives of the two great political parties of the State and Union, upon the principles in issue between those parties, and this vast concourse of people shows the deep feeling which pervades the public mind in regard to the questions dividing us.

Prior to 1854 this country was divided into two great political parties, known as the Whig and Democratic parties. Both were national and patriotic, advocating principles that were universal in their application. An old line Whig could proclaim his principles in Louisiana and Massachusetts alike. Whig principles had no boundary sectional line; they were not limited by the Ohio River, nor by the Potomac, nor by the line of the free and slave States, but applied and were proclaimed wherever the Constitution ruled or the American flag waved over the American soil. So it was, and so it is with the great Democratic party, which, from the days of Jefferson until this period, has proven itself to be the historic party of this nation. While the Whig and Democratic parties differed in regard to a bank, the tariff, distribution, the specie circular, and the sub-treasury, they agreed on the great slavery question which now agitates the Union. I say that the Whig party and the Democratic party agreed on this slavery question, while they differed on those matters of expediency to which I have referred. The Whig party and the Democratic party jointly adopted the Compromise measures of 1850 as the basis of a proper and just solution of this slavery question in all its forms. Clay was the great leader, with Webster on his right and Cass on his left, and sustained by the patriots in the Whig and Democratic ranks who had devised and enacted the Compromise measures of 1850.

In 1851, the Whig party and the Democratic party united in Illinois in adopting resolutions indorsing and approving the principles of the Compromise measures of 1850, as the proper adjustment of that question. In 1852, when the Whig party assembled in Convention at Baltimore for the purpose of nominating a candidate for the Presidency, the first thing it did was to declare the Compromise measures of 1850, in substance and in principle, a suitable adjustment of that question. [Here the speaker was interrupted by loud and long continued applause] My friends, silence will be more acceptable to me in the discussion of these questions than applause. I desire to address myself to your judgment, your understanding, and your consciences, and not to your passions or your enthusiasm. When the Democratic Convention assembled in Baltimore in the same year, for the purpose of nominating a Democratic candidate for the Presidency, it also adopted the compromise measures of 1850 as the basis of Democratic action. Thus you see that up to 1853-'54, the Whig party and the Democratic party both stood on the same platform with regard to the slavery question. That platform was the right of the people of each State and each Territory to decide their local and domestic institutions for themselves, subject only to the federal constitution.

During the session of Congress of 1853-'54, I introduced into the Senate of the United States a bill to organize the Territories of Kansas and Nebraska on that principle which had been adopted in the compromise measures of 1850, approved by the Whig party and the Democratic party in Illinois in 1851, and endorsed by the Whig party and the Democratic party in national convention in 1852. In order that there might be no misunderstanding in relation to the principle involved in the Kansas and Nebraska bill, I put forth the true intent and meaning of the act in these words: "It is the true intent and meaning of this act not to legislate slavery into any State or Territory, or to exclude it therefrom, but to leave the people thereof perfectly free to form and regulate their domestic institutions in their own way, subject only to the federal constitution." Thus you see that up to 1854, when the Kansas and Nebraska bill was brought into Congress for the purpose of carrying out the principles which both parties had up to that time endorsed and approved, there had been no division in this country in regard to that principle except the opposition of the abolitionists. In the House of Representatives of the Illinois Legislature, upon a resolution asserting that principle, every Whig and every Democrat in the House voted in the affirmative, and only four men voted against it, and those four were old line Abolitionists.

In 1854, Mr. Abraham Lincoln and Mr. Trumbull entered into an arrangement, one with the other, and each with his respective friends, to dissolve the old Whig party on the one hand, and to dissolve the old Democratic party on the other, and to connect the members of both into an Abolition party under the name and disguise of a Republican party. The terms of that arrangement between Mr. Lincoln and Mr. Trumbull have been published to the world by Mr. Lincoln's special friend, James H. Matheny, Esq., and they were, that Lincoln should have Shields's place in the United States Senate, which was then about to become vacant, and that Trumbull should have my seat when my term expired. Lincoln went to work to abolitionize the Old Whig party all over the State, pretending that he was then as good a Whig as ever; and Trumbull went to work in his part of the State preaching Abolitionism in its milder and lighter form, and trying to abolitionize the Democratic party, and bring old Democrats handcuffed and bound hand and foot into the Abolition camp.

In pursuance of the arrangement, the parties met at Springfield in October, 1854, and proclaimed their new platform. Lincoln was to bring into the Abolition camp the old line Whigs, and transfer them over to Giddings, Chase, Fred Douglass, and Parson Lovejoy, who were ready to receive them and christen them in their new faith. They laid down on that occasion a platform for their new Republican party, which was to be thus constructed. I have the resolutions of the State Convention then held, which was the first mass State Convention ever held in Illinois by the Black Republican party, and I now hold them in my hands, and will read a part of them, and cause the others to be printed. Here are the most important and material resolutions of this Abolition platform:

1. Resolved, That we believe this truth to be self-evident, that when parties become subversive of the ends for which they are established, or incapable of restoring the government to the true principles of the constitution, it is the right and duty of the people to dissolve the political bands by which they may have been connected therewith, and to organize new parties, upon such principles and with such views as the circumstances and exigencies of the nation may demand.

2. Resolved, That the times imperatively demand the reorganization of parties, and, repudiating all previous party attachments, names and predilections, we unite ourselves together in defense of the liberty and Constitution of the country, and will hereafter co-operate as the Republican party, pledged to the accomplishment of the following purposes: to bring the administration of the government back to the control of first principles; to restore Nebraska and Kansas to the position of free Territories; that, as the constitution of the United States, vests in the States, and not in Congress, the power to legislate for the extradition of fugitives from labor, to repeal and entirely abrogate the fugitive slave law; to restrict slavery to those States in which it exists; to prohibit the admission of any more Slave States into the Union; to abolish slavery in the District of Columbia; to exclude slavery from all the territories over which the general government has exclusive jurisdiction; and to resist the acquirements of any more Territories unless the practice of slavery therein forever shall have been prohibited.

3. Resolved, That in furtherance of these principles we will use such constitutional and lawful means as shall seem best adapted to their accomplishment, and that we will support no man for office, under the General or State Government, who is not positively and fully committed to the support of these principles, and whose personal character and conduct is not a guaranty that he is reliable, and who shall not have abjured old party allegiance and ties.

Now, gentlemen, your Black Republicans have cheered every one of those propositions, and yet I venture to say that you cannot get Mr. Lincoln to come out and say that he is now in favor of each one of them. That these propositions, one and all, constitute the platform of the Black Republican party of this day, I have no doubt; and when you were not aware for what purpose I was reading them, your Black Republicans cheered them as good Black Republican doctrines. My object in reading these resolutions, was to put the question to Abraham Lincoln this day, whether he now stands and will stand by each article in that creed and carry it out. I desire to know whether Mr. Lincoln to-day stands, as he did in 1854, in favor of the unconditional repeal of the Fugitive-Slave law. I desire him to answer whether he stands pledged to-day, as he did in 1854, against the admission of any more Slave States into the Union, even if the people want them. I want to know whether he stands pledged against the admission of a new State into the Union with such a Constitution as the people of that State may see fit to make. I want to know whether he stands to-day pledged to the abolition of slavery in the District of Columbia. I desire him to answer whether he stands pledged to the prohibition of the slave-trade between the different States. I desire to know whether he stands pledged to prohibit slavery in all the Territories of the United States, North as well as South of the Missouri Compromise line. I desire him to answer whether he is opposed to the acquisition of any more territory, unless slavery is prohibited therein.

I want his answer to these questions. Your affirmative cheers in favor of this Abolition platform are not satisfactory. I ask Abraham Lincoln to answer these questions, in order that, when I trot him down to lower Egypt, I may put the same questions to him. My principles are the same everywhere. I can proclaim them alike in the North, the South, the East, and the West. My principles will apply wherever the Constitution prevails, and the American flag waves. I desire to know whether Mr. Lincoln's principles will bear transplanting from Ottawa to Jonesboro? I put these questions to him to-day distinctly, and ask an answer. I have a right to an answer, for I quote from the platform of the Republican party, made by himself and others at the time that party was formed, and the bargain made by Lincoln to dissolve and kill the old Whig party, and transfer its members, bound hand and foot, to the Abolition party, under the direction of Giddings and Fred Douglass.

In the remarks I have made on this platform, and the position of Mr. Lincoln upon it, I mean nothing personally disrespectful or unkind to that gentleman. I have known him for nearly twenty-five years. There were many points of sympathy between us when we first got acquainted. We were both comparatively boys, and both struggling with poverty in a strange land. I was a schoolteacher in the town of Winchester, and he a flourishing grocery-keeper in the town of Salem. He was more successful in his occupation than I was in mine, and hence more fortunate in this world's goods. Lincoln is one of those peculiar men who perform with admirable skill everything which they undertake. I made as good a schoolteacher as I could, and when a cabinet maker I made a good bedstead and tables, although my boss said I succeeded better with bureaus and secretaries than with anything else; but I believe that Lincoln was always more successful in business than I, for his business enabled him to get into the Legislature. I met him there, however, and had sympathy with him, because of the uphill struggle we both had in life. He was then just as good at telling an anecdote as now. He could beat any of the boys wrestling, or running a foot-race, in pitching quoits or tossing a copper; could ruin more liquor than all the boys of the town together, and the dignity and impartiality with which he presided at a horse-race or fist-fight excited the admiration and won the praise of everybody that was present and participated. I symphathized with him, because he was struggling with difficulties, and so was I.

Mr. Lincoln served with me in the Legislature in 1836, when we both retired, and he subsided, or became submerged, and he was lost sight of as a public man for some years. In 1846, when Wilmot introduced his celebrated proviso, and the Abolition tornado swept over the country, Lincoln again turned up as a member of Congress from the Sangamon district. I was then in the Senate of the United States, and was glad to welcome my old friend and companion. Whilst in Congress, he distinguished himself by his opposition to the Mexican war, taking the side of the common enemy against his own country; and when he returned home he found that the indignation of the people followed him everywhere, and he was again submerged or obliged to retire into private life, forgotten by his former friends. He came up again in 1854, just in time to make this Abolition or Black Republican platform, in company with Giddings, Lovejoy, Chase, and Fred Douglass, for the Republican party to stand upon.

Trumbull, too, was one of our own contemporaries. He was born and raised in old Connecticut, was bred a Federalist, but removing to Georgia, turned Nullifier, when nullification was popular, and as soon as he disposed of his clocks and wound up his business, migrated to Illinois, turned politician and lawyer here, and made his appearance in 1841 as a member of the Legislature. He became noted as the author of the scheme to repudiate a large portion of the State debt of Illinois, which, if successful, would have brought infamy and disgrace upon the fair escutcheon of our glorious State. The odium attached to that measure consigned him to oblivion for a time. I helped to do it. I walked into a public meeting in the hall of the House of Representatives, and replied to his repudiating speeches, and resolutions were carried over his head denouncing repudiation, and asserting the moral and legal obligation of Illinois to pay every dollar

of the debt she owed, and every bond that bore her seal. Trumbull's malignity
has followed me since I thus defeated his infamous scheme.

These two men having formed this combination to abolitionize the old
Whig party and the old Democratic party, and put themselves into the Senate of
the United States, in pursuance of their bargain, are now carrying out that arrangement. Matheny states that Trumbull broke faith; that the bargain was that
Lincoln should be the Senator in Shields's place, and Trumbull was to wait for
mine; and the story goes, that Trumbull cheated Lincoln, having control of four
or five abolitionized Democrats who were holding over in the Senate; he would
not let them vote for Lincoln, which obliged the rest of the Abolitionists to support him in order to secure an Abolition Senator. There are a number of authorities for the truth of this besides Matheny, and I suppose that even Mr. Lincoln
will not deny it.

Mr. Lincoln demands that he shall have the place intended for Trumbull, as
Trumbull cheated him and got his, and Trumbull is stumping the State traducing
me for the purpose of securing the position for Lincoln, in order to quiet him. It
was in consequence of this arrangement that the Republican Convention was
impanneled to instruct for Lincoln and nobody else, and it was on this account
that they passed resolutions that he was their first, their last, and their only
choice. Archy Williams was nowhere, Browning was nobody, Wentworth was
not to be considered; they had no man in the Republican party for the place except Lincoln, for the reason that he demanded that they should carry out the arrangement.

Having formed this new party for the benefit of deserters from Whiggery,
and deserters from Democracy, and having laid down the Abolition platform
which I have read, Lincoln now takes his stand and proclaims his Abolition doctrines. Let me read a part of them. In his speech at Springfield to the convention
which nominated him for the Senate, he said:

"In my opinion it will not cease until a crisis shall have been reached and
passed. 'A house divided against itself cannot stand.' I believe this government
cannot endure permanently half Slave and half Free. I do not expect the Union
to be dissolved—I do not expect the house to fall—*but I do expect it will cease
to be divided.* It will become all one thing, or all the other. Either the opponents
of slavery *will arrest the further spread of it,* and place it where the public mind
shall rest in the belief *that it is in the course of ultimate extinction:* or its advocates *will push it forward till it shall became alike lawful in all the States*—old
as well as new, North as well as South."["Good," "good," and cheers.]

I am delighted to hear you Black Republicans say "good." I have no doubt
that doctrine expresses your sentiments, and I will prove to you now, if you will
listen to me, that it is revolutionary and destructive of the existence of this government. Mr. Lincoln, in the extract from which I have read, says that this government cannot endure permanently in the same condition in which it was made

by its framers,—divided into Free and Slave States. He says that it has existed for about seventy years thus divided, and yet he tells you that it cannot endure permanently on the same principles and in the same relative condition in which our fathers made it. Why can it not exist divided into Free and Slave States? Washington, Jefferson, Franklin, Madison, Hamilton, Jay, and the great men of that day, made this Government divided into free States and slave States, and left each State perfectly free to do as it pleased on the subject of slavery. Why can it not exist on the same principles on which our fathers made it? They knew when they framed the Constitution that in a country as wide and broad as this, with such a variety of climate, production, and interest, the people necessarily required different laws and institutions in different localities. They knew that the laws and regulations which would suit the granite hills of New Hampshire would be unsuited to the rice plantations of South Carolina, and they therefore provided that each State should retain its own Legislature and its own sovereignty, with the full and complete power to do as it pleased within its own limits, in all that was local and not national.

One of the reserved rights of the States was the right to regulate the relations between master and servant, on the slavery question. At the time the Constitution was framed, there were thirteen States in the Union, twelve of which were slaveholding States and one a free State. Suppose this doctrine of uniformity preached by Mr. Lincoln, that the States should all be free or all be slave had prevailed, and what would have been the result? Of course, the twelve slaveholding States would have overruled the one a Free State, and slavery would have been fastened by a Constitutional provision on every inch of the American Republic, instead of being left, as our fathers wisely left it, to each State to decide for itself. Here I assert that uniformity in the local laws and institutions of the different States in neither possible or desirable. If uniformity had been adopted when the Government was established, it must inevitably have been the uniformity of slavery everywhere, or else the uniformity of negro citizenship and negro equality everywhere.

We are told by Lincoln that he is utterly opposed to the Dred Scott decision, and will not submit to it, for the reason that he says it deprives the negro of the rights and privileges of citizenship. That is the first and main reason which he assigns for his warfare on the Supreme Court of the United Sates and its decision. I ask you, are you in favor of conferring upon the negro the rights and privileges of citizenship? Do you desire to strike out of our State Constitution that clause which keeps slaves and free negroes out of the State, and allow the free negroes to flow in, and cover your prairies with black settlements? Do you desire to turn this beautiful State into a free negro colony, in order that when Missouri abolishes slavery she can send one hundred thousand emancipated slaves into Illinois, to become citizens and voters, on an equality with yourselves? If you desire negro citizenship, if you desire to allow them to come into the State and settle with the white man, if you desire them to vote on an equality with yourselves, and to make them eligible to office, to serve on juries, and to adjudge your rights, then support Mr. Lincoln and the Black Republican party, who are in favor of the citizenship of the negro. For one, I am opposed to negro citizenship in any and every form. I believe this Government was made on the white basis. I believe it was made by white men, for the benefit of white men and their posterity for ever, and I am in favor of confining citizenship to white men, men of European birth and descent, instead of conferring it upon negroes, Indians, and other inferior races.

Mr. Lincoln, following the example and lead of all the little Abolition orators, who go around and lecture in the basements of schools and churches, reads from the Declaration of Independence, that all men were created equal, and then asks, how can you deprive a negro of that equality which God and the Declaration of Independence award to him? He and they maintain that negro equality is guaranteed by the laws of God, and that it is asserted in the Declaration of Independence. If they think so, of course they have a right to say so, and so vote. I do not question Mr. Lincoln's conscientious belief that the negro was made his equal, and hence is his brother, but for my own part, I do not regard the negro as my equal, and positively deny that he is my brother or any kin to me whatever. Lincoln has evidently learned by heart Parson Lovejoy's catechism. He can repeat it as well as Farnsworth, and he is worthy of a medal from Father Giddings and Fred Douglass for his Abolitionism. He holds that the negro was born his equal and yours, and that he was endowed with equality by the Almighty, and that no human law can deprive him of these rights, which were guaranteed to him by the Supreme Ruler of the universe.

Now, I do not believe that the Almighty ever intended the negro to be the equal of the white man. If he did, he has been a long time demonstrating the fact. For thousands of years the negro has been a race upon the earth, and during all that time, in all latitudes and climates, wherever he has wandered or been taken, he has been inferior to the race which he has there met. He belongs to an inferior race, and must always occupy an inferior position. I do not hold that because the negro is our inferior that therefore he ought to be a slave. By no means can such a conclusion be drawn from what I have said. On the contrary, I hold that humanity and Christianity both require that the negro shall have and enjoy every right, every privilege, and every immunity consistent with the safety of the society in which he lives. On that point, I presume, there can be no diversity of opinion. You and I are bound to extend to our inferior and dependent beings every right, every privilege, every facility and immunity consistent with the public good.

The question then arises, What rights and privileges are consistent with the public good? This is a question which each State and each Territory must decide for itself—Illinois has decided it for herself. We have provided that the negro shall not be a slave, and we have also provided that he shall not be a citizen, but protect him in his civil rights, in his life, his person and his property, only depriving him of all political rights whatsoever, and refusing to put him on an equality with the white man. That policy of Illinois is satisfactory to the Democratic party and to me, and if it were to the Republicans, there would then be no question upon the subject. But the Republicans say that he ought to be made a citizen, and when he becomes a citizen he becomes your equal, with all your rights and privileges. They assert the Dred Scott decision to be monstrous because it denies that the negro is or can be a citizen under the Constitution. Now, I hold that Illinois had a right to abolish and prohibit slavery as she did, and I hold that Kentucky has the same right to continue and protect slavery that Illinois had to abolish it. I hold that New York had as much right to abolish slavery as Virginia has to continue it, and that each and every State of this Union is a sovereign power, with the right to do as it pleases upon this question of slavery, and upon all its domestic institutions.

Slavery is not the only question which comes up in this controversy. There is a far more important one to you, and that is, what shall be done with the free negro? We have settled the slavery question as far as we are concerned; we have prohibited it in Illinois forever, and in doing so, I think we have done wisely, and there is no man in the State who would be more strenuous in his opposition to the introduction of slavery than I would. But when we settled it for ourselves, we exhausted all our power over that subject. We have done our whole duty, and can do no more. We must leave each and every other State to decide for itself the same question. In relation to the policy to be pursued toward the free negroes, we have said that they shall not vote; whilst Maine, on the other hand, has said that they shall vote. Maine is a sovereign State, and has the power to regulate the qualifications of voters within her limits. I would never consent to confer the right of voting and of citizenship upon a negro, but still I am not going to quarrel with Maine for differing from me in opinion. Let Maine take care of her own negroes and fix the qualifications of her own voters to suit herself, without interfering with Illinois, and Illinois will not interfere with Maine. So with the State of New York. She allows the negro to vote, provided he owns two hundred and fifty dollars' worth of property, but not otherwise. While I would not make any distinction whatever between a negro who held property and one who did not; yet if the sovereign State of New York chooses to make that distinction, it is her business and not mine, and I will not quarrel with her for it. She can do as she pleases on this question if she minds her own business, and we will do the same thing.

Now, my friends, if we will only act conscientiously and rigidly upon this great principle of popular sovereignty, which guaranties to each State and Territory the right to do as it pleases on all things, local and domestic, instead of Congress interfering, we will continue at peace one with another. Why should Illinois be at war with Missouri, or Kentucky with Ohio, or Virginia with New York, merely because their institutions differ? Our fathers intended that our institutions should differ. They knew that the North and the South, having different climates, productions, and interests, required different institutions. This doctrine of Mr. Lincoln, of uniformity among the institutions of the different States, is a new doctrine, never dreamed of by Washington, Madison, or the framers of this government. Mr. Lincoln and the Republican party set themselves up as wiser than these men who made this Government, which has flourished for seventy years under the principle of popular sovereignty, recognizing the right of each State to do as it pleased. Under that principle, we have grown from a nation of three or four millions to a nation of about thirty millions of people; we have crossed the Allegheny mountains and filled up the whole Northwest, turning the prairie into a garden, and building up churches and schools, thus spreading civilization and Christianity where before there was nothing but savage barbarism. Under that principle we have become, from a feeble nation, the most powerful on the face of the earth, and if we only adhere to that principle, we can go forward increasing in territory, in power, in strength, and in glory until the Republic of America shall be the North Star that shall guide the friends of freedom throughout the civilized world.

And why can we not adhere to the great principle of self-government, upon which our institutions were originally based. I believe that this new doctrine preached by Mr. Lincoln and his party will dissolve the Union if it succeeds. They are trying to array all the Northern States in one body against the South, to excite a sectional war between the free States and the slave States, in order that the one or the other may be driven to the wall.

I am told that my time is out. Mr. Lincoln will now address you for an hour and a half, and I will then occupy an half hour in replying to him.

MR. LINCOLN'S REPLY IN THE OTTAWA DEBATE

My Fellow-citizens:

When a man hears himself somewhat misrepresented, it provokes him—at least, I find it so with myself; but when misrepresentation becomes very gross and palpable, it is more apt to amuse him. The first thing I see fit to notice, is the fact that Judge Douglas alleges, after running through the history of the old Democratic and the old Whig parties, that Judge Trumbull and myself made an arrangement in 1854, by which I was to have the place of General Shields in the United States Senate, and Judge Trumbull was to have the place of Judge Douglas. Now, all I have to say upon that subject is, that I think no man—not even Judge Douglas—can prove it, *because it is not true*. I have no doubt he is *"conscientious"* in saying it.

As to those resolutions that he took such a length of time to read, as being the platform of the Republican party in 1854, I say I never had anything to do with them, and I think Trumbull never had. Judge Douglas cannot show that either of us ever did have anything to do with them. I believe *this* is true about those resolutions. There was a call for a Convention to form a Republican party at Springfield, and I think that my friend Mr. Lovejoy, who is here upon this stand, had a hand in it. I think this is true, and I think if he will remember accurately, he will be able to recollect that he tried to get me into it, and I would not go in. I believe it is also true that I went away from Springfield when the Convention was in session, to attend court in Tazewell County. It is true they did place my name, though without authority, upon the committee, and afterward wrote me to attend the meeting of the committee; but I refused to do so, and I never had anything to do with that organization. This is the plain truth about all that matter of the resolutions.

Now, about this story that Judge Douglas tells of Trumbull bargaining to sell out the old Democratic party, and Lincoln agreeing to sell out the old Whig party, I have the means of *knowing* about that: Judge Douglas cannot have; and I know there is no substance to it whatever. Yet I have no doubt he is *"conscientious"* about it. I know that after Mr. Lovejoy got into the Legislature that winter, he complained of me that I had told all the old Whigs of his district that the old Whig party was good enough for them, and some of them voted against him because I told them so. Now, I have no means of totally disproving such charges as this which the Judge makes. A man cannot prove a negative, but he has a right to claim that when a man makes an affirmative charge, he must offer some proof to show the truth of what he says. I certainly cannot introduce testimony to show the negative about things, but I have a right to claim that if a man says he *knows* a thing, then he must show *how* he knows it. I always have a right to claim this, and it is not satisfactory to me that he may be "conscientious" on the subject.

Now, gentlemen, I hate to waste my time on such things, but in regard to that general Abolition tilt that Judge Douglas makes, when he says that I was engaged at that time in selling out and Abolitionizing the Old Whig party, I hope you will permit me to read a part of a printed speech that I made then at Peoria, which will show altogether a different view of the position I took in that contest of 1854.

A voice.—"Put on your specs."

Mr. Lincoln.—Yes, sir, I am obliged to do so. I am no longer a young man.

"This is the *repeal* of the Missouri Compromise. The foregoing history may not be precisely accurate in every particular, but I am sure it is sufficiently so for all the uses I shall attempt to make of it, and in it we have before us, the chief materials enabling us to correctly judge whether the repeal of the Missouri Compromise is right or wrong.

"I think, and shall try to show, that it is wrong,—wrong in its direct effect, letting slavery into Kansas and Nebraska, and wrong in its prospective principle, allowing it to spread to every other part of the wide world where men can be found inclined to take it.

"This *declared* indifference, but, as I must think, covert *real* zeal for the spread of slavery, I cannot but hate. I hate it because of the monstrous injustice of slavery itself. I hate it because it deprives our republican example of its just influence in the world,—enables the enemies of free institutions, with plausibility, to taunt us as hypocrites; causes the real friends of freedom to doubt our sincerity, and especially because it forces so many really good men amongst ourselves into an open war with the very fundamental principles of civil liberty,—criticizing the Declaration of Independence, and insisting that there is no right principle of action but *self-interest*.

"Before proceeding, let me say I think I have no prejudice against the Southern people. They are just what we would be in their situation. If slavery did not now exist among them, they would not introduce it. If it did now exist amongt us, we should not instantly give it up. This I believe of the masses North and South. Doubtless there are individuals on both sides, who would not hold slaves under any circumstances; and others who would gladly introduce slavery anew, if it were out of existence. We know that some Southern men do free their slaves, go North, and become tip-top Abolitionists; while some Northern ones go South, and become most cruel slave-masters.

"When Southern people tell us they are no more responsible for the origin of slavery than we, I acknowledge the fact. When it is said that the institution exists, and that it is very difficult to get rid of it, in any satisfactory way, I can understand and appreciate the saying. I surely will not blame them for not doing what I should not know how to do myself. If all earthly power were given me, I should not know what to do, as to the existing institution. My first impulse would be to free all the slaves, and send them to Liberia,—to their own native land. But a moment's reflection would convince me that whatever of high hope (as I think there is) there may be in this, in the long run, its sudden execution is impossible. If they were all landed there in a day, they would all perish in the next ten days; and there are not surplus shipping and surplus money enough in the world to carry them there in many times ten days. What then? Free them all, and keep them among us as underlings? Is it quite certain that this betters their condition? I think I would not hold one in slavery, at any rate; yet the point is not clear enough to me to denounce people upon. What next? Free them, and make them politically and socially our equals? My own feelings will not admit of this; and if mine would, we well know that those of the great mass of white people will not. Whether this feeling accords with justice and sound judgment is not the sole question, if, indeed, it is any part of it. A universal feeling, whether well or ill-founded, cannot be safely disregarded. We cannot, then, make them equals. It does seem to me that systems of gradual emancipation might be adopted; but for their tardiness in this, I will not undertake to judge our brethren of the South.

"When they remind us of their constitutional rights, I acknowledge them, not grudgingly, but fully and fairly; and I would give them any legislation for the reclaiming of their fugitives which should not, in its stringency, be more likely to carry a free man into slavery, than our ordinary criminal laws are to hang an innocent one.

"But all this, to my judgment, furnishes no more excuse for permitting slavery to go into our own free territory, than it would for reviving the African slave-trade by law. The law which forbids the bringing of slaves *from* Africa, and that which has so long forbid the taking of them *to* Nebraska, can hardly be distinguished on any moral principle; and the repeal of the former could find quite as plausible excuses as that of the latter."

I have reason to know that Judge Douglas *knows* that I said this. I think he has the answer here to one of the questions he put to me. I do not mean to allow him to catechise me unless he pays back for it in kind. I will not answer questions one after another, unless he reciprocates; but as he has made this inquiry, and I have answered it before, he has got it without my getting anything in return. He has got my answer on the fugitive-Slave law.

Now, gentlemen, I don't want to read at any greater length, but this is the true complexion of all I have ever said in regard to the institution of slavery and the black race. This is the whole of it, and anything that argues me into his idea of perfect social and political equality with the negro is but a specious and fantastic arrangement of words, by which a man can prove a horse-chestnut to be a chestnut horse.

I will say here, while upon this subject, that I have no purpose, directly or indirectly, to interfere with the institution of slavery in the States where it exists. I believe I have no lawful right to do so, and I have no inclination to do so. I have no purpose to introduce political and social equality between the white and the black races. There is a physical difference between the two, which, in my judgment, will probably forever forbid their living together upon the footing of perfect equality; and inasmuch as it becomes a necessity that there must be a difference, I, as well as Judge Douglas, am in favor of the race to which I belong having the superior position. I have never said anything to the contrary, but I hold that, notwithstanding all this, there is no reason in the world why the negro is not entitled to all the natural rights enumerated in the Declaration of Independence—the right to life, liberty, and the pursuit of happiness. I hold that he is as much entitled to these as the white man. I agree with Judge Douglas he is not my equal in many respects—certainly not in color, perhaps not in moral or intellectual endowment. But in the right to eat the bread, without the leave of anybody else, which his own hand earns, he is my equal and the equal of Judge Douglas, and the equal of every living man.

Now I pass on to consider one or two more of these little follies. The Judge is woefully at fault about his early friend Lincoln being a "grocery keeper." I don't know as it would be a great sin, if I had been; but he is mistaken. Lincoln never kept a grocery anywhere in the world. It is true that Lincoln did work the latter part of one winter in a little still-house, up at the head of a hollow.

And so I think my friend, the Judge, is equally at fault when he charges me at the time when I was in Congress of having opposed our soldiers who were fighting in the Mexican war. The Judge did not make his charge very distinctly, but I can tell you what he can prove, by referring to the record. You remember I was an old Whig, and whenever the Democratic party tried to get me to vote that the war had been righteously begun by the President, I would not do it. But whenever they asked for any money, or land-warrants, or anything to pay the soldiers there, during all that time, I gave the same vote that Judge Douglas did. You can think as you please as to whether that was consistent. Such is the truth; and the Judge has the right to make all he can out of it. But when he, by a general charge, conveys the idea that I withheld supplies from the soldiers who were fighting in the Mexican war, or did anything else to hinder the soldiers, he is, to say the least, grossly and altogether mistaken, as a consultation of the records will prove to him.

As I have not used up so much of my time as I had supposed, I will dwell a little longer upon one or two of these minor topics upon which the Judge has spoken. He has read from my speech in Springfield, in which I say that "a house divided against itself cannot stand." Does the Judge say it *can* stand? I don't know whether he does or not. The Judge does not seem to be attending to me just now, but I would like to know if it is his opinion that a house divided against itself *can stand*. If he does, then there is a question of veracity, not between him and me, but between the Judge and an authority of a somewhat higher character.

Now, my friends, I ask your attention to this matter for the purpose of saying something seriously. I know the Judge may readily enough agree with me that the maxim which was put forth by the Saviour is true, but he may allege that I misapply it; and the Judge has a right to urge that, in my application, I do misapply it and then I have a right to show that I do *not* misapply it. When he undertakes to say that because I think this nation, so far as the question of slavery is concerned, will all become one thing or all the other, I am in favor of bringing about a dead uniformity in the various States in all their institutions, he argues erroneously. The great variety of the local institutions in the States, springing from differences in the soil, differences in the face of the country, and in the climate, are bonds of Union. They do not make "a house divided against itself," but they make a house united. If they produce in one section of the country what is called for by the wants of another section, and this other section can supply the wants of the first, they are not matters of discord, but bonds of union, true bonds of union.

But can this question of slavery be considered as among *these* varieties in the institutions of the country? I leave it to you to say whether, in the history of our Government, this institution of slavery has not always failed to be a bond of union, and, on the contrary, been an apple of discord and an element of division in the house. I ask you to consider whether, so long as the moral constitution of men's minds shall continue to be the same, after this generation and assemblage shall sink into the grave, and another race shall arise, with the same moral and intellectual development we have—whether, if that institution is standing in the same irritating position in which it now is, it will not continue an element of division? If so, then I have a right to say that, in regard to this question, the Union is a house divided against itself; and when the Judge reminds me that I have often said to him that the institution of slavery has existed for eighty years in some States, and yet it does not exist in some others, I agree to the fact, and I account for it by looking at the position in which our fathers originally placed it,—restricting it from the new Territories where it had not gone, and legislating to cut off its source by the abrogation of the slave-trade, thus putting the seal of legislation *against its spread.*

The public mind *did* rest in the belief that it was in the course of ultimate extinction. But lately, I think—and in this I charge nothing on the Judge's motives—lately, I think, that he, and those acting with him, have placed that institution on a new basis, which looks to the *perpetuity and nationalization of slavery.* And while it is placed upon this new basis, I say, and I have said, that I believe we shall not have peace upon the question until the opponents of slavery arrest the further spread of it, and place it where the public mind shall rest in the belief that it is in the course of ultimate extinction; or, on the other hand, that its advocates will push it forward until it shall become alike lawful in all the States, old as well as new, North as well as South. Now I believe if we could arrest the spread, and place it where Washington and Jefferson and Madison placed it, it *would be* in the course of ultimate extinction, and the public mind *would,* as for eighty years past, believe that it was in the course of ultimate extinction. The crisis would be past, and the institution might be let alone for a hundred years, if it should live so long, in the States where it exists, yet it would be going out of existence in the way best for both the black and the white races.

A Voice.—"Then do you repudiate popular sovereignty?"

Mr. Lincoln.—Well, then, let us talk about popular sovereignty. What is popular sovereignty? Is it the right of the people to have slavery or not have it, as they see fit, in the territories? I will state—and I have an able man to watch me—my understanding is that Popular Sovereignty, as now applied to the question of slavery, does allow the people of a Territory to have slavery if they want to, but does not allow them *not* to have it if they *do not* want it. I do not mean that if this vast concourse of people were in a Territory of the United States, any one of them would be obliged to have a slave if he did not want one; but I do say that, as I understand the Dred Scott decision, if any one man wants slaves, all the rest have no way of keeping that one man from holding them.

When I made my speech at Springfield, of which the Judge complains, and from which he quotes, I really was not thinking of the things which he ascribes to me at all. I had no thought in the world that I was doing anything to bring about a war between the Free and Slave States. I had no thought in the world that I was doing anything to bring about a political and social equality of the black and white races. It never occurred to me that I was doing anything, or favoring anything to reduce to a dead uniformity all the local institutions of the various States. But I must say, in all fairness to him, if he thinks I am doing something which leads to these bad results, it is none the better that I did not mean it. It is just as fatal to the country, if I have any influence in producing it, whether I intend it or not. But can it be true, that placing this institution upon the original basis—the basis upon which our fathers placed it—can have any tendency to set the Northern and the Southern States at war with one another, or that it can have any tendency to make the people of Vermont raise sugar-cane, because they raise it in Louisiana, or that it can compel the people of Illinois to cut pine logs on the Grand Prairie, where they will not grow, because they cut pine logs in Maine, where they do grow?

The Judge says this is a new principle started in regard to this question. Does the Judge claim that he is working on the plan of the founders of government? I think he says in some of his speeches—indeed, I have one here now—that he saw evidence of a policy to allow slavery to be south of a certain line, while north of it it should be excluded, and he saw an indisposition on the part of the country to stand upon that policy, and therefore he set about studying the subject upon *original principles*, and upon *original principles* he got up the Nebraska bill! I am fighting it upon these "original principles"—fighting it in the Jeffersonian, Washingtonian, and Madisonian fashion.

Now, my friends, I wish you to attend for a little while to one or two other things in that Springfield speech. My main object was to show, so far as my humble ability was capable of showing to the people of this country, what I believed was the truth—that there was a *tendency*, if not a conspiracy among those who have engineered this slavery question for the last four or five years, to make slavery perpetual and universal in this nation. Having made that speech principally for that object, after arranging the evidences that I thought tended to prove my proposition, I concluded with this bit of comment:

"We cannot absolutely know that these exact adaptations are the result of pre-concert, but when we see a lot of framed timbers, different portions of which we know have been gotten out at different times and places, and by different workmen—Stephen, Franklin, Roger, and James, for instance,—and when we see these timbers joined together, and see they exactly make the frame of a house or a mill, all the tenons and mortices exactly fitting, and all the lengths and proportions of the different pieces exactly adapted to their respective places, and not a piece too many or too few,—not omitting even the scaffolding,—or if a single piece be lacking, we see the place in the frame exactly fitted and prepared yet to bring such piece in—in such a case we feel it impossible not to believe that Stephen and Franklin, and Roger and James, all understood one another from the beginning, and all worked upon a common plan or draft drawn before the first blow was struck."

When my friend, Judge Douglas, came to Chicago on the 9th of July, this speech having been delivered on the 16th of June, he made an harangue there, in which he took hold of this speech of mine, showing that he had carefully read it; and while he paid no attention to *this* matter at all, but complimented me as being a "kind, amiable, and intelligent gentleman," notwithstanding I had said this, he goes on and deduces, or draws out, from my speech this tendency of mine to set the States at war with one another, to make all the institutions uniform, and set the niggers and white people to marrying together. Then, as the Judge had complimented me with these pleasant titles (I must confess to my weakness), I was a little "taken," for it came from a great man. I was not very much accustomed to flattery, and it came the sweeter to me. I was rather like the Hoosier, with the gingerbread, when he said he reckoned he loved it better than any other man, and got less of it. As the Judge had so flattered me, I could not make up my mind that he meant to deal unfairly with me; so I went to work to show him that he misunderstood the whole scope of my speech, and that I really never intended to set the people at war with one another.

As an illustration, the next time I met him, which was at Springfield, I used this expression, that I claimed no right under the Constitution, nor had I any inclination, to enter into the Slave States and interfere with the institutions of slavery. He says upon that: Lincoln will not enter into the Slave States, but will go to the banks of the Ohio, on this side, and shoot over! He runs on, step by step, in the horse-chestnut style of argument, until in the Springfield speech he says, "Unless he shall be successful in firing his batteries, until he shall have extinguished slavery in all the States, the Union shall be dissolved." Now I don't think that was exactly the way to treat "a kind, amiable, intelligent gentleman." I know if I had asked the Judge to show when or where it was I had said that, if I didn't succeed in firing into the slave States until slavery should be extinguished, the Union should be dissolved, he could not have shown it. I understand what he would do. He would say, "I don't mean to quote from you, but this was the *result* of what you say." But I have the right to ask, and I do ask now, Did you not put it in such a form that an ordinary reader or listener would take it as an expression from me?

In a speech at Springfield, on the night of the 17th, I thought I might as well attend to my own business a little, and I recalled his attention as well as I could to this charge of conspiracy to nationalize slavery. I called his attention to the fact that he had acknowledged, in my hearing twice, that he had carefully read the speech, and, in the language of the lawyers, as he had twice read the speech, and still had put in no plea or answer, I took a default on him. I insisted that I had a right then to renew that charge of conspiracy. Ten days afterward I met the Judge at Clinton,—that is to say, I was on the ground, but not in the discussion,—and heard him make a speech. Then he comes in with his plea to this charge, for the first time; and his plea when put in, as well as I can recollect it, amounted to this: that he never had any talk with Judge Taney or the President of the United States with regard to the Dred Scott decision before it was made. I (Lincoln) ought to know that the man who makes a charge without knowing it to be true, falsifies as much as he who knowingly tells a falsehood; and lastly, that he would pronounce the whole thing a falsehood; but he would make no personal application of the charge of falsehood, not because of any regard for the "kind, amiable, intelligent gentleman," but because of his own personal self-respect!

I have understood since then (but will not hold the Judge to it if he is not willing) that he has broken through the "self-respect," and has got to saying the thing *out*. The Judge nods to me that it is so. It is fortunate for me that I can keep as good-humored as I do, when the Judge acknowledges that he has been trying to make a question of veracity with me. I know the Judge is a great man, while I am only a small man, but *I feel that I have got him*. I demur to that plea. I waive all objections that it was not filed till after default was taken, and demur to it upon the merits. What if Judge Douglas never did talk with Chief Justice Taney and the President, before the Dred Scott decision was made; does it follow that he could not have had as perfect an understanding without talking as with it? I am not disposed to stand upon my legal advantage. I am disposed to take his denial as being like an answer in chancery, that he neither had any knowledge, information, or belief in the existence of such a conspiracy. I am disposed to take his answer as being as broad as though he had put it in these words. And now, I ask, even if he had done so, have not I a right to *prove it on him*, and to offer the evidence of more than two witnesses, by whom to prove it; and if the evidence proves the existence of the conspiracy, does his broad answer denying all knowledge, information, or belief, disturb the fact? It can only show that he was *used* by conspirators, and was not a *leader* of them.

Now, in regard to his reminding me of the moral rule that persons who tell what they do not know to be true, falsify as much as those who knowingly tell falsehoods. I remember the rule, and it must be borne in mind that in what I have read to you, I do not say that I *know* such a conspiracy to exist. To that I reply, *I believe it*. If the Judge says that I do *not* believe it, then *he* says what *he* does not know, and falls within his own rule, that he who asserts a thing which he does not know to be true, falsifies as much as he who knowingly tells a falsehood.

I want to call your attention to a little discussion on that branch of the case, and the evidence which brought my mind to the conclusion which I expressed as my *belief*. If, in arraying that evidence, I had stated anything which was false or erroneous, it needed but that Judge Douglas should point it out, and I would have taken it back with all the kindness in the world. I do not deal in that way. If I have brought forward anything not a fact, if he will point it out, it will not even ruffle me to take it back. But if he will not point out anything erroneous in the evidence, is it not rather for him to show, by a comparison of the evidence, that I have *reasoned* falsely, than to call the "kind, amiable, intelligent gentleman" a liar? If I have reasoned to a false conclusion, it is the vocation of an able debater to show by argument that I have wandered to an erroneous conclusion. I want to ask your attention to a portion of the Nebraska bill, which Judge Douglas has quoted: "It being the true intent and meaning of this act, not to legislate slavery into any Territory or State, nor to exclude it therefrom, but to leave the people thereof perfectly free to form and regulate their domestic institutions in their own way, subject only to the Constitution of the United States." Thereupon Judge Douglas and others began to argue in favor of ",,"—the right of the people to have slaves if they wanted them, and to exclude slavery if they did not want them. "But," said, in substance, a Senator from Ohio (Mr. Chase, I believe), "we more than suspect that you do not mean to allow the people to exclude slavery if they wish to, and if you do mean it, accept an amendment which I propose expressly authorizing the people to exclude slavery."

I believe I have the amendment here before me, which was offered, and under which the people of the Territory, through their proper representatives, might, if they saw fit, prohibit the existence of slavery therein. And now I state it as a *fact,* to be taken back if there is any mistake about it, that Judge Douglas and those acting with him *voted that amendment down.* I now think that those men who voted it down, had a *real reason* for doing so. They know what that reason was. It looks to us, since we have seen the Dred Scott decision pronounced, holding that, "under the Constitution," the people cannot exclude slavery—I say it looks to outsiders, poor, simple, "amiable, intelligent gentlemen," as though the niche was left as a place to put that Dred Scott decision in,—a niche which would have been spoiled by adopting the amendment. And now, I say again, if *this* was not the reason, it will avail the Judge much more to calmly and good-humoredly point out to these people what that *other* reason was for voting the amendment down, than, swelling himself up, to vociferate that he may be provoked to call somebody a liar.

Again: there is in that same quotation from the Nebraska bill this clause—"It being the true intent and meaning of this bill not to legislate slavery into any Territory or *State.*" I have always been puzzled to know what business the word "State" had in that connection, Judge Douglas knows. *He put it there.* He knows what he put it there for. We outsiders cannot say what he put it there for. The law they were passing was not about States, and was not making provisions for States. What was it placed there for? After seeing the Dred Scott decision, which holds that the people cannot exclude slavery from a *Territory,* if another Dred Scott decision shall come, holding that they cannot exclude it from a *State,* we shall discover that when the word was originally put there, it was in view of something which was to come in due time, we shall see that it was the *other half* of something. I now say again, if there is any different reason for putting it there, Judge Douglas, in a good humored way, without calling anybody a liar, *can tell what the reason was.*

When the Judge spoke at Clinton, he came very near making a charge of falsehood against me. He used, as I found it printed in a newspaper, which, I remember, was very nearly like the real speech, the following language:—

"I did not answer the charge [of conspiracy] before, for the reason that I did not suppose there was a man in America with a heart so corrupt as to believe such a charge could be true. I have too much respect for Mr. Lincoln to suppose he is serious in making the charge."

I confess this is rather a curious view, that out of respect for me he should consider I was making what I deemed rather a grave charge in fun. I confess it strikes me rather strangely. But I let it pass. As the Judge did not for a moment believe that there was a man in America whose heart was so "corrupt" as to make such a charge, and as he places me among the "men in America" who have hearts base enough to make such a charge, I hope he will excuse me if I hunt out another charge very like this; and if it should turn out that in hunting I should find that other, and it should turn out to be Judge Douglas himself who made it, I hope he will reconsider this question of the deep corruption of heart he has thought fit to ascribe to me. In Judge Douglas's speech of March 22, 1858, which I hold in my hand, he says: —

"In this connection there is another topic to which I desire to allude. I seldom refer to the course of newspapers, or notice the articles which they publish in regard to myself; but the course of the Washington *Union* has been so extraordinary, for the last two or three months, that I think it well enough to make some allusion to it. It has read me out of the Democratic party every other day, at least for two or three months, and keeps reading me out, and, as if it had not succeeded, still continues to read me out, using such terms as 'traitor,' 'renegade,' 'deserter,' and other kind and polite epithets of that nature. Sir, I have no vindication to make of my Democracy against the Washington *Union*, or any other newspapers. I am willing to allow my history and action for the last twenty years to speak for themselves as to my political principles, and my fidelity to political obligations. The Washington *Union* has a personal grievance. When its editor was nominated for public printer I declined to vote for him, and stated that at some time I might give my reasons for doing so. Since I declined to give that vote, this scurrilous abuse, these vindictive and constant attacks have been repeated almost daily on me. Will my friend from Michigan read the article to which I allude?"

This is a part of the speech. You must excuse me from reading the entire article of the Washington *Union*, as Mr. Stuart read it for Mr. Douglas. The Judge goes on and sums up, as I think, correctly:—

"Mr. President, you here find several distinct propositions advanced boldly by the Washington *Union* editorially, and apparently *authoritatively*; and any man who questions any of them is denounced as an Abolitionist, a Free-soiler, a fanatic. The propositions are, first, that the primary object of all government at its original institution is the protection of person and property; second, that the Constitution of the United States declares that the citizens of each State shall be entitled to all the privileges and immunities of citizens in the several States; and that, therefore, thirdly, all State laws, whether organic or otherwise, which prohibit the citizens of one State from settling in another with their slave property, and especially declaring it forfeited, are direct violations of the original intention of the Government and Constitution of the United States; and, fourth, that the emancipation of the slaves of the Northern States was a gross outrage on the rights of property, inasmuch as it was involuntarily done on the part of the owner.

"Remember that this article was published in the *Union* on the 17th of November, and on the 18th appeared the first article giving the adhesion of the *Union* to the Lecompton Constitution. It was in these words: —

"'KANSAS AND HER CONSTITUTION—The vexed question is settled. The problem is solved. The dead point of danger is passed. All serious trouble to Kansas affairs is over and gone'—

"And a column nearly of the same sort. Then, when you come to look into the Lecompton Constitution, you find the same doctrine incorporated in it which was put forth editorially in the *Union*. What is it?

"'ARTICLE 7, *Section 1*. The right of property is before and higher than any Constitutional sanction; and the right of the owner of a slave to such slave and its increase is the same and as inviolable as the right of the owner of any property whatever.'

"Then in the schedule is a provision that the Constitution may be amended after 1864 by a two-thirds vote.

"'But no alteration shall be made to affect the right of property in the ownership of slaves.'

"It will be seen by these clauses in the Lecompton Constitution, that they are identical in spirit with the *authoritative* article in the Washington *Union* of the day previous to its indorsement of this Constitution."

I pass over some portions of the speech, and I hope that any one who feels interested in this matter will read the entire section of the speech, and see whether I do the Judge injustice. He proceeds:—

"When I saw that article in the *Union* of the 17th of November, followed by the glorification of the Lecompton Constitution on the 18th of November, and this clause in the Constitution asserting the doctrine that a State has no right to prohibit slavery within its limits, I saw that there was a *fatal blow* being struck at the sovereignty of the States of this Union."

I stop the quotation there, again requesting that it may all be read. I have read all of the portion I desire to comment upon. What is this charge that the Judge thinks I must have a very corrupt heart to make? It was a purpose on the part of certain high functionaries to make it impossible for the people of one State to prohibit the people of any other State from entering it with their "property," so called, and making it a slave State. In other words, it was a charge implying a design to make the institution of slavery national. And now I ask your attention to what Judge Douglas has himself done here. I know he made that part of the speech as a reason why he had refused to vote for a certain man for public printer, but when we get at it, the charge itself is the very one I made against him, that he thinks I am so corrupt for uttering. Now, whom does he make that charge against? Does he make it against that newspaper editor merely? No; he says it is identical in spirit with the Lecompton Constitution, and so the framers of that Constitution are brought in with the editor of the newspaper in that "fatal blow being struck." He did not call it a "conspiracy." In his language it is a "fatal blow being struck." And if the words carry the meaning better when changed from a "conspiracy" into a "fatal blow being struck," I will change *my* expression and call it "fatal blow being struck." We see the charge made not merely against the editor of the *Union*, but all the framers of the Lecompton Constitution; and not only so, but the article was an *authoritative* article. By whose authority? Is there any question but he means it was by the authority of the President and his Cabinet—the Administration?

Is there any sort of question but he means to make that charge? Then there are the editors of the *Union*, the framers of the Lecompton Constitution, the President of the United States and his Cabinet, and all the supporters of the Lecompton Constitution, in Congress and out of Congress, who are all involved in this "fatal blow being struck." I commend to Judge Douglas's consideration the question of *how corrupt a man's heart must be to make such a charge!*

Now, my friends, I have but one branch of the subject, in the little time I have left, to which to call your attention, and as I shall come to a close at the end of that branch, it is probable that I shall not occupy quite all the time allotted to me. Although on these questions I would like to talk twice as long as I have, I could not enter upon another head and discuss it properly without running over my time. I ask the attention of the people here assembled and elsewhere, to the course that Judge Douglas is pursuing every day as bearing upon this question of making slavery national. Not going back to the records, but taking the speeches he makes, the speeches he made yesterday and day before, and makes constantly all over the country,—I ask your attention to them. In the first place, what is necessary to make the institution national? Not war. There is no danger that the people of Kentucky will shoulder their muskets, and, with a young nigger stuck on every bayonet, march into Illinois and force them upon us. There is no danger of our going over there and making war upon them. Then what is necessary for the nationalization of slavery? It is simply the next Dred Scott decision. It is merely for the Supreme Court to decide that no *State* under the Constitution can exclude it, just as they have already decided that under the Constitution neither Congress nor the Territorial Legislature can do it. When that is decided and acquiesced in, the whole thing is done.

This being true, and this being the way, as I think, that slavery is to be made national, let us consider what Judge Douglas is doing every day to that end. In the first place, let us see what influence he is exerting on public sentiment. In this and like communities, public sentiment is everything. With public sentiment, nothing can fail; without it nothing can succeed. Consequently he who moulds public sentiment goes deeper than he who enacts statutes or pronounces decisions. He makes statutes and decisions possible or impossible to be executed. This must be borne in mind, as also the additional fact that Judge Douglas is a man of vast influence, so great that it is enough for many men to profess to believe anything, when they once find out that Judge Douglas professes to believe it. Consider also the attitude he occupies at the head of a large party,—a party which he claims has a majority of all the voters in the country. This man sticks to a decision which forbids the people of a Territory from excluding slavery, and he does so not because he says it is right in itself,—he does not give any opinion on that,—but because it has been decided by the court; and being decided by court, he is, and you are bound to take it in your political action as law, not that he judges at all of its merits, but because a decision of the court is to him a "Thus saith the Lord." He places it on that ground alone, and you will bear in mind that, thus committing himself unreservedly to this decision commits him to the next one just as firmly as to this. He did not commit himself on account of the merit or demerit of the decision, but it is a "Thus saith the Lord." The next decision, as much as this, will be a "Thus saith the Lord."

There is nothing that can divert or turn him away from this decision. It is nothing that I point out to him that his great prototype, General Jackson, did not believe in the binding force of decisions. It is nothing to him that Jefferson did not so believe. I have said that I have often heard him approve of Jackson's course in disregarding the decision of the Supreme Court pronouncing a National Bank constitutional. He says, I did not hear him say so. He denies the accuracy of my recollection. I say he ought to know better than I, but I will make no question about this thing, though it still seems to me that I heard him say it twenty times. I will tell him, though, that he now claims to stand on the Cincinnati platform, which affirms that Congress *cannot* charter a National Bank, in the teeth of that old standing decision that Congress *can* charter a bank.

And I remind him of another piece of history on the question of respect for judicial decisions: and it is a piece of Illinois history, belonging to a time when the large party to which Judge Douglas belonged were displeased with a decision of the Supreme Court of Illinois; because they had decided that a Governor could not remove a Secretary of State. You will find the whole story in Ford's History of Illinois, and I know that Judge Douglas will not deny that he was then in favor of overslaughing that decision by the mode of adding five new Judges, so as to vote down the four old ones. Not only so, but it ended in *the Judge's sitting down on that very bench as one of the five new Judges to break down the four old ones*. It was in this way precisely that he got his title of Judge. Now, when the Judge tells me that men appointed conditionally to sit as members of a court, will have to be catechised beforehand upon some subject, I say, "You know, Judge; you have tried it." When he says a court of this kind will lose the confidence of all men, will be prostituted and disgraced by such a proceeding, I say, "You know best, Judge; you have been through the mill."

But I cannot shake Judge Douglas's teeth loose from the Dred Scott decision. Like some obstinate animal (I mean no disrespect), that will hang on when he has once got his teeth fixed, you may cut off a leg, or you may tear away an arm, still he will not relax his hold. And so I may point out to the Judge, and say that he is bespattered all over, from the beginning of his political life to the present time, with attacks upon judicial decisions; I may cut off limb after limb of his public record, and strive to wrench him from a single dictum of the court,—yet I cannot divert him from it. He hangs, to the last, to the Dred Scott decision. These things show there is a purpose *strong as death and eternity* for which he adheres to this decision, and for which he will adhere to *all other decisions* of the same court.

A Hibernian. — "Give us something besides Dred Scott."

Mr. Lincoln. —Yes; no doubt you want to hear something that don't hurt. Now, having spoken of the Dred Scott decision, one more word and I am done. Henry Clay, my *beau ideal* of a statesman, the man for whom I fought all my humble life,—Henry Clay once said of a class of men who would repress all tendencies to liberty and ultimate emancipation, that they must, if they would do this, go back to the era of our Independence, and muzzle the cannon which thunders its annual joyous return; they must blow out the moral lights around us; they must penetrate the human soul, and eradicate there the love of liberty; and then, and not till then, could they perpetuate slavery in this country! To my thinking, Judge Douglas is, by his example and vast influence, doing that very thing in this community, when he says that the negro has nothing in the Declaration of Independence. Henry Clay plainly understood the contrary.

Judge Douglas is going back to the era of our Revolution, and to the extent of his ability, muzzling the cannon which thunders its annual joyous return. When he invites any people, willing to have slavery, to establish it, he is blowing out the moral lights around us. When he says he "cares not whether slavery is voted down or voted up,"—that it is a sacred right of self-government,—he is, in my judgment, penetrating the human soul and eradicating the light of reason and the love of liberty in this American people. And now I will only say that when, by all these means and appliances, Judge Douglas shall succeed in bringing public sentiment to an exact accordance with his own views—when these vast assemblages shall echo back all these sentiments; when they shall come to repeat his views and to avow his principles, and to say all that he says on these mighty questions,—then it needs only the formality of the second Dred Scott decision, which he indorses in advance, to make slavery alike lawful in all the States, old as well as new, North as well as South.

My friends, that ends the chapter. The Judge can take his half hour.

Mr. Douglas' Rejoinder

Fellow citizens: I will now occupy the half hour allotted to me in replying to Mr. Lincoln. The first point to which I will call your attention is, as to what I said about the organization of the Republican party in 1854, and the platform that was formed on the 5th of October, of that year, and I will then put the question to Mr. Lincoln, whether or not he approves of each article in that platform and ask for a specific answer. I did not charge him with being a member of the committee which reported that platform. I charged that that platform was the platform of the Republican party adopted by them. The fact that it was the platform of the Republican party is not denied, but Mr. Lincoln now says, that although his name was on the committee which reported it, he does not think he was there, but thinks he was in Tazewell, holding court. Now, I want to remind Mr. Lincoln that he was at Springfield when that Convention was held and those resolutions adopted.

The point I am going to remind Mr. Lincoln of is this: that after I had made my speech in 1854, during the fair, he gave me notice that he was going to reply to me the next day. I was sick at the time, but I staid over in Springfield to hear his reply and to reply to him. On that day this very Convention, the resolutions adopted by which I have read, was to meet in the Senate chamber. He spoke in the hall of the House; and when he got through his speech,—my recollection is distinct, and I shall never forget it,—Mr. Codding walked in as I took the stand to reply, and gave notice that the Republican State Convention would meet instantly in the Senate chamber, and called upon the Republicans to retire there and go into this very Convention, instead of remaining and listening to me.

Mr. Lincoln.—Judge, add that I went along with them.

Mr. Douglas.—Gentlemen, Mr. Lincoln tells me to add that he went along with them to the Senate chamber. I will not add that, because I do not know whether he did or not.

Mr. Lincoln.—I know he did not.

Mr. Douglas.—I do not know whether he knows it or not, that is not the point, and I will yet bring him on to the question.

In the first place, Mr. Lincoln was selected by the very men who made the Republican organization, on that day, to reply to me. He spoke for them and for that party, and he was the leader of the party; and on the very day he made his speech in reply to me, preaching up this same doctrine of negro equality under the Declaration of Independence, this Republican party met in Convention. Another evidence that he was acting in concert with them is to be found in the fact that that Convention waited an hour after its time of meeting to hear Lincoln's speech, and Codding, one of their leading men, marched in the moment Lincoln got through, and gave notice that they did not want to hear me, and would proceed with the business of the Convention. Still another fact. I have here a newspaper printed at Springfield, Mr. Lincoln's own town, in October, 1854, a few days afterward, publishing these resolutions, charging Mr. Lincoln with entertaining these sentiments, and trying to prove that they were also the sentiments of Mr. Yates, then candidate for Congress. This has been published on Mr. Lincoln over and over again, and never before has he denied it.

But, my friends, this denial of his that he did not act on the committee, is a miserable quibble to avoid the main issue, which is, that this Republican platform declares in favor of the unconditional repeal of the Fugitive-Slave law. Has Lincoln answered whether he indorsed that or not? I called his attention to it when I first addressed you, and asked him for an answer, and I then predicted that he would not answer. How does he answer? Why, that he was not on the committee that wrote the resolutions. I then repeated the next proposition contained in the resolutions, which was to restrict slavery in those States in which it exists, and asked him whether he indorsed it. Does he answer yes, or no? He says in reply, "I was not on the committee at the time; I was up in Tazewell." The next question I put to him was, whether he was in favor of prohibiting the admission of any more slave States into the Union. I put the question to him distinctly, whether, if the people of the Territory, when they had sufficient population to make a State, should form their Constitution recognizing slavery, he would vote for or against its admission. He is a candidate for the United States Senate, and it is possible, if he should be elected, that he would have to vote directly on that question. I asked him to answer me and you, whether he would vote to admit a State into the Union, with slavery or without it, as its own people might choose. He did not answer that question. He dodges that question also, under the cover that he was not on the Committee at the time, that he was not present when the platform was made. I want to know if he should happen to be in the Senate when a State applied for admission, with a Constitution acceptable to her own people, [whether?] he would vote to admit that State, if slavery was one of its institutions. He avoids the answer.

Mr. Lincoln.—No, Judge.

It is true he gives the Abolitionists to understand by a hint that he would not vote to admit such a State. And why? He goes on to say that the man who would talk about giving each State the right to have slavery, or not, as it pleased, was akin to the man who would muzzle the guns which thundered forth the annual joyous return of the day of our independence. He says that that kind of talk is casting a blight on the glory of this country. What is the meaning of that? That he is not in favor of each State to have the right of doing as it pleases on the slavery question? I will put the question to him again and again, and I intend to force it out of him.

Then again, this platform which was made at Springfield by his own party, when he was its acknowledged head, provides that Republicans will insist on the abolition of slavery in the District of Columbia, and I asked Lincoln specifically whether he agreed with them in that? [Did you get an answer?] He is afraid to answer it. He knows I will trot him down to Egypt. I intend to make him answer there, or I will show the people of Illinois that he does not intend to answer these questions. The convention to which I have been alluding goes a little further, and pledges itself to exclude slavery from all the Territories over which the General Government has exclusive jurisdiction north of 36 deg. 30 min., as well as south. Now I want to know whether he approves that provision. I want him to answer, and when he does, I want to know his opinion on another point, which is, whether he will redeem the pledge of this platform and resist the acquirement of any more territory unless slavery therein shall be forever prohibited. I want him to answer this last question.

Each of the questions I have put to him are practical questions,—questions based upon the fundamental principles of the Black Republican party, and I want to know whether he is the first, last, and only choice of a party with whom he does not agree in principle. He does not deny but that that principle was unanimously adopted by the Republican party; he does not deny that the whole Republican party is pledged to it; he does not deny that a man who is not faithful to it is faithless to the Republican party; and now I want to know whether that party is unanimously in favor of a man who does not adopt that creed and agree with them in their principles: I want to know whether the man who does not agree with them, and who is afraid to avow his differences, and who dodges the issue, is the first, last, and only choice of the Republican party.

A Voice.—"How about the conspiracy?"

Never mind, I will come to that soon enough. But the platform which I have read to you not only lays down these principles, but it adds:—

"*Resolved,* That, in furtherance of these principles we will use such constitutional and lawful means as shall seem best adapted to their accomplishment, and that we will support no man for office, under the general or state government, who is not positively and fully committed to the support of these principles, and whose personal character and conduct are not a guarantee that he is reliable, and who shall not have abjured old party allegiance and ties."

The Black Republican party stands pledged that they will never support Lincoln until he has pledged himself to that platform, but he cannot devise his answer. He has not made up his mind whether he will or not. He talked about everything else he could think of to occupy his hour and a half, and when he could not think of anything more to say, without an excuse for refusing to answer these questions, he sat down long before his time was out.

In relation to Mr. Lincoln's charge of conspiracy against me, I have a word to say. In his speech today he quotes a playful part of his speech at Springfield, about Stephen, and James, and Franklin, and Roger, and says that I did not take exception to it. I did not answer it, and he repeats it again. I did not take exception to this figure of his. He has a right to be as playful as he pleases in throwing his arguments together, and I will not object; but I did take objection to his second Springfield speech, in which he stated that he intended his first speech as a charge of corruption or conspiracy against the Supreme Court of the United States, President Pierce, B, and myself. That gave the offensive character to the charge. He then said that when he made it he did not know whether it was true or not; but inasmuch as Judge Douglas had not denied it, although he had replied to the other parts of his speech three times, he repeated it as a charge of conspiracy against me, thus charging me with moral turpitude. When he put it in that form I did say that inasmuch as he repeated the charge simply because I had not denied it, I would deprive him of the opportunity of ever repeating it again, by declaring that it was, in all its bearings, an infamous lie. He says he will repeat it until I answer his folly and nonsense about Stephen, and Franklin, and Roger, and Bob, and James.

He studied that out, prepared that one sentence with the greatest care, committed it to memory, and put it in his first Springfield speech, and now he carries that speech around and reads that sentence to show how pretty it is. His vanity is wounded because I will not go into that beautiful figure of his about the building of a house. All I have to say is, that I am not green enough to let him make a charge which he acknowledges he does not know to be true, and then take up my time in answering it, when I know it to be false, and nobody else knows it to be true.

I have not brought a charge of moral turpitude against him. When he, or any other man, brings one against me, instead of disproving it I will say that it is a lie, and let him prove it if he can.

I have lived twenty-five years in Illinois. I have served you with all the fidelity and ability which I possess, and Mr. Lincoln is at liberty to attack my public action, my votes, and my conduct; but when he dares to attack my moral integrity, by a charge of conspiracy between myself, Chief Justice Taney and the Supreme Court, and two Presidents of the United States, I will repel it.

Mr. Lincoln has not character enough for integrity and truth, merely on his own *ipse dixit* to arraign President Buchanan, President Pierce, and nine judges of the Supreme Court, not one of whom would be complimented by being put on an equality with him. There is an unpardonable presumption in a man putting himself up before thousands of people, and pretending that his *ipse dixit*, without proof, without fact, and without truth, is enough to bring down and destroy the purest and best of living men.

Fellow-citizens, my time is fast expiring; I must pass on. Mr. Lincoln wants to know why I voted against Mr. Chase's amendment to the Nebraska bill. I will tell him. In the first place, the bill already conferred all the power which Congress had, by giving the people the whole power over the subject. Chase offered a proviso that they might abolish slavery, which by implication would convey the idea that they could prohibit by not introducing that institution. General Cass asked him to modify his amendment, so as to provide that the people might either prohibit or introduce slavery, and thus make it fair and equal. Chase refused to so modify his proviso, and then Gen. Cass and all the rest of us, voted it down. These facts appear on the journals and debates of Congress, where Mr. Lincoln found the charge, and if he had told the whole truth, there would have been no necessity for me to occupy your time in explaining the matter.

Mr. Lincoln wants to know why the word "State," as well as "Territory," was put into the Nebraska bill! I will tell him. It was put there to meet just such false arguments as he has been adducing. That first, not only the people of the Territories should do as they pleased, but that when they come to be admitted as States, they should come into the Union with or without slavery, as the people determined. I meant to knock in the head this Abolition doctrine of Mr. Lincoln's, that there shall be no more slave States, even if the people want them. And it does not do for him to say, or for any other Black Republican to say, that there is nobody in favor of the doctrine of no more slave States, and that nobody wants to interfere with the right of the people to do as they please. What was the origin of the Missouri difficulty and the Missouri compromise? The people of

Missouri formed a constitution as a slave State, and asked admission into the Union, but the Free Soil party of the North being in a majority, refused to admit her because she had slavery as one of her institutions. Hence this first slavery agitation arose upon a State, and not upon a Territory; and yet Mr. Lincoln does not know why the word "State" was placed in the Kansas-Nebraska bill. The whole Abolition agitation arose on that doctrine of prohibiting a State from coming in with slavery or not, as it pleased, and that same doctrine is here in this Republican platform of 1854; it has never been repealed; and every Black Republican stands pledged by that platform, never to vote for any man who is not in favor of it. Yet Mr. Lincoln does not know that there is a man in the world who is in favor of preventing a State from coming in as it pleases, notwithstanding. The Springfield platform says that they, the Republican party, will not allow a State to come in under such circumstances. He is an ignorant man.

Now you see that upon these very points I am as far from bringing Mr. Lincoln up to the line as I ever was before. He does not want to avow his principles. I do want to avow mine, as clear as sunlight in mid-day. Democracy is founded upon the eternal principle of right. The plainer these principles are avowed before the people, the stronger will be the support which they will receive. I only wish I had the power to make them so clear that they would shine in the heavens for every man, woman, and child to read. The first of those principles that I would proclaim would be in opposition to Mr. Lincoln's doctrine of uniformity between the different States, and I would declare instead the sovereign right of each State to decide the slavery question as well as all other domestic questions for themselves, without interference from any other State or power whatsoever.

When that principle is recognized, you will have peace and harmony and fraternal feeling between all the States of this Union; until you do recognize that doctrine, there will be sectional warfare agitating and distracting the country. What does Mr. Lincoln propose? He says that the Union cannot exist divided into free and slave States. If it cannot endure thus divided, then he must strive to make them all free or all slave, which will inevitably bring about a dissolution of the Union.

Gentlemen, I am told that my time is out, and I am obliged to stop.

Interpretation

Douglas opened the first in the series of seven debates with Lincoln by claiming that the old Whig and Democratic parties had agreed to the Compromise of 1850, and with it "the right of the people of each State and each Territory to decide their local and domestic institutions for themselves, subject only to the Federal Constitution." This same principle, he maintains, was at the heart of his own Kansas and Nebraska bill. But Lincoln and his friend Trumbull then cooperated in dissolving these old parties and forming in their place the new Republican party as an Abolitionist party in disguise. Douglas demands to know whether Lincoln still stood on the various "abolitionist" planks of that Republican platform, and whether he will proclaim the same principles in southern Illinois (much more friendly to slavery) as he does in the north.

Before proceeding further, Douglas explains his relation to these founders of the new Republican party (he calls it Black Republican), speaking familiarly of Lincoln (since they had known each other for a long time), noting his greater success in business and detailing, no doubt with mischievous irony, the (rather low) activities he engaged in, such as drinking, wrestling and officiating at horse-races and fist-fights. He then turns his attention to Lincoln's *House Divided* speech of a few months before. The founding fathers, Douglas insists, were guided by the same principle that now guides him. They left it to the people of each state, amid varying circumstances, to decide how they wanted to treat slavery. But Lincoln's abolitionism prevents him from accepting this principle and causes him to refuse to accept the Supreme Court's Dred Scott decision denying citizenship blacks, asserting his own unbending opposition to granting citizenship to them, Douglas challenges his audience to decide whether they favor it, appealing as strongly as he can to their anti-black sentiments. This government, he insists, was made by and for whites, not for "negroes, Indians, and other inferior races." Derisively responding to Lincoln's well-known habit of appealing to the Declaration of Independence on the equality of the races, Douglas declares the universal teaching of history to be that blacks "belong to an inferior race, and must always occupy an inferior position." This may not necessitate slavery, for "inferior and dependent beings" should be granted as much advantage as the public safety allows. But the disposition of the matter must be left to the people of each state, who may in some cases grant citizenship and the right to vote to blacks, and in others consign them to slavery. This is what our forefathers intended, and on its basis we "have become, from a feeble nation, the most powerful on the face of the earth" and can keep "increasing in territory, in power, in strength, and in glory" and "guide the friends of freedom throughout the civilized world." Lincoln's principles, on the other hand, can only lead to a "sectional war between the Free States and the Slave States."

Lincoln begins his response to this powerful assault by denying the charge that he cooperated with Trumbull in replacing the old parties or consented to the new Republican party's platform. He quotes at length from his Peoria address of four years before, beginning with an attack on the moral indifference embodied in the Kansas and Nebraska Act of allowing the people to vote slavery in or out. "This *declared* indifference, but, as I must think, covert *real* zeal for the spread of slavery, I cannot but hate. I hate it because of the monstrous injustice of slavery itself." He then (in the passage quoted) goes on to admit that he really does not know what to do about the freed slaves. Sending them to Liberia won't work. Keeping them as underlings might not better their condition. "What next? Free them, and make them politically and socially our equals?"

By this excerpt from his earlier speech and the discussion he now adds, Lincoln testifies to the central importance of this issue. Since his treatment of it here has many parallels in the other debates and elsewhere, let us again (as before with the Peoria speech) examine it with some care. Lincoln says his own feelings will not admit of making the negroes politically and socially equal to whites, but even if his would, those of "the great mass of white people will not." But are "feelings" the last word? "Whether this feeling accords with justice and sound judgment is not the sole question, if, indeed, it is any part of it. A universal feeling, whether well or ill-founded, cannot be safely disregarded." By raising this consideration, Lincoln suggests that anti-negro feeling on the part of white people—he calls it "universal"—may not accord with justice and sound judgment, in which case it would be a mere prejudice. Having raised this issue—thus making sure that we know that, by the standard of truth, sound judgment and not feeling is the criterion—Lincoln shows the difference between what is true and what is politically viable. The feelings of the great mass of white people must prevail because of their political power. Notice that Lincoln sees fit to withhold his own judgment on the matter, as distinguished from the feelings he expresses. Nor does he give us the basis for his feelings, which could be a reluctance to offend other whites rather than a direct revulsion for blacks.

He concludes this part of his argument with: "We cannot, then, make them equals." Having said this, it is hard to understand his next sentence, declaring that "systems of gradual emancipation might be adopted." Perhaps he has two different situations in mind. Whites might not consent to live with blacks if an overall emancipation takes place at one time, but a gradual emancipation might overcome this difficulty. Only a few sentences later, however, Lincoln seems to take this back, declaring flatly that "There is a physical difference between the two, which, in my judgment, will probably forever forbid their living together upon the footing of perfect equality." Here the idea of superiority and inferiority gives way to physical differences—apparently a reference to differences in appearance between the races. That is an enormous concession to a possible equality of mind and soul, the crucial indices of superiority and inferiority and hence of slavery itself. Lincoln immediately adds that these physical differences themselves entail the relationship of superiority or inferiority, and, like Judge Douglas, admits he is "in favor of the race to which I belong having the superior position." This admission only weakens the justification for negro slavery. It is hardly complimentary to the white race, since it rests not on any superior qualification possessed by that race but on nothing more than Lincoln's preferring to be on top rather than underneath—especially since Judge Douglas is already there watching. At this point, however, and in the face of this seeming case for racial inequality, Lincoln adduces the Declaration of Independence, insisting that the black is the white's equal in possessing the same natural rights to life, liberty and the pursuit of happiness. "I agree with Judge Douglas he is not my equal in many respects—certainly not in color, perhaps not in moral or intellectual endowment. But in the right to eat the bread, without the leave of anybody else, which his own hand earns, he is my equal, and the equal of Judge Douglas, and the equal of every living man."

To be "equal" or "unequal" in color is a very strange expression: we would normally say "the same" or "different." But inequality of color is the only inequality Lincoln refers to as "certain." Regarding the much more important moral or intellectual inequality between the races, he will only say "perhaps." This is a most important "perhaps," since it shows that Lincoln is far from sharing the conviction of moral and intellectual superiority so widespread among whites and underpinning their prejudice against blacks. From this the possibility arises that antipathy for blacks based on color might be counterbalanced by demonstrated moral and intellectual capacity on their part, and toward this end gradual emancipation might be an essential means, since it would permit whites to adjust their views as their experience of free blacks improves. If this is true, gradual emancipation can re-emerge as a serious alternative.

Assuming this to be Lincoln's innermost reasoning, it is obvious that such thoughts could not be expressed openly without the most drastic repercussions, including sure electoral defeat. In order to appreciate fully his need for caution in expressing himself, we need only put ourselves in his place. Again and again, Douglas pilloried the "Black" Republicans, accusing Lincoln of wanting political and social equality for blacks and using every possible occasion to blast him for befriending blacks at the cost of whites, for favoring miscegenation, and so on. Lincoln's only recourse was to adhere to the principles of the Declaration, insisting on the injustice of slavery, while leaving unclear the ultimate disposition of the black race—surely a weakness in his position, but one he could not avoid. The policy required, at the same time, that he pretend to share the general prejudice against the black while giving small indications of his true thoughts and real long range hopes. He was not being hypocritical, but he did, repeatedly, dissimulate for good ends.

This may account for Lincoln's willingness to drop his thoughts about colonization rather abruptly in this speech. It also makes us wonder how serious he was later as president when, in a last-minute and unsuccessful effort, he tried to convince a small band of blacks at the White House to join in his colonization plans. He must have known the idea was as unpopular with blacks as it was impractical. In short, the blacks were here to stay. It also accounts for two other facts: Lincoln's reluctance to free the slaves all at once, even as a war measure, and, after he had freed them, his eagerness to find ways of gradually absorbing them into the political life of the nation.

A bit later, Lincoln defends his use of the House Divided metaphor. He does not try to criticize Douglas' historical review of the compromises between North and South that had prevailed before 1854. Instead he concentrates on the repeal that year of the Missouri Compromise in Douglas' Kansas-Nebraska Act and the Dred Scott decision of 1857. Together these pose a new threat—"the *perpetuity and nationalization of slavery*"—that justifies the "house divided" metaphor. The founders had acted decisively to limit the extension of slavery. They kept it out of the new Territories through legislation, and also by law cut off the slave trade (a prohibition allowed by the Constitution itself). These are the crucial points missed by Douglas, who would allow slavery to spread whe-rever a majority of whites want it. And Douglas does not seem to realize that his support for "popular sovereignty" and his support for the *Dred Scott* decision are inconsistent with each other. For pursuant to that decision, a vote to keep slavery out of a state or territory cannot succeed, since anyone who then wishes to bring slaves into the area will have the protection of the Supreme Court in doing so. What Lincoln fears, as the next logical step, is a Supreme Court decision adding that not only Congress and Territorial legislatures (as already decided by *Dred Scott*) but the States themselves have no constitutional right to exclude slavery: "When that is decided and acquiesced in, the whole thing is done."

Lincoln denies that his policy of returning the institution of slavery to the founders' plan for it "can have any tendency to set the Northern and the South-ern States at war with one another," as Douglas had charged. It is hard to con-sider this his true judgment. Though civil war was still more than two years away when Lincoln gave his *House Divided* speech, the threat he posed to the South—the South of 1858—was clear. Despite the historical evidence he pre-sented, most Southerners would not return to the pre-1854 situation, or consent to slavery's being kept out of new areas, or—even worse—admit that it was ultimately doomed to extinction. Nor does Lincoln relent from renewing, in this First Debate, his charge that a pro-slavery conspiracy was afoot, involving not only Douglas but the president (Buchanan) and Chief Justice Taney as well. All along, as the controversy became more intense, he must have realized that the South would be extremely upset with his views, and upset even more should he ever mount higher in politics. To appreciate his true situation, as he himself un-derstood it, we must think it entirely possible that he saw little or no way of avoiding the civil war, consistent with preserving the Union as it was originally envisioned by the founders. Try as he might to avoid this outcome, his chances of success would remain slim.

The contest with Douglas was more than a set of debates in the ordinary sense. It involved the formation of what Lincoln calls "public sentiment," for "he who moulds public sentiment goes deeper than he who enacts statutes or pronounces decisions." The contest, in short, was for the mind and soul of America, or of as much of America as would listen and learn from it. On his side

Douglas had the repeal of the Missouri Compromise, the Kansas-Nebraska Act, the democratic appeal (false though it was) of his principle of "popular sovereignty," strong popular prejudice against political and social equality for the black, upon which he called constantly, and, finally, the Supreme Court's recently pronounced view of the constitutional place of the black. It is with this last element of Douglas' strength that Lincoln again takes issue at the end of his speech. He accuses Douglas of simply obeying the Court's *Dred Scott* decision without saying why that decision is right. It was a "Thus saith the Lord." Lincoln himself will not consider Supreme Court decisions sacrosanct. He cites both Jefferson and Jackson, against Douglas, reminds Douglas of the opposing views of the matter he had previously held, and finally recounts in humorous fashion the story of Douglas' adventure into the judgeship which gave him the title "Judge."

Lincoln ends with an appeal to Henry Clay. Citing by heart one of Clay's most beautiful passages, he re-asserts with its help the basic point—that the Declaration of Independence covered blacks as well as whites. Douglas is doing his utmost not only to protect slavery where it is but to make it impossible for states and territories alike to outlaw it, should they wish to. In his concluding response, Douglas again assails Lincoln for surreptitiously departing from the Republican platform and once more demands answers to his questions. He wants Lincoln to concede that he would oppose admitting a new state that had chosen to have slavery, and, generally, that he opposes each state having the right of doing as it pleases on the slavery question. Angrily, he denounces as "an infamous lie" Lincoln's charge of conspiracy, accusing him of "unpardonable presumption" in tarnishing the reputations of "the purest and best of living men"—a reference, it seems, to President Buchanan, President Pierce and the nine judges of the Supreme Court. He goes so far as to call Lincoln "an ignorant man."

Douglas ends with a proud avowal of his principles. "Democracy is founded upon the eternal principle of right," and this requires letting the people of each state decide the slavery question for themselves. Only the recognition of this principle can bring an end to the "sectional warfare agitating and distracting the country," whereas Lincoln's House Divided view will inevitably bring about the "dissolution of the Union." There was some truth to this charge, but Douglas seems not to care about the relative weight of the slave and free states in the Union, let alone the fate of the black. Nor does he see the implications of the *Dred Scott* decision, which Lincoln correctly understood as making it possible for slaves and slavery to be brought into any part of the Union, regardless of whether slavery has been outlawed there or not. Having removed the geographic limits set on slavery by the Missouri Compromise, Douglas, with his Kansas-Nebraska Act, opened up the contention between slave and free forces to all new areas, north and south. The result was, not the amelioration of the racial problem, as Douglas had promised and kept promising, but its enormous amplification and intensification. What, then, were the real alternatives? Either Lincoln's position, with its obvious dangers of imminent civil war, or Douglas', with its piecemeal struggles and eventual explosion, possibly under circumstances much less favorable to the North.

Chapter 10

Second Lecture on Discoveries and Inventions, February 11, 1859

This unusual lecture was delivered at Illinois College and to several societies in Illinois devoted to the discussion of public issues.

Text

We have all heard of Young America. He is the most *current* youth of the age. Some think him conceited, and arrogant; but has he not reason to entertain a rather extensive opinion of himself? Is he not the inventor and owner of the *present*, and sole hope of the *future*? Men, and things, everywhere, are ministering unto him. Look at his apparel, and you shall see cotten fabrics from Manchester and Lowell; flax-linen from Ireland; wool-cloth from silk from France; furs from the Arctic regions, with a buffalo-robe from the Rocky Mountains, as a general out-sider. At his table, besides plain bread and meat made at home, are sugar from Louisiana; coffee and fruits from the tropics; salt from Turk's Island; fish from New-foundland; tea from China, and spices from the Indies. The whale of the Pacific furnishes his candle-light; he has a diamond-ring from Brazil; a gold-watch from California, and a spanish cigar from Havanna. He not only has a present supply of all these, and much more; but thousands of hands are engaged in producing fresh supplies, and other thousands, in bringing them to him. The iron horse is panting, and impatient, to carry him everywhere, in no time; and the lightening stands ready harnessed to take and bring his tidings in a trifle less than no time. He owns a large part of the world, by right of possessing it; and all the rest by right of *wanting* it, and *intending* to have it. As Plato had for the immortality of the soul, so Young America has "a pleasing hope—a fond desire—a longing after" territory. He has a great passion—a perfect rage—for the *"new"*; particularly new men for office, and the new earth mentioned in the revelations, in which, being no more sea, there must be about three times as much land as in the present. He is a great friend of humanity; and his desire for land is not selfish, but merely an impulse to extend the area of freedom. He is anxious to fight for the liberation of enslaved nations and colonies, provided, always, they *have* land, and have *not* any liking for his interference. As to those who have no land, and would be glad of help from any quarter, he considers *they* can afford to wait a few hundred years longer. In knowledge he is particularly rich. He knows all that can possibly be known; inclines to believe in spiritual rappings, and is the unquestioned inventor of *"Manifest Destiny."* His horror is for all that is old, particularly "Old Fogy"; and if there be any thing old which he can endure, it is only old whiskey and old tobacco.

If the said Young America really is, as he claims to be, the owner of all present, it must be admitted that he has considerable advantage of Old Fogy. Take, for instance, the first of all fogies, father Adam. There he stood, a very perfect physical man, as poets and painters inform us; but he must have been very ignorant, and simple in his habits. He had had no sufficient time to learn much by observation; and he had no near neighbors to teach him anything. No part of his breakfast had been brought from the other side of the world; and it is quite probable, he had no conception of the world having any other side. In all of these things, it is very plain, he was no equal of Young America; the most that can be said is, that *according to his chance* he may have been quite as much of a man as his very self-complaisant descendant. Little as was what he knew, let the Youngster discard all he has learned from others, and then show, if he can, any advantage on his side. In the way of *land,* and *live stock,* Adam was quite in the ascendant. He had dominion over all the earth, and all the living things upon, and round about it. The land has been sadly divided out since; but never fret, Young America will *re-annex* it.

The great difference between Young America and Old Fogy, is the result of *Discoveries, Inventions,* and *Improvements.* These, in turn, are the result of *observation, reflection* and *experiment.* For instance, it is quite certain that ever since water has been boiled in covered vessels, men have seen the lids of the vessels rise and fall a little, with a sort of fluttering motion, by force of the steam; but so long as this was not specially observed, and reflected and experimented upon, it came to nothing. At length however, after many thousand years, some man observes this long-known effect of hot water lifting a pot-lid, and begins a train of reflection upon it. He says "Why, to be sure, the force that lifts the pot-lid, will lift any thing else, which is no heavier than the pot-lid." "And, as man has much hard lifting to do, can not this hot-water power be made to help him?" He has become a little excited on the subject, and he fancies he hears a voice answering "Try me" He does try it; and the *observation, reflection,* and *trial* gives to the world the control of that tremendous, and now well known agent, called steam-power. This is not the actual history in detail, but the general principle.

But was this first inventor of the application of steam, wiser or more ingenious than those who had gone before him? Not at all. Had he not learned much of them, he never would have succeeded—probably, never would have thought of making the attempt. To be fruitful in invention, it is indispensable to have a *habit* of observation and reflection; and this *habit,* our steam friend acquired, no doubt, from those who, to him, were old fogies. But for the difference in *habit* of observation, why did yankees, almost instantly, discover gold in California, which had been trodden upon, and over-looked by indians and Mexican greasers, for centuries? Gold-mines are not the only mines overlooked in the same way. There are more mines above the Earth's surface than below it. All nature—the whole world, material, moral, and intellectual,—is a mine; and, in Adam's day, it was a wholly unexplored mine. Now, it was the destined work of Adam's race to develope, by discoveries, inventions, and improvements, the hidden treasures of this mine. But Adam had nothing to turn his attention to the work. If he should do anything in the way of invention, he had first to invent the art of invention—the *instance* at least, if not the *habit* of observation and reflection. As might be expected he seems not to have been a very observing man at first; for it appears he went about naked a considerable length of time, before he even noticed that obvious fact. But when he did observe it, the observation was not lost upon him; for it immediately led to the first of all inventions, of which we have any direct account—*the fig-leaf apron.*

The inclination to exchange thoughts with one another is probably an original impulse of our nature. If I be in pain I wish to let you know it, and to ask your sympathy and assistance; and my pleasurable emotions also, I wish to communicate to, and share with you. But to carry on such communication, some *instrumentality* is indispensable. Accordingly speech—articulate sounds rattled off from the tongue—was used by our first parents, and even by Adam, before the creation of Eve. He gave names to the animals while she was still a bone in his side; and he broke out quite volubly when she first stood before him, the best present of his maker. From this it would appear that speech was not an invention of man, but rather the direct gift of his Creator. But whether Divine gift, or invention, it is still plain that if a mode of communication had been left to invention, *speech* must have been the first, from the superior adaptation to the end, of the organs of speech, over every other means within the whole range of nature. Of the organs of speech the tongue is the principal; and if we shall test it, we shall find the capacities of the tongue, in the utterance of articulate sounds, absolutely wonderful. You can count from one to one hundred, quite distinctly in about forty seconds. In doing this two hundred and eighty three distinct sounds or syllables are uttered, being seven to each second; and yet there shall be enough difference between every two, to be easily recognized by the ear of the hearer. What other *signs* to represent *things* could possibly be produced so rapidly? or, even, if ready made, could be *arranged* so rapidly to express the sense? *Motions* with the hands, are no adequate substitute. *Marks* for the recognition of the eye—*writing*—although a wonderful auxiliary for speech, is no worthy substitute for it. In addition to the more slow and laborious process of getting up a communication in writing, the materials—pen, ink, and paper—are not always at hand. But one always has his tongue with him, and the breath of his life is the ever-ready material with which it works. Speech, then, by enabling different individuals to interchange thoughts, and thereby to combine their powers of observation and reflection, greatly facilitates useful discoveries and inventions. What one observes, and would himself infer nothing from, he tells to another, and that other at once sees a valuable hint in it. A result is thus reached which neither *alone* would have arrived at.

And this reminds me of what I passed unnoticed before, that the very first invention was a joint operation. Eve having shared with Adam in the getting up of the apron. And, indeed, judging from the fact that sewing has come down to our times as "woman's work" it is very probable she took the leading part; he, perhaps, doing no more than to stand by and thread the needle. That proceeding may be reckoned as the mother of all "Sewing societies"; and the first and most perfect "world's fair" all inventions and all inventors then in the world, being on the spot.

But speech alone, valuable as it ever has been, and is, has not advanced the condition of the world much. This is abundantly evidenced when we look at the degraded condition of all those tribes of human creatures who have no considerable additional means of communicating thoughts. *Writing*—the art of communicating thoughts to the mind, through the eye—is the great invention of the world. Great in the astonishing range of analysis and combination which necessarily underlies the most crude and general conception of it—great, very great in enabling us to converse with the dead, the absent, and the unborn, at all distances of time and of space; and great, not only in its direct benefits, but greatest help, to all other inventions. Suppose the art, with all conception of it, were this day lost to the world, how long, think you, would it be, before even Young America could get up the letter A. with any adequate notion of using it to advantage? The precise period at which writing was invented, is not known; but it certainly was as early as the time of Moses; from which we may safely infer that it's inventors were very old fogies.

Webster, at the time of the writing of his Dictionary, speaks of the English Language as then consisting of seventy or eighty thousand words. If so, the language in which the five books of Moses were written must, at that time, now thirty three or four hundred years ago, have consisted of at least one quarter as many, or, twenty thousand. When we remember that words are *sounds* merely, we shall conclude that the idea of representing those sounds by *marks*, so that whoever should at any time after see the marks, would understand what sounds they meant, was a bold and ingenius conception, not likely to occur to one man of a million, in the run of a thousand years. And, when it did occur, a distinct mark for each word, giving twenty thousand different marks first to be learned, and afterwards remembered, would follow as the second thought, and would present such a difficulty as would lead to the conclusion that the whole thing was impracticable. But the *necessity* still would exist; and we may readily suppose that the idea was conceived, and lost, and reproduced, and dropped, and taken up again and again, until at last, the thought of dividing sounds into parts, and making a mark, not to represent a whole sound, but only part of one, and then of combining these marks, not very many in number, upon the principles of permutation, so as to represent any and all of the whole twenty thousand words, and even any additional number was somehow conceived and pushed into practice. This was the invention of *phoenetic* writing, as distinguished from the clumsy picture writing of some of the nations. That it was difficult of conception and execution, is apparent, as well by the foregoing reflections, as by the fact that so many tribes of men have come down from Adam's time to ours without ever having possessed it. It's utility may be conceived, by the reflection that, to *it* we owe everything which distinguishes us from savages. Take it from us, and the Bible, all history, all science, all government, all commerce, and nearly all social intercourse go with it.

The great activity of the tongue, in articulating sounds, has already been mentioned; and it may be of some passing interest to notice the wonderful powers of the *eye*, in conveying ideas to the mind from writing. Take the same example of the numbers from *one* to *one hundred*, written down, and you can run your eye over the list, and be assured that every number is in it, in about one half the time it would require to pronounce the words with the voice; and not only so, but you can, in the same short time, determine whether every word is spelled correctly, by which it is evident that every separate letter, amounting to eight hundred and sixty four, has been recognized, and reported to the mind, within the incredibly short space of twenty seconds, or one third of a minute.

I have already intimated my opinion that in the world's history, certain inventions and discoveries occurred, of peculiar value, on account of their great efficiency in facilitating all other inventions and discoveries. Of these were the arts of writing and of printing—the discovery of America, and the introduction of Patent-laws. The date of the first, as already stated, is unknown; but it certainly was as much as fifteen hundred years before the Christian era; the second—printing—came in 1436, or nearly three thousand years after the first. The others followed more rapidly—the discovery of America in 1492, and the first patent laws in 1624. Though not apposite to my present purpose, it is but justice to the fruitfulness of that period, to mention two other important events—the Lutheran Reformation in 1517, and, still earlier, the invention of negroes, or, of the present mode of using them, in 1434. But, to return to the consideration of printing, it is plain that it is but the *other* half—and in real utility, the *better* half—of writing; and that both together are but the assistants of speech in the communication of thoughts between man and man. When man was possessed of speech alone, the chances of invention, discovery, and improvement, were very limited; but by the introduction of each of these, they were greatly multiplied. When writing was invented, any important observation, likely to lead to a discovery, had at least a chance of being written down, and consequently, a better chance of never being forgotten; and of being seen, and reflected upon, by a much greater number of persons; and thereby the chances of a valuable hint being caught, proportionately augmented. By this means the observation of a single individual might lead to an important invention, years, and even centuries after he was dead. In one word, by means of writing, the seeds of invention were more permanently preserved, and more widely sown. And yet, for the three thousand years during which printing remained undiscovered after writing was in use, it was only a small portion of the people who could write, or read writing; and consequently the field of invention, though much extended, still continued very

limited. At length printing came. It gave ten thousand copies of any written matter, quite as cheaply as ten were given before; and consequently a thousand
minds were brought into the field where there was but one before. This was a
great *gain*; and history shows a great *change* corresponding to it, in point of
time. I will venture to consider *it*, the true termination of that period called "the
dark ages." Discoveries, inventions, and improvements followed rapidly, and
have been increasing their rapidity ever since. The effects could not come, all at
once. It required time to bring them out; and they are still coming. The *capacity*
to read, could not be multiplied as fast as the *means* of reading. Spelling-books
just began to go into the hands of the children; but the teachers were not very
numerous, or very competent; so that it is safe to infer they did not advance so
speedily as they do now-a-days. It is very probable—almost certain—that the
great mass of men, at that time, were utterly unconscious, that their *conditions*,
or their *minds* were capable of improvement. They not only looked upon the
educated few as superior beings; but they supposed themselves to be naturally
incapable of rising to equality. To immancipate the mind from this false and
under estimate of itself, is the great task which printing came into the world to
perform. It is difficult for us, *now* and *here*, to conceive how strong this slavery
of the mind was; and how long it did, of necessity, take, to break it's shackles,
and to get a habit of freedom of thought, established. It is, in this connection, a
curious fact that a new country is most favorable—almost necessary—to the
immancipation of thought, and the consequent advancement of civilization and
the arts. The human family originated as is thought, somewhere in Asia, and
have worked their way princip[al]ly Westward. Just now, in civilization, and the
arts, the people of Asia are entirely behind those of Europe; those of the East of
Europe behind those of the West of it; while we, here in America, *think* we discover, and invent, and improve, faster than any of them. *They* may think this is
arrogance; but they can not deny that Russia has called on us to show her how to
build steam-boats and railroads—while in the older parts of Asia, they scarcely
know that such things as S.Bs & RR.s. exist. In anciently inhabited countries,
the dust of ages—a real downright old-fogy-ism—seems to settle upon, and
smother the intellects and energies of man. It is in this view that I have mentioned the discovery of America as an event greatly favoring and facilitating
useful discoveries and inventions.

Next came the Patent laws. These began in England in 1624; and, in this
country, with the adoption of our constitution. Before then [these?], any man
might instantly use what another had invented; so that the inventor had no special advantage from his own invention. The patent system changed this; secured
to the inventor, for a limited time, the exclusive use of his invention; and thereby
added the fuel of *interest* to the *fire* of genius, in the discovery and production of
new and useful things.

Interpretation

This is the second lecture thus named, the first having been delivered almost a year before on April 6, 1858. The supposition that they comprise two halves of one lecture is highly unlikely, since the example of Adam's fig-leaf apron, the first of all inventions, is used in both and would be plainly repetitious if they were expected to form a single whole. The style of the first is different too—more of a cataloguing of types of inventions, without a broader framework. Given Lincoln's rhetorical abilities, it is even difficult to imagine him thinking it suitable for a lecture at all.

The 1859 text is clearly more mature and complete, but it too has some unusual features. Why does it begin with an extensive satire on Young America, apparently taking the side of "Old Fogies" like Adam, yet later heap praise on this very America? Why does it end hanging in air with a paragraph about patent laws rather than with anything that really sounds like a conclusion? Why, along the way, does Lincoln mention the Lutheran Revolution of 1517 and the beginning of negro slavery (he actually speaks of "inventing" negroes) as if they were both inventions properly placed alongside the others he names?

The general picture conveyed by the lecture is this. Invention is the chief characteristic of man, and the source of human progress. Mankind, created by God in a less than perfect condition, becomes more civilized and generally improves his lot by inventions—inventions that, far from being regular or inevitable, at least at first seem largely matters of chance. His improvement is of his own making, not God's, and of this improvement America is the peak. Thus, the story of mankind that begins with Old Fogy Adam ends with Young America and the advent of a new democratic age. Having begun with the Bible, it proceeds soon afterward to leave the Bible behind, and ends with it very far behind.

To this happy picture the opening of the talk stands in marked contrast. Young America is portrayed as something like a smug, spoiled, even arrogant adolescent, ministered to by the rest of the world through commerce, thinking of himself as the "inventor and owner of the present, and sole hope for the future," a lover of his own liberty and eager to spread liberty to others, so long as it brings more territory to himself. It is not a picture of thoughtful maturity. The yearning for the immortality of the soul, identified by Lincoln with Plato rather than the Bible, constitutes almost the polar opposite of what Young America represents, which is physical convenience and pleasure, on the one hand, and political expansion, on the other—all with the help of a rapidly multiplying technology.

Let's work our way through the speech gradually to see what it all means. In the midst of his satire (with epic overtones) on Young America, Lincoln shows that he fully understands how unbiblical it is by his reference to the Book of Revelations (21:1), with its vision of "a new heaven and a new earth," and the conversion of the seas to land. The way Young America looks upon this is simply as the tripling of the amount of land now in existence, with the promise of feeding even more his thirst for territory. His knowledge is very rich—in fact, "he knows all that can possibly be known." Yet Lincoln adds, in the same breath, that he "inclines to believe in spiritual rappings, and is the unquestioned inventor of "Manifest Destiny." How can the possessor of all knowledge believe in these rappings? Evidently Young America's knowledge does not keep him from being superstitious, or from bending a lingering belief in divine providence to suit his interests and make westward expansion to the Pacific America's destiny. The "knowledge" Lincoln refers to is undoubtedly modern science, with all of its great advances, particularly in the natural sciences. But by itself it does not bring virtue, nor an end to beliefs that have no basis in reason. We have not become better human beings, just more knowledgeable, and our passions, far from coming under rational control, simply have a larger field on which to operate.

These sobering reflections give way, in the lecture, to an analysis of human progress. "The great difference," Lincoln tells us, "between Young America and Old Fogy is the result of Discoveries, Inventions and Improvements. These, in turn, are the result of observation, reflection and experiment."

Without new intellectual habits, such progress can't occur. And then these spectacular words: "All nature—the whole world, material, moral and intellectual—is a mine; and in Adam's day it was a wholly unexplored mine." So Adam was deficient, but is it not noteworthy that neither before nor after the fall does the Bible give any sign that he was deficient in this way, and certainly no sign that his race was destined, through "discoveries, inventions and improvements," to develop the "hidden treasures of this mine"—the three-fold mine of Lincoln's words?

Inquiring into the origin of discovery and invention, Lincoln now turns more fully to the Bible, which for most of his audience declares the beginning of all things. Father Adam was the first of fogies. His physical perfection is attested to by poets and painters—i.e., not by the Bible, which, while not stating as much directly, allows an inference in this respect from the goodness of creation itself. But Adam was "very ignorant, and simple in his habits"—a great defect, in Lincoln's view, and therefore in somewhat shaky alliance with the idea of Adam's original goodness or perfection. Ignorance is Adam's great defect, not the sinfulness he and Eve soon demonstrate in the Garden of Eden. To their original sin, to this breach with God, Lincoln pays no direct attention at all, but by not mentioning it, this foremost characteristic of Biblical man leaps out as having been omitted.

This point is most clearly demonstrated in Lincoln's account of Adam's first invention, the fig-leaf apron. Adam "seems not to have been a very observing man at first; for it appears he went about naked a considerable length of time before he even noticed that obvious fact. But when he did observe it, the observation was not lost upon him." Whereupon he invented the fig-leaf apron. Nothing about Adam and Eve's disobedience to God and their eating of the tree of the knowledge of good and evil, for that was what caused them to be ashamed of their nakedness, not any simple "noticing" on Adam's part. Lincoln's account is only partly Biblical, and because of that really unbiblical.

Lincoln's next topic is the origin of speech: "The inclination to exchange thoughts with one another is probably an original impulse of our nature." Adam named the animals even before the creation of Eve, and "broke out quite volubly when she first stood before him." It "appears" from this, Lincoln says, that "speech was not an invention of man but a direct gift of his Creator." But, whether invention or Divine gift, "it is still plain that if a mode of communication had been left to invention, speech must have been the first." This is because the organs of speech are conducive to it. Here the description becomes entirely natural rather than religious, and quite distinctively Lincolnian. Waxing lyrical at the "absolutely wonderful" capacity of the tongue to form articulate sounds, he even has us make a little experiment for counting these sounds up. He marvels at how quickly writing enables the eye to follow ideas, again using arithmetical examples of his own making, almost as if to parallel modern science.

Having established the fact that speech is universal to man, but not born with him—that it had to be invented or created—Lincoln admits that by itself it did not do much to advance the "condition of the world." Look at the "degraded condition" of tribes that fail to go beyond speech. Writing is "the great invention of the world"—great in what underlies it and makes it possible, great in its extension of communication, and great in facilitating other inventions. Lincoln says writing goes back at least to the time of Moses, which he reckons at some thirty-three or thirty-four hundred years before (i.e., around 1500 B.C.), but he does not ascribe it to the Creator: it was invented by "very old fogies."

Without revealing the source of his information, Lincoln tells us that the English language in his day contained something like four times the number of words used in the five books of Moses. This in itself seems to signify the superiority of later times. But the point he wants to emphasize is that the invention of writing required "a bold and ingenious conception"—starting with the novel idea that a mark could represent a sound, advancing to making marks for whole words and finally breaking down words into phonetic parts, into letters. The original idea was so bold that it was "not likely to occur to one man of a million, in a run of a thousand years." To the development and perfection of writing we "owe everything that distinguished us from savages. Take it from us, and the Bible, all history, all science, all government, all commerce, and nearly all social intercourse go with it." This has some surprising implications. Does the coming of the Bible itself depend on the very singular invention of writing? Was the Bible something men wrote? And how could Adam's race have been "destined" to bring about improvements if improvements depended substantially on the singular discovery of writing?

Having surprised us by considering speech as almost an invention, and writing as the greatest invention, Lincoln now proceeds to what are normally considered inventions and discoveries. Those of greatest value in "facilitating all other inventions and discoveries," after writing itself, were printing, the discovery of America and the introduction of patent laws. Printing came in 1436, almost 3 thousand years after writing. The last two came in 1492 and 1624 respectively. It's here that Lincoln mentions, not as apposite to his subject but as doing "justice to the fruitfulness of that period," two rather strange additions: the Lutheran Reformation of 1517, and "the invention of negroes, or, of the present mode of using them," which he traces back to 1434.

It is rather ironical to regard, as an example of the "fruitfulness" of that time, the "invention" of negroes as slaves. Lincoln must have in mind the first uses by the Portuguese of West African blacks as slaves, an event now dated slightly later than the 1634 he uses. Strangely, in the midst of his outline of human progress through invention, slavery is thrown in—as if to signify the limitations of progress. As for the Lutheran Reformation, Lincoln does not quite dare call it an "invention," as he does with negro slavery, for this would make of it a simple human product, completely lacking in divine inspiration—and it was Luther who began the movement leading to the Protestantism shared by most Americans. Nor does he indicate why it has any relation to his talk whatsoever. Taken together, these two examples do suggest that historical events are inventions too, that they are part of innovative thoughts generally—of all the things we think of and act upon for specific purposes. In that sense all conscious actions are inventions, just as all inventions are conscious actions.

For the rest of his talk, Lincoln will discuss three discoveries after writing, starting with printing. Printing is the other and better half of writing. Writing helped discovery and invention, but it took three thousand years for printing to be discovered. By it, the number of those who could communicate was vastly expanded: "This was a great gain" and constituted the true end of "the dark ages." After it, numerous discoveries followed rapidly, and have been occurring even more rapidly ever since. The greatest effect of this progress was moral and political. Till then, "the great mass of men were utterly unconscious that their conditions, or their minds were capable of improvement." Lincoln concludes that "To immancipate the mind from this false and under estimate of itself, is the great task which printing came into the world to perform." It broke the "slavery of the mind," and made it possible to establish freedom of thought.

The point of view Lincoln adopts here is wholly that of the Enlightenment. It is not the furtherance of the Bible, nor even of its reinvigoration in Luther's reformation, that is the object of progress. It is freedom of thought, and with it the possibility of democracy—a word Lincoln somehow refrains from introducing. In fact, all history prior to that point is part of the "dark ages," including classical antiquity, so what we must have here is the greatest of all revolutions in human affairs. This enables Lincoln to make his transition to the discovery of America, as his third peak. A new country was most favorable to the "immancipation" of thought and "the consequent advancement of civilization and the arts." So it is really a combination of this freedom with the general concerns of civilization and the arts that constitutes the object of the whole progress. The human family, Lincoln says, is thought to have originated in Asia and from there kept moving westward. And so it is with civilization and the arts, with Asia lagging behind Europe, and Europe lagging behind America.

The tone of this remark is hardly Biblical. The "is thought" points us in the direction of modern history and science, not only because the placement indicated by the Bible is ignored but because, as it turns out, the birthplace of Biblical religion was in an Asia that remains backward. And now we come upon a reminder of the lecture's opening, for "we here in America think we discover, and invent, and improve, faster" than the entire rest of the world. They may think we're arrogant, but Russia asks us to build steamboats and railroads for her, and Asia hardly knows they exist. "In anciently inhabited countries, the dust of ages—a real downright old-fogyism—seems to settle upon, and smother the intellect and energies of man."

After this, the lecture ends abruptly with a simple reference to the English and American introduction of patent laws as an advantage that would greatly assist "the discovery and production of new and useful things." But the steamboat and the railroad hardly suffice as indicators of a general improvement in civilization, nor is the mining of hidden material and even intellectual riches any sign of what happens in the moral world. Momentarily, Lincoln has adopted the standpoint of Young America, and taken its side against all comers. But we cannot forget his satirical opening portrait, and that may be the concluding paragraph the lecture needs. After reading about patents we should return to this opening, which questions the moral maturity of Young America. It is the freedom of the mind, the releasing of human energies, the new confidence of the average man, not the material riches, that is America's most valuable possession. And Lincoln's whole point in the lecture is to show how dependent on the Old Fogies of the past Young America really is. The difference between Young America and Adam is due not simply to the former's own efforts, raising himself by his own bootstraps, but to the accumulated "discoveries, inventions and improvements" that preceded them.

Is Lincoln an optimist or a pessimist about modern progress? Somewhere in between. But he lived at a time when modern technology was in its boyhood. What would he have thought amid the atomic bombs, television, tapes, aircraft, birth control devices and computers of today? What would the coming of communism and fascism have signified to him? Remember American expansionism, and its potentiality for war. Remember the invention of Negroes. It is not likely that Lincoln would have too greatly underestimated man's capacity for evildoing, though he might well have been surprised, even shocked, by the forms it took in the twentieth century.

Chapter 11

The Address on Agriculture, September 30, 1859

Lincoln gave this address at the annual fair of the Wisconsin State Agricultural Society in Milwaukee.

Text

Members of the Agricultural Society and Citizens of Wisconsin:

Agricultural Fairs are becoming an institution of the country; they are useful in more ways than one; they bring us together, and thereby make us better acquainted, and better friends than we otherwise should be. From the first appearance of man upon the earth, down to very recent times, the words *"stranger"* and *"enemy"* were *quite* or *almost*, synonymous. Long after civilized nations had defined robbery and murder as high crimes, and had affixed severe punishments to them, when practiced among and upon their own people respectively, it was deemed no offence, but even meritorious, to rob, and murder, and enslave *strangers*, whether as nations or as individuals. Even yet, this has not totally disappeared. The man of the highest moral cultivation, in spite of all that abstract principle can do, likes him whom he does know, much better than him whom he does not know. To correct the evils, great and small, which spring from want of sympathy, and from positive enmity, among *strangers*, as nations, or as individuals, is one of the highest functions of civilization. To this end, our Agricultural Fairs contribute in no small degree. They make more pleasant, and more strong, and more durable, the bond of social and political union among us.

Again, if as, Pope declares, "happiness is our being's end and aim," our fairs contribute much to that end and aim, as occasions of recreation—as holidays. Constituted as man is, he has positive need of occasional recreation; and whatever can give him this, associated with virtue and advantage, and free from vice and disadvantage, is a positive good. Such recreation our Fairs afford. They

195

are a present pleasure, to be followed by no pain, as a consequence; they are a present pleasure, making the future more pleasant.

But the chief use of agricultural Fairs is to aid in improving the great calling of *Agriculture*, in all its departments, and minute divisions; to make mutual exchange of agricultural discovery, information and knowledge; so that, at the end, *all* may know everything, which may have been known to but *one* or to but a *few*, at the beginning—to bring together especially all which is supposed to not be generally known, because of recent discovery or invention.

And not only to bring together, and to impart all that has been accidentally discovered or invented upon ordinary motive; but, by exciting emulation, for premiums, and for the pride and honor of success—of triumph, in some sort—to stimulate that discovery and invention into extraordinary activity. In this, these Fairs are kindred to the patent clause in the Constitution of the United States; and to the department and practical system, based upon that clause.

One feature I believe, of every fair, is a regular *address*. The Agricultural Society of the young, prosperous, and soon to be great State of Wisconsin, has done me the high honor of selecting me to make that address on this occasion—an honor for which I make my profound and grateful acknowledgement.

I presume I am not expected to employ the time assigned me, in the mere flattery of farmers, as a class. My opinion of them is that, in proportion to numbers, they are neither better nor worse than other people. In the nature of things they are more numerous than any other class; and I believe there really are more attempts at flattering them than any other; the reason of which I cannot perceive, unless it be that they can cast more votes than any other. On reflection, I am not quite sure that there is not cause of suspicion against you in selecting me, in some sort a politician and in no sort a farmer, to address you.

But farmers, being the most numerous class, it follows that their interest is the largest interest. It also follows that that interest is most worthy of all to be cherished and cultivated—that if there be inevitable conflict between that interest and any other, that other should yield.

Again, I suppose it is not expected of me to impart to you much specific information on Agriculture. You have no reason to believe, and do not believe, that I possess it. If that were what you seek in this address, any one of your own number, or class, would be more able to furnish it.

You, perhaps, do expect me to give some general interest to the occasion; and to make some general suggestions, on practical matters. I shall attempt nothing more. And in such suggestions by me, quite likely very little will be new to you, and a large part of the rest possibly already known to be erroneous.

My first suggestion is an inquiry as to the effect of greater *thoroughness* in all the departments of agriculture than now prevails in the Northwest—perhaps I might say in America. To speak entirely within bounds, it is known that fifty bushels of wheat, or one hundred bushels of Indian corn, can be produced from an acre. Less than a year ago I saw it stated that a man, by extraordinary care and labor, had produced of wheat, what was equal to two hundred bushels from an acre. But take fifty of wheat, and one hundred of corn, to be the *probability*, and compare with it the actual crops of the country. Many years ago I saw it stated in a Patent Office Report that eighteen bushels to the acre was the average crop throughout the wheat growing region of the United States; and this year an intelligent farmer of Illinois assured me that he did not believe the land harvested in that State this season, had yielded more than an average of eight bushels to the acre. The brag crop I heard of in our vicinity was two thousand bushels from ninety acres. Many crops were threshed, producing no more than three bushels to the acre; much was cut, and then abandoned as not worth threshing; and much was abandoned as not worth cutting. As to Indian corn, and indeed, most other crops, the case has not been much better. For the last four years I do not believe the ground planted with corn in Illinois, has produced an average of twenty bushels to the acre. It is true, that heretofore we have had better crops, with no better cultivation; but I believe it is also true that the soil has never been pushed up to one-half of its capacity.

What would be the effect upon the farming interest to push the soil up to something near its full capacity? Unquestionably it will take more labor to produce *fifty* bushels from an acre, than it will to produce *ten* bushels from the same acre. But will it take more labor to produce fifty bushes from *one* acre, than from *five*? Unquestionably, thorough cultivation will require more labor to the *acre*; but will it require more to the *bushel*? If it should require just as *much* to the bushel, there are some *probable*, and several *certain* advantages in favor of the thorough practice. It is probable it would develope those unknown causes, or develope unknown cures for those causes, which of late years have cut down our crops below their former average. It is almost certain, I think, that in the deeper plowing, analysis of soils, experiments with manures and varieties of seeds, observance of seasons, and the like, these cures would be found.

It is certain that thorough cultivation would spare half, or more than half, the cost of land, simply because the same product would be got from half, or from less than half the quantity of land. This proposition is self-evident, and can be made no plainer by repetitions or illustrations. The cost of land is a great item, even in new countries; and constantly grows greater and greater, in comparison with other items, as the country grows older.

It also would spare a large proportion of the making and maintaining of inclosures—the same, whether these inclosures should be hedges, ditches or fences. This, again, is a heavy item—heavy at first, and heavy in its continual demand for repairs. I remember once being greatly astonished by an apparently authentic exhibition of the proportion the cost of inclosures bears to all the other expenses of the farmer, though I can not remember exactly, what that proportion was. Any farmer, if he will, can ascertain, it in his own case, for himself.

Again, a great amount of "locomotion" is spared by thorough cultivation. Take fifty bushels of wheat, ready for harvest, standing upon a *single* acre; and it can be harvested in any of the known ways, with less than half the labor which would be required if it were spread over *five* acres. This would be true, if cut by the old hand sickle; true, to a greater extent if by the scythe and cradle; and to a still greater extent, if by the machinery now in use. These machines are chiefly valuable, as a means of substituting animal power for the power of men in this branch of farm-work. In the highest degree of perfection yet reached, in applying the horse power to harvesting, fully nine-tenths of the power is expended by the animal in carrying himself and dragging the machine over the field; leaving certainly not more than one-tenth to be applied directly to the only end of the whole operation—the gathering in the grain, and clipping of the straw. When grain is very thin on the ground, it is always more or less intermingled with weeds, chess and the like; and a large part of the power is expended in cutting these. It is plain that when the crop is very thick upon the ground, the larger proportion of the power is directly applied to gathering in and cutting it, and the smaller, to that which is totally useless as an end. And what I have said of harvesting is true, in a greater or less degree, of mowing, plowing, gathering in of crops generally, and, indeed, of almost all farm work.

The effect of thorough cultivation upon the farmer's own mind, and, in reaction through his mind, back upon his business, is perhaps quite equal to any other of its effects. Every man is proud of what he does *well*, and no man is proud of what he does *not* do well. With the former, his heart is in his work; and he will do twice as much of it with less fatigue. The latter he performs a little imperfectly, looks at it in disgust, turns from it, and imagines himself exceedingly tired. The little he has done, comes to nothing, for want of finishing.

The man who produces a good full crop will scarcely ever let any part of it go to waste. He will keep up the enclosure about it, and allow neither man nor beast to trespass upon it. He will gather it in due season, and store it in perfect security. Thus he labors with satisfaction, and saves himself the whole fruit of his labor.

The other, starting with no purpose for a full crop, labors less, and with less satisfaction; allows his fences to fall, and cattle to trespass; gathers not in due season, or not at all; and stores insecurely, or not at all. Thus the labor he has performed, is wasted away, little by little, till in the end, he derives scarcely anything from it.

The ambition for broad acres leads to poor farming even with men of energy. I scarcely ever knew a mammoth farm to sustain itself, much less to return a profit upon the outlay. I have more than once known a man to spend a respectable fortune upon one, fail and leave it, and then some man of more modest aims, get a small fraction of the ground, and make a good living upon it. Mammoth farms are like tools or weapons, which are too heavy to be handled. Ere long they are thrown aside, at a great loss.

The successful application of *steam power*, to farm work is a *desideratum*—especially a steam-plow. It is not enough that a machine operated by steam will really plow. To be successful, it must, all things considered, plow *better* than can be done with animal power. It must do all the work as well, and *cheaper*; or more *rapidly*, so as to get through more perfectly in *season*; or in some way afford an advantage over plowing with animals, else it is no success. I have never seen a machine intended for a steam-plow. Much praise and admiration are bestowed upon some of them; and they may be, for aught I know, already successful; but I have not perceived the demonstration of it. I have thought a good deal, in an abstract way, about a steam-plow. That one which shall be so contrived as to apply the larger proportion of its power to the cutting and turning the soil, and the smallest to the moving itself over the field, will be the best one. A very small stationary engine would draw a large gang of plows through the ground from a short distance to itself; but when it is not stationary, but has to move along like a horse, dragging the plows after it, it must have additional power to carry itself; and the difficulty grows by what is intended to overcome it; for what adds power, also adds size and weight to the machine, thus increasing again, the demand for power. Suppose you should construct the machine so as to cut a succession of short furrows, say a rod in length, transversely to the course the machine is locomoting, something like the shuttle in weaving. In such case the whole machine would move north only the width of a furrow, while in length the furrow would be a rod from east to west. In such case a very large proportion of the power would be applied to the actual plowing. But in this, too, there would be a difficulty, which would be the getting of the plow *into* and *out* of the ground, at the ends of all these short furrows.

I believe, however, ingenious men will, if they have not already, overcome the difficulties I have suggested. But there is still another, about which I am less sanguine. It is the supply of *fuel*, and especially of *water*, to make steam. Such supply is clearly practicable, but can the expense of it be borne? Steamboats live upon the water, and find their fuel at stated places. Steam-mills and other stationary steam machinery, have their stationary supplies of fuel and water. Railroad-locomotives have their regular wood and water station. But the steam-plow is less fortunate. It does not live upon the water; even if it be once at a water station, it will work away from it, and when it gets away can not return without leaving its work, at a great expense of its time and strength. It will occur that a wagon and horse team might be employed to supply it with fuel and water; but this, too, is expensive; and the question recurs, "Can the expense be borne?" When this is added to all other expenses, will not the plowing cost more than in the old way?

It is to be hoped that the steam plow will be finally successful, and if it shall be, *"thorough cultivation"*—putting the soil to the top of its capacity—producing the largest crop possible from a given quantity of ground will be most favorable to it. Doing a large amount of work upon a small quantity of ground, it will be, as nearly as possible, stationary while working, and as free as possible from locomotion; thus expending its strength, as much as possible, upon its work, and as little as possible in travelling. Our thanks, and something more substantial than thanks, are due to every man engaged in the effort to produce a successful steam plow. Even the unsuccessful will bring something to light, which, in the hands of others, will contribute to the final success. I have not pointed out difficulties in order to discourage, but in order that being seen, they may be the more readily overcome.

The world is agreed that *labor* is the source from which human wants are mainly supplied. There is no dispute upon this point. From this point, however, men immediately diverge. Much disputation is maintained as to the best way of applying and controlling the labor element. By some it is assumed that labor is available only in connection with capital—that nobody labors, unless somebody else, owning capital, somehow, by the use of that capital, induces him to do it. Having assumed this, they proceed to consider whether it is best that capital shall *hire* laborers, and thus induce them to work by their own consent; or *buy* them, and drive them to it without their consent. Having proceeded so far, they naturally conclude that all laborers are necessarily either *hired* laborers or *slaves*. They further assume that whoever is once a hired laborer, is fatally fixed in that condition for life; and thence, again, that his condition is as bad as, or worse than that of a slave. This is the *"mud-sill"* theory.

But another class of reasoners hold the opinion that there is no *such* relation between capital and labor as assumed; and that there is no such thing as a freeman being fatally fixed for life, in the condition of a hired laborer, that both these assumptions are false, and all inferences from them groundless. They hold that labor is prior to, and independent of, capital; that, in fact, capital is the fruit of labor, and could never have existed if labor had not *first* existed; that labor can exist without capital, but that capital could never have existence without labor. Hence they hold that labor is the superior—greatly the superior—of capital.

They do not deny that there is, and probably always will be, a relation between labor and capital. The error, as they hold, is in assuming that the *whole* labor of the world exists within that relation. A few men own capital; and that few avoid labor themselves, and with their capital, hire or buy another few to labor for them. A large majority belong to neither class—neither work for others, nor have others working for them. Even in all our slave States, except South Carolina, a majority of the whole people of all colors, are neither slaves nor masters. In these free States, a large majority are neither *hirers* nor hired. Men, with their families—wives, sons and daughters—work for themselves, on their farms, in their houses and in their shops, taking the whole product to themselves, and asking no favors of capital on the one hand, nor of hirelings or slaves on the other. It is not forgotten that a considerable number of persons mingle their own labor with capital; that is, labor with their own hands, and also buy slaves or hire freemen to labor for them; but this is only a *mixed*, and not a *distinct* class. No principle stated is disturbed by the existence of this mixed class.

Again, as has already been said, the opponents of the *"mud-sill"* theory insist that there is not, of necessity, any such thing as the free hired laborer being fixed to that condition for life. There is demonstration for saying this. Many independent men, in this assembly, doubtless a few years ago were hired laborers. And their case is almost, if not quite, the general rule. The prudent, penniless beginner in the world labors for wages awhile, saves a surplus with which to buy tools or land for himself; then labors on his own account another while, and at length hires another new beginner to help him. This, say its advocates, is *free* labor—the just and generous and prosperous system, which opens the way for all—gives hope to all, and energy and progress, and improvement of condition to all. If any continue through life in the condition of the hired laborer, it is not the fault of the system, but because of either a dependent nature which prefers it, or improvidence, folly, or singular misfortune. I have said this much about the elements of labor generally, as introductory to the consideration of a new phase which that element is in process of assuming. The old general rule was that *educated* people did not perform manual labor. They managed to eat their bread, leaving the toil of producing it to the uneducated. This was not an insupportable evil to the working bees, so long as the class of drones remained very small. But *now*, especially in these free States, nearly all are educated—quite too nearly all, to leave the labor of the uneducated, in any way adequate to the support of the whole. It follows from this that henceforth educated people too must labor. Otherwise, education itself would become a positive and intolerable evil. No country can sustain, in idleness, more than a small per centage of its numbers. The great majority must labor at something useful—something productive. From these premises the problem springs, "How can *labor* and *education* be the most satisfactory combined?"

By the *"mud-sill"* theory it is assumed that labor and education are incompatible and any practical combination of them impossible. According to that theory, a blind horse upon a tread-mill is a perfect illustration of what a laborer should be—all *the* better for being blind, that he can not tread out of place, or kick understandingly. According to that theory, the educating of laborers is not only useless, but pernicious, and dangerous. In fact, it is, in some sort, deemed a misfortune that laborers should have heads at all. Those same heads are regarded as explosive materials, only to be safely kept in damp places, as far as possible from that peculiar sort of fire which ignites them. A Yankee who could invent a strong-*handed* man without a head would secure the everlasting gratitude of the *"mud-sill"* advocates.

But Free Labor says "No!" Free Labor argues that, as the Author of man makes every individual with one head, and one pair of hands, it was probably intended that heads and hands should cooperate as friends, and that that particular head, should direct and control that particular pair of hands. As each man has one mouth to be fed, and one pair of hands to furnish food, it was probably intended that that particular pair of hands should feed that particular mouth—that each head is the natural guardian, director and protector of the hands and mouth inseparably connected with it; and that being so, every head should be cultivated, and improved, by whatever will add to its capacity for performing its charge. In one word Free Labor insists on universal education.

I have so far stated the opposite theories of *"mud-sill"* and "free labor," without declaring any preference of my own between them. On an occasion like this, I ought not to declare any; I suppose, however, I shall not be mistaken, in assuming as a fact, that the people of Wisconsin prefer free labor, with its natural companion, education.

This leads to the further reflection that no other human occupation opens so wide a field for the profitable and agreeable combination of labor with cultivated thought, as agriculture. I know of nothing so pleasant to the mind, as the discovery of anything which is at once *new* and *valuable*—nothing which so lightens and sweetens toil as the hopeful pursuit of such discovery. And how vast, and how varied a field is agriculture, for such discovery. The mind, already trained to thought in the country school, or higher school, cannot fail to find there an exhaustless source of profitable enjoyment. Every blade of grass is a study; and to produce two where there was but one, is both a profit and a pleasure. And not grass alone, but soils, seeds, and seasons; hedges, ditches, and fences; draining, droughts, and irrigation; plowing, hoeing, and harrowing; reaping, mowing, and threshing;—saving crops, pests of crops, diseases of crops, and what will prevent or cure them; implements, utensils, and machines, their relative merits, and how to improve them; hogs, horses, and cattle; sheep, goats, and poultry; trees, shrubs, fruits, plants, and flowers; the thousand things of which these are specimens, each a world of study within itself.

In all this, book-learning is available. A capacity and taste, for reading, gives access to whatever has already been discovered by others. It is the key, or one of the keys, to the already solved problems. And not only so. It gives a relish and facility for successfully pursuing the yet unsolved ones. The rudiments of science are available and highly valuable. Some knowledge of botany assists in dealing with the vegetable world—with all growing crops; chemistry assists in the analysis of soils, selection and application of manures, and in numerous other ways. The mechanical branches of natural philosophy, are ready helps in almost everything, but especially in reference to implements and machinery.

The thought recurs that education—cultivated thought—can best be combined with agricultural labor, or any labor, on the principle of *thorough* work—that careless, half performed, slovenly work, makes no place for such combination. And thorough work, again, renders sufficient, the smallest quantity of ground to each man. And this again, conforms to what must occur in a world less inclined to wars, and more devoted to the arts of peace, than heretofore. Population must increase rapidly—more rapidly than in former times—and ere long the most valuable of all arts will be the art of deriving a comfortable subsistence from the smallest area of soil. No community whose every member possesses this art, can ever be the victim of oppression of any of its forms. Such community will be alike independent of crowned kings, money kings, and land kings.

But, according to your programme the awarding of premiums awaits the closing of this address. Considering the deep interest necessarily pertaining to that performance, it would be no wonder if I am already heard with some impatience. I will detain you but a moment longer. Some of you will be successful, and such will need but little philosophy to take them home in cheerful spirits; others will be disappointed, and will be in a less happy mood. To such, let it me say, "Lay it not too much to heart." Let them adopt the maxim, "Better luck next time;" and then, by renewed exertion, make that better luck for themselves.

And, by the successful and the unsuccessful, let it be remembered, that while occasions like the present bring their sober and durable benefits, the exultations and mortifictions of them are but temporary; that the victor shall soon be the vanquished, if he relax in his exertion; and that the vanquished this year, may be victor the next, in spite of all competition.

It is said an Eastern monarch once charged his wise men to invent him a sentiment to be ever in view, and which should be true and appropriate in all times and situations. They presented him the words: *"And this, too, shall pass away."* How much it expresses! How chastening in the hour of pride; how consoling in the depths of affliction! *"And this, too, shall pass away."* And yet let us hope it is not *quite* true. Let us hope, rather, that by the best cultivation of the physical world, beneath and around us; and the intellectual and moral world within us, we shall secure an individual, social, and political prosperity and happiness, whose course shall be onward and upward, and which, while the earth endures, shall not pass away.

Interpretation

Lincoln begins this important speech by attributing three benefits to agricultural fairs: strengthening the bonds of friendship, of "social and political union"; affording a kind of recreation associated with "virtue and advantage"; and stimulating agriculture itself.

As background to the first of these, Lincoln tells us that men have always tended to regard strangers as enemies whom they were at liberty to harm. Even after civilization defined robbery and murder as crimes and prohibited them within societies, they were allowed and even encouraged when practiced against strangers. By bringing people together in a friendly setting, and reducing the "want of sympathy" and "positive enmity" toward strangers, fairs perform "one of the highest functions of civilization." Notice that fairs are institutions *within* civilized societies, so that the antagonism we feel toward strangers is a force that persists among ourselves, despite our civilized laws. Lincoln does not go so far as to deny that men are naturally social—after all, their friendships within civilized societies form naturally—but he does believe that the fear and distrust we feel toward those we don't know prevents us from treating them well. The functions of civilization vary, and Lincoln does not try to state them all, but "one of the highest" is to afford opportunities for friendship and cooperation to develop: fairs help civilize further those already civilized.

In connection with the second benefit, Lincoln quotes the eighteenth century English poet, Alexander Pope. If "happiness is our being's end and aim," and man needs "occasional recreation," whatever can provide him with it that is "associated with virtue and advantage, and free from vice and disadvantage," is good for him. "They are a present pleasure, to be followed by no pain, as a consequence; they are a present pleasure, making the future more pleasant." If Lincoln thought fairs were sinks of iniquity, they would not qualify. But in fact they are associated with good people and good deeds (like raising excellent herds) and not with immoral things. The pleasure they bring, and their consequent contribution to our happiness, is unsullied. We may note that Lincoln's recourse to the poet Pope and his statement about happiness implies an understanding of "man's end and aim" that is entirely natural and independent of the Bible. The virtue he has in mind is natural virtue, the advantage, natural advantage.

These two benefits of agricultural fairs are important, but their "chief aim" is to spread agricultural knowledge, and, by encouraging contests, to stimulate the search for new knowledge. Lincoln compares fairs to the patent clause of the Constitution, which also gives encouragement to invention, he then asks what an appropriate object of his talk to the Agricultural Society might be. Not to flatter farmers as a class: "they are neither better nor worse than other people." Given Thomas Jefferson's well-known praise of the independent farmer, this is a surprising comment coming from one of his most fervent admirers. Far from flattering, as politicians are wont to do, all Lincoln will concede is that farmers are "the most numerous class," and that their interest, as the largest, "is most worthy of all to be cherished and cultivated." Again, no praise for the farmer and his way of life, in comparison, say, to the urban masses whose rootlessness Jefferson deplored.

In addition, Lincoln surmises that his audience would not expect "much specific information" about agriculture from him, so his twofold object will be to give to the occasion some "general interest," and to "make some general suggestions on practical matters." His first topic is the need for thoroughness in agriculture, for intensively cultivating smaller plots rather than accumulating acreage. Here Lincoln surprises by his detailed knowledge of agricultural production, its recent slippage and the various technical elements that might contribute to its improvement. He does provide "much specific information" after all! He emphasizes the importance of doing a job well and taking pride in it, but he also pays a great deal of attention to technological innovations like the steam plow, to the invention of which he looks forward. Altogether, he seems eager to ensure the successful perseverance of the small farmer and to discourage large-scale farming on "mammoth farms."

Lincoln's second topic is more removed from agricultural production and of broader significance. It involves the place of labor in human life. All agree, he says, that "*labor* is the source from which human wants are mainly supplied," but thereafter views diverge. One, the so-called mud-sill theory (the "mud-sill is the lowest supporting member of a building, resting right on the ground) holds that capital is the prior cause by which the economic system is put into motion, that nobody works unless stimulated to it by capital. Secondly, it claims that labor can either be hired or slave, and that the hired laborer is close to the slave in that his condition is fixed for life.

The opposing theory is that labor is prior to and superior to capital, which is the fruit of labor, and that no free man is fixed for life as a hired laborer. "In these free states," most men "neither work for others, nor have others work for them." Helped by their families, they "work for themselves, on their farms, in their houses and in their shops." This is the system of "free labor," and allows for men rising in the world by their own labor. It "opens the way for all—gives hope to all, and energy, and progress, and improvement of condition to all." So normal is this upward progress that Lincoln is willing to speak of those who remain hired laborers throughout life as lacking in some way. Since Lincoln is addressing a group of farmers, the hired laborer he has in mind is one who works on farms or in shops. He does not single out factory workers for special mention. No doubt those who work in factories in large numbers and live in big cities constitute a special case, and it may be harder for them to accumulate enough capital to go out on their own. But the pathway to advancement is never fully blocked for anyone. Perhaps it was to stress the possibility of advancement for all, whether in the countryside, small towns or cities, that Lincoln chooses not to extol the independent farmer even before an audience of farmers. And we must not forget that the principle on which it all rests—that labor is prior to and superior to capital—is pronounced by the man who helped found the Republican Party long considered the natural home of capitalism itself!

Lincoln continues with a related point. A "new phase" of life has been recently introduced, whereby all or almost all people are educated. Previously, the educated were few and could be supported in idleness by the many who worked. Now, it is imperative that the many who are educated also "labor at something productive." According to the "mud-sill" theory, educating laborers is "not only useless, but pernicious and dangerous." "Free labor" starts with a different premise. It understands the various human organs to have specific functions relative to the whole. The head is the "natural guardian, director, and protector of the hands and mouth," and should therefore be educated to perform its charge. The head must direct the hand to provide food for the mouth. In short, "free labor insists on universal education."

Lincoln gives the impression that the education he has in mind is entirely practical, that it is always geared to furnishing our physical needs. But it manages to go beyond that. Agriculture—and now it is singled out for special praise— is the occupation that best combines "labor with cultivated thought." "I know of nothing," he says, "so pleasant to the mind, as the discovery of anything which is at once *new* and *valuable*—nothing which so lightens and sweetens toil as the hopeful pursuit of such discovery." In agriculture Lincoln lists several of the many possible objects of study and asserts that to pursue them book-learning is helpful, particularly in the sciences of botany, chemistry and mechanics. He does not say how these sciences were themselves developed, nor whether they grew out of practical or purely theoretical concerns. But one can easily imagine his applying to his own studies and writings (and to those of scientists, philosophers and poets) the statement that he knows "of nothing so pleasant to the mind, as the discovery of anything which is at once *new* and *valuable*." He does not compare the pleasures of the mind with those of the body, nor was it appropriate for him to do so on this occasion.

Education, or cultivated thought, should help with the principle of thorough work on small acreage that Lincoln had stressed earlier. In this he sees political significance as well. In connection with the art of "deriving a comfortable subsistence from the smallest area of soil," Lincoln tells us that "no community, whose every member possesses this art, can ever be the victim of oppression in any of its forms. Such community will be alike independent of crowned kings, money kings, and land kings." Here we see Lincoln's thought converge with Jefferson's and even go beyond it. He seems to be recommending that "every member" of the community possess this art: even those who are not full-time farmers should do some farming of their own. If everyone had such economic independence, they could not be oppressed by either crowned, money or land kings—i.e., by those deriving power and wealth from status, finance and commerce, or large amounts of land, all threats to the self-rule of the people.

Turning, finally, to the distribution of prizes about to occur on the program, Lincoln gives encouragement to both winners and losers. The winners will need "little philosophy" to cheer them up, but those who are disappointed should "adopt the maxim, 'Better luck next time,' and then, by renewed exertion, make that better luck for themselves." He warns both that their "exultations and mortifications . . . are but temporary; that the victor shall soon be the vanquished, if he relax in his exertion; and that the vanquished this year, may be the victor the next, in spite of all competition." There are no fixed winners and losers! Exertion is all! Make your own luck! That's the message.

Lincoln does not leave it at this. He ends with a story about the Eastern monarch who, charging his wise men to come up with a sentence that is always true, supplied the words: *"And this, too, shall pass away."* Lincoln comments: "How chastening in the hour of pride!—how consoling in the depths of affliction!" Yet he does not want it to be *quite* true: "Let us hope, rather, that by the best cultivation of the physical world, beneath and around us, and the intellectual and moral world within us," we keep adding to "individual, social, and political prosperity and happiness." Let us hope, in short, that we can make endless progress on all fronts which, "while the earth endures, shall not pass away." So the speech apparently ends on a very optimistic note, but a moment before Lincoln had apparently given his cachet to those wise men and their saying that all things pass away. That conclusion was based on more than hope. And as if to remind us of this, he adds the qualifier, "while the earth endures." He does not do this with something like Judgment Day in mind, which would connect us with the moral and spiritual world of the Bible and of things that do not pass away, but as a reflection on the perishability of all material things, including the earth. This perishability sets an ultimate natural limit to human power, ambition and striving for improvement—a conclusion not quite in keeping with the festive occasion but true nevertheless. Lincoln was an advocate of modern progress—of cultivating nature and the world within us, and of a democratic education accompanying and strengthening it—but not without qualification. Like those eastern wise men, he knew all was changeable, including progress itself.

Chapter 12

The Cooper Union Address, February 27, 1860

Lincoln had been invited to give this address by the Young Men's Republican Union at the Cooper Union for the Advancement of Science and Art in Manhattan. It was Lincoln's first opportunity to present his views to an eastern audience.

Text

Mr. President and fellow citizens of New York:—

The facts with which I shall deal this evening are mainly old and familiar; nor is there anything new in the general use I shall make of them. If there shall be any novelty, it will be in the mode of presenting the facts, and the inferences and observations following that presentation.

In his speech last autumn, at Columbus, Ohio, as reported in "The New-York Times," Senator Douglas said:

"Our fathers, when they framed the Government under which we live, understood this question just as well, and even better, than we do now."

I fully indorse this, and I adopt it as a text for this discourse. I so adopt it because it furnishes a precise and an agreed starting point for a discussion between Republicans and that wing of the Democracy headed by Senator Douglas. It simply leaves the inquiry: *"What was the understanding those fathers had of the question mentioned?"*

What is the frame of government under which we live?

The answer must be: "The Constitution of the United States." That Constitution consists of the original, framed in 1787, (and under which the present government first went into operation,) and twelve subsequently framed amendments, the first ten of which were framed in 1789.

Who were our fathers that framed the Constitution? I suppose the "thirty-nine" who signed the original instrument may be fairly called our fathers who framed that part of the present Government. It is almost exactly true to say they framed it, and it is altogether true to say they fairly represented the opinion and sentiment of the whole nation at that time. Their names, being familiar to nearly all, and accessible to quite all, need not now be repeated.

I take these "thirty-nine," for the present, as being "our fathers who framed the Government under which we live."

What is the question which, according to the text, those fathers understood "just as well, and even better than we do now?"

It is this: Does the proper division of local from federal authority, or anything in the Constitution, forbid our *Federal Government* to control as to slavery in *our Federal Territories*?

Upon this, Senator Douglas holds the affirmative, and Republicans the negative. This affirmation and denial form an issue; and this issue—this question—is precisely what the text declares our fathers understood "better than we."

Let us now inquire whether the "thirty-nine," or any of them, ever acted upon this question; and if they did, how they acted upon it—how they expressed that better understanding?

In 1784, three years before the Constitution—the United States then owning the Northwestern Territory, and no other, the Congress of the Confederation had before them the question of prohibiting slavery in that Territory; and four of the "thirty-nine" who afterward framed the Constitution, were in that Congress, and voted on that question. Of these, Roger Sherman, Thomas Mifflin, and Hugh Williamson voted for the prohibition, thus showing that, in their understanding, no line dividing local from federal authority, nor anything else, properly forbade the Federal Government to control as to slavery in federal territory. The other of the four—James M'Henry—voted against the prohibition, showing that, for some cause, he thought it improper to vote for it.

In 1787, still before the Constitution, but while the Convention was in session framing it, and while the Northwestern Territory still was the only territory owned by the United States, the same question of prohibiting slavery in the territory again came before the Congress of the Confederation; and two more of the "thirty-nine" who afterward signed the Constitution, were in that Congress, and voted on the question. They were William Blount and William Few; and they both voted for the prohibition—thus showing that, in their understanding, no line dividing local from federal authority, nor anything else, properly forbids the Federal Government to control as to slavery in Federal territory. This time the prohibition became a law, being part of what is now well known as the Ordinance of '87.

The question of federal control of slavery in the territories, seems not to have been directly before the Convention which framed the original Constitution; and hence it is not recorded that the "thirty-nine," or any of them, while engaged on that instrument, expressed any opinion on that precise question.

In 1789, by the first Congress which sat under the Constitution, an act was passed to enforce the Ordinance of '87, including the prohibition of slavery in the Northwestern Territory. The bill for this act was reported by one of the "thirty-nine," Thomas Fitzsimmons, then a member of the House of Representatives from Pennsylvania. It went through all its stages without a word of opposition, and finally passed both branches without yeas and nays, which is equivalent to a unanimous passage. In this Congress there were sixteen of the thirty-nine fathers who framed the original Constitution. They were John Langdon, Nicholas Gilman, Wm. S. Johnson, Roger Sherman, Robert Morris, Thos. Fitzsimmons, William Few, Abraham Baldwin, Rufus King, William Paterson, George Clymer, Richard Bassett, George Read, Pierce Butler, Daniel Carroll, James Madison.

This shows that, in their understanding, no line dividing local from federal authority, nor anything in the Constitution, properly forbade Congress to prohibit slavery in the federal territory; else both their fidelity to correct principle, and their oath to support the Constitution, would have constrained them to oppose the prohibition.

Again, George Washington, another of the "thirty-nine," was then President of the United States, and, as such approved and signed the bill; thus completing its validity as a law, and thus showing that, in his understanding, no line dividing local from federal authority, nor anything in the Constitution, forbade the Federal Government, to control as to slavery in federal territory.

No great while after the adoption of the original Constitution, North Carolina ceded to the Federal Government the country now constituting the State of Tennessee; and a few years later Georgia ceded that which now constitutes the States of Mississippi and Alabama. In both deeds of cession it was made a condition by the ceding States that the Federal Government should not prohibit slavery in the ceded country. Besides this, slavery was then actually in the ceded country. Under these circumstances, Congress, on taking charge of these countries, did not absolutely prohibit slavery within them. But they did interfere with it—take control of it—even there, to a certain extent. In 1798, Congress organized the Territory of Mississippi. In the act of organization, they prohibited the bringing of slaves into the Territory, from any place without the United States, by fine, and giving freedom to slaves so brought. This act passed both branches of Congress without yeas and nays. In that Congress were three of the "thirty-nine" who framed the original Constitution. They were John Langdon, George Read and Abraham Baldwin. They all, probably, voted for it. Certainly they would have placed their opposition to it upon record, if, in their understanding, any line dividing local from federal authority, or anything in the Constitution, properly forbade the Federal Government to control as to slavery in federal territory.

In 1803, the Federal Government purchased the Louisiana country. Our former territorial acquisitions came from certain of our own States; but this Louisiana country was acquired from a foreign nation. In 1804, Congress gave a territorial organization to that part of it which now constitutes the State of Louisiana. New Orleans, lying within that part, was an old and comparatively large city. There were other considerable towns and settlements, and slavery was extensively and thoroughly intermingled with the people. Congress did not, in the Territorial Act, prohibit slavery; but they did interfere with it—take control of it—in a more marked and extensive way than they did in the case of Mississippi. The substance of the provision therein made, in relation to slaves, was:

First. That no slave should be imported into the territory from foreign parts.

Second. That no slave should be carried into it who had been imported into the United States since the first day of May, 1798.

Third. That no slave should be carried into it, except by the owner, and for his own use as a settler; the penalty in all the cases being a fine upon the violator of the law, and freedom to the slave.

This act also was passed without yeas and nays. In the Congress which passed it, there were two of the "thirty-nine." They were Abraham Baldwin and Jonathan Dayton. As stated in the case of Mississippi, it is probable they both voted for it. They would not have allowed it to pass without recording their opposition to it, if, in their understanding, it violated either the line properly dividing local from federal authority, or any provision of the Constitution.

In 1819-20, came and passed the Missouri question. Many votes were taken, by yeas and nays, in both branches of Congress, upon the various phases of the general question. Two of the "thirty-nine"—Rufus King and Charles Pinckney—were members of that Congress. Mr. King steadily voted for slavery prohibition and against all compromises, while Mr. Pinckney as steadily voted against slavery prohibition and against all compromises. By this, Mr. King showed that, in his understanding, no line dividing local from federal authority, nor anything in the Constitution, was violated by Congress prohibiting slavery in federal territory; while Mr. Pinckney, by his votes, showed that, in his understanding, there was some sufficient reason for opposing such prohibition in that case.

The cases I have mentioned are the only acts of the "thirty-nine," or of any of them, upon the direct issue, which I have been able to discover.

To enumerate the persons who thus acted, as being four in 1784, two in 1787, seventeen in 1789, three in 1798, two in 1804, and two in 1819-20—there would be thirty of them. But this would be counting John Langdon, Roger Sherman, William Few, Rufus King, and George Read each twice, and Abraham Baldwin, three times. The true number of those of the "thirty-nine" whom I have shown to have acted upon the question, which, by the text, they understood better than we, is twenty-three, leaving sixteen not shown to have acted upon it in any way.

Here, then, we have twenty-three out of our thirty-nine fathers "who framed the government under which we live," who have, upon their official responsibility and their corporal oaths, acted upon the very question which the text affirms they "understood just as well, and even better than we do now;" and twenty-one of them—a clear majority of the whole "thirty-nine"—so acting upon it as to make them guilty of gross political impropriety and wilful perjury, if, in their understanding, any proper division between local and federal authority, or anything in the Constitution they had made themselves, and sworn to support, forbade the Federal Government to control as to slavery in the federal territories. Thus the twenty-one acted; and, as actions speak louder than words, so actions, under such responsibility, speak still louder.

Two of the twenty-three voted against Congressional prohibition of slavery in the federal territories, in the instances in which they acted upon the question. But for what reasons they so voted is not known. They may have done so because they thought a proper division of local from federal authority, or some provision or principle of the Constitution, stood in the way; or they may, without any such question, have voted against the prohibition, on what appeared to them to be sufficient grounds of expediency. No one who has sworn to support the Constitution can conscientiously vote for what he understands to be an unconstitutional measure, however expedient he may think it; but one may and ought to vote against a measure which he deems constitutional, if, at the same time, he deems it inexpedient. It, therefore, would be unsafe to set down even the two who voted against the prohibition, as having done so because, in their understanding, any proper division of local from federal authority, or anything in the Constitution, forbade the Federal Government to control as to slavery in federal territory.

The remaining sixteen of the "thirty-nine," so far as I have discovered, have left no record of their understanding upon the direct question of federal control of slavery in the federal territories. But there is much reason to believe that their understanding upon that question would not have appeared different from that of their twenty-three compeers, had it been manifested at all.

For the purpose of adhering rigidly to the text, I have purposely omitted whatever understanding may have been manifested by any person, however distinguished, other than the thirty-nine fathers who framed the original Constitution; and, for the same reason, I have also omitted whatever understanding may have been manifested by any of the "thirty-nine" even, on any other phase of the general question of slavery. If we should look into their acts and declarations on those other phases, as the foreign slave trade, and the morality and policy of slavery generally, it would appear to us that on the direct question of federal control of slavery in federal territories, the sixteen, if they had acted at all, would probably have acted just as the twenty-three did. Among that sixteen were several of the most noted anti-slavery men of those times—as Dr. Franklin, Alexander Hamilton and Gouverneur Morris—while there was not one now known to have been otherwise, unless it may be John Rutledge, of South Carolina.

The sum of the whole is, that of our thirty-nine fathers who framed the original Constitution, twenty-one—a clear majority of the whole—certainly understood that no proper division of local from federal authority, nor any part of the Constitution, forbade the Federal Government to control slavery in the federal territories; while all the rest probably had the same understanding. Such, un-questionably, was the understanding of our fathers who framed the original Constitution; and the text affirms that they understood the question "better than we."

But, so far, I have been considering the understanding of the question manifested by the framers of the original Constitution. In and by the original instrument, a mode was provided for amending it; and, as I have already stated, the present frame of "the Government under which we live" consists of that original, and twelve amendatory articles framed and adopted since. Those who now insist that federal control of slavery in federal territories violates the Constitution, point us to the provisions which they suppose it thus violates; and, as I understand, that all fix upon provisions in these amendatory articles, and not in the original instrument. The Supreme Court, in the Dred Scott case, plant themselves upon the fifth amendment, which provides that no person shall be deprived of "life, liberty or property without due process of law;" while Senator Douglas and his peculiar adherents plant themselves upon the tenth amendment, providing that "the powers not delegated to the United States by the Constitution" "are reserved to the States respectively, or to the people."

Now, it so happens that these amendments were framed by the first Congress which sat under the Constitution—the identical Congress which passed the act already mentioned, enforcing the prohibition of slavery in the Northwestern Territory. Not only was it the same Congress, but they were the identical, same individual men who, at the same session, and at the same time within the session, had under consideration, and in progress toward maturity, these Constitutional amendments, and this act prohibiting slavery in all the territory the nation then owned. The Constitutional amendments were introduced before, and passed after the act enforcing the Ordinance of '87; so that, during the whole pendency of the act to enforce the Ordinance, the Constitutional amendments were also pending.

The seventy-six members of that Congress, including sixteen of the framers of the original Constitution, as before stated, were pre- eminently our fathers who framed that part of "the Government under which we live," which is now claimed as forbidding the Federal Government to control slavery in the federal territories.

Is it not a little presumptuous in any one at this day to affirm that the two things which that Congress deliberately framed, and carried to maturity at the same time, are absolutely inconsistent with each other? And does not such affirmation become impudently absurd when coupled with the other affirmation from the same mouth, that those who did the two things, alleged to be inconsistent, understood whether they really were inconsistent better than we—better than he who affirms that they are inconsistent?

It is surely safe to assume that the thirty-nine framers of the original Constitution, and the seventy-six members of the Congress which framed the amendments thereto, taken together, do certainly include those who may be fairly called "our fathers who framed the Government under which we live." And so assuming, I defy any man to show that any one of them ever, in his whole life, declared that, in his understanding, any proper division of local from federal authority, or any part of the Constitution, forbade the Federal Government to control as to slavery in the federal territories. I go a step further. I defy any one to show that any living man in the whole world ever did, prior to the beginning of the present century, (and I might almost say prior to the beginning of the last half of the present century,) declare that, in his understanding, any proper division of local from federal authority, or any part of the Constitution, forbade the Federal Government to control as to slavery in the federal territories. To those who now so declare, I give, not only "our fathers who framed the Government under which we live," but with them all other living men within the century in which it was framed, among whom to search, and they shall not be able to find the evidence of a single man agreeing with them.

Now, and here, let me guard a little against being misunderstood. I do not mean to say we are bound to follow implicitly in whatever our fathers did. To do so, would be to discard all the lights of current experience—to reject all progress—all improvement. What I do say is, that if we would supplant the opinions and policy of our fathers in any case, we should do so upon evidence so conclusive, and argument so clear, that even their great authority, fairly considered and weighed, cannot stand; and most surely not in a case whereof we ourselves declare they understood the question better than we.

If any man at this day sincerely believes that a proper division of local from federal authority, or any part of the Constitution, forbids the Federal Government to control as to slavery in the federal territories, he is right to say so, and to enforce his position by all truthful evidence and fair argument which he can. But he has no right to mislead others, who have less access to history, and less leisure to study it, into the false belief that "our fathers who framed the Government under which we live" were of the same opinion—thus substituting falsehood and deception for truthful evidence and fair argument. If any man at this day sincerely believes "our fathers who framed the Government under which we live," used and applied principles, in other cases, which ought to have led them to understand that a proper division of local from federal authority or some part of the Constitution, forbids the Federal Government to control as to slavery in the federal territories, he is right to say so. But he should, at the same time, brave the responsibility of declaring that, in his opinion, he understands their principles better than they did themselves; and especially should he not shirk that responsibility by asserting that they "understood the question just as well, and even better, than we do now."

But enough! *Let all who believe that "our fathers, who framed the Government under which we live, understood this question just as well, and even better, than we do now," speak as they spoke, and act as they acted upon it. This is all Republicans ask—all Republicans desire—in relation to slavery. As those fathers marked it, so let it be again marked, as an evil not to be extended, but to be tolerated and protected only because of and so far as its actual presence among us makes that toleration and protection a necessity. Let all the guarantees those fathers gave it, be, not grudgingly, but fully and fairly, maintained.* For this Republicans contend, and with this, so far as I know or believe, they will be content.

And now, if they would listen—as I suppose they will not—I would address a few words to the Southern people.

I would say to them:—You consider yourselves a reasonable and a just people; and I consider that in the general qualities of reason and justice you are not inferior to any other people. Still, when you speak of us Republicans, you do so only to denounce us a reptiles, or, at the best, as no better than outlaws. You will grant a hearing to pirates or murderers, but nothing like it to "Black Republicans." In all your contentions with one another, each of you deems an unconditional condemnation of "Black Republicanism" as the first thing to be attended to. Indeed, such condemnation of us seems to be an indispensable prerequisite—license, so to speak—among you to be admitted or permitted to speak at all. Now, can you, or not, be prevailed upon to pause and to consider whether this is quite just to us, or even to yourselves? Bring forward your charges and specifications, and then be patient long enough to hear us deny or justify.

You say we are sectional. We deny it. That makes an issue; and the burden of proof is upon you. You produce your proof; and what is it? Why, that our party has no existence in your section—gets no votes in your section. The fact is substantially true; but does it prove the issue? If it does, then in case we should, without change of principle, begin to get votes in your section, we should thereby cease to be sectional. You cannot escape this conclusion; and yet, are you willing to abide by it? If you are, you will probably soon find that we have ceased to be sectional, for we shall get votes in your section this very year. You will then begin to discover, as the truth plainly is, that your proof does not touch the issue. The fact that we get no votes in your section, is a fact of your making, and not of ours. And if there be fault in that fact, that fault is primarily yours, and remains until you show that we repel you by some wrong principle or practice. If we do repel you by any wrong principle or practice, the fault is ours; but this brings you to where you ought to have started—to a discussion of the right or wrong of our principle. If our principle, put in practice, would wrong your section for the benefit of ours, or for any other object, then our principle, and we with it, are sectional, and are justly opposed and denounced as such. Meet us, then, on the question of whether our principle, put in practice, would wrong your section; and so meet it as if it were possible that something may be said on our side. Do you accept the challenge? No! Then you really believe that the principle which "our fathers who framed the Government under which we live" thought so clearly right as to adopt it, and indorse it again and again, upon their official oaths, is in fact so clearly wrong as to demand your condemnation without a moment's consideration.

Some of you delight to flaunt in our faces the warning against sectional parties given by Washington in his Farewell Address. Less than eight years before

Washington gave that warning, he had, as President of the United States, approved and signed an act of Congress, enforcing the prohibition of slavery in the Northwestern Territory, which act embodied the policy of the Government upon that subject up to and at the very moment he penned that warning; and about one year after he penned it, he wrote LaFayette that he considered that prohibition a wise measure, expressing in the same connection his hope that we should at some time have a confederacy of free States.

Bearing this in mind, and seeing that sectionalism has since arisen upon this same subject, is that warning a weapon in your hands against us, or in our hands against you? Could Washington himself speak, would he cast the blame of that sectionalism upon us, who sustain his policy, or upon you who repudiate it? We respect that warning of Washington, and we commend it to you, together with his example pointing to the right application of it.

But you say you are conservative—eminently conservative—while we are revolutionary, destructive, or something of the sort. What is conservatism? Is it not adherence to the old and tried, against the new and untried? We stick to, contend for, the identical old policy on the point in controversy which was adopted by "our fathers who framed the Government under which we live;" while you with one accord reject, and scout, and spit upon that old policy, and insist upon substituting something new. True, you disagree among yourselves as to what that substitute shall be. You are divided on new propositions and plans, but you are unanimous in rejecting and denouncing the old policy of the fathers. Some of you are for reviving the foreign slave trade; some for a Congressional Slave-Code for the Territories; some for Congress forbidding the Territories to prohibit Slavery within their limits; some for maintaining Slavery in the Territories through the judiciary; some for the "gur-reat pur-rinciple" that "if one man would enslave another, no third man should object," fantastically called "Popular Sovereignty;" but never a man among you is in favor of federal prohibition of slavery in federal territories, according to the practice of "our fathers who framed the Government under which we live." Not one of all your various plans can show a precedent or an advocate in the century within which our Government originated. Consider, then, whether your claim of conservatism for yourselves, and your charge or destructiveness against us, are based on the most clear and stable foundations.

Again, you say we have made the slavery question more prominent than it formerly was. We deny it. We admit that it is more prominent, but we deny that we made it so. It was not we, but you, who discarded the old policy of the fathers. We resisted, and still resist, your innovation; and thence comes the greater prominence of the question. Would you have that question reduced to its former proportions? Go back to that old policy. What has been will be again, under the same conditions. If you would have the peace of the old times, readopt the precepts and policy of the old times.

You charge that we stir up insurrections among your slaves. We deny it; and what is your proof? Harper's Ferry! John Brown!! John Brown was no Republican; and you have failed to implicate a single Republican in his Harper's Ferry enterprise. If any member of our party is guilty in that matter, you know it or you do not know it. If you do know it, you are inexcusable for not designating the man and proving the fact. If you do not know it, you are inexcusable for asserting it, and especially for persisting in the assertion after you have tried and failed to make the proof. You need to be told that persisting in a charge which one does not know to be true, is simply malicious slander.

Some of you admit that no Republican designedly aided or encouraged the Harper's Ferry affair, but still insist that our doctrines and declarations necessarily lead to such results. We do not believe it. We know we hold to no doctrine, and make no declaration, which were not held to and made by "our fathers who framed the Government under which we live." You never dealt fairly by us in relation to this affair. When it occurred, some important State elections were near at hand, and you were in evident glee with the belief that, by charging the blame upon us, you could get an advantage of us in those elections. The elections came, and your expectations were not quite fulfilled. Every Republican man knew that, as to himself at least, your charge was a slander, and he was not much inclined by it to cast his vote in your favor. Republican doctrines and declarations are accompanied with a continual protest against any interference whatever with your slaves, or with you about your slaves. Surely, this does not encourage them to revolt. True, we do, in common with "our fathers, who framed the Government under which we live," declare our belief that slavery is wrong; but the slaves do not hear us declare even this. For anything we say or do, the slaves would scarcely know there is a Republican party. I believe they would not, in fact, generally know it but for your misrepresentations of us, in their hearing. In your political contests among yourselves, each faction charges the other with sympathy with Black Republicanism; and then, to give point to the charge, defines Black Republicanism to simply be insurrection, blood and thunder among the slaves.

Slave insurrections are no more common now than they were before the Republican party was organized. What induced the Southampton insurrection, twenty-eight years ago, in which, at least three times as many lives were lost as at Harper's Ferry? You can scarcely stretch your very elastic fancy to the conclusion that Southampton was "got up by Black Republicanism." In the present state of things in the United States, I do not think a general, or even a very extensive slave insurrection is possible. The indispensable concert of action cannot be attained. The slaves have no means of rapid communication; nor can incendiary freemen, black or white, supply it. The explosive materials are everywhere in parcels; but there neither are, nor can be supplied, the indispensable connecting trains.

Much is said by Southern people about the affection of slaves for their masters and mistresses; and a part of it, at least, is true. A plot for an uprising could scarcely be devised and communicated to twenty individuals before some one of them, to save the life of a favorite master or mistress, would divulge it. This is the rule; and the slave revolution in Hayti was not an exception to it, but a case occurring under peculiar circumstances. The gunpowder plot of British history, though not connected with slaves, was more in point. In that case, only about twenty were admitted to the secret; and yet one of them, in his anxiety to save a friend, betrayed the plot to that friend, and, by consequence, averted the calamity. Occasional poisonings from the kitchen, and open or stealthy assassinations in the field, and local revolts extending to a score or so, will continue to occur as the natural results of slavery; but no general insurrection of slaves, as I think, can happen in this country for a long time. Whoever much fears, or much hopes for such an event, will be alike disappointed.

In the language of Mr. Jefferson, uttered many years ago, "It is still in our power to direct the process of emancipation, and deportation, peaceably, and in such slow degrees, as that the evil will wear off insensibly; and their places be, *pari passu*, filled up by free white laborers. If, on the contrary, it is left to force itself on, human nature must shudder at the prospect held up."

Mr. Jefferson did not mean to say, nor do I, that the power of emancipation is in the Federal Government. He spoke of Virginia; and, as to the power of emancipation, I speak of the slaveholding States only. The Federal Government, however, as we insist, has the power of restraining the extension of the institution—the power to insure that a slave insurrection shall never occur on any American soil which is now free from slavery.

John Brown's effort was peculiar. It was not a slave insurrection. It was an attempt by white men to get up a revolt among slaves, in which the slaves refused to participate. In fact, it was so absurd that the slaves, with all their ignorance, saw plainly enough it could not succeed. That affair, in its philosophy, corresponds with the many attempts, related in history, at the assassination of kings and emperors. An enthusiast broods over the oppression of a people till he fancies himself commissioned by Heaven to liberate them. He ventures the attempt, which ends in little else than his own execution. Orsini's attempt on Louis Napoleon, and John Brown's attempt at Harper's Ferry were, in their philosophy, precisely the same. The eagerness to cast blame on old England in the one case, and on New England in the other, does not disprove the sameness of the two things.

And how much would it avail you, if you could, by the use of John Brown, Helper's Book, and the like, break up the Republican organization? Human action can be modified to some extent, but human nature cannot be changed. There is a judgment and a feeling against slavery in this nation, which cast at least a million and a half of votes. You cannot destroy that judgment and feeling—that sentiment—by breaking up the political organization which rallies around it. You can scarcely scatter and disperse an army which has been formed into order in the face of your heaviest fire; but if you could, how much would you gain by forcing the sentiment which created it out of the peaceful channel of the ballot-box, into some other channel? What would that other channel probably be? Would the number of John Browns be lessened or enlarged by the operation?

But you will break up the Union rather than submit to a denial of your Constitutional rights.

That has a somewhat reckless sound; but it would be palliated, if not fully justified, were we proposing, by the mere force of numbers, to deprive you of some right, plainly written down in the Constitution. But we are proposing no such thing.

When you make these declarations, you have a specific and well-understood allusion to an assumed Constitutional right of yours, to take slaves into the federal territories, and to hold them there as property. But no such right is specifically written in the Constitution. That instrument is literally silent about any such right. We, on the contrary, deny that such a right has any existence in the Constitution, even by implication.

Your purpose, then, plainly stated, is that you will destroy the Government, unless you be allowed to construe and enforce the Constitution as you please, on all points in dispute between you and us. You will rule or ruin in all events.

This, plainly stated, is your language. Perhaps you will say the Supreme Court has decided the disputed Constitutional question in your favor. Not quite so. But waiving the lawyer's distinction between dictum and decision, the Court have decided the question for you in a sort of way. The Court have substantially said, it is your Constitutional right to take slaves into the federal territories, and to hold them there as property. When I say the decision was made in a sort of way, I mean it was made in a divided Court, by a bare majority of the Judges, and they not quite agreeing with one another in the reasons for making it; that it is so made as that its avowed supporters disagree with one another about its meaning, and that it was mainly based upon a mistaken statement of fact—the statement in the opinion that "the right of property in a slave is distinctly and expressly affirmed in the Constitution."

An inspection of the Constitution will show that the right of property in a slave is not "*distinctly* and *expressly* affirmed" in it. Bear in mind, the Judges do not pledge their judicial opinion that such right is *impliedly* affirmed in the Constitution; but they pledge their veracity that it is "*distinctly* and *expressly*" affirmed there—"distinctly," that is, not mingled with anything else—"expressly," that is, in words meaning just that, without the aid of any inference, and susceptible of no other meaning.

If they had only pledged their judicial opinion that such right is affirmed in the instrument by implication, it would be open to others to show that neither the word "slave" nor "slavery" is to be found in the Constitution, nor the word "property" even, in any connection with language alluding to the things slave, or slavery; and that wherever in that instrument the slave is alluded to, he is called a "person;"—and wherever his master's legal right in relation to him is alluded to, it is spoken of as "service or labor which may be due,"—as a debt payable in service or labor. Also, it would be open to show, by contemporaneous history, that this mode of alluding to slaves and slavery, instead of speaking of them, was employed on purpose to exclude from the Constitution the idea that there could be property in man.

To show all this, is easy and certain.

When this obvious mistake of the Judges shall be brought to their notice, is it not reasonable to expect that they will withdraw the mistaken statement, and reconsider the conclusion based upon it?

And then it is to be remembered that "our fathers, who framed the Government under which we live"—the men who made the Constitution—decided this same Constitutional question in our favor, long ago—decided it without division among themselves, when making the decision; without division among themselves about the meaning of it after it was made, and, so far as any evidence is left, without basing it upon any mistaken statement of facts.

Under all these circumstances, do you really feel yourselves justified to break up this Government unless such a court decision as yours is, shall be at once submitted to as a conclusive and final rule of political action? But you will not abide the election of a Republican president! In that supposed event, you say, you will destroy the Union; and then, you say, the great crime of having destroyed it will be upon us! That is cool. A highwayman holds a pistol to my ear, and mutters through his teeth, "Stand and deliver, or I shall kill you, and then you will be a murderer!"

To be sure, what the robber demanded of me—my money—was my own; and I had a clear right to keep it; but it was no more my own than my vote is my own; and the threat of death to me, to extort my money, and the threat of destruction to the Union, to extort my vote, can scarcely be distinguished in principle.

A few words now to Republicans. *It is exceedingly desirable that all parts of this great Confederacy shall be at peace, and in harmony, one with another. Let us Republicans do our part to have it so. Even though much provoked, let us do nothing through passion and ill temper. Even though the southern people will not so much as listen to us, let us calmly consider their demands, and yield to them if, in our deliberate view of our duty, we possibly can.* Judging by all they say and do, and by the subject and nature of their controversy with us, let us determine, if we can, what will satisfy them.

Will they be satisfied if the Territories be unconditionally surrendered to them? We know they will not. In all their present complaints against us, the Territories are scarcely mentioned. Invasions and insurrections are the rage now. Will it satisfy them, if, in the future, we have nothing to do with invasions and insurrections? We know it will not. We so know, because we know we never had anything to do with invasions and insurrections; and yet this total abstaining does not exempt us from the charge and the denunciation.

The question recurs, what will satisfy them? Simply this: We must not only let them alone, but we must somehow, convince them that we do let them alone. This, we know by experience, is no easy task. We have been so trying to convince them from the very beginning of our organization, but with no success. In all our platforms and speeches we have constantly protested our purpose to let them alone; but this has had no tendency to convince them. Alike unavailing to convince them, is the fact that they have never detected a man of us in any attempt to disturb them.

These natural, and apparently adequate means all failing, what will convince them? This, and this only: cease to call slavery *wrong*, and join them in calling it *right*. And this must be done thoroughly—done in *acts* as well as in *words*. Silence will not be tolerated—we must place ourselves avowedly with them. Senator Douglas' new sedition law must be enacted and enforced, suppressing all declarations that slavery is wrong, whether made in politics, in presses, in pulpits, or in private. We must arrest and return their fugitive slaves with greedy pleasure. We must pull down our Free State constitutions. The whole atmosphere must be disinfected from all taint of opposition to slavery, before they will cease to believe that all their troubles proceed from us.

I am quite aware they do not state their case precisely in this way. Most of them would probably say to us, "Let us alone, do nothing to us, and say what you please about slavery." But we do let them alone—have never disturbed them—so that, after all, it is what we say, which dissatisfies them. They will continue to accuse us of doing, until we cease saying.

I am also aware they have not, as yet, in terms, demanded the overthrow of our Free-State Constitutions. Yet those Constitutions declare the wrong of slavery, with more solemn emphasis, than do all other sayings against it; and when all these other sayings shall have been silenced, the overthrow of these Constitutions will be demanded, and nothing be left to resist the demand. It is nothing to the contrary, that they do not demand the whole of this just now. Demanding what they do, and for the reason they do, they can voluntarily stop nowhere short of this consummation. Holding, as they do, that slavery is morally right, and socially elevating, they cannot cease to demand a full national recognition of it, as a legal right, and a social blessing.

Nor can we justifiably withhold this, on any ground save our conviction that slavery is wrong. If slavery is right, all words, acts, laws, and constitutions against it, are themselves wrong, and should be silenced, and swept away. If it is right, we cannot justly object to its nationality—its universality; if it is wrong, they cannot justly insist upon its extension—its enlargement. All they ask, we could readily grant, if we thought slavery right; all we ask, they could as readily grant, if they thought it wrong. Their thinking it right, and our thinking it wrong, is the precise fact upon which depends the whole controversy. Thinking it right, as they do, they are not to blame for desiring its full recognition, as being right; but, thinking it wrong, as we do, can we yield to them? Can we cast our votes with their view, and against our own? In view of our moral, social, and political responsibilities, can we do this?

Wrong as we think slavery is, we can yet afford to let it alone where it is, because that much is due to the necessity arising from its actual presence in the nation; but can we, while our votes will prevent it, allow it to spread into the

National Territories, and to overrun us here in these Free States? If our sense of duty forbids this, then let us stand by our duty, fearlessly and effectively. Let us be diverted by none of those sophistical contrivances wherewith we are so industriously plied and belabored—contrivances such as groping for some middle ground between the right and the wrong, vain as the search for a man who should be neither a living man nor a dead man—such as a policy of "don't care" on a question about which all true men do care—such as Union appeals beseeching true Union men to yield to Disunionists, reversing the divine rule, and calling, not the sinners, but the righteous to repentance—such as invocations to Washington, imploring men to unsay what Washington said, and undo what Washington did.

Neither let us be slandered from our duty by false accusations against us, nor frightened from it by menaces of destruction to the Government nor of dungeons to ourselves. LET US HAVE FAITH THAT RIGHT MAKES MIGHT, AND IN THAT FAITH, LET US, TO THE END, DARE TO DO OUR DUTY AS WE UNDERSTAND IT.

Interpretation

Senator Douglas had asserted that the founding fathers understood the question of the extension of slavery *"just as well, and even better, than we do now."* Seizing upon this admission, Lincoln makes his own investigation of what the founders' understanding was. The question at issue is: "Does the proper division of local from federal authority, or anything in the Constitution, forbid our *Federal Government* to control as to slavery in *our Federal Territories*?" The views to be sought, primarily, are those of the thirty-nine individuals who signed the original Constitution—the founding fathers in the strict sense.

Lincoln shows his originality and industry in this amazing piece of historical research, learning how many of these same individuals sat in the First and other Congresses and discovering their votes regarding the Northwest Ordinance of 1787 and other relevant matters. He shows that a clear majority (twenty-one) certainly believed the Federal Government has the authority to control slavery in the Federal Territories, and the remainder probably did as well. As for the claim that the Fifth and Tenth Amendments (added to the new Constitution, by the same First Congress) contained grounds for denying such control to the Federal Government, Lincoln simply extends his case in the same way—by examining what the First Congress did, again with reference to the Northwest Ordinance, and comes up with the same conclusion.

In an important statement of principle, Lincoln is willing to admit that we are not completely bound to follow what the founding fathers did, for this would leave no room for experience and the possibility of improvement. But supplanting their "opinions and policy" should only be done "upon evidence so conclusive and argument so clear, that even their great authority, fairly considered and weighed, cannot stand." We can see that the question under consideration involved not a Federal authority directly and plainly stipulated in the Constitution (over the extension of slavery) but one inferred from other provisions. In any case, the obligation owed to the founding fathers is very strong but not absolute. Douglas and others like him, he says, deserve to be taken severely to task, not so much for differing from the founding fathers as for pretending that they do not. The founders marked slavery "as an evil not to *be extended, but to be tolerated and protected only because of and so far as its actual presence among us makes that toleration and protection a necessity. Let all the guaranties those fathers gave it, be, not grudgingly, but fully and fairly maintained."* (Lincoln has in mind the "fugitive slave" provisions of Article IV, Sect.2). This shows how far Lincoln was willing to go in the direction of conciliating the South and its slaveholders—and believed the North was obliged to go by the Constitution itself— so long as the extension of slavery could be opposed and its ultimate fate thereby settled.

The second part of the address explicitly directed now to "the Southern people"—if they would but listen—considers their charges against the Republicans, the Black Republicans, as they liked to call them. One by one Lincoln repels the charges that the Republicans are a sectional party, that they are revolutionary rather than conservative, like the South, that they have made the slavery question more prominent than it was, that they are stirring up slave insurrections. On this last point Lincoln sees fit to dilate. Slave insurrections, while possible—as shown by the Southampton insurrection, twenty-eight years before—are nevertheless very unlikely. As for John Brown's attempt at Harper's Ferry to instigate such insurrections, Lincoln's judgment is harsh: "An enthusiast broods over the oppression of a people till he fancies himself commissioned by Heaven to liberate them." We can see that such efforts would quickly destroy the Union Lincoln was at such pains to preserve, and with the slaves suffering most of all.

The Southerners also assert that they would rather break up the Union than see their constitutional rights denied. This compels Lincoln to confront the pro-Southern *Dred Scott* decision, which he summarizes as holding that there is a "Constitutional right to take slaves into the federal territories, and to hold them there as property." Lincoln points out that this decision was made by a bare majority of the Court, and even then with disagreements among the majority. It was based, moreover, on a "mistaken statement of fact"—that the right to property in slaves is "distinctly and expressly affirmed in the Constitution." This Lincoln flatly denies. On the contrary, he claims, correctly, that the terms "slavery" and "slave" appear nowhere in the Constitution, not even in those places where it would be most natural to have used them. Lincoln's says the founders wanted to "exclude from the Constitution the idea that there could be property in man." In other words, whatever their temporary concessions to the institution of slavery, the founders, anticipating and hoping that it would come to an end before long, did not want to give it a permanent place in a document devoted to "the blessings of liberty."

Lincoln's final remarks are directed to his fellow Republicans. He pleads for peace and harmony, for giving due consideration to every Southern demand. Yet he also makes clear that nothing will satisfy the South unless the Republicans "cease to call slavery *wrong*, and join them in calling it *right*." Ultimately the South would feel compelled to call for the elimination of anti-slavery clauses in Northern state constitutions so as to extend it everywhere, just because they think it right. For "If slavery is right, all words, acts, laws, and constitutions against it are themselves wrong." If it is wrong, however, the South cannot insist on its extension. He could have gone much further, for he omits the full corollary of his statement—that if slavery is wrong, all words, acts, laws and constitutions for it are also wrong. Note that he is willing to draw the most severe and comprehensive consequences from the true moral status of slavery. That is the crux of the matter: "Their thinking it (slavery) right, and our thinking it wrong, is the precise fact upon which depends the whole controversy." Evidently, these moral beliefs are somewhat independent of, and more fundamental than, the Constitution itself.

It is strange that Lincoln neglects appealing at this point to the Declaration of Independence. He treats the wrongness of slavery as a bedrock moral judgment that is self-subsistent rather than traceable to some source, philosophical or religious. Lincoln's silence about the Declaration here suggests that it is not always prudent to analyze the sources of fundamental beliefs. Even when one of these is the Declaration, as in this case, doing so would have the effect of drawing allegiance away from the Constitution and to the Declaration, thus undermining the practical compromise with slavery that the founders incorporated into the Constitution.

The speech ends on a defiant note. Lincoln calls upon Republicans to oppose the spread of slavery into the Territories and possibly the Free States themselves. He appeals to their sense of duty, urging them to beware of sophistical notions that would attempt an impossible compromise on the key issue. "LET US HAVE FAITH THAT RIGHT MAKES MIGHT, AND IN THAT FAITH, LET US, TO THE END, DARE TO DO OUR DUTY AS WE UNDERSTAND IT." This final exhortation is capitalized in the text. Because he will not yield on the wrongness of slavery, he knows he cannot, in fact, satisfy the South, or prevent the imminent explosion. If Lincoln strikes us as stubborn, he is—on the wrongness of slavery. If he conceded to the South on this issue, slavery could and would spread, even to the North, increasingly causing the Union to be dominated by pro-slavery forces and intensifying civil discord. On the other hand, he could not invite the South to secede, allowing each confederacy to go its own way. That separation would lead to a bitter and belligerent rivalry, from the outset setting an example of republican disintegration, and, at the same time, sealing forever the fate of the black slaves in the South. Holding onto the Union and opposing the spread of slavery, even at the risk of civil war, was the only sound policy.

III. Civil War Speeches

Chapter 13

The First Inaugural Address, March 4, 1861

By the time President Lincoln delivered this inaugural address, seven states had already withdrawn from the Union and formed the Confederacy. This is his response to the secession.

Text

Fellow-citizens of the United States:

In compliance with a custom as old as the government itself, I appear before you to address you briefly, and to take, in your presence, the oath prescribed by the Constitution of the United States, to be taken by the President "before he enters on the execution of this office."

I do not consider it necessary at present for me to discuss those matters of administration about which there is no special anxiety or excitement.

Apprehension seems to exist among the people of the Southern States, that by the accession of a Republican Administration, their property, and their peace, and personal security, are to be endangered. There has never been any reasonable cause for such apprehension. Indeed, the most ample evidence to the contrary has all the while existed, and been open to their inspection. It is found in nearly all the published speeches of him who now addresses you. I do but quote from one of those speeches when I declare that "I have no purpose, directly or indirectly, to interfere with the institution of slavery in the States where it exists. I believe I have no lawful right to do so, and I have no inclination to do so." Those who nominated and elected me did so with full knowledge that I had made this, and many similar declarations, and had never recanted them. And more than this, they placed in the platform, for my acceptance, and as a law to themselves, and to me, the clear and emphatic resolution which I now read:

Resolved, That the maintenance inviolate of the rights of the States, and especially the right of each State to order and control its own domestic institutions according to its own judgment exclusively, is essential to that balance of power on which the perfection and endurance of our political fabric depend; and we denounce the lawless invasion by armed force of the soil of any State or Territory, no matter under what pretext, as among the gravest of crimes."

I now reiterate these sentiments: and in doing so, I only press upon the public attention the most conclusive evidence of which the case is susceptible, that the property, peace and security of no section are to be in any wise endangered by the now incoming Administration. I add too, that all the protection which, consistently with the Constitution and the laws, can be given, will be cheerfully given to all the States when lawfully demanded, for whatever cause—as cheerfully to one section as to another.

There is much controversy about the delivering up of fugitives from service or labor. The clause I now read is as plainly written in the Constitution as any other of its provisions:

"No person held to service or labor in one State, under the laws thereof, escaping into another, shall, in consequence of any law or regulation therein, be discharged from such service or labor, but shall be delivered up on claim of the party to whom such service or labor may be due."

It is scarcely questioned that this provision was intended by those who made it, for the reclaiming of what we call fugitive slaves; and the intention of the law-giver is the law. All members of Congress swear their support to the whole Constitution—to this provision as much as to any other. To the proposition, then, that slaves whose cases come within the terms of this clause, "shall be delivered up," their oaths are unanimous. Now, if they would make the effort in good temper, could they not, with nearly equal unanimity, frame and pass a law, by means of which to keep good that unanimous oath?

There is some difference of opinion whether this clause should be enforced by national or by state authority; but surely that difference is not a very material one. If the slave is to be surrendered, it can be of but little consequence to him, or to others, by which authority it is done. And should any one, in any case, be content that his oath shall go unkept, on a merely unsubstantial controversy as to *how* it shall be kept?

Again, in any law upon this subject, ought not all the safeguards of liberty known in civilized and humane jurisprudence to be introduced, so that a free man be not, in any case, surrendered as a slave? And might it not be well, at the same time to provide by law for the enforcement of that clause in the Constitution which guarantees that "the citizens of each State shall be entitled to all privileges and immunities of citizens in the several States"?

I take the official oath to-day, with no mental reservations, and with no purpose to construe the Constitution or laws, by any hypercritical rules. And while I do not choose now to specify particular acts of Congress as proper to be enforced, I do suggest that it will be much safer for all, both in official and private stations, to conform to, and abide by, all those acts which stand unrepealed, than to violate any of them, trusting to find impunity in having them held to be unconstitutional.

It is seventy-two years since the first inauguration of a President under our national Constitution. During that period fifteen different and greatly distinguished citizens, have, in succession, administered the executive branch of the government. They have conducted it through many perils; and, generally, with great success. Yet, with all this scope for [of] precedent, I now enter upon the same task for the brief constitutional term of four years, under great and peculiar difficulty. A disruption of the Federal Union, heretofore only menaced, is now formidably attempted.

I hold, that in contemplation of universal law, and of the Constitution, the Union of these States is perpetual. Perpetuity is implied, if not expressed, in the fundamental law of all national governments. It is safe to assert that no government proper, ever had a provision in its organic law for its own termination. Continue to execute all the express provisions of our national Constitution, and the Union will endure forever—it being impossible to destroy it, except by some action not provided for in the instrument itself.

Again, if the United States be not a government proper, but an association of States in the nature of contract merely, can it, as a contract, be peaceably unmade, by less than all the parties who made it? One party to a contract may violate it—break it, so to speak; but does it not require all to lawfully rescind it?

Descending from these general principles, we find the proposition that, in legal contemplation, the Union is perpetual, confirmed by the history of the Union itself. The Union is much older than the Constitution. It was formed in fact, by the Articles of Association in 1774. It was matured and continued by the Declaration of Independence in 1776. It was further matured and the faith of all the then thirteen States expressly plighted and engaged that it should be perpetual, by the Articles of Confederation in 1778. And finally, in 1787, one of the declared objects for ordaining and establishing the Constitution, was *"to form a more perfect Union."*

But if [the] destruction of the Union, by one, or by a part only, of the States, be lawfully possible, the Union is *less* perfect than before the Constitution, having lost the vital element of perpetuity.

It follows from these views that no State, upon its own mere motion, can lawfully get out of the Union,—that *resolves* and *ordinances* to that effect are legally void, and that acts of violence, within any State or States, against the authority of the United States, are insurrectionary or revolutionary, according to circumstances.

I therefore consider that in view of the Constitution and the laws, the Union is unbroken; and to the extent of my ability I shall take care, as the Constitution itself expressly enjoins upon me, that the laws of the Union be faithfully executed in all the States. Doing this I deem to be only a simple duty on my part; and I shall perform it, so far as practicable, unless my rightful masters, the American people, shall withhold the requisite means, or in some authoritative manner, direct the contrary. I trust this will not be regarded as a menace, but only as the declared purpose of the Union that it will constitutionally defend and maintain itself.

In doing this there needs to be no bloodshed or violence; and there shall be none, unless it be forced upon the national authority. The power confided to me will be used to hold, occupy, and possess the property and places belonging to the government, and to collect the duties and imposts; but beyond what may be necessary for these objects, there will be no invasion—no using of force against or among the people anywhere. Where hostility to the United States, in any interior locality, shall be so great and so universal, as to prevent competent resident citizens from holding the Federal offices, there will be no attempt to force obnoxious strangers among the people for that object. While the strict legal right may exist in the government to enforce the exercise of these offices, the attempt to do so would be so irritating, and so nearly impracticable with all, that I deem it better to forego, for the time, the uses of such offices.

The mails, unless repelled, will continue to be furnished in all parts of the Union. So far as possible, the people everywhere shall have that sense of perfect security which is most favorable to calm thought and reflection. The course here indicated will be followed, unless current events and experience shall show a modification or change to be proper; and in every case and exigency my best discretion will be exercised according to circumstances actually existing, and with a view and a hope of a peaceful solution of the national troubles, and the restoration of fraternal sympathies and affections.

That there are persons in one section or another who seek to destroy the Union at all events, and are glad of any pretext to do it, I will neither affirm nor deny; but if there be such, I need address no word to them. To those, however, who really love the Union may I not speak?

Before entering upon so grave a matter as the destruction of our national fabric, with all its benefits, its memories and its hopes, would it not be wise to ascertain precisely why we do it? Will you hazard so desperate a step, while there is any possibility that any portion of the ills you fly from have no real existence? Will you, while the certain ills you fly to, are greater than all the real ones you fly from? Will you risk the commission of so fearful a mistake?

All profess to be content in the Union, if all constitutional rights can be maintained. Is it true, then, that any right, plainly written in the Constitution, has been denied? I think not. Happily the human mind is so constituted, that no party can reach to the audacity of doing this. Think, if you can, of a single instance in which a plainly written provision of the Constitution has ever been denied. If, by the mere force of numbers, a majority should deprive a minority of any clearly written constitutional right, it might, in a moral point of view, justify revolution—certainly would, if such right were a vital one. But such is not our case. All the vital rights of minorities, and of individuals, are so plainly assured to them, by affirmations and negations, guaranties and prohibitions, in the Constitution, that controversies never arise concerning them. But no organic law can ever be framed with a provision specifically applicable to every question which may occur in practical administration. No foresight can anticipate, nor any document of reasonable length contain express provisions for all possible questions. Shall fugitives from labor be surrendered by national or by State authority? The Constitution does not expressly say. *May* Congress prohibit slavery in the territories? The Constitution does not expressly say. *Must* Congress protect slavery in the territories? The Constitution does not expressly say.

From questions of this class spring all our constitutional controversies, and we divide upon them into majorities and minorities. If the minority will not acquiesce, the majority must, or the government must cease. There is no other alternative; for continuing the government, is acquiescence on one side or the other. If a minority, in such case, will secede rather than acquiesce, they make a precedent which, in turn, will divide and ruin them; for a minority of their own will secede from them whenever a majority refuses to be controlled by such minority. For instance, why may not any portion of a new confederacy, a year or two hence, arbitrarily secede again, precisely as portions of the present Union now claim to secede from it? All who cherish disunion sentiments, are now being educated to the exact temper of doing this.

Is there such perfect identity of interests among the States to compose a new Union, as to produce harmony only, and prevent renewed secession?

Plainly, the central idea of secession, is the essence of anarchy. A majority, held in restraint by constitutional checks and limitations, and always changing easily with deliberate changes of popular opinions and sentiments, is the only true sovereign of a free people. Whoever rejects it, does, of necessity, fly to anarchy or to despotism. Unanimity is impossible; the rule of a minority, as a permanent arrangement, is wholly inadmissible; so that, rejecting the majority principle, anarchy or despotism in some form is all that is left.

I do not forget the position assumed by some, that constitutional questions are to be decided by the Supreme Court; nor do I deny that such decisions must be binding in any case, upon the parties to a suit, as to the object of that suit, while they are also entitled to very high respect and consideration in all parallel cases by all other departments of the government. And while it is obviously possible that such decision may be erroneous in any given case, still the evil effect following it, being limited to that particular case, with the chance that it may be over-ruled, and never become a precedent for other cases, can better be borne than could the evils of a different practice. At the same time, the candid citizen must confess that if the policy of the government upon vital questions, affecting the whole people, is to be irrevocably fixed by decisions of the Supreme Court, the instant they are made, in ordinary litigation between parties, in personal actions, the people will have ceased to be their own rulers, having to that extent practically resigned their government into the hands of that eminent tribunal. Nor is there in this view any assault upon the court or the judges. It is a duty from which they may not shrink, to decide cases properly brought before them; and it is no fault of theirs if others seek to turn their decisions to political purposes.

One section of our country believes slavery is *right*, and ought to be extended, while the other believes it is *wrong*, and ought not to be extended. This is the only substantial dispute. The fugitive slave clause of the Constitution, and the law for the suppression of the foreign slave trade, are each as well enforced, perhaps, as any law can ever be in a community where the moral sense of the people imperfectly supports the law itself. The great body of the people abide by the dry legal obligation in both cases, and a few break over in each. This, I think, cannot be perfectly cured; and it would be worse in both cases *after* the separation of the sections, than before. The foreign slave trade, now imperfectly suppressed, would be ultimately revived without restriction, in one section; while fugitive slaves, now only partially surrendered, would not be surrendered at all, by the other.

Physically speaking, we cannot separate. We can not remove our respective sections from each other, nor build an impassable wall between them. A husband and wife may be divorced, and go out of the presence, and beyond the reach of each other; but the different parts of our country cannot do this. They cannot but remain face to face; and intercourse, either amicable or hostile, must continue between them. Is it possible, then, to make that intercourse more advantageous or more satisfactory, *after* separation than *before*? Can aliens make treaties easier than friends can make laws? Can treaties be more faithfully enforced between aliens than laws can among friends? Suppose you go to war, you cannot fight always; and when, after much loss on both sides, and no gain on either, you cease fighting, the identical old questions, as to terms of intercourse, are again upon you.

This country, with its institutions, belongs to the people who inhabit it. Whenever they shall grow weary of the existing Government, they can exercise their *constitutional* right of amending it, or their *revolutionary* right to dismember or overthrow it. I cannot be ignorant of the fact that many worthy and patriotic citizens are desirous of having the national Constitution amended. While I make no recommendation of amendments, I fully recognize the rightful authority of the people over the whole subject to be exercised in either of the modes prescribed in the instrument itself; and I should, under existing circumstances, favor rather than oppose a fair opportunity being afforded the people to act upon it.

I will venture to add that to me the Convention mode seems preferable, in that it allows amendments to originate with the people themselves, instead of only permitting them to take or reject propositions, originated by others, not especially chosen for the purpose, and which might not be precisely such as they would wish to either accept or refuse. I understand a proposed amendment to the Constitution, which amendment, however, I have not seen, has passed Congress, to the effect that the federal government shall never interfere with the domestic institutions of the States, including that of persons held to service. To avoid misconstruction of what I have said, I depart from my purpose not to speak of particular amendments, so far as to say that holding such a provision to now be implied constitutional law, I have no objection to its being made express and irrevocable.

The Chief Magistrate derives all his authority from the people, and they have referred none upon him to fix terms for the separation of the States. The people themselves can do this if also they choose; but the executive, as such, has nothing to do with it. His duty is to administer the present government, as it came to his hands, and to transmit it, unimpaired by him, to his successor.

Why should there not be a patient confidence in the ultimate justice of the people? Is there any better or equal hope, in the world? In our present differences, is either party without faith of being in the right? If the Almighty Ruler of nations, with his eternal truth and justice, be on your side of the North, or on yours of the South, that truth, and that justice, will surely prevail, by the judgment of this great tribunal, the American people.

By the frame of the government under which we live, this same people have wisely given their public servants but little power for mischief; and have, with equal wisdom, provided for the return of that little to their own hands at very short intervals.

While the people retain their virtue and vigilance, no administration, by any extreme of wickedness or folly, can very seriously injure the government in the short space of four years.

My countrymen, one and all, think calmly and *well*, upon this whole subject. Nothing valuable can be lost by taking time. If there be an object to *hurry* any of you, in hot haste, to a step which you would never take *deliberately,* that object will be frustrated by taking time; but no good object can be frustrated by it. Such of you as are now dissatisfied still have the old Constitution unimpaired, and, on the sensitive point, the laws of your own framing under it; while the new administration will have no immediate power, if it would, to change either. If it were admitted that you who are dissatisfied, hold the right side in the dispute, there still is no single good reason for precipitate action. Intelligence, patriotism, Christianity, and a firm reliance on Him, who has never yet forsaken this favored land, are still competent to adjust, in the best way, all our present difficulty.

In *your* hands, my dissatisfied fellow countrymen, and not in *mine,* is the momentous issue of civil war. The government will not assail *you.* You can have no conflict without being yourselves the aggressors. *You* have no oath registered in Heaven to destroy the government, while *I* shall have the most solemn one to "preserve, protect, and defend it."

I am loath to close. We are not enemies, but friends. We must not be enemies. Though passion may have strained, it must not break our bonds of affection. The mystic chords of memory, stretching from every battle-field, and patriot grave, to every living heart and hearth-stone, all over this broad land, will yet swell the chorus of the Union, when again touched, as surely they will be, by the better angels of our nature.

Interpretation

In a last ditch effort to prevent civil war, Lincoln cites his own views and those of the Republican platform promising not to "interfere with the institution of slavery in the States where it exists," and strongly condemning attempts, like John Brown's, to free the slaves by force. He goes so far as to urge the adoption of a careful fugitive slave law, acknowledging that the Constitution itself requires it.

Having given these assurances, Lincoln turns to the "great and peculiar difficulty" with which he, as the sixteenth president, is already faced: "A disruption of the Federal Union, heretofore only menaced, is now formidably attempted." Without calling it a "secession," Lincoln presents the arguments, both general and historical, for considering such disruptions unconstitutional, and either "insurrectionary or revolutionary, according to circumstances." The general point is that all governments are set up to be perpetual. And if it is argued that the "United States be not a government proper, but an association of States in the nature of contract merely," can one of the parties to such a contract simply break it on its own? Historically, the evidence from before the Constitution, going as far back as the Articles of Association of 1774, and from the preamble to the Constitution itself demonstrates the clear intention to be perpetual.

In view of this conclusion, Lincoln expresses his determination to defend and maintain the Union. Bloodshed and violence need not occur unless forced upon the national authority. He will hold the places belonging to the national government, and collect duties and imposts, but any invasion (of the states in rebellion) or attempt to fill unfilled Federal offices with "obnoxious strangers" is ruled out. It is better "to forego, for the time, the uses of such offices." Lincoln wants to give "calm thought and reflection" a chance to take hold, and therefore speaks in the most cautious terms, promising to tailor his actions (as chief executive and commander-in-chief) to particular circumstances.

Having examined the great constitutional issue posed by secession and indicated the course of action he will take to defend the Constitution and the Union, Lincoln now addresses himself to those "who really love the Union," enjoining them to consider what wisdom and justice require. He grants a vital principle: "If, by the mere force of numbers, a majority should deprive a minority of any clearly written constitutional right, it might, in a moral point of view, justify revolution—certainly would, if such a right were a vital one." The dissension about slavery, however, concerns not such clearly protected constitutional rights but issues—like whether Congress may prohibit slavery in the territories—left open by the Constitution.

If, on such issues, the minority does not yield to the majority, the government must cease to exist. If this minority should secede and form a separate confederacy, that confederacy would be subject to further secessions from it: "Plainly, the central idea of secession, is the essence of anarchy." Or, making the basic point as well as anyone has: "A majority, held in check by constitutional checks and limitations, and always changing easily with deliberate changes of popular opinions and sentiments is the only true sovereign of a free people."

Southerners who argued for secession justified it either on constitutional or revolutionary grounds. According to the former, the states, as the ultimate unit of government, are free to leave the Union, just as they were free to join it. According to the latter, the states have a right not to be tyrannized over and to alter the government over them as they see fit. Lincoln must have thought the revolutionary argument more worrisome, since he pays greater attention to it. It appears, at first, that the looser language he permitted himself in examining the Mexican War will not do here. He does not again speak of a people, or part of a people, rightfully changing the government to which they are subject, or establishing a new one, at their pleasure. Once a constitutional union has been freely formed, the only perfect ground for revolution by part of the people can occur when a majority deprives a minority of some *vital, clearly written, constitutional* right. Judged by this standard, the South's concern that remaining in the Union would jeopardize the institution of slavery in the long run does not suffice to justify the revolutionary act of secession. Nor do the South's present fears, which Lincoln has done everything in his power to allay. It is not enough to secede because of fears that are baseless.

Lincoln considers the objection, favorable to the South, that the Supreme Court's *Dred Scott* decision forbade Congress to keep slavery out of the territories. His position is the same he took in his speech on that case: "if the policy of the government upon vital questions, affecting the whole people, is to be irrevocably fixed by decisions of the Supreme Court, the instant they are made, in ordinary litigation between parties, in personal actions, the people will have ceased to be their own rulers, having to that extent practically resigned their government into the hands of that eminent tribunal."

Rather than repeat his arguments against Taney's opinion, Lincoln prefers to admit a deep division in the country on the subject of the rightness of slavery and its extension. Even so, he maintains, it is better to remain one country than to separate into hostile nations, since we cannot separate physically. The constitution of the country can be changed by the people, and again Lincoln ventures upon dangerous ground. Here is how he puts it: "This country, with its institutions, belongs to the people who inhabit it. Whenever they shall grow weary of the existing government, they can exercise their *constitutional* right of amending it, or their *revolutionary* right to dismember, or overthrow it."

First Lincoln indicates a willingness to accept an amendment protecting slavery in the states from federal interference. As to revolutionary right, in connection with the Mexican War Lincoln had argued in favor of the unrestricted right of a people, *or part of a people*, to "revolutionize." The revolution he envisions as a possibility here, however, is one he seems to think of as undertaken by the whole people, north and south together, should they "grow weary of the existing government." But what if a part of the people (the South) grows weary of the existing government? Earlier in the speech, Lincoln had better protected against this dangerous alternative when he required actual (not imagined) violations of constitutional rights for the right to revolution to become operative. To be operative, the "growing weary" could not just depend on subjective feelings but on real facts indicating that the "weariness" was deserved! This problem of keeping the "right to revolution" reasonable is inherent in every stipulation of it as a general right. The Declaration of Independence is more cautious, justifying our revolution against Great Britain by "a long train of tyrannical abuses" and not just by our weariness of the existing government. On the basis of the Declaration, Lincoln might also have argued that popular revolutions for the sake of enslaving others, rather than for greater freedom, are not justified at all.

Lincoln closes by urging "patient confidence in the ultimate justice of the people"—the best hope in the world. If the "Almighty ruler of nations," with His eternal truth and justice, favors one side or the other, will not that view prevail by the judgment of this "great tribunal, the American people"? While the people retain their "virtue and vigilance," little harm can be done to the government by any administration in its four year term. Again Lincoln cautions against precipitate action, and expresses confidence that "intelligence, patriotism, Christianity, and a firm reliance on Him, who has never yet forsaken this favored land" will find a way out of the present difficulty.

The ending is momentous. Lincoln tells his "dissatisfied fellow countrymen" that the issue of civil war is in their hands, not his, reminding them of his presidential oath, registered in heaven, to "preserve, protect and defend" the government. His final glorious appeal is couched in terms of a complex musical metaphor. He imagines chords (harmonious sounds) of memory connecting every living heart and hearthstone, every individual and family, to the battlefields and graves of our national history. These chords, these memories of great sacrifices undertaken together, touched by the better angels of our nature, will swell the chorus of the Union—will, like the harps angels touch, stimulate the singing together, in chorus, north and south, of support for the Union. But, however gorgeous the metaphor, it was not to be.

Chapter 14

Letter to Horace Greeley, August 22, 1862

Two days before, Horace Greeley had published in the New York Tribune, *his paper, an editorial speaking in the name of Twenty Millions and urging Lincoln to end slavery by enforcing the Second Confiscation Act. Greeley published Lincoln's response in the* Tribune *of August 25.*

Text

Executive Mansion,
Washington, August 22, 1862.

Hon. Horace Greeley:
Dear Sir.

I have just read yours of the 19th. addressed to myself through the New-York Tribune. If there be in it any statements, or assumptions of fact, which I may know to be erroneous, I do not now and here, controvert them. If there be in it any inferences which I may believe to be falsely drawn, I do not now and here, argue against them. If there be perceptable [*sic*] in it an impatient and dictatorial tone, I waive it in deference to an old friend, whose heart I have always supposed to be right.

As to the policy I "seem to be pursuing" as you say, I have not meant to leave any one in doubt.

I would save the Union. I would save it the shortest way under the Constitution. The sooner the national authority can be restored; the nearer the Union will be "the Union as it was." If there be those who would not save the Union, unless they could at the same time *save* slavery, I do not agree with them. If there be those who would not save the Union unless they could at the same time *destroy* slavery, I do not agree with them. My paramount object in this struggle *is* to save the Union, and is *not* either to save or to destroy slavery. If I could save the Union without freeing *any* slave I would do it, and if I could save it by freeing *all* the slaves I would do it; and if I could save it by freeing some and leaving others alone I would also do that. What I do about slavery, and the colored race,

I do because I believe it helps to save the Union; and what I forbear, I forbear because I do *not* believe it would help to save the Union. I shall do *less* whenever I shall believe what I am doing hurts the cause, and I shall do *more* whenever I shall believe doing more will help the cause. I shall try to correct errors when shown to be errors; and I shall adopt new views so fast as they shall appear to be true views.

I have here stated my purpose according to my view of *official* duty; and I intend no modification of my oft-expressed *personal* wish that all men every where could be free.

Yours,
A. Lincoln

Interpretation

Lincoln begins this concise, memorable and almost defiant response to Greeley's open letter in the *New York Tribune* (his paper) by setting aside, without further comment, whatever errors of fact and inference he might have found in it and "waiving" its "impatient and dictatorial tone" in deference to an "old friend, whose heart I have always supposed to be right." Lincoln only supposes Greeley's heart to be right, implying that he knows Greeley's intellect is not. But friendship must be given its due, even in the midst of political controversy.

Greeley had criticized Lincoln for failing to provide the country with a clear policy and neglecting to take steps toward emancipating the slaves. Lincoln responds by stating his whole policy in a single unswerving paragraph. It was to save the Union, to restore the national authority, and not to either save or destroy slavery. If he could save the Union by freeing none of the slaves, all of the slaves or some of the slaves, he would. What he does about the "colored race" is done only with an eye to saving the Union. This, Lincoln concludes, is what his official duty requires, as distinguished from his "oft-expressed *personal* wish that all men everywhere could be free."

In order to keep emancipation from being at least one of his main objectives, Lincoln has to reduce the strength of its authority as a demand, a moral and political demand. That's why he speaks of it so weakly—as a mere personal wish—whereas its true status, in his own mind, was really that of a demand of justice itself, to be satisfied whenever circumstances allowed. But Lincoln is on sound constitutional grounds. His sworn duty, as president, was to "preserve, protect and defend the Constitution of the United States." Saving the Union meant saving it as it was in 1860, before the rebellion, and the Constitution did allow for the existence of slavery in the states.

There were also political reasons for not making emancipation a direct object of national policy. In large sections of the country outside the deep South, emancipation would have been very unpopular, and even with the South it was important to avoid giving the impression that the Union, from the beginning, was out to destroy slavery—an abolitionist position that Lincoln certainly never shared. But let us look further down the line. To save the Union *was* in fact to set slavery on the course to extinction, and to fail in saving the Union *was* in fact to guarantee the perpetuation of slavery. In the latter case, the South would be free to preserve slavery as it wished; in the former, the North's victory, while not immediately leading to emancipation, would so confine the South's ambitions as to make that conclusion inevitable, however long it might take. Why could Lincoln be confident this policy of containment would spell slavery's ultimate doom in the South? Probably because of the slow but definite effect of the Declaration of Independence in bringing Southerners around in their thinking, combined with the growing predominance and influence of free states within the Union.

Lincoln's position, stated here with some asperity, was sound in every respect. What it did was to provide for, and guarantee, eventual emancipation without ever making it the Union's direct object in the Civil War. But let us not forget his asserted willingness to free all the slaves (he does not say on what constitutional ground) if necessary to saving the Union. Only a month later, on September 22, Lincoln told the nation that he would issue the Emancipation Proclamation on the very first day of the new year, 1863, justifying it as a war measure—with limitations on the extent of emancipation necessitated by that fact. He did not reveal his plan to do so in this letter to Greeley.

Chapter 15

The Emancipation Proclamation, January 1, 1863

This is the most famous document of Lincoln's administration. The original version was prepared by Lincoln and submitted to his cabinet on July 22, a month before Horace Greeley's editorial.

Text

A PROCLAMATION.

Whereas, on the twentysecond day of September, in the year of our Lord one thousand eight hundred and sixty two, a proclamation was issued by the President of the United States, containing, among other things, the following, to wit:

"That on the first day of January, in the year of our Lord one thousand eight hundred and sixty-three, all persons held as slaves within any State or designated part of a State, the people whereof shall then be in rebellion against the United States, shall be then, thenceforward and forever free; and the Executive Government of the United States, including the military and naval authority thereof, will recognize and maintain the freedom of such persons, and will do no act or acts to repress such persons, or any of them, in any efforts they may make for their actual freedom.

"That the Executive will, on the first day of January aforesaid, by proclamation, designate the States and parts of States, if any, in which the people thereof, respectively, shall then be in rebellion against the United States; and the fact that any State, or the people thereof, shall on that day be, in good faith, represented in the Congress of the United States by members chosen thereto at elections wherein a majority of the qualified voters of such State shall have participated, shall, in the absence of strong countervailing testimony, be deemed conclusive evidence that such State, and the people thereof, are not then in rebellion against the United States."

Now, therefore I, Abraham Lincoln, President of the United States, by virtue of the power in me vested as Commander-in-Chief, of the Army and Navy of the United States in time of actual armed rebellion against the authority and government of the United States, and as a fit and necessary war measure for suppressing said rebellion, do, on this first day of January, in the year of our Lord one thousand eight hundred and sixty three, and in accordance with my purpose so to do publicly proclaimed for the full period of one hundred days, from the day first above mentioned, order and designate as the States and parts of States wherein the people thereof respectively, are this day in rebellion against the United States, the following, to wit:

Arkansas, Texas, Louisiana, (except the Parishes of St. Bernard, Plaquemines, Jefferson, St. Johns, St. Charles, St. James, Ascension, Assumption, Terrebonne, Lafourche, St. Mary, St. Martin, and Orleans, including the City of New Orleans) Mississippi, Alabama, Florida, Georgia, South-Carolina, North-Carolina, and Virginia, (except the forty-eight counties designated as West Virginia, and also the counties of Berkley, Accomac, Northampton, Elizabeth-City, York, Princess Ann, and Norfolk, including the cities of Norfolk & Portsmouth[)]; and which excepted parts are for the present left precisely as if this proclamation were not issued.

And by virtue of the power, and for the purpose aforesaid, I do order and declare that all persons held as slaves within said designated States, and parts of States are and henceforward shall be free; and that the Executive government of the United States, including the military and naval authorities thereof, will recognize and maintain the freedom of said persons.

And I hereby enjoin upon the people so declared to be free to abstain from all violence, unless in necessary self-defence; and I recommend to them that in all cases when allowed, they labor faithfully for reasonable wages.

And I further declare and make known, that such persons of suitable condition, will be received into the armed service of the United States to garrison forts, positions, stations, and other places, and to man vessels of all sorts in said service.

And upon this act, sincerely believed to be an act of justice, warranted by the Constitution, upon military necessity, I invoke the considerate judgment of mankind, and the gracious favor of Almighty God.

In witness whereof, I have hereunto set my hand and caused the seal of the United States to be affixed.

[L. S.]   Done at the City of Washington, this first day of January, in the year of our Lord one thousand eight hundred and sixty three, and of the Independence of the United States of America the eighty-seventh.

By the President:

                                          Abraham Lincoln

                                          William H. Seward
                                          Secretary of State

Interpretation

On September 22 of the previous year, Lincoln had announced the emancipation he intended to proclaim and place into operation on the following January 1, hoping that, during this period of one hundred days, some states or parts of states in rebellion would return to the Union fold. In that announcement, he had also promised to all "slave-states, so called," not or no longer in rebellion, that he would "again recommend" to Congress two things: giving financial assistance to voluntary programs of emancipation and continuing the effort "to colonize persons of African descent, with their consent, upon this continent, or elsewhere." Finally, he had ordered the military to obey Congress' recent action of July 17 prohibiting the return of fugitive slaves to their owners and setting such slaves free.

Now, on January 1, 1863, Lincoln begins by designating the states and parts of states still in rebellion, and then, acting by his authority as Commander-in-chief of the Army and Navy, orders—as a "fit and necessary war measure for suppressing said rebellion"—that "all persons held as slaves within said designated States, and parts of States, are, and henceforward shall be free, and that the Executive government of the United States, including the military and naval authorities thereof, will recognize and maintain the freedom of said persons."

Eight whole states—Arkansas, Texas, Mississippi, Alabama, Florida, Georgia, South Carolina and North Carolina—are designated as in rebellion, and two—Louisiana and Virginia—with parts specifically excepted from the order. There and only there the slaves are freed. Lincoln enjoins on the newly freed people "to abstain from all violence, unless in necessary self-defence," and recommends that they "labor faithfully for reasonable wages," when allowed. He also orders that "such persons of suitable condition" be taken into the armed services to garrison places in the army and man vessels in the navy. He closes the proclamation by invoking "the considerate judgment of mankind and the gracious favor of Almighty God" for what he sincerely believes "to be an act of justice, warranted by the Constitution, upon military necessity."

This is the justly famous Emancipation Proclamation. Its brevity and simple executive directness convey little idea of the care given not only to its composition but even more to its very conception and origination. It has been criticized for its limitations: for leaving slavery untouched in the "border states" not in rebellion, for affecting slavery even in the rebel states only so far as the army had reached or could actively reach, for not denouncing the institution of slavery, and, of course, for coming so late.

Previously, on August 14, 1862, Lincoln had assembled a group of blacks in the White House and said to them, "Your race are suffering, in my judgment, the greatest wrong inflicted on any people." Yet only a few days later, in seeming disregard of this injustice, he wrote Horace Greeley that "My paramount object in this struggle is to save the Union, and is *not* either to save or destroy slavery."

As we have already seen, the two objectives are interrelated: to save the Union was his sworn duty as President, and saving the Union was also the only way in which slavery could be destroyed, however long it might take. Granting that the president had no constitutional right, nor did Congress (except through amendment) to abolish slavery on moral grounds, it was the civil war itself that afforded him an opportunity to effect emancipation constitutionally. Slaves, considered as mere property, were of use to the rebel enemy, and depriving an enemy of useful property was well within Lincoln's powers as Commander-in-Chief. Hence the form of the Emancipation Proclamation, the operative section of which begins with an assertion of the full power and authority of the President: "I, Abraham Lincoln, President of the United States, by virtue of the power in me vested as Commander-in-Chief of the Army and Navy of the United States."

It was a daring act nonetheless. It abolished slavery forever in the rebellious states, whether the Union armies had gotten there or not, thereby giving slaves an enormous motive to flee, if they could, and to contribute less to, or impede, the rebel cause, if they couldn't. Their masters could no longer presume on their obedience. It is true that only the coming of the Union armies could guarantee the liberty of most, and, finally, a Union victory in the war, but Antietam had just been won and prospects looked better. The Proclamation even gave freedmen a direct opportunity to assist in victory by welcoming them into the Union army and navy, where they could give proof of their gratitude, loyalty and fighting ability. And even if they stayed where they were, the Proclamation empowered them for the first time to act as free wage-earners, arranging suitable terms with their erst-while masters. A parchment entitlement in most cases, but symbolically real and in ultimate effect revolutionary.

Only in the very last sentence does Lincoln refer to his order as an "act of justice" constitutionally warranted on the grounds of "military necessity." This "act of justice" says it all to the heeding ear. There was no need to dwell upon the injustices of slavery. With one official document and one signature, they are gone—not gone in fact but in principle, the facts to follow as soon as possible. How unjust to this good and wise man to consider him anything but (as he was thought to be for so long) the greatest friend and benefactor the black race ever had in this country! He was, in truth, the Great Emancipator. Realizing the limitations of the Proclamation, Lincoln set to work immediately on creating the Thirteenth Amendment, the intent of which was to prohibit slavery everywhere in the Union. The "new birth of freedom" was well on its way, and a new day for members of the black race, and their white brothers, had dawned.

Chapter 16

Letter to Erastus Corning, June 12, 1863

This is Lincoln's response to resolutions Ohio Democrats passed at a public meeting, denouncing him for violating the constitution by authorizing "certain military arrests and proceedings following them." Their protests were ignited by General Burnside's arrest of Ohio Congressman Clement V. Vallandigham for speaking against the war.

Text

Executive Mansion,
Washington, June 12, 1863.

Hon. Erastus Corning and others
Gentlemen
Your letter of May 19th, inclosing the resolutions of a public meeting held at Albany, New York, on the 16th of the same month, was received several days ago.

The resolutions, as I understand them, are resolvable into two propositions—first, the expression of a purpose to sustain the cause of the Union, to secure peace through victory, and to support the administration in every constitutional and lawful measure to suppress the rebellion; and secondly, a declaration of censure upon the administration for supposed unconstitutional action, such as the making of military arrests. And, from the two propositions a third is deduced, which is that the gentlemen composing the meeting are resolved on doing their part to maintain our common government and country, despite the folly or wickedness, as they may conceive, of any administration. This position is eminently patriotic, and as such I thank the meeting, and congratulate the nation for it. My own purpose is the same; so that the meeting and myself have a common object, and can have no difference, except in the choice of means or measures for effecting that object.

And here I ought to close this paper, and would close it, if there were no apprehension that more injurious consequences than any merely personal to myself might follow the censures systematically cast upon me for doing what, in my view of duty, I could not forbear. The resolutions promise to support me in every constitutional and lawful measure to suppress the rebellion; and I have not knowingly employed, nor shall knowingly employ, any other. But the meeting, by their resolutions, assert and argue that certain military arrests, and proceedings following them, for which I am ultimately responsible, are unconstitutional. I think they are not. The resolutions quote from the Constitution the definition of treason, and also the limiting safe-guards and guarantees therein provided for the citizen on trials for treason, and on his being held to answer for capital or otherwise infamous crimes, and in criminal prosecutions, his right to a speedy and public trial by an impartial jury. They proceed to resolve "that these safe-guards of the rights of the citizen against the pretentions of arbitrary power were intended more especially for his protection in times of civil commotion." And, apparently, to demonstrate the proposition, the resolutions proceed: "They were secured substantially to the English people after years of protracted civil war, and were adopted into our constitution at the close of the revolution." Would not the demonstration have been better, if it could have been truly said that these safe-guards had been adopted, and applied *during* the civil wars and *during* our revolution, instead of *after* the one, and at the *close* of the other. I too am devotedly for them *after* civil war, and *before* civil war, and at all times "except when, in cases of Rebellion or Invasion, the public Safety may require" their suspension. The resolutions proceed to tell us that these safeguards "have stood the test of seventy-six years of trial, under our republican system, under circumstances which show that while they constitute the foundation of all free government, they are the elements of the enduring stability of the Republic." No one denies that they have so stood the test up to the beginning of the present rebellion, if we except a certain occurrence at New-Orleans hereafter to be mentioned; nor does any one question that they will stand the same test much longer after the rebellion closes. But these provisions of the constitution have no application to the case we have in hand, because the arrests complained of were not made for treason—that is, not for *the* treason defined in the Constitution, and upon the conviction of which the punishment is death—nor yet were they made to hold persons to answer for any capital, or otherwise infamous crimes; nor were the proceedings following, in any constitutional or legal sense, "criminal prosecutions." The arrests were made on totally different grounds, and the proceedings following accorded with the grounds of the arrests. Let us consider the real case with which we are dealing, and apply to it the parts of the constitution plainly made for such cases.

Prior to my installation here it had been inculcated that any State had a lawful right to secede from the national Union, and that it would be expedient to exercise the right whenever the devotees of the doctrine should fail to elect a President to their own liking. I was elected contrary to their liking; and accordingly, so far as it was legally possible, they had taken seven States out of the Union, had seized many of the United States forts, and had fired upon the United

States flag, all before I was inaugurated, and, of course, before I had done any official act whatever. The rebellion thus began soon ran into the present civil war; and, in certain respects, it began on very unequal terms between the parties. The insurgents had been preparing for it more than thirty years, while the government had taken no steps to resist them. The former had carefully considered all the means which could be turned to their account. It undoubtedly was a well pondered reliance with that in their own unrestricted effort to destroy Union, Constitution, and law, all together, the government would, in great degree, be restrained by the same Constitution and law from arresting their progress. Their sympathizers pervaded all departments of the government and nearly all communities of the people. From this material, under cover of "liberty of speech," "liberty of the press," and *"habeas corpus,"* they hoped to keep on foot amongst us a most efficient corps of spies, informers, suppliers, and aiders and abettors of their cause in a thousand ways. They knew that in times such as they were inaugurating, by the Constitution itself the *"habeas corpus"* might be suspended; but they also knew they had friends who would make a question as to who was to suspend it; meanwhile their spies and others might remain at large to help on their cause. Or if, as has happened, the Executive should suspend the writ, without ruinous waste of time, instances of arresting innocent persons might occur, as are always likely to occur in such cases; and then a clamor could be raised in regard to this, which might be at least of some service to the insurgent cause. It needed no very keen perception to discover this part of the enemy's programme, so soon as by open hostilities their machinery was fairly put in motion. Yet, thoroughly imbued with a reverence for the guaranteed rights of individuals, I was slow to adopt the strong measures which by degrees I have been forced to regard as being within the exceptions of the Constitution, and as indispensable to the public Safety. Nothing is better known to history than that courts of justice are utterly incompetent to such cases. Civil courts are organized chiefly for trials of individuals, or, at most, a few individuals acting in concert—and this in quiet times, and on charges of crimes well defined in the law. Even in times of peace bands of horse-thieves and robbers frequently grow too numerous and powerful for the ordinary courts of justice. But what comparison, in numbers, have such bands ever borne to the insurgent sympathizers even in many of the loyal States? Again, a jury too frequently has at least one member more ready to hang the panel than to hang the traitor. And yet again, he who dissuades one man from volunteering, or induces one soldier to desert, weakens the Union cause as much as he who kills a Union soldier in battle. Yet this dissuasion or inducement may be so conducted as to be no defined crime of which any civil court would take cognizance.

Ours is a case of Rebellion—so called by the resolutions before me—in fact, a clear, flagrant, and gigantic case of rebellion; and the provision of the Constitution that "The privilege of the writ of *habeas corpus* shall not be suspended unless when, in cases of rebellion or invasion, the public safety may require it" is the provision which specially applies to our present case. This provision plainly attests the understanding of those who made the Constitution that ordinary courts of justice are inadequate to "cases of Rebellion"—attests their that, in such cases, men may be held in custody whom the courts, acting on ordinary rules, would discharge. *Habeas corpus* does not discharge men who are proved to be guilty of defined crime; and its suspension is allowed by the Constitution on purpose that men may be arrested and held who cannot be proved to be guilty of defined crime, "when, in cases of rebellion or invasion the public safety may require it."

This is precisely our present case—a case of rebellion wherein the public safety does require the suspension. Indeed, arrests by process of courts, and arrests in cases of rebellion do not proceed altogether upon the same basis. The former is directed at the small percentage of ordinary and continuous perpetration of crime, while the latter is directed at sudden and extensive uprisings against the government, which, at most, will succeed or fail, in no great length of time. In the latter case arrests are made not so much for what has been done, as for what probably would be done. The latter is more for the preventive and less for the vindictive than the former. In such cases the purposes of men are much more easily understood than in cases of ordinary crime. The man who stands by and says nothing when the peril of his government is discussed, cannot be misunderstood. If not hindered, he is sure to help the enemy; much more if he talks ambiguously—talks for his country with "buts," and "ifs" and "ands." Of how little value the constitutional provision I have quoted will be rendered if arrests shall never be made until defined crimes shall have been committed, may be illustrated by a few notable examples. General John C. Breckinridge, General Robert E. Lee, General Joseph E. Johnston, General John B. Magruder, General William B. Preston, General Simon B. Buckner, and Commodore Franklin Buchanan, now occupying the very highest places in the rebel war service, were all within the power of the government since the rebellion began, and were nearly as well known to be traitors then as now. Unquestionably if we had seized and held them, the insurgent cause would be much weaker. But no one of them had then committed any crime defined in the law. Every one of them, if arrested would have been discharged on *habeas corpus*, were the writ allowed to operate. In view of these and similar cases, I think the time not unlikely to come when I shall be blamed for having made too few arrests rather than too many.

By the third resolution the meeting indicate their opinion that military arrests may be constitutional in localities where rebellion actually exist, but that such arrests are unconstitutional in localities where rebellion or insurrection does not actually exist. They insist that such arrests shall not be made "outside of the lines of necessary military occupation, and the scenes of insurrection." Inasmuch, however, as the Constitution itself makes no such distinction, I am unable to believe that there is any such constitutional distinction. I concede that the class of arrests complained of can be constitutional only when, in cases of rebellion or invasion, the public safety may require the and I insist that in such cases, they are constitutional wherever the public safety does require them—as well in places to which they may prevent the rebellion extending, as in those where it may be already prevailing; as well where they may restrain mischievous interference with the raising and supplying of armies to suppress the rebellion as where the rebellion may actually be; as well where they may restrain the enticing men out of the army, as where they would prevent mutiny in the army; equally constitutional at all places where they will conduce to the public safety, as against the dangers of rebellion or invasion. Take the particular case mentioned by the meeting. It is asserted in substance, that Mr. Vallandigham was, by a military commander, seized and tried "for no other reason than words addressed to a public meeting, in criticism of the course of the administration, and in condemnation of the military orders of that general." Now, if there be no mistake about this, if this assertion is the truth and the whole truth, if there was no other reason for the arrest, then I concede that the arrest was wrong. But the arrest, as I understand, was made for a very different reason. Mr. Vallandigham avows his hostility to the war on the part of the Union; and his arrest was made because he was laboring, with some effect, to prevent the raising of troops, to encourage desertions from the army, and to leave the rebellion without an adequate military force to suppress it. He was not arrested because he was damaging the political prospects of the administration or the personal interests of the commanding general, but because he was damaging the army, upon the existence and vigor of which the life of the nation depends. He was warring upon the military, and this gave the military constitutional jurisdiction to lay hands upon him. If Mr. Vallandigham was not damaging the military power of the country, then his arrest was made on mistake of fact, which I would be glad to correct on reasonably satisfactory evidence.

I understand the meeting whose resolutions I am considering, to be in favor of suppressing the rebellion by military force—by armies. Long experience has shown that armies cannot be maintained unless desertion shall be punished by the severe penalty of death. The case requires, and the law and the Constitution sanction, this punishment. Must I shoot a simple-minded soldier boy who deserts, while I must not touch a hair of a wiley agitator who induces him to desert? This is none the less injurious when effected by getting a father, or brother, or friend, into a public meeting, and there working upon his feelings till he is persuaded to write the soldier boy that he is fighting in a bad cause, for a wicked administration of a contemptable government, too weak to arrest and punish him if he shall desert. I think that in such a case, to silence the agitator, and save the boy is not only constitutional, but, withal a great mercy.

If I be wrong on this question of constitutional power, my error lies in believing that certain proceedings are constitutional when, in cases of rebellion or invasion, the public safety requires them, which would not be constitutional when, in absence of rebellion or invasion, the public safety does not require them: in other words, that the Constitution is not in its application in all respects the same in cases of rebellion or invasion, involving the public safety, as it is in times of profound peace and public security. The Constitution itself makes the distinction, and I can no more be persuaded that the government can constitutionally take no strong measure in time of rebellion, because it can be shown that the same could not be lawfully taken in time of peace, than I can be persuaded that a particular drug is not good medicine for a sick man because it can be shown to not be good food for a well one. Nor am I able to appreciate the danger apprehended by the meeting, that the American people will by means of military arrests during the rebellion lose the right of public discussion, the liberty of speech and the press, the law of evidence, trial by jury, and *habeas corpus*, throughout the indefinite peaceful future which I trust lies before them, any more than I am able to believe that a man could contract so strong an appetite for emetics during temporary illness, as to persist in feeding upon them through the remainder of his healthful life.

In giving the resolutions that earnest consideration which you request of me, I cannot overlook the fact that the meeting speak as "Democrats." Nor can I, with full respect for their known intelligence, and the fairly presumed deliberation with which they prepared their resolutions, be permitted to suppose that this occurred by accident, or in any way other than that they preferred to designate themselves "Democrats" rather than "American citizens." In this time of national peril I would have preferred to meet you upon a level one step higher than any party platform, because I am sure that from such more elevated position we could do better battle for the country we all love than we possibly can from those lower ones where, from the force of habit, the prejudices of the past, and selfish hopes of the future, we are sure to expend much of our ingenuity and strength in finding fault with and aiming blows at each other. But since you have denied me this, I will yet be thankful, for the country's sake, that not all Democrats have done so. He on whose discretionary judgment Mr. Vallandigham was arrested and tried is a Democrat, having no old party affinity with me, and the judge who rejected the constitutional view expressed in these resolutions, by refusing to discharge Mr. Vallandigham on *habeas corpus*, is a Democrat of better days than these, having received his judicial mantle at the hands of President Jackson. And still more, of all those Democrats who are nobly exposing their lives and shedding their blood on the battle-field, I have learned that many approve the course taken with Mr. V. while I have not heard of a single one condemning it. I cannot assert that there are none such. And the name of President Jackson recalls an instance of pertinent history. After the battle of New-Orleans, and while the fact that the treaty of peace had been concluded was well known in the city, but before official knowledge of it had arrived, General Jackson still maintained martial or military law. Now that it could be said the war was over, the clamor against martial law, which had existed from the first, grew more furious. Among other things, a Mr. Louiallier published a denunciatory newspaper article. General Jackson arrested him. A lawyer by the name of Morel procured the U.S. Judge Hall to order a writ of *habeas corpus* to release Mr. Louiallier. General Jackson arrested both the lawyer and the judge. A Mr. Hollander ventured to say of some part of the matter that "it was a dirty trick." General Jackson arrested him. When the officer undertook to serve the writ of *habeas corpus*, General Jackson took it from him, and sent him away with a copy. Holding the judge in custody a few days, the general sent him beyond the limits of his encampment, and set him at liberty with an order to remain till the ratification of peace should be regularly announced, or until the British should have left the Southern coast. A day or two more elapsed, the ratification of the treaty of peace was regularly announced, and the judge and others were fully liberated. A few days more, and the judge called Gen. Jackson into court and fined him $1000 for having arrested him and the others named. The general paid the fine, and there the matter rested for nearly thirty years, when Congress refunded principal and interest. The late Senator Douglas, then in the House of Representatives, took a leading part in the debates in which the constitutional question was much discussed. I am not prepared to say whom the journals would show to have voted for the measure.

It may be remarked—first, that we had the same Constitution then as now; secondly; that we then had a case of invasion, and that now we have a case of rebellion; and, thirdly, that the permanent right of the people to public discussion, the liberty of speech and the press, the trial by jury, the law of evidence, and the *habeas corpus*, suffered no detriment whatever by that conduct of General Jackson, or its subsequent approval by the American congress.

And yet, let me say that, in my own discretion, I do not know whether I would have ordered the arrest of Mr. Vallandigham. While I can not shift the responsibility from myself, I hold that, as a general rule, the commander in the field is the better judge of the necessity in any particular case. Of course I must practice a general directory and revisory power in the matter.

One of the resolutions expresses the opinion of the meeting that arbitrary arrests will have the effect to divide and distract those who should be united in suppressing the rebellion, and I am specifically called on to discharge Mr. Vallandigham. I regard this as, at least, a fair appeal to me, on the expediency of exercising a constitutional power which I think exists. In response to such appeal I have to say, it gave me pain when I learned that Mr. Vallandigham had been arrested (that is, I was pained that there should have seemed to be a necessity for arresting him) and that it will afford me great pleasure to discharge him so soon as I can by any means believe the public safety will not suffer by it.

I further say that, as the war progress, it appears to me, opinion, and action, which were in great confusion at first, take shape and fall into more regular channels, so that the necessity for strong dealing with them gradually decreases. I have every reason to desire that it would cease altogether; and far from the least is my regard for the opinions and wishes of those who, like the meeting at Albany, declare their purpose to sustain the government in every constitutional and lawful measure to suppress the rebellion. Still, I must continue to do so much as may seem to be required by the public safety.

A. Lincoln.

Intepretation

After commending the Democrats meeting in Albany, New York, for their dedication to the Union cause, Lincoln turns to their severe censure of his action authorizing military authorities to suspend the writ of *habeas corpus*—i.e., to arrest and detain people without a proper trial. He begins by allowing that the constitutionally defined crime of treason is not involved, nor any capital crime, nor—further—any criminal prosecution whatsoever. What *is* involved?

"Let us consider the real case with which we are dealing," says Lincoln, "and apply it to the parts of the Constitution plainly made for such cases." Consider the situation: the insurgents, whose "sympathizers pervaded all departments of the government and nearly all communities of the people," have relied on our normal liberties (of speech, press and *habeas corpus*) to "keep on foot a most efficient corps of spies, informers, suppliers, and abettors of their cause in a thousand ways." They knew the Constitution itself made an exception, allowing the suspension of the writ of *habeas corpus* when "in cases of rebellion or invasion the public safety may require it," but they also knew "they had friends who would make a question as to who was to suspend it," thus enabling them to place additional obstacles in the Union's way.

Lincoln's reference to the question of who has the power to suspend the writ derives from the fact that the clause in question appears in Article I, section 9, which lists the things Congress may not do. Congress may not suspend the writ of *habeas corpus* except in these emergencies (of rebellion or invasion), and if required for the public safety. Did the location of this vital empowerment imply that it was Congress and Congress alone that could do the suspending? Lincoln acknowledges the Executive did the suspension—to avoid "ruinous waste of time." Was he stretching the Constitution too far?

Lincoln does not offer a full and direct defense of this assumption of responsibility on the part of the Executive. But he does offer a most complete analysis of why the civil courts, with their normal judicial processes, cannot be relied upon in cases of "rebellion or invasion." They cannot effectively deal with the large number of people that may be siding with the enemy, whether rebels or invaders. This is why the Constitution itself, envisioning this condition, allows men to be arrested and held who "cannot be proved to be guilty of defined crime." In fact, it is primarily to prevent what they *might* do rather than punish what they *have done* that they are detained without benefit of the writ.

As to the question whether Congress alone has the right to suspend the writ, time is of the essence in such drastic emergencies: the life or death of the nation is at stake. The decision to suspend must be made swiftly, and thoroughly, without "ruinous waste of time." But, especially in a situation of great unrest and great divisions within the population, Congress is less able to act than the Executive. The President, one man, is commander-in-chief and responsible for the defense of the nation. In such times, he would necessarily be at the helm, since the emergency is intrinsically military in nature. In such times, moreover, Congress may have difficulty assembling, let alone deciding. So the practical logic is entirely with Lincoln.

While it is hard to believe that men of experience like the founding fathers were unable to anticipate these eventualities, they may have hesitated to invest the president with this power explicitly, fearing that by adding to his already great and unprecedented powers they might make ratification of the Constitution even more difficult than it already was. For it would not have required great sagacity to envision what Lincoln calls the "real case" of such national emergencies, with the president heading up a nation at war against either domestic or foreign foes. Lincoln might also have mentioned (though he does not) the difference between the oaths on taking office that the Constitution prescribes for members of Congress and the president. Article VI, paragraph 3 requires the members of Congress (and others) to be bound by oath or affirmation to "support this Constitution," whereas the presidential pledge explicitly spelled out in Article II, section 1, paragraph 7, binds the president to "preserve, protect and defend the Constitution of the United States." This makes the president rather than Congress the final protector of the Constitution and may have been intended for just the kind of emergency the Union faced in 1861. Given all these elements, the constitutional case for the president's assuming the power to suspend the writ of *habeas corpus* is as compelling as any non-explicit empowerment can be.

Lincoln is very bold in showing how far he would go in extending the suspension of the writ. "The man who stands by and says nothing when the peril of his government is discussed, cannot be misunderstood." Even more, the man who "talks ambiguously—talks for his country with 'buts,' and 'ifs' and 'ands.'" These would all be subject to arrest. Lincoln goes so far as to express regret—or come close to expressing regret—that he had not arrested seven rebel military leaders whom he names (including Robert E. Lee) when they were "within the power of the government" and "nearly as well known to be traitors then as now." He even thinks there may come a time when he will be blamed for making too few arrests rather than too many!

As to the contention expressed at the same meeting that military arrests in areas where rebellion does not exist are unconstitutional, Lincoln replies that the Constitution makes no such distinction. If the "public safety" requires preventing an extension of the rebellion in certain places, or preventing men from interfering with the raising and supplying of armies in any place, the constitutional empowerment applies. This is the principle covering the case of a Mr. Vallandigham (Lincoln does not identify him as a congressman from Ohio), who was arrested because "he was laboring, with some effect, to prevent the raising of troops, to encourage desertions from the army, and to leave the rebellion without an adequate military force to suppress it."

Lincoln's point could not be more clearly or more memorably expressed:

"Must I shoot a simple-minded soldier boy who deserts, while I must not touch a hair of a wily agitator who induces him to desert? This is none the less injurious when effected by getting a father, or brother or friend into a public meeting and there working upon his feelings till he is persuaded to write the soldier boy that he is fighting in a bad cause, for a wicked administration of a contemptible government, too weak to arrest and punish him if he shall desert. I think that, in such a case, to silence the agitator and save the boy is not only constitutional, but withal a great mercy."

Lincoln continues by reverting to the idea that the Constitution itself means to operate differently in times of rebellion or invasion as compared to "times of profound peace and public security." He makes it perfectly clear that the nation will return to its normal liberties when the emergency ends, that it will be as disinclined to persist with these emergency measures in normal times as a well man will persist in taking emetics. And since the Albany Democrats have addressed him as Democrats rather than in the higher capacity of Americans simply, Lincoln sees fit to respond with a few words at that level. The general arresting Vallandigham, he tells us, is a Democrat, and the judge denying him the writ of *habeas corpus* as well. He then strikes the longest comic note in his letter by narrating the relevant actions of an earlier Democrat, General Andrew Jackson, during the last moments of the battle of New Orleans. Jackson's example shows that the actions necessitated by a time of invasion (or rebellion, now) will not persist once the emergency is over.

Lincoln ends on a more conciliatory note by recurring to the sensitive matter of Vallandigham and promising to discharge him "as soon as I can by any means believe the public safety will not suffer by it." As the war proceeds, "opinion and action" have fallen into "more regular channels," reducing the necessity for dealing with them strongly, and Lincoln hopes that this necessity will cease altogether, not least out of regard for the feelings of those, like the Albany Democrats, who "declare their purpose to sustain the government in every constitutional and lawful measure to suppress the rebellion."

Chapter 17

Letter to James C. Conkling, August 26, 1863

Conkling, an old friend of Lincoln's, had tried to gather together the Union men of both parties in order to offset the influence of Northern Democrats who wanted an arranged peace with the South.

Text

Executive Mansion,
Washington, August 26, 1863

Hon. James C. Conkling
My Dear Sir.
Your letter inviting me to attend a mass-meeting of unconditional Union-men, to be held at the Capitol of Illinois, on the 3d day of September, has been received.

It would be very agreeable to me, to thus meet my old friends, at my own home; but I can not, just now, be absent from here, so long as a visit there, would require.

The meeting is to be of all those who maintain unconditional devotion to the Union; and I am sure my old political friends will thank me for tendering, as I do, the nation's gratitude to those other noble men, whom no partizan malice, or partizan hope, can make false to the nation's life.

There are those who are dissatisfied with me. To such I would say: You desire peace; and you blame me that we do not have it. But how can we attain it? There are but three conceivable ways. First, to suppress the rebellion by force of arms. This I am trying to do. Are you for it? If you are, so far we are agreed. If you are not for it, a second way is to give up the Union. I am against this. Are you for it? If you are, you should say so plainly. If you are not for *force*, nor yet for *dissolution*, there only remains some imaginable *compromise*. I do not believe any compromise, embracing the maintenance of the Union, is now possible. All I learn leads to a directly opposite belief. The strength of the rebellion, is its military—its army. That army dominates all the country, and all the people, within its range. Any offer of terms made by any man or men within that range, in opposition to that army, is simply nothing for the present; because such man or men, have no power whatever to enforce their side of a compromise, if one were made with them. To illustrate. Suppose refugees from the South, and peace men of the North, get together in convention, and frame and proclaim a compromise embracing a restoration of the Union; in what way can that compromise be used to keep Lee's army out of Pennsylvania? Meade's army can keep Lee's army out of Pennsylvania; and, I think, can ultimately drive it out of existence. But no paper compromise, to which the controllers of Lee's army are not agreed, can at all affect that army. In an effort at such compromise we should waste time, which the enemy would improve to our disadvantage; and that would be all. A compromise, to be effective, must be made either with those who control the rebel army, or with the people first liberated from the domination of that army, by the success of our own army. Now allow me to assure you, that no word or intimation, from that rebel army, or from any of the men controlling it, in relation to any peace compromise, has ever come to my knowledge or belief. All charges and insinuations to the contrary, are deceptive and groundless. And I promise you, that if any such proposition shall hereafter come, it shall not be rejected, and kept a secret from you. I freely acknowledge myself the servant of the people, according to the bond of service—the United States Constitution; and that, as such, I am responsible to them.

But to be plain, you are dissatisfied with me about the negro. Quite likely there is a difference of opinion between you and myself upon that subject. I certainly wish that all men could be free, while I suppose you do not. Yet I have neither adopted, nor proposed any measure, which is not consistent with even your view, provided you are for the Union. I suggested compensated emancipation; to which you replied you wished not to be taxed to buy negroes. But I had not asked you to be taxed to buy negroes, except in such way, as to save you from greater taxation to save the Union exclusively by other means.

You dislike the emancipation proclamation; and, perhaps, would have it retracted. You say it is unconstitutional—I think differently. I think the constitution invests its Commander-in-chief, with the law of war, in time of war. The most that can be said, if so much, is, that slaves are property. Is there—has there ever been—any question that by the law of war, property, both of enemies and friends, may be taken when needed? And is it not needed whenever taking it, helps us, or hurts the enemy? Armies, the world over, destroy enemie's property when they can not use it; and even destroy their own to keep it from the enemy. Civilized belligerents do all in their power to help themselves, or hurt the enemy, except a few things regarded as barbarous or cruel. Among the exceptions are the massacre of vanquished foes, and non-combatants, male and female.

But the proclamation, as law, either is valid, or is not valid. If it is not valid, it needs no retraction. If it is valid, it can not be retracted, any more than the dead can be brought to life. Some of you profess to think its retraction would operate favorably for the Union. Why better *after* the retraction, than *before* the issue? There was more than a year and a half of trial to suppress the rebellion before the proclamation issued, the last one hundred days of which passed under an explicit notice that it was coming, unless averted by those in revolt, returning to their allegiance. The war has certainly progressed as favorably for us, since the issue of proclamation as before. I know, as fully as one can know the opinions of others, that some of the commanders of our armies in the field who have given us our most important successes believe the emancipation policy and the use of the colored troops constitute the heaviest blow yet dealt to the Rebellion, and that at least one of these important successes could not have been achieved when it was but for the aid of black soldiers. Among the commanders holding these views are some who have never had any affinity with what is called abolitionism or with the Republican party policies but who held them purely as military opinions. I submit these opinions as being entitled to some weight against the objections often urged that emancipation and arming the blacks are unwise as military measures and were not adopted as such in good faith.

You say you will not fight to free negroes. Some of them seem willing to fight for you; but, no matter. Fight you, then, exclusively to save the Union. I issued the proclamation on purpose to aid you in saving the Union. Whenever you shall have conquered all resistance to the Union, if I shall urge you to continue fighting, it will be an apt time, then, for you to declare you will not fight to free negroes.

I thought that in your struggle for the Union, to whatever extent the negroes should cease helping the enemy, to that extent it weakened the enemy in his resistance to you. Do you think differently? I thought that whatever negroes can be got to do as soldiers, leaves just so much less for white soldiers to do, in saving the Union. Does it appear otherwise to you? But negroes, like other people, act upon motives. Why should they do any thing for us, if we will do nothing for them? If they stake their lives for us, they must be prompted by the strongest motive—even the promise of freedom. And the promise being made, must be kept.

The signs look better. The Father of Waters again goes unvexed to the sea. Thanks to the great Northwest for it. Nor yet wholly to them. Three hundred miles up, they met New England, Empire, Key-stone, and Jersey, hewing their way right and left. The Sunny South too, in more colors than one, also lent a hand. On the spot, their part of the history was jotted down in black and white. The job was a great national one; and let none be banned who bore an honorable part in it. And while those who have cleared the great river may well be proud, even that is not all. It is hard to say that anything has been more bravely, and well done, than at Antietam, Murfreesboro, Gettysburg, and on many fields of lesser note. Nor must Uncle Sam's web-feet be forgotten. At all the watery margins they have been present. Not only on the deep sea, the broad bay, and the rapid river, but also up the narrow muddy bayou, and wherever the ground was a little damp, they have been, and made their tracks. Thanks to all. For the great republic—for the principle it lives by, and keeps alive—for man's vast future—thanks to all.

Peace does not appear so distant as it did. I hope it will come soon, and come to stay; and so come as to be worth the keeping in all future time. It will then have been proved that, among free men, there can be no successful appeal from the ballot to the bullet; and that they who take such appeal are sure to lose their case, and pay the cost. And then, there will be some black men who can remember that, with silent tongue, and clenched teeth, and steady eye, and well-poised bayonnet, they have helped mankind on to this great consummation; while, I fear, there will be some white ones, unable to forget that, with malignant heart, and deceitful speech, they strove to hinder it.

Still, let us not be over-sanguine of a speedy final triumph. Let us be quite sober. Let us diligently apply the means, never doubting that a just God, in his own good time, will give us the rightful result.

> Yours very truly
> A. Lincoln

Interpretation

Too occupied to accept Conkling's invitation to attend a meeting of "unconditional Union-men" in Springfield, Illinois, Lincoln sent this letter instead, with the request to Conkling that he read it to the meeting—"very slowly." At first Lincoln's tone is hardly argumentative. He would have found it very agreeable, he says, to see his old friends, and thanks those other "noble men" at the meeting for resisting the partisan temptation to be "false to the nation's life."

Suddenly Lincoln departs from the friendly accord with which he began: "There are those who are dissatisfied with me." The first ground for dissatisfaction that he considers at some length is his supposed refusal to accept a compromise with the South. His rejoinder is that he has not received any such offer from the South, that a compromise arranged without the consent of the rebel army would be useless (the only alternative being a compromise coming from those liberated by the Union army), and that any offer that does come to him will be revealed to the people, whose servant he is under the Constitution.

With equal abruptness, Lincoln then reveals the real issue rankling those very Union-men: "But to be plain, you are dissatisfied with me about the negro." Lincoln speaks as if they *all* are. And the main difference between him and them? "I certainly wish that all men could be free, while I suppose you do not." Lincoln could have put his view much more strongly in terms of the inalienable right to freedom possessed by all men, i.e., in terms of the Declaration of Independence, but, having no desire to incur even greater resentment in these whites, or to be accused of fomenting blacks uprisings, he softens the point, expressing it only in the form of a personal wish.

Not only did these Union-men (and others) oppose an earlier plan of his for "compensated emancipation," but they claim the emancipation proclamation to be unconstitutional. To defend its constitutionality, so questioned by these *northerners*, Lincoln appeals not to the Declaration of Independence, with its inalienable rights, but to the "law of war" with which he is invested by the Constitution as Commander-in-chief in time of war. The "law of war" is that code by which civilized nations wage war, and it permits the appropriation of property belonging to the enemy—in this case the slave. Lincoln's expression is peculiar: "The most that can be said, if so much, is, that slaves are property." Freeing the slave is therefore justified constitutionally simply as a military measure. But the "if so much" seems to cast doubt as to whether slaves can really be property, or, better, whether human beings can rightly be slaves.

As for the possibility of retracting the proclamation, Lincoln speaks somewhat mysteriously: if invalid as a law it needs no retraction, and "if it is valid, it can not be retracted—any more than the dead can be brought to life." The word "valid" here seems to mean "sound" rather than simply "passed in the proper way," for if it only meant the latter, it should be possible to retract it. And why does an invalid law need no retraction? Will its invalidity be so apparent that no one will regard it as deserving obedience? As for a valid law, why is it impossible to retract it? Lincoln seems to have in mind a notion of law that attributes to it a status independent of human action. Thus, an invalid (let us say, unsound) law is no law at all: it does not exist. If it is valid (i.e., sound), it exists regardless of any effort on our part and cannot be retracted.

We must leave unsolved the mystery of his meaning in these few sentences. Lincoln goes on to consider the charge that emancipation has hurt rather than helped the Union cause. On the contrary, some Union commanders, he says, believe "emancipation and the use of colored troops" to be "the heaviest blow yet dealt to the Rebellion," and that at least one military success "could not have been achieved without black soldiers." He goes on with a certain sarcasm: "You say you will not fight to free negroes. Some of them seem willing to fight for you; but, no matter." By putting words in their mouth, Lincoln imagines how some of his white audience in Illinois would continue their objections to his policies. His response is that getting blacks to "cease helping the enemy," or to join up against the enemy, must help the white soldiers fighting in the Union's cause. Those blacks who become soldiers must be motivated to risk their lives, and what motivates them is "the promise of freedom." So it turns out, by Lincoln's analysis, that the black man is not fighting *for* the white soldier but for himself. But he is fighting, and his fighting does in fact help the white soldiers and the Union. All Lincoln asks of the white soldier is that he fight not for the black but for the Union—the Union protecting the freedom he already has.

Lincoln pauses to summarize and celebrate the war's progress, starting with the opening of the Mississippi, expressed in these marvelous words: "The Father of Waters again goes unvexed to the sea." He mentions the successes at Antietam, Murfreesboro and Gettysburg, thanks all those who participated, white and black, for the "great republic," for its principle (presumably liberty and equality) and "man's vast future." So with the prospect of peace not as remote as it had been, the successful conclusion of the war will show that, "among free men, there can be no successful appeal from the ballot to the bullet." At the war's end, he tells us. the black soldiers will remember that "with silent tongue, and clenched teeth, and steady eye, and well-poised bayonet, they have helped mankind on to this great consummation; while, I fear, there will be some white ones, unable to forget that, with malignant heart, and deceitful speech, they strove to hinder it."

This is a striking portrait of the brave and battle-ready black soldier, who, striving for his own freedom, realizes that he has also fought for mankind. The portrait is made even more daring by the contrast Lincoln draws with those white soldiers (he means from the North, not the South, as represented by the Illinois meeting to which he was invited) who will only be able to remember their hindering mankind—hindering it, that is, out of ill will for the black and his freedom.

"Read it very slowly," Lincoln had told Conkling. He wanted its message to sink in—a message not only arguing for the emancipation and the use of black troops, but shaming and castigating those whites who probably invited him to Springfield so that on these very points they could castigate him.

Chapter 18

The Gettysburg Address, November 19, 1863

The occasion was the dedication of a new cemetery at Gettysburg for those who had fallen in the recent battle. The main speaker for the occasion was Edward Everett, not Lincoln.

Text

Four score and seven years ago our fathers brought forth on this continent, a new nation, conceived in Liberty, and dedicated to the proposition that all men are created equal.

Now we are engaged in a great civil war, testing whether that nation, or any nation so conceived and so dedicated, can long endure. We are met on a great battle-field of that war. We have come to dedicate a portion of that field, as a final resting place for those who here gave their lives that that nation might live. It is altogether fitting and proper that we should do this.

But, in a larger sense, we can not dedicate—we can not consecrate—we can not hallow—this ground. The brave men, living and dead, who struggled here, have consecrated it, far above our poor power to add or detract. The world will little note, nor long remember what we say here, but it can never forget what they did here. It is for us the living, rather, to be dedicated here to the unfinished work which they who fought here have thus far so nobly advanced. It is rather for us to be here dedicated to the great task remaining before us—that from these honored dead we take increased devotion to that cause for which they gave the last full measure of devotion—that we here highly resolve that these dead shall not have died in vain—that this nation, under God, shall have a new birth of freedom—and that government of the people, by the people, for the people, shall not perish from the earth.

Abraham Lincoln.

November 19, 1863

Interpretation

The thought in this miniature masterpiece is not as easy to follow as might appear from its enormous popularity. It consists of three increasingly long paragraphs. Its opening reference to "four score and seven years ago" brings the origin of the nation back, not to 1789 and the Constitution, but to 1776 and the Declaration of Independence. In this way, Lincoln takes a course opposite to the one in the *Perpetuation* speech, where reverence for the Constitution and the laws (not for the Declaration of Independence) was openly called for. The background metaphor for the first paragraph is that of human birth, except that the new nation was "brought forth on this continent" by fathers, not mothers. This nation was "conceived in Liberty"—where "conceived" can refer to both generative origin and an act of thought simultaneously. It could mean either that the nation owed its origin to forethought that was free, that was not subject to some external power. Or it could mean that the very spirit of the nation originally was one of Liberty, so that the new nation was begun from and with this spirit of liberty.

While begun in liberty, the new nation was nevertheless "dedicated to the proposition that all men are created equal." Its conception and its dedication are therefore different. Dedication signifies something like the nation's purpose or highest aim—perhaps like baptism, in the case of Christian birth. But in some ways the parallel to human birth breaks down, since we do not by nature dedicate our children to some end in the same sense that a nation can be so dedicated. There is a sense of deliberation involved in bringing forth a nation—in conceiving it and giving it basic direction—that would not be present in the case of ordinary human conception and birth. And in the case of the nation, that original deliberation, that conceiving and setting forth of the new nation, took place in the Declaration of Independence.

So it is to the Declaration that Lincoln asks us to turn our minds as we witness the ceremonies at Gettysburg. The Declaration of Independence had proclaimed that "all men are created equal," and "endowed by their Creator with certain inalienable rights, among them life, liberty and the pursuit of happiness." It introduced this thought by the ringing phrase, "We hold these truths to be self-evident." Lincoln changes this. He seems to sum up by the word "liberty" the three inalienable rights (the central one being the right to liberty) stipulated by the Declaration, transforming them from inalienable rights into something like a spirit of liberty in which the new nation was conceived. He then makes equality the very purpose, the very object of dedication of the new nation, just as the Declaration places "all men are created equal" before listing the rights with which they are endowed. Their equality, in fact, consists in their all having equally the very same inalienable rights. But Lincoln changes the status of equality itself. That "all men are created equal" was considered by the Declaration a self-evident truth. In the Gettysburg Address, it is called a "proposition," not a self-evident truth. And by treating inalienable rights as he does, Lincoln implies that the same holds for them. He does not want to call any of them self-evident truths.

By making equality rather than liberty the object to which American society is dedicated, Lincoln may have wanted to stress the unique character of the Declaration's principles. Other societies, like ancient Athens, have also had liberty and equality as their principles, but not for slaves, whereas the Declaration envisages a world where all men are created equal, for the first time delegitimizing slavery, caste systems, aristocracies and monarchies by birth, and the like, everywhere. But why not keep the Declaration's powerful idiom, "self-evident truths?" Lincoln does not mean to question whether the equality of mankind is true. The proposition, he implies, is heartily worth being dedicated to. But to call something a "self-evident truth" gives it an air of invincibility—it cannot but win out—whereas Lincoln implies at once, in the second paragraph, that a nation so conceived (in liberty) and dedicated (to equality) may not long endure. Freedom and equality are not obviously solid supports of enduring government: there is something problematic about them. This great civil war is a sufficient proof of that fact, and it is therefore a test of whether such a nation can long endure.

Here we must be clear in our minds. Lincoln is not focusing on the problem of slavery. He is considering the essential character of a nation built on freedom and equality, not the fact that in some areas within it whites keep these principles from applying to blacks. It is the fact of civil war itself that preoccupies him, with the South's deciding to secede rather than accept Lincoln's wholly legitimate election as president. The problem is deeper: it derives from the very principles of freedom and equality, which encourage the various parts of the democracy—individuals as well as states—to think they can do as they please and consent to be ruled only by whom they please. There is a temptation and tendency for the nation to fly apart as if subject to a centrifugal force. The refusal to obey laws, and the withdrawal of consent and allegiance, will always be a greater danger in nations so conceived than in those constructed on other principles. A great civil war is now being fought to force a renegade part of the Union to remain within the Union against its will, to quell a great rebellion born of the very spirit of liberty and equality felt by citizens and states alike. It is very much like the breakdown of civic order discussed in the *Perpetuation* speech, in which mobs take the law into their own hands and then escape the consequences of their law-breaking. Nor is it plain, or pre-determined, which side—the Union or the rebels—will prevail in this struggle.

Notably absent from most of Lincoln's speech is any appeal to an all-powerful God working to ensure the victory of those fighting for compulsory union. The struggle must be undertaken by men, and while the Union has just won a great battle at Gettysburg, the fact that the battle was fought as far north as Gettysburg sufficiently attests to the daring and strength of the South.

Another feature of the speech is that Lincoln does not even mention, let alone dwell upon, the fact that the Union has just won a great victory. He does say that the occasion is meant to dedicate a portion of the field of battle to those "who here gave their lives that that nation might live," and refers to their deeds in other places as well, but the very words "Union" and "rebels" do not appear in the speech. It's as if a fratricidal war is rather shameful and should not be proudly paraded. He has no desire to see this great division perpetuated in words.

The third and largest paragraph goes on to discuss the act of dedicating a part of this battlefield. "There is a sense," Lincoln says, "in which we can not dedicate—we can not consecrate—we can not hallow—this ground." Notice the change to a religious tone with the words "consecrate" and "hallow." "The brave men, living and dead, who struggled here, have consecrated this ground"—have made it holy. By their great deeds and sacrifices, human beings can have an effect usually attributed to divine beings. And in yet another memorable phrase, Lincoln tells us that "the world will little note, nor long remember what we say here, but it can never forget what they did here." Can he have meant this? Can we believe that so devoted a lover of Shakespeare and so serious a reader of the Bible failed to realize that it is not simply the deeds but the words about the deeds that endow them with lasting value and significance? Lincoln's speech was meant to remind the world of what the soldiers did here, but, even more, of the larger significance of their deeds. And so effective has this speech been that it has to a considerable extent outshone and even effaced the deeds it celebrates.

The final section of the last paragraph calls for a renewed dedication on the part of us the living. Instead of dedicating the ground, we are now dedicating ourselves to a cause. In the spirit of the devotion shown by these honored dead, we must dedicate ourselves to "the great task remaining," which is "that this nation, under God, shall have "a new birth of freedom—and that government of the people, by the people, for the people, shall not perish from the earth." So this great task has two parts. The first is to ensure that this nation—under God's dominion, but by our own doing, not His—shall have a new birth of freedom. Returning explicitly now to the original metaphor of birth, this phrase must refer to the "proposition that all men are equal" to which the country is dedicated. At the very beginning of the year, Lincoln had issued the *Emancipation Proclamation*, thus finally realizing the promise of equality in the Declaration. The new birth of freedom will be a freedom shared by blacks and whites alike. This is the only reference—and an indirect one at that—to slavery in the whole speech. The new birth of freedom is based on old principles, for Lincoln had described the new nation as having been dedicated, from the outset, to the proposition that all men are created equal. That proposition had already begun to be made a "truth" in the sense of a political reality, but only if the Union wins the war can it become a permanent truth. Only victory over the slave-holding South can make this extension of freedom—this new birth of freedom—a permanent achievement of American society.

The second resolve of the living must be that government of, by and for the people shall not perish from the earth. This is the only time in the speech that Lincoln spells out the full democratic meaning of liberty and equality. "Of the people" means belonging to them, "by the people" means that those who govern are drawn from the people, which guarantees their acting "for the people"—i.e., in their behalf. By spelling out the meaning of democracy in this way, Lincoln can bring home the full significance, first, of either losing or winning the war, and then, afterwards, of taking those precautions that might help secure democracy over the long haul. For the principles of liberty and equality, and the democracy based on them, are not easy to sustain. Like all other governments, they have difficulties arising from within themselves. They can, in fact, perish from the earth—perish utterly. Great human effort will therefore be required—militarily in the short run and politically in the long run. Toward this long-range aim Lincoln contributes most by his clear-sighted analysis of democracy's inherent defects. And through this speech he marshalls the religious spirit of Americans and helps sanctify the cause of preserving the Union and American democracy together, preserving, in full maturity, a nation "conceived in liberty and dedicated to the proposition that all men are created equal."

Chapter 19

The Second Inaugural, March 4, 1865

This is Lincoln's justly famous speech on entering—quite unexpectedly, to him—the office of the presidency a second time.

Text

At this second appearing to take the oath of the presidential office, there is less occasion for an extended address than there was at the first. Then a statement, somewhat in detail, of a course to be pursued, seemed fitting and proper. Now, at the expiration of four years, during which public declarations have been constantly called forth on every point and phase of the great contest which still absorbs the attention, and engrosses the energies of the nation, little that is new could be presented. The progress of our arms, upon which all else chiefly depends, is as well known to the public as to myself; and it is, I trust, reasonably satisfactory and encouraging to all. With high hope for the future, no prediction in regard to it is ventured.

On the occasion corresponding to this four years ago, all thoughts were anxiously directed to an impending civil war. All dreaded it—all sought to avert it. While the inaugeral [*sic*] address was being delivered from this place, devoted altogether to *saving* the Union without war, insurgent agents were in the city seeking to *destroy* it without war—seeking to dissole [*sic*] the Union, and divide effects, by negotiation. Both parties deprecated war; but one of them would *make* war rather than let the nation survive; and the other would *accept* war rather than let it perish. And the war came.

One eighth of the whole population were colored slaves, not distributed generally over the Union, but localized in the Southern part of it. These slaves constituted a peculiar and powerful interest. All knew that this interest was, somehow, the cause of the war. To strengthen, perpetuate, and extend this interest was the object for which the insurgents would rend the Union, even by war; while the government claimed no right to do more than to restrict the territorial enlargement of it. Neither party expected for the war, the magnitude, or the duration, which it has already attained. Neither anticipated that the *cause* of the conflict might cease with, or even before, the conflict itself should cease. Each looked for an easier triumph, and a result less fundamental and astounding. Both read the same Bible, and pray to the same God; and each invokes His aid against the other. It may seem strange that any men should dare to ask a just God's assistance in wringing their bread from the sweat of other men's faces; but let us judge not that we be not judged. The prayers of both could not be answered; that of neither has been answered fully. The Almighty has his own purposes. "Woe unto the world because of offences! for it must needs be that offences come; but woe to that man by whom the offence cometh!" If we shall suppose that American Slavery is one of those offences which, in the providence of God, must needs come, but which, having continued through His appointed time, He now wills to remove, and that He gives to both North and South, this terrible war, as the woe due to those by whom the offence came, shall we discern therein any departure from those divine attributes which the believers in a Living God always ascribe to Him? Fondly do we hope—fervently do we pray—that this mighty scourge of war may speedily pass away. Yet, if God wills that it continue, until all the wealth piled by the bond-man's two hundred and fifty years of unrequited toil shall be sunk, and until every drop of blood drawn with the lash, shall be paid by another drawn with the sword, as was said three thousand years ago, so still it must be said "the judgments of the Lord, are true and righteous altogether."

With malice toward none; with charity for all; with firmness in the right, as God gives us to see the right, let us strive on to finish the work we are in; to bind up the nation's wounds; to care for him who shall have borne the battle, and for his widow, and his orphan—to do all which may achieve and cherish a just and lasting peace, among ourselves, and with all nations.

Interpretation

Four years before, Lincoln had devoted the nine pages of his First Inaugural address to telling the nation, and the South, in particular, what could be expected from his administration. For his Second Inaugural, he needed only two pages, but they are two of his most powerful. It was no longer necessary, he says, to discuss further the course to be taken by the government, nor even the encouraging military progress already met with in the "great contest" still absorbing the nation. Four years before, at the very moment when his First Inaugural sought to save the Union without war, "insurgent agents" in the capitol were trying to *destroy* it without war: "Both parties deprecated war; but one of them would *make* war rather than let the nation survive; and the other would *accept* war rather than let it perish. And the war came."

With this Biblical intoning, Lincoln turns to the cause of the war. Everyone knew the war was somehow due to the "peculiar and powerful interest" constituted by the "colored slaves," who were one eighth of the population and lived mainly in the south. The insurgents wanted to perpetuate and extend this interest, the government no more than to prevent its extension. The war came and exceeded all expectations, growing larger and lasting longer. Nor did either side anticipate that "the cause of the conflict (slavery) might cease with, or even before, the conflict itself should cease."

The rest of the third paragraph (by far the longest of the four) contains an intricate religious reflection on the war. Both sides "read the same Bible, and pray to the same God," and each invokes His aid against the other. "It may seem strange," Lincoln says, "that any men should dare to ask a just God's assistance in wringing their bread from the sweat of other men's faces; but let us judge not that we be not judged." Having introduced the Bible as the source of the religion of both sides, Lincoln persists in keeping it before us. Quite noticeably he forbears from appealing to the Declaration of Independence as a foundational document held in common by North and South, probably because they disagree in their interpretation of it in connection with negro slavery. Lincoln gives the impression that the God of the Bible is just and opposes slavery, so that the slavery issue he had earlier reduced to the question of the extension of slavery really comes down to the question whether slavery is just. With Christ's famous line from Matthew (7:1) about "judging not," Lincoln asks us to abstain from judging the supporters of slavery so that we ourselves may not be judged. But has not his own phrase—"wringing their bread from the sweat of other men's faces"—aroused our moral indignation and made us think badly of slave-owners? How can we both judge and not judge? Lincoln seems to want to make us angry and then dampen that anger down, but can the moral indignation be that easily dampened?

We must realize that Biblical thought, in both Old and New Testaments, does not contain a direct attack on slavery, whatever its indirect and long-range effects. That is what made it possible for the South to combine being Christian with keeping slaves. When Lincoln suggests that a just God would oppose slavery, he is actually appealing to a kind of moral common sense or to the spirit of the Declaration, where all men are endowed by their Creator with equal rights. Such a God would find slavery offensive. But Lincoln forbears from mentioning the principles of the Declaration and immediately adds that the Almighty has His own purposes, quoting (without giving the source) from the Gospel of St. Matthew (18:7), where Christ says, "Woe unto the world because of offences! for it must needs be that offences come; but woe to that man by whom the offence cometh!" If we suppose American slavery to be an offence that God in His providence determines must come, and that He gives this terrible war to both North and South as the woe due to those by whom the offence came, would this, Lincoln asks, signify "any departure from those divine attributes which the believers in a Living God always ascribe to Him?"

This is the question with which Lincoln's supposition ends. Thus understood, this "terrible war" is a divine punishment for the sin or offence of slavery—a sin Lincoln attributes to both North and South, presumably because the North had helped in various ways to support that institution, not least by adopting the Constitution itself. So the meaning of the war must be traced back to the Bible rather than the Declaration, to the sense of sin shared by Americans as Christians rather than to the sense of rights they share as rational beings. Here in the Bible is the ground common to North and South on which to build his case. In the Gettysburg Address it was the Declaration and not the Bible that was in the forefront of Lincoln's attention to the war, and it was the problem of union rather than the problem of slavery. But here slavery occupies center stage, and nowhere are its evils depicted more succinctly or unforgettably.

We hope and pray, Lincoln continues, that this "mighty scourge of war" will end quickly, but (in weak paraphrase) if God wills it to continue until the wealth piled up by two hundred and fifty years of slave labor is destroyed and every drop of blood drawn by the lash is paid for by one drawn by the sword, it must still be said—and here he quotes from the Book of Psalms 19:9—that "the judgments of the Lord are true and righteous altogether." This summary indictment of slavery cannot be excelled. Slavery consists in compelling human beings to serve as property that produces wealth—compelling them, ultimately, with the lash. And here the judgments of the Lord seem appropriately just, for He would be making the punishments match the sins. It would be "measure for measure." By implication, anything short of this would be attributable to God's mercy rather than His justice.

We wonder why it was necessary for Lincoln to complicate the picture by introducing the idea that slavery is part of God's providential scheme, and having his elaborate supposition lead to a question about the attributes of the Living God. He could have left it at viewing slavery as a wrong or sin or offence for which Americans are responsible and justly punished. Instead, he supposes that slavery, while evil and thus an offence is actually brought about by God Himself for His own purposes, His providential yet inscrutable purposes. Even so, according to Christ, the men who brought it about or maintain it are justly punished for doing so. That is what the statement in Matthew requires, and it shows that Old and New Testament are at one in sanctifying divine retribution. But does this not inevitably raise the question as to whether it is just to punish men for a necessity brought about by God Himself? And, further, is the idea of a compulsory providential plan consistent with human freedom, responsibility and virtue, or with the idea not only of just punishment but of just rewards?

Lincoln did not have to introduce this complication. He did not have to raise a question about the Living God and His relationship to the world He created. And by speaking of the religious interpretation of slavery as a "supposition," rather than stating it directly as his own view, he allows for the possibility that we cannot be sure of it. It is possible that this may not be the proper interpretation of slavery. It is even possible that Lincoln does not share the religious supposition as such, just as he did not necessarily include himself among "the believers in a Living God." Thus, at the same time that he presents a religious interpretation of the Civil War most likely to resonate with Americans, to win their approval and to be remembered, he gives some indication that questions remain about it.

What effect did Lincoln seek by this expansive religious reflection as he assumed the presidency for the second time? First, and most obviously, the question of slavery can become central because the question of union, with which the Gettysburg Address was primarily concerned, is, with victory in sight for the Union forces, well on its way to solution. Second, Lincoln can now express himself most forcibly about the evil and injustice of slavery, going far beyond the terse language he used in the Emancipation Proclamation or his earlier expressions of a "personal wish" that all men be free. The fullness of his hatred of the institution can finally be revealed. Third, with the help of the Bible (and not the Declaration of Independence), he sets forth an understanding of the war as a divine punishment and the institution of slavery as an evil for which both sides in the war must share responsibility and for which both are being justly punished. Taken by itself, Lincoln's language about appropriating the wealth from the "bondsman's toil" and blood drawn by the lash would mainly lay responsibility on the South, and the strength of this language allows no one, North or South, to forget what this predominantly Southern evil entailed. But Lincoln persists in laying neither sole nor even primary responsibility on the South, thereby making it possible to re-integrate the South into the Union. Fourth, by reminding North and South of their common Biblical heritage, he helps re-open the reservoir of good will across the nation. Finally, and unobtrusively, he suggests questions about the religious interpretation of the Civil War that he himself sets forth.

The end of the speech reaches new heights of sublimity. The idea that slavery is an offence against God and the war a punishment for that offence is forgotten, or laid aside: God's retribution is not to be a model and incentive for human retribution, even more because the North would have to punish itself as well as the South. God's role is now confined to providing moral insight. Presuming a Union victory without actually mentioning it, Lincoln tells the people how we must act to bring this crisis of our history to a close. We must act without malice, with charity, but also with "firmness in the right, as God gives us to see the right." While seeing the right seems to be a third and separate category, the appeals opposing malice and invoking charity preceding it must also be part of that right. And while they sound entirely Christian, they are not presented that way. They are the right thing to do—the right that God gives us to see, once—with Lincoln's help—He opens our eyes, because they are right in themselves and as visible to us as they are to Him. When Lincoln urges caring for "him who shall have borne the battle," for his widow and his orphan, he again leaves the impression, unsaid, that it is the Southern as well as the Northern soldier he has in mind. The object of it all is a just and lasting peace, among ourselves and with all nations. War was necessary, but only as a means to peace, a just peace, which Lincoln presumes here to be the fundamental condition of human good.

Nearing success in a war over slavery, and with the emancipation of the slaves already proclaimed, one would have thought that a final vindication of the Declaration of Independence, the very foundation of Lincoln's pre-war argument, would constitute the heart of his Second Inaugural. It does not. On the subject of the evil of slavery, the war and the need for charity after the war, Lincoln found the Bible a more suitable element than the Declaration, but it is the Bible so selected from and modified as to comport well with the needs of a free society. Thus, refusing with regard to Southern slave-holders or ex-slave-holders to assume a punitive role, Lincoln, had he lived, would have wholly opposed all efforts to reduce the South to helpless dependency. The charity he urges at the end is more than a concession by the North due to shared guilt over slavery. By opening his last paragraph with this call to set aside malice and act charitably, Lincoln endows the attitudes he invokes with an independence and priority suggesting an independent source—something like a natural high-mindedness that will not stoop to vengeance. Even after all the killing and all the destruction, malice must be cleared from the mind as an unworthy and dangerous disposition, and a noble charity must replace it. Nor is this only a moral appeal in the simple sense, since it is also a dictate of prudence. People who must continue to live together as one nation cannot suffer a permanent division into victor and vanquished, superior and inferior, righteous and sinners. This is why Lincoln always viewed the question as to whether the rebel states were outside the Union as merely theoretical and capable of doing much mischief. To him the rebels constituted an errant part that temporarily and mistakenly left their natural and proper place in the Union.

Chapter 20

The Last Public Address, April 11, 1865

Text

We meet this evening, not in sorrow, but in gladness of heart. The evacuation of Petersburg and Richmond, and the surrender of the principal insurgent army, give hope of a righteous and speedy peace whose joyous expression can not be restrained. In the midst of this, however, He from whom all blessings flow, must not be forgotten. A call for a national thanksgiving is being prepared, and will be duly promulgated. Nor must those whose harder part gives us the cause of re-joicing, be overlooked. Their honors must not be parcelled out with others. I myself was near the front, and had the high pleasure of transmitting much of the good news to you; but no part of the honor, for plan or execution, is mine. To Gen. Grant, his skilful officers, and brave men, all belongs. The gallant Navy stood ready, but was not in reach to take active part.

By these recent successes the re-inauguration of the national authority—reconstruction—which has had a large share of thought from the first, is pressed much more closely upon our attention. It is fraught with great difficulty. Unlike a case of a war between independent nations, there is no authorized organ for us to treat with. No one man has authority to give up the rebellion for any other man. We simply must begin with, and mould from, disorganized and discordant elements. Nor is it a small additional embarrassment that we, the loyal people, differ among ourselves as to the mode, manner, and means of reconstruction.

As a general rule, I abstain from reading the reports of attacks upon myself, wishing not to be provoked by that to which I can not properly offer an answer. In spite of this precaution, however, it comes to my knowledge that I am much censured for some supposed agency in setting up, and seeking to sustain, the new State government of Louisiana. In this I have done just so much as, and no more than, the public knows. In the Annual Message of Dec. 1863 and accom-panying Proclamation, I presented *a* plan of re-construction (as the phrase goes) which, I promised, if adopted by any State, should be acceptable to, and sus-tained by, the Executive government of the nation. I distinctly stated that this was not the only plan which might possibly be acceptable; and I also distinctly protested that the Executive claimed no right to say when, or whether members should be admitted to seats in Congress from such States. This plan was, in ad-vance, submitted to the then Cabinet, and distinctly approved by every member of it. One of them suggested that I should then, and in that connection, apply the Emancipation Proclamation to the theretofore excepted parts of Virginia and Louisiana; that I should drop the suggestion about apprenticeship for freed-people, and that I should omit the protest against my own power, in regard to the admission of members to Congress; but even he approved every part and parcel of the plan which has since been employed or touched by the action of Louisiana. The new constitution of Louisiana, declaring emancipation for the whole State, practically applies the Proclamation to the part previously excepted. It does not adopt apprenticeship for freed-people; and it is silent, as it could not well be otherwise, about the admission of members to Congress. So that, as it applies to Louisiana, every member of the Cabinet fully approved the plan. The message went to Congress, and I received many commendations of the plan, written and verbal; and not a single objection to it, from any professed emancipationist, came to my knowledge, until after the news reached Washington that the people of Louisiana had begun to move in accordance with it. From about July 1862, I had corresponded with different persons, supposed to be interested, seeking a reconstruction of a State government for Louisiana. When the message of 1863, with the plan before mentioned, reached New-Orleans, Gen. Banks wrote me that he was confident the people, with his military co-operation, would reconstruct, substantially on that plan. I wrote him, and some of them to try it; they tried it, and the result is known. Such only has been my agency in getting up the Louisiana government. As to sustaining it, my promise is out, as before stated. But, as bad promises are better broken than kept, I shall treat this as a bad promise, and break it, whenever I shall be convinced that keeping it is adverse to the public interest. But I have not yet been so convinced.

I have been shown a letter on this subject, supposed to be an able one, in which the writer expresses regret that my mind has not seemed to be definitely fixed on the question whether the seceding States, so called, are in the Union or out of it. It would perhaps, add astonishment to his regret, were he to learn that since I have found professed Union men endeavoring to make that question, I have *purposely* forborne any public expression upon it. As appears to me that question has not been, nor yet is, a practically material one, and that any discussion of it, while it thus remains practically immaterial, could have no effect other than the mischievous one of dividing our friends. As yet, whatever it may hereafter become, that question is bad, as the basis of a controversy, and good for nothing at all—a merely pernicious abstraction.

We all agree that the seceded States, so called, are out of their proper practical relation with the Union; and that the sole object of the government, civil and military, in regard to those States is to again get them into that proper practical relation. I believe it is not only possible, but in fact, easier to do this, without deciding, or even considering, whether these States have ever been out of the Union, than with it. Finding themselves safely at home, it would be utterly immaterial whether they had ever been abroad. Let us all join in doing the acts necessary to restoring the proper practical relations between these States and the Union; and each forever after, innocently indulge his own opinion whether, in doing the acts, he brought the States from without, into the Union, or only gave them proper assistance, they never having been out of it.

The amount of constituency, so to speak, on which the new Louisiana government rests, would be more satisfactory to all, if it contained fifty, thirty, or even twenty thousand, instead of only about twelve thousand, as it does. It is also unsatisfactory to some that the elective franchise is not given to the colored man. I would myself prefer that it were now conferred on the very intelligent, and on those who serve our cause as soldiers. Still the question is not whether the Louisiana government, as it stands, is quite all that is desirable. The question is, "Will it be wiser to take it as it is, and help to improve it; or to reject, and disperse it?" "Can Louisiana be brought into proper practical relation with the Union *sooner* by *sustaining*, or by *discarding* her new State government?"

Some twelve thousand voters in the heretofore slave-state of Louisiana have sworn allegiance to the Union, assumed to be the rightful political power of the State, held elections, organized a State government, adopted a free-state constitution, giving the benefit of public schools equally to black and white, and empowering the Legislature to confer the elective franchise upon the colored man. Their Legislature has already voted to ratify the constitutional amendment recently passed by Congress, abolishing slavery throughout the nation. These twelve thousand persons are thus fully committed to the Union, and to perpetual freedom in the state—committed to the very things, and nearly all the things the nation wants—and they ask the nations recognition and its assistance to make good their committal. Now, if we reject, and spurn them, we do our utmost to disorganize and disperse them. We in effect say to the white men "You are worthless, or worse—we will neither help you, nor be helped by you." To the blacks we say "This cup of liberty which these, your old masters, hold to your lips, we will dash from you, and leave you to the chances of gathering the spilled and scattered contents in some vague and undefined when, where, and how." If this course, discouraging and paralyzing both white and black, has any tendency to bring Louisiana into proper practical relations with the Union, I have, so far, been unable to perceive it. If, on the contrary, we recognize, and sustain the new government of Louisiana the converse of all this is made true. We encourage the hearts, and nerve the arms of the twelve thousand to adhere to their work, and argue for it, and proselyte for it, and fight for it, and feed it, and grow it, and ripen it to a complete success. The colored man too, in seeing all united for him, is inspired with vigilance, and energy, and daring, to the same end. Grant that he desires the elective franchise, will he not attain it sooner by saving the already advanced steps toward it, than by running backward over them? Concede that the new government of Louisiana is only to what it should be as the egg is to the fowl, we shall sooner have the fowl by hatching the egg than by smashing it? Again, if we reject Louisiana, we also reject one vote in favor of the proposed amendment to the national Constitution. To meet this proposition, it has been argued that no more than three fourths of those States which have not attempted secession are necessary to validly ratify the amendment. I do not commit myself against this, further than to say that such a ratification would be questionable, and sure to be persistently questioned; while a ratification by three-fourths of all the States would be unquestioned and unquestionable.

I repeat the question, "Can Louisiana be brought into proper practical relation with the Union *sooner* by *sustaining* or by *discarding* her new State Government?"

What has been said of Louisiana will apply generally to other States. And yet so great peculiarities pertain to each state, and such important and sudden changes occur in the same state; and withal, so new and unprecedented is the whole case, that no exclusive, and inflexible plan can be safely prescribed as to details and colatterals [*sic*]. Such exclusive, and inflexible plan, would surely become a new entanglement. Important principles may, and must, be inflexible.

In the present *"situation"* as the phrase goes, it may be my duty to make some new announcement to the people of the South. I am considering, and shall not fail to act, when satisfied that action will be proper.

Interpretation

The crowd wanted a triumph: Lincoln gave them a lecture. War-weary themselves, they wanted to celebrate victory with their war-weary president and hear him tell how it was won. And no one could have better related the trials of the war, its lows and its highs, its terrible sacrifices, the great changes it wrought, the way it was brought to a close than Lincoln. But he chose not to do so. It was as if, only two days after Lee's surrender at Appomattox, he wanted to add a postscript to the Second Inaugural from a month before, delineating some of the problems of reconstruction now pressing in on them and the proper uses of long-sought victory. The future, not even the most recent past, was preoccupying him.

After recognizing the imminence of "a righteous and speedy peace whose joyous expression can not be restrained," Lincoln seems to think that that occasion for joy, while very near, is not yet there. So he begins his rather sober, even prosaic, account by allowing that "He from Whom all blessings flow, must not be forgotten," which will soon be done by a "national thanksgiving" that is being prepared. In the Second Inaugural he had linked the war with powerful reflections on the "Living God," but they are not continued here. Lincoln goes on to bestow all the honors of victory on General Grant and his army, "whose harder part gives us the cause of rejoicing." He mentions himself only as having been near the front and having had "the high pleasure of transmitting much of the good news to you," but, he adds, "no part of the honor, for plan or execution, is mine." His whole role in prosecuting the war from beginning to end and achieving that victory is left unspoken, but the victory itself is treated very briefly too.

What is on Lincoln's mind is Louisiana's application for re-instatement—the first of its kind—and he gives us a lesson in prudence, of reason at work on a contentious issue of immediate and far-reaching importance. The reasoning is complicated, so it is unclear just how much of it he expected the crowd he was addressing to absorb. He introduces the problem by acknowledging, generally, that "the re-inauguration of the national authority—reconstruction" is "fraught with great difficulty." The central rebel authority cannot speak for the "disorganized and discordant elements" that must now seek re-instatement. "Nor is it," Lincoln observes, "a small additional embarrassment that we, the loyal people, differ among ourselves as to the mode, manner, and means of reconstruction."

In his annual message to Congress of December 1863, Lincoln had proposed a plan for guiding the rebel states in reconstructing themselves and received unanimous approval for it from the cabinet and favorable comment from members of Congress. One cabinet member had suggested that Lincoln require freedom for the blacks in the excepted parts of Louisiana and Virginia, drop the idea of "apprenticeship for freed-people," and also omit his deferring entirely to Congress for authority in the matter. Evidently, Lincoln did not make these changes, but, on its own, Louisiana's proposed constitution freed the slaves and omitted apprenticeship. The cabinet unanimously approved this proposed constitution for Louisiana, but it has evidently received unexpected opposition in Congress, and Lincoln has been criticized for improperly influencing its formation. That's why he recounts its history.

At the outset, Lincoln takes up the question "whether the seceded states, so called, are in the Union or out of it." He has "*purposely* forborne any public expression on it," taking it to be, at that time, immaterial as a practical matter, "mischievous" in its effect of "dividing our friends," and "a merely pernicious abstraction." In order to get the seceded States back into "their proper practical relation with the Union," it is easier to do this "without deciding, or even considering, whether these states have ever been out of the Union." One can see that Lincoln does not want to regard the rebel states as beaten enemies that must now overcome obstacles or suffer punishments in order to return to the Union, His thought is, "Let's get these brothers back into the family." And it is important to note his suggestion of apprenticeship for "freed-people"—certainly a radical but sensible idea that presumes their remaining on these shores. It is the first step toward integrating the blacks within American society: an education in useful occupation by which they can support themselves and be of benefit to others. This is the direction perfected afterward by Booker T. Washington.

Lincoln admits disappointment at the fact that the new Louisiana "constituency" contains only twelve thousand, and tells us that "It is also unsatisfactory to some that the elective franchise is not given to the colored man." "I would myself," he says, "prefer that it were now conferred on the very intelligent, and on those who serve our cause as soldiers." Why Lincoln does not also demand the vote for all black men he does not say. By the logic of equal rights, they will have to be given it at some point. He may have had in mind appealing to qualities—like intelligence and military service—that might more easily receive recognition in the South and start the process going. As it is, the difficulty is shown by the fact that the new constitution does not give blacks the vote at all.

So what should be done? In Lincoln's words, "Will it be wiser to take it as it is, and help to improve it, or to reject, and disperse it?" He argues for accepting it. He begins by listing all the good things the twelve thousand voters in Louisiana have done. They have "sworn allegiance to the Union," formed an elected government, "adopted a free-state constitution, giving the benefit of public schools equally to black and white, and empowering the Legislature to confer the elective franchise upon the colored man." Not only that: their new Legislature has already "voted to ratify the constitutional amendment (the Thirteenth) abolishing slavery throughout the nation." It is impressive to see an equal public education accorded to both races, and the idea behind leaving it to the Legislature to grant voting rights to blacks must have been the perceived necessity for their first receiving some education. The absence of apprenticeship training is not made up for by the guarantee of public education, but it is important in itself and its implication. For it means that Louisiana is committing itself, in principle, to the ultimate full political and legal equality of the races.

Lincoln's response to the question he poses is that rejecting the new constitution would bring only disparagement to the whites and discouragement to the blacks in Louisiana. On the contrary, by accepting the new constitution, "We encourage the hearts, and nerve the arms of the twelve thousand to adhere to their work, and argue for it, and proselyte for it, and fight for it, and feed it, and grow it, and ripen it to a complete success." He undoubtedly has in mind the proselytizing necessary to bringing the mass of other Louisianans to support it. And accepting it will have a similarly good effect on the blacks: "The colored man too, in seeing all united for him, is inspired with vigilance, and energy, and daring, to the same end. Grant that he desires the elective franchise, will he not attain it sooner by saving the already advanced steps toward it, than by running backward over them? Finally, some consideration should be given to the fact that the new Louisiana Legislature has already ratified the new amendment to the constitution (the Thirteenth) abolishing slavery everywhere in the country.

Lincoln ends by saying that the question with all the seceded states will be to bring them, like Louisiana, into "proper practical relation with the Union." Yet circumstances will vary so much that no detailed plan can be prescribed for all, even though "important principles may, and must, be inflexible." He may have to make a further announcement to the people of the South: "I am considering, and shall not fail to act, when satisfied that action will be proper." These are the last words of Lincoln's last public address. There is no farewell, no proper conclusion. It is like work in progress—thoughts in the midst of work. He had this rare ability to join inflexible principles to the needs of particular cases, avoiding abstract theories and plans that make it impossible to deal in a practical way with particular cases. This is the very essence of the wise and just man. Three days later Lincoln was shot, and he died on the fourth, leaving us only the priceless legacy of his deeds and words.

Index

Pope, Alexander, 195, 204
popular sovereignty, 117-18, 120-21,
  133, 136, 144, 155, 161, 164, 179,
  180, 217
predestination, 55

right to revolution, 66, 239
Scott, Dred, 1, 64, 123, 125-27, 129,
  131-34, 137-41, 144, 153, 155, 161,
  163, 164-65, 168-69, 170, 176, 179,
  180, 214, 225, 238
Shakespeare, William, 1, 40, 53, 121,
  270
Speed, Joshua, 5
steam plow, 199, 205

Taney, Roger B., 123, 125, 127, 129,
  134, 141, 144, 163-64, 174, 179, 238

Vallandigham, Clement V., 249, 253-
  55, 257, 258
Van Buren, Martin, 57, 72

Washington, George, 27-28, 38-40, 48,
  62, 74, 115, 121-22, 153, 155, 161,
  211, 216-17, 223
Webster, Daniel, 113, 115, 148, 186
Whig party, 148-50, 152, 157
Wilmot Proviso, 91, 94-97, 117

Young America, 183-84, 186, 189-90,
  193

About the Author

David Lowenthal is professor emeritus of political science at Boston College, the author of *Shakespeare and the Good Life: Ethics and Politics in Dramatic Form* and *Present Dangers: Rediscovering the First Amendment*, and the translator of Montesquieu's *Considerations on the Causes of the Greatness of the Romans and Their Decline*.